# THE SUPREME COURT
# ON FREEDOM OF THE PRESS:
## DECISIONS AND DISSENTS

# THE SUPREME COURT
# ON
# FREEDOM OF THE PRESS:

## DECISIONS AND DISSENTS

❖

## *William A. Hachten*

❖

**THE IOWA STATE UNIVERSITY PRESS**     **AMES, IOWA**

WILLIAM A. HACHTEN is Professor of Journalism, University of Wisconsin, where he has taught since 1959. He holds the B.A. degree from Stanford University, the M.S. degree from the University of California at Los Angeles, and the Ph.D. degree from the University of Minnesota. He has been guest professor at the Berlin Institute for Mass Communication in Developing Nations (1964), and has done field research on mass media in tropical Africa (1965). In 1968 he was awarded a Fulbright-Hays fellowship for research on mass communication in Africa. His professional experience has included reporting and copy editing for California and Minnesota newspapers. Besides this book, he is author of several journal articles allying the fields of journalism and political science.

© 1968 The Iowa State University Press
Ames, Iowa, U.S.A. All rights reserved

Composed and printed by
The Iowa State University Press

First edition, 1968
*Second printing, 1970*

Library of Congress Catalog Card Number: 68–17492
International Standard Book Number: 0–8138–0704–2

FOR HARVA, ELIZABETH, AND MARIANNE

# PREFACE

THERE IS AN AFFINITY between journalists and the law. Many newspapermen begin their careers on the police or the courthouse beat and become fascinated with the law and its intricacies. Lawyers and judges, for their part, are often keen observers and critics of the press. In the course of their day-to-day coverage of the news, journalists sometimes have become unwitting actors in legal contests and occasionally, because an issue of freedom of the press was involved, even litigants in great constitutional decisions. The *New York Times* libel case *(Times v. Sullivan),* the Dr. Sam Sheppard murder trial, the Alabama election day editorial case *(Mills v. Alabama),* the "Desperate Hours" privacy contest *(Time v. Hill),* and the televising of the Billie Sol Estes trial are all recent examples.

In my study of constitutional law as a graduate student at the University of Minnesota, I became deeply interested in what the Supreme Court of the United States has said about liberty in general and freedom of expression in particular. The law and the media of communication run through all of American life. When issues involving communication have come before the Supreme Court, the resulting Court decisions have held words charged with almost magical power and persuasiveness. Some of the noblest writing in the English language has resulted when the Court's decisions have touched upon freedom of thought and expression.

The Court's words, of course, have all the force of law—constitutional law—in those written passages specifically addressed to the legal point at hand in a specific case. But while a Supreme Court decision is the law, it is sometimes more than that. In judicial asides called *dicta* (talk), or in concurring or dissenting opinions, the Justices often go beyond the decision to expound political or social philosophy. Sometimes a novel idea or an illuminating turn of phrase may forecast—or become the basis for—the future path of the law. And in many decisions of the Supreme Court one can discern a good deal of the political philosophy and the ethics of American journalism.

What the giants of the modern court—Justices Oliver Wendell Holmes, Louis Brandeis, Charles Evans Hughes, Hugo Black, Felix Frankfurter, William O. Douglas, Earl Warren, and others—have written about freedom of the press, newspapers, journalists, news services, broadcasting, motion pictures, and the laws regulating them, has had an influence far beyond the juridicial.

American journalism's *raison d'etre*, its ethical and political justifications, I believe, can be found in the decisions excerpted in this book. I am convinced that to understand the political and social role of journalism in modern American life, as well as the legal limits of freedom of the press, one must take careful cognizance of what the Supreme Court has said.

This book therefore is not primarily concerned with the current state of the law of the press; it is concerned with the ideas and principles underpinning the freedom of our system of mass communication as they have been enunciated in decisions of the Supreme Court of the United States. It is an effort to pull together the Court's major statements and comments concerning the communication of information and ideas in a free and self-governing society.

I want to show the words the Justices themselves uttered—whether as part of a Court majority or in dissent—in the context of resolving great constitutional questions. My feeling is that there is too little understanding, in and out of journalism and mass communication, of what freedom of the press is about or the breadth of that freedom.

At the outset, I will admit to a bias. As a former newspaperman and as a teacher of journalism, my sympathies lean toward the libertarian views of the First Amendment—especially toward those of Justices Black and Douglas—who believed that freedom of expression is a "preferred freedom" and should be given the widest possible latitude. I would be the last to deny that there is great merit in the brilliantly reasoned opinions of Justice Frankfurter. He argued for a "balancing of interests" approach to First Amendment questions and urged the Court to exercise judicial self-restraint. But I am more strongly drawn to the position of Justice Black, who believed that when the Constitution says that "Congress shall make no law . . . abridging freedom . . . of the press" it means just that—Congress shall make no law.

As a result, a tendency to overrepresent the views of Justices Black and Douglas may be present in the selection of opinions reprinted here. I do not apologize. Anyone who feels strongly about freedom of the press, whether active in journalism or not, must feel especially sympathetic to their viewpoint. But defending freedom of the press is not, as this book shows, the prerogative of merely a few members of the Court; it is so firmly embedded in constitutional law that all Justices of the Supreme Court give it steadfast support.

This study was supported in part by the Research Committee of the Graduate School of the University of Wisconsin, from special funds voted by the Wisconsin State Legislature. Professor Dwight L. Teeter prepared Chapter 8, "Freedom to Report News versus the Right of Privacy," and made valuable editing suggestions throughout the manuscript. I thank Donald Shaw for assistance on the research and Professor Harold L. Nelson for commenting on the manuscript. I am most indebted to my wife, Harva, a working journalist, for her editing improvements, for typing the manuscript, and for her encouragement.

WILLIAM A. HACHTEN

*Madison, Wisconsin*

# CONTENTS

# TABLE OF DECISIONS

# JUSTICES QUOTED IN DECISIONS

*Years served on Supreme Court are indicated*

❄

BLACK, HUGO L. (1937 to _____)
*Associated Press v. United States,* court opinion
*Barenblatt v. United States,* dissent
*Beauharnais v. Illinois,* dissent
*Braden v. United States,* dissent
*Breard v. Alexandria,* dissent
*Bridges vs. California,* court opinion
*Curtis Publishing Co. v. Butts,* dissent; *Associated Press v. Walker,* concurrence
*Dennis v. United States,* dissent
*Eastern Railroad Presidents Conference v. Noerr Motor Freight,* court opinion
*Farmers Educational & Cooperative Union v. WDAY, Inc.,* court opinion
*Garrison v. Louisiana,* concurrence
*Ginzburg v. United States,* dissent
*Kingsley International Pictures v. Regents of New York,* concurrence
*Kovacs v. Cooper,* dissent
*Martin v. Struthers,* court opinion
*Milk Wagon Drivers Union v. Meadowmoor Dairies,* dissent
*Mills v. Alabama,* court opinion
*New York Times v. Sullivan,* concurrence
*Public Utilities Commission v. Pollak,* separate opinion
*Smith v. California,* concurrence
*Talley v. California,* court opinion

xvii

*Freedman v. Maryland,* concurrence
*Garrison v. Louisiana,* concurrence
*Ginzburg v. United States,* dissent
*Hannegan v. Esquire,* court opinion
*Kingsley Books v. Brown,* dissent
*Kingsley International Pictures v. Regents of New York,* concurrence
*Lamont v. Postmaster General,* court opinion
*Mabee v. White Plains Publishing Co.,* court opinion
*Public Utilities Commission v. Pollak,* dissent
*Roth v. United States,* dissent
*Saia v. New York,* court opinion
*Smith v. California,* concurrence
*Superior Films v. Ohio,* concurrence
*Terminiello v. Chicago,* court opinion
*Time, Inc. v. Hill,* concurrence
*Times Film Corp. v. Chicago,* dissent
*United States v. Rumely,* concurrence
*Wilkinson v. United States,* dissent

FIELD, STEPHEN (1863 to 1897)
*Ex Parte Jackson,* court opinion

FORTAS, ABE (1965 to _____)
*Time, Inc. v. Hill,* dissent

FRANKFURTER, FELIX (1939 to 1962)
*Associated Press v. United States,* concurrence
*Baumgartner v. United States,* court opinion
*Beauharnais v. Illinois,* court opinion
*Bridges v. California,* dissent
*Dennis v. United States,* concurrence
*Federal Communications Commission v. Pottsville Broadcasting Co.,* court opinion
*Irvin v. Dowd,* concurrence
*Kingsley Books v. Brown,* court opinion
*Kingsley International Pictures v. Regents of New York,* concurrence
*Kovacs v. Cooper,* concurrence
*Maryland v. Baltimore Radio Show,* separate opinion
*Milk Wagon Drivers Union v. Meadowmoor Dairies,* court opinion
*National Broadcasting Co. v. United States,* court opinion
*Pennekamp v. Florida,* concurrence
*Saia v. New York,* dissent

GOLDBERG, ARTHUR I. (1962 to 1965)
  *New York Times v. Sullivan,* concurrence

HARLAN, JOHN MARSHALL (1955 to _____)
  *Estes v. Texas,* concurrence
  *Time, Inc. v. Hill,* concurrence in part and dissent in part

HOLMES, OLIVER WENDELL (1902 to 1931)
  *Abrams v. United States,* dissent
  *Gitlow v. New York,* dissent
  *Milwaukee Social Democratic Publishing Co. v. Burleson,* dissent
  *Schenck v. United States,* court opinion

HUGHES, CHARLES EVANS (1910 to 1915; 1930 to 1940)
  *Lovell v. Griffin,* court opinion
  *Near v. Minnesota,* court opinion

JACKSON, ROBERT H. (1941 to 1954)
  *Beauharnais v. Illinois,* dissent
  *Terminiello v. Chicago,* dissent
  *West Virginia State Board of Education v. Barnette,* court opinion

MURPHY, FRANK (1940 to 1948)
  *Associated Press v. United States,* dissent
  *Craig v. Harney,* concurrence
  *Jones v. Opelika,* dissent
  *National Broadcasting Co. v. United States,* dissent
  *Pennekamp v. Florida,* concurrence

PITNEY, MAHLON (1912 to 1922)
  *International News Service v. Associated Press,* court opinion

REED, STANLEY (1938 to 1957)
  *Breard v. Alexandria,* court opinion
  *Jones v. Opelika,* court opinion
  *Kovacs v. Cooper,* court opinion
  *Martin v. Struthers,* dissent
  *Pennekamp v. Florida,* court opinion

ROBERTS, OWEN J. (1930 to 1944)
  *Associated Press v. National Labor Relations Board,* court opinion

# THE SUPREME COURT
# ON FREEDOM OF THE PRESS:

## DECISIONS AND DISSENTS

*Chapter One*

# INTRODUCTION: THE FIRST AMENDMENT AND THE PRESS

Freedom of the press in America begins but does not end with the First Amendment to the United States Constitution:

*Congress shall make no law respecting an establishment of religion, or prohibiting the free exercise thereof; or abridging the freedom of speech, or of the press; or the right of the people peaceably to assemble, and to petition the Government for a redress of grievances.*

The relevant words for this study are: "Congress shall make no law . . . abridging the freedom . . . of the press." Freedom of the press is based primarily upon those words and upon the written decisions of the Supreme Court of the United States.

The First Amendment is old, yet its words and the meanings in them have been renewed and revitalized by decisions of the Supreme Court. Interestingly enough, most of these decisions are less than fifty years old.

The Supreme Court has always rendered its decisions on freedom of expression in the light of the First Amendment's specific restrictions upon congressional power to legislate in the area. In so doing, the Court has often taken into consideration the intentions of the men who wrote the Constitution.

That there have been difficulties and disagreements in ascertaining the intentions of the framers of the Constitution is not surprising. The historical chronology of the First Amendment, however, is easier to chart.

And the historical circumstances surrounding the First Amendment's inception are important to know just as it is essential to understand that there were intellectual antecedents in the ideas of Socrates, the trials of Galileo, the tracts of Milton, the writings of Locke and the Enlightenment, the arguments of Erskine, the trial of Zenger, and the speeches of Jefferson and Madison. The great ideas of these men run through the decisions of the U.S. Supreme Court like leitmotivs.

As originally drafted and ratified, the United States Constitution contained no guarantee of press freedom, even though nine of the original thirteen colonies had previously amended their charters to include such guarantees. Alexander Hamilton defended the omission on the ground that liberty of the press was indefinable and depended only upon public opinion and the general spirit of the people and government for its security.[1] The citizens of the states were not satisfied, however, and the absence of the guarantee of free speech and press was repeatedly condemned in state conventions; in fact, Virginia, New York, and Rhode Island included a declaration of this right in their ratifications of the federal Constitution.

Therefore, at the first session of the new Congress, a Bill of Rights, including the First Amendment, was proposed for adoption by the states and became a part of the Constitution December 15, 1791.

As Zechariah Chafee wrote, "The free speech clauses of the American [State] Constitutions are not merely expressions of political faith without binding legal force. Their history shows that they limit legislative action as much as any other part of the Bill of Rights."[2]

The Supreme Court, however, rarely agrees unanimously on the extent of legislative limitation in this area, and the differing points of view expressed by the Justices generally reflect differing opinions on just what the men who wrote the First Amendment had in mind.

Many authorities, including some Supreme Court Justices, feel as Chafee did, that by the unqualified prohibitions, the framers intended to accomplish a double purpose: they "sought to preserve the fruits of the old victory abolishing the censor-

---

[1] Zechariah Chafee, Jr., *Free Speech in the United States* (Cambridge: Harvard University Press, 1948), p. 5.
[2] *Ibid.*, p. 4.

ship, and to achieve a new victory abolishing seditious prosecutions."[3]

In other words, this view holds that the Constitution gave the people a broad and untrammeled right to criticize their government and its leaders. Justice Hugo L. Black has stated that the First Amendment conferred such an unfettered right on the people to criticize official conduct that even civil libel suits could not be instituted against a citizen criticizing his governors. However, other authorities contend that the authors of the Bill of Rights did not believe in such freedom to criticize, particularly in politics. Professor Leonard W. Levy has written:

> The evidence drawn particularly from the period 1776 to 1791 indicates that the generation that framed the first state declarations of rights and the First Amendment was hardly as libertarian as we have traditionally assumed. They did not intend to give free rein to criticism of the government that might be deemed seditious libel, although the concept of seditious libel was—and still is—the principal basis of muzzling political dissent. There is even reason to believe that the Bill of Rights was more the chance product of political expediency on all sides than of principled commitment to personal liberties. A broad libertarian theory of free speech and press did not emerge in the United States until the Jeffersonians, when a minority party, were forced to defend themselves against the Federalist Sedition Act of 1798.[4]

These are the broad outlines of two differing historical interpretations—viewpoints which have been applied and refined in relation to the free speech and press aspects of the First Amendment largely in this century.

Professor John P. Roche said that excluding the Sedition Act of 1798 it is impossible to find any national laws penalizing dissenting *opinion* before World War I. Until the epidemic of criminal anarchy laws spread after President McKinley's assassination, the states had little legislation on the subject.[5]

Because of the dearth of test cases to give meaning and definition to the First Amendment—to put meat on the bones of the law—most of the law we need to know about freedom

---

[3] John P. Roche, "The Curbing of the Militant Majority," *The Reporter* 29:2 (July 18, 1963), p. 36. The "old victory" over censorship and prior restraint had been won in England in 1695.

[4] Levy, *Legacy of Suppression* (Cambridge: Harvard University Press, 1960), pp. vii–viii.

[5] Roche, p. 36.

of the press has been made since 1917. Most of the decisions in this book date from that time.

Since World War I, the Supreme Court of the United States has faced a large number of vexing constitutional disputes that have involved, in one way or another, the right of freedom of expression guaranteed by the First Amendment. But it wasn't until 1925 that an expanded variety of problems of free expression came into the jurisdiction of the Supreme Court. In that year the Court, in the significant *Gitlow* decision,[6] expanded the due process clause of the Fourteenth Amendment to include the rights of the First Amendment. This meant that the Court's protection of freedom of the press was extended to include actions originating in state and local courts.

Since then, during this past half-century of great social and political change, appeals have come from all quarters of society—from anarchists, syndicalists, Communists, and other political extremists; from a persecuted religious sect such as the Jehovah's Witnesses; from conservative newspaper publishers opposing New Deal legislation; from motion picture distributors, professional hatemongers, leaders of civil rights movements; and occasionally even from a working newsman.

The diversity of the litigants reminds us that freedom of the press is an individual right belonging to all Americans. When anyone wins a victory for free expression at the bar of the Supreme Court, it enhances and enlarges freedom for all. As Justice Felix Frankfurter said in *Pennekamp v. Florida:* "The liberty of the press is no greater and no less than . . . the liberty of every citizen of the United States."[7]

The Supreme Court has had to cope with the technological revolution that has shaped mass communications in this century. In the days of small, hand-printed news sheets, James Madison and the architects of the First Amendment could not foresee giant high-speed rotary presses, network television, communications satellites, mobile loudspeakers, motion pictures, radio, or world-wide news agencies strung together by teletype and telephone.

But had they had such foresight, it is unlikely that they would have rewritten the First Amendment. It is part of the genius of our Constitution that each generation can adapt the document's broad and enduring principles to the changing needs of the time.

[6] See p. 21.
[7] 328 U.S. 331 (1946).

The Constitution has proved flexible enough to deal with such challenges to freedom of expression as the rise of modern corporate giants of mass communications, the technological necessity of government licensing and regulation of radio and television, a multimillion dollar traffic in commercial obscenity, the organized conspiracy of a domestic Communist party, the extensive social legislation required to meet the challenges of the Great Depression era, and the highly centralized industrial society that agrarian eighteenth-century America has become.

These and other tests of freedom of the press have come to the Supreme Court in the form of specific legal contests in which an issue involving the Constitution was to be resolved. This book is a collection of many of these decisions. The purpose is to show what the Justices themselves wrote about the press and its rights when deciding those issues. Sometimes, the significant ideas are found in the Court opinion, which, of course, is the law. Sometimes only the dissent is quoted, because it may have the most pertinent comments for the press. In some instances, the arguments of the dissent were later adopted as the ruling opinion in subsequent decisions.

This book does not endeavor to cover the whole spectrum of the First Amendment, with all its ramifications for freedom of assembly, speech, petition, national security and loyalty problems, religion, and association. It has a much finer focus: the Court's views relating to freedom of the press as applied to the media of mass communications. The intention has been to sift out of the vast number of Supreme Court decisions those particularly pertinent to the "press," as here defined: the dissemination of ideas, news, and information by the printed word in newspapers, pamphlets, books, and periodicals, as well as the spoken word conveyed by radio, in speeches, by television, and in motion pictures.

It is well to ask if there is any difference between freedom of speech and freedom of the press. Professor Chafee thought not, and said that free speech and free press virtually coincide as legal concepts. He wrote:

I have not found the courts mentioning any significant difference between these two freedoms. There is, however, a difference in fact so far as governmental control is concerned, for newspapers are more vulnerable than speakers. The government (unless checked by the Constitution) can impose restraints on them which would not be applicable to orators, like heavy taxation in Tory England and Louisiana, requirements of large bonds guaranteeing against violation of libel or sedition laws, injunctions against future issues, exclusion from the mails, etc.[8]

Several chapters in this study—on censorship and prior restraint, licensing, unjust taxation, contempt, libel immunity, postal regulations, and distribution—are mostly concerned with the print media because the battles for freedom of the press have been largely fought in contests involving printed matter.

But this is also because, as Chafee noted, in years past "the press" had been interpreted rather narrowly by the courts: "They have been inclined to limit it to the popular sense of newspapers (and probably books and pamphlets) without embracing other media of communication such as broadcasting and motion pictures."[9]

Since Chafee wrote these words in 1947, the Court has been bringing the electronic media under the same umbrella that protects newspapers. Some of the most significant developments in freedom of the press in recent years have come from efforts to provide for broadcasting, magazines, books, and especially motion pictures, the same protections against prior restraint and censorship that newspapers enjoy.

A few of the decisions quoted appear to involve only freedom of speech, freedom of religion, or the rights of pickets, or of Communist party members. But because the principles enunciated are directly relevant to "the press" or mass communications, they have an appropriate place in this book. By the same token, numerous other important decisions are not included because they do not focus on the concerns of journalism and mass communication.

Some of the cases concern free expression activities of eccentric individualists, political pariahs, or members of unorthodox religious sects. Their problems and travails may seem far removed from those of the media of mass communications; but actually the principles involved are often directly relevant to press freedom, and the Supreme Court never forgets, of course, that freedom of the press belongs to every citizen of the Republic. The rights of all citizens often have been strengthened

[8] Chafee, *Government and Mass Communications* (Chicago: University of Chicago Press, 1947), pp. 34–35.
[9] *Ibid.*

by the determination of such non-conformists to carry their personal legal contests all the way to the Supreme Court.

### HISTORICAL PRECEDENTS ARE FOLLOWED

To adjudicate freedom of the press cases, the Court has often relied upon the principles, legal precedents, and traditions that are the heritage of the long political struggle for freedom of the press that began in England and continued in colonial and republican America. These principles are very much alive in American constitutional law and the modern court frequently cites them. The libertarian ideas expressed long ago by John Milton, John Locke, Thomas Jefferson, Thomas Erskine, and John Stuart Mill still turn up in contemporary decisions.

In the discriminatory taxation case of *Grosjean v. American Press Co.*,[10] Justice George Sutherland recounted the noxious history of "taxes on knowledge." He pointed out that the kind of tax Huey Long levied against the critical Louisiana newspapers "is bad because, in the light of its history and its present setting, it is seen to be a deliberate and calculated device in the guise of a tax to limit the circulation of information to which the public is entitled in virtue of the constitutional guaranties."

In *Lovell v. Griffin,* which involved stringent licensing of Jehovah's Witnesses when distributing printed tracts, Chief Justice Charles Evans Hughes recalled press history when he wrote:

The struggle for freedom of the Press was primarily directed against the power of the licensor. It was against that power that John Milton directed his assault by his "Appeal for the Liberty of Unlicensed Printing," and the liberty of the press became initially a right to publish "without a license what formerly could be published only with one."[11]

And Justice Black, concurring in the libel case of *New York Times v. Sullivan,* echoed the words of Thomas Jefferson when he wrote: "But I doubt that a country can live in freedom where its people can be made to suffer physically or finan-

[10] 297 U.S. 233 (1936).
[11] 303 U.S. 444 (1938).

cially for criticizing their government, its actions, or its officials."[12]

These are reflections of the traditional (or more properly, libertarian) approach that freedom of expression exists best where government interference or regulation is least. A differing line of thought occasionally used by some members of the modern Court in press freedom cases gives government a role to play. In this view, government is given the assignment of protecting and somtimes securing the people's right of freedom of expression, thus assuring that the media of mass communication perform in a socially responsible manner.

Professor William E. Hocking, an advocate of this view, wrote:

Government remains the residuary legatee of responsibility for an adequate press performance. It is bound to consider whether self-administered standards and normal self-righting elements within community life are sufficient to meet the public interest and eliminate emerging abuses. If they are not sufficient, government action may be indicated.[13]

Unquestionably, government can play a positive and dynamic role as it has since 1940 in the area of federal law enforcement of civil rights. Professor Robert W. Carr, in *Federal Protection of Civil Rights: Quest for a Sword*[14] pointed out that in the 1944 case of *Pollock v. Williams*,[15] Justice Robert H. Jackson stated that every individual in America is protected against slavery and involuntary servitude by "both a shield and a sword." In this context, the "sword" is dynamic government action or regulation; the "shield" is the traditional protection of the Constitution.

The sword and shield concept, by permitting some government intervention in the media, is thought to serve the broader interests of the First Amendment. It legitimizes the need for and constitutionality of the increasing regulatory functions that the federal government has assumed in mass communications in the twentieth century—notably through the Federal Communications Commission, the Federal Trade Com-

---

[12] 376 U.S. 254 (1964).

[13] Hocking, *Freedom of the Press: A Framework of Principle* (Chicago: University of Chicago Press, 1947), pp. 182–83.

[14] Carr, *Federal Protection of Civil Rights: Quest for a Sword* (Ithaca: Cornell University Press, 1947), p. 3.

[15] 322 U.S. 4 (1944).

mission, the National Labor Relations Board, and the application of the anti-trust laws. And it is part of the trend that Roche refers to as the "intervention of the centralized state" which through such legislative actions as the Wagner Act and "the Supreme Court decisions in school segregation, reapportionment, search and seizure, right to counsel, and other cases have played a notable part in the expansion of individual freedom."[16]

As Professor J. Edward Gerald noted:

In our day, the sharpest phases of the controversy over assuring freedom of press have been developed by government intervention in private affairs, on the theory that freedom is not a passive force but must be socially directed to carry out the principles of the First and Fourteenth Amendments.[17]

Justice Black expressed the sword concept in the famous anti-trust case, *Associated Press v. United States*, when he wrote:

It would be strange indeed, however, if the grave concern for freedom of the press which prompted adoption of the First Amendment should be read as a command that the government was without power to protect that freedom. The First Amendment, far from providing an argument against the application of the Sherman Act, here provides powerful reasons to the contrary. . . . Surely, a command that the government itself shall not impede the free flow of ideas does not afford nongovernmental combinations a refuge if they impose restraints upon that constitutionally guaranteed freedom. Freedom to publish means freedom for all and not for some. Freedom to publish is guaranteed by the Constitution but freedom to combine to keep others from publishing is not. Freedom of the press from governmental interference under the First Amendment does not sanction repression of that freedom by private interests. The First Amendment affords not the slightest support for the contention that a combination to restrain trade in news and views has any constitutional immunity.[18]

The mass media of communication today are obliged, then, to be responsible and to serve the public interest. If not, government intervention in the broad interests of the First Amendment may be necessary. This is, it should be noted, a

---

[16] Roche, p. 38.
[17] Gerald, *The Press and the Constitution 1931–1947* (Minneapolis: University of Minnesota Press, 1948), p. 4.
[18] 326 U.S. 1 (1945).

controversial viewpoint. Many authorities on constitutional law would argue that there is nothing in the Constitution that requires the mass media to be "responsible" and to serve the "public interest." However, in *Pennekamp v. Florida,* Justice Frankfurter found historical precedent for the responsibility theme:

> A free press is vital to a democratic society because its freedom gives it power. Power in a democracy implies responsibility in its exercise. No institution in a democracy, either governmental or private, can have absolute power. Nor can the limits of power which enforce responsibility be finally determined by the limited power itself. In plain English, freedom carries with it responsibility even for the press; freedom of the press is not a freedom from responsibility for its exercise. Most state constitutions expressly provide for liability for abuse of the press's freedom. That there was such legal liability was so taken for granted by the framers of the First Amendment that it was not spelled out. Responsibility for its abuse was imbedded in the law. The first Amendment safeguarded the right. . . . The public function which belongs to the press makes it an obligation of honor to exercise this function only with the fullest sense of responsibility. Without such a lively sense of responsibility a free press may readily become a powerful instrument of injustice.[19]

It should be noted that Justice Frankfurter, who undeniably made great contributions to the law, was an Anglophile and often drew upon British legal authority in press freedom issues. On the other hand there is strong support for Justice Black's statement in *Bridges v. California* that "no purpose in ratifying the Bill of Rights was clearer than that of securing for the people of the United States much greater freedom of religion, expression, assembly, and petition than the people of Great Britain had ever enjoyed."[20] If Professor Levy's research is valid, Justice Black's view may no longer be good history but it is still good constitutional law.

In any case, the differing viewpoints tend to alternate as themes running through various decisions included in this book. The libertarian view historically rooted in Milton, Jefferson, and Madison is the more dominant. An interesting point of difference between the two approaches is that the traditional libertarian view has been applied mainly to individual

[19] 328 U.S. 331 (1946).
[20] 314 U.S. 252 (1941).

rights to speak or print; the responsibility or government-intervention idea, so far a minor theme, is more often invoked when the mass media are considered in their corporate sense, as when a giant broadcasting network or a news association is involved, and it seems more concerned with amorphous group rights—i.e., "the people's right to know" or the "public interest."

### "PREFERRED FREEDOM" v. "BALANCING OF INTERESTS"

It is often risky and sometimes actually misleading to label certain Justices as "conservative" or "liberal." The specific issue before the Court and its circumstances are decisive.

However, the Justices may be categorized on the basis of one basic question: How much latitude should be given to freedom of the press? Is it a "preferred freedom" that should be given priority when in conflict with other rights? Or should the Court apply a "balancing of interests" approach and compromise the claims of press freedom with other claims to constitutional protection?

During the 1940's the "preferred right" view of the First Amendment was espoused, and in *Jones v. Opelika,* Chief Justice Harlan Fiske Stone wrote:

The First Amendment is not confined to safeguarding freedom of speech . . . against discriminatory attempts to wipe them out. On the contrary, the Constitution by virtue of the First and Fourteenth Amendments, has put these freedoms in a preferred position. Their commands are not restricted to cases where the protected privilege is sought out for attack.[21]

The "preferred right" position has been consistently advocated by Justices Black and Douglas, and is basically the law today. Justice Black stated the "preferred freedom" view in *Smith v. California:*

Certainly the First Amendment's language leaves no room for inference that abridgments of speech and press can be made just because they are slight. That Amendment provides, in simple words, that "Congress shall make no law . . . abridging the freedom of speech, or of the press." The First Amendment, which is the supreme law of the land, has thus fixed its own value on freedom of speech and press by putting these freedoms wholly "beyond the reach" of federal power to abridge. No other provision of the Con-

[21] 316 U.S. 584 (1942).

stitution purports to dilute the scope of these unequivocal commands of the First Amendment. Consequently, I do not believe that any federal agencies, including Congress and this court, have power or authority to subordinate speech and press to what they think are "more important interests."[22]

The most consistent critic of this view was Justice Frankfurter. He argued that the Court should exercise more judicial self-restraint while protecting press rights. There was little question he was referring to Justices Black and Douglas when he wrote with the majority in *Dennis v. United States:*

There are those who find in the Constitution a wholly unfettered right of expression. Such literalness treats the words of the Constitution as though they were found on a piece of outworn parchment instead of being words that have called into being a nation with a past to be preserved for the future. The soil in which the Bill of Rights grew was not a soil of arid pedantry. The historic antecedents of the First Amendment preclude the notion that its purpose was to give unqualified immunity to every expression that touched on matters within the range of political interest. . . . The demands of free speech in a democratic society as well as the interest in national security are better served by candid and informed weighing of the competing interests, within the confines of the judicial process, than by announcing dogmas too inflexible for the non-euclidean problems to be solved.[23]

And in *Pennekamp v. Florida,* in which a Florida newspaper appealed a state contempt conviction, Justice Frankfurter's views, often shared by the Court majority, were:

Since at the core of our problem is a proper balance between two basic conditions of our constitutional democracy—freedom of utterance and impartial justice—we cannot escape the exercise of judgment on the particular circumstances of the particular case. And we must always bear in mind that since a judgment from a State court comes here as the voice of the State, it must be accorded every fair intendment that in reason belongs to action by a state.[24]

Whether based on "preferred freedom" or "balancing of interests," the decisions cited in this book make it abundantly clear that the Supreme Court of the United States is an assiduous champion of freedom of the press. These are not the view-

[22] 361 U.S. 147 (1959).
[23] 341 U.S. 494 (1951).
[24] 328 U.S. 331 (1946).

points of a handful of isolated radicals, or impractical academicians, or individual journalists, but the carefully considered opinions of the highest Court of the land. The words the Justices say here about the press and its role in a free society are firmly imbedded in U.S. constitutional law. For the last third of a century the Supreme Court of the United States has enlarged and nationalized the protection of the rights guaranteed by the First Amendment, as it has for other protections of the Bill of Rights. An increasingly wide latitude has been accorded to press rights in area after area where they have conflicted with other rights or the claims of government—contempt of court, freedom from censorship, criticism of government officials, postal regulations, unjust taxation, police and health regulations, civil and criminal defamation, broadcasting, and motion picture freedoms. It is probably accurate to state that there is greater freedom of the press today than at any time in the history of our Republic.

Roche wrote that "the contemporary American, despite the existence of a huge centralized state, is today free to enjoy a range of personal liberty unknown to his ancestors."[25]

For all Americans, the body of Supreme Court decisions on freedom of the press, in addition to being law, is a precious lode of political theory, of social commentary, and of the history of free journalism. Certainly these decisions constitute one of the great legacies and safeguards of a free people.

[25] Roche, p. 38.

*Chapter Two*

**ដ**

# FREEDOM OF EXPRESSION:
# PROBLEMS OF LOYALTY AND SECURITY

**ដ**

DURING the long period from 1787 until World War I, few Supreme Court decisions involved freedom of expression. Except for President Abraham Lincoln's suppression of northern critics of government policies during the Civil War, no action of the national government raised free expression issues until 1917.[1] The passage of the Espionage Act in 1917 and the Sedition Act in 1918, however, resulted in a number of prosecutions focusing public attention on issues of freedom of expression. The question raised was: How far *does* freedom of speech and press extend to critics of the government during time of war?

### THE "CLEAR AND PRESENT DANGER" TEST

The two members of the Supreme Court during World War I most responsible for adapting the First Amendment to this challenge were Justices Oliver Wendell Holmes and Louis D. Brandeis. The tool they fashioned was the "clear and present danger" test. This expression first appeared in the *Schenck* decision. Justice Holmes's great service, according to Zechariah Chafee, was in influencing the Court to accept this new test of guilt as a means of defining and restricting governmental control over free expression. But by the time the "clear and present danger" test was adopted in *Schenck,* it was too late to help

[1] The infamous Alien and Sedition Acts of 1798 were not brought before the Court.

the 1,956 persons prosecuted and the 877 persons convicted of violations of loyalty and security during and immediately after World War I.

In *Schenck* and subsequently in their dissents in *Abrams* and *Gitlow,* and in their concurrence in *Whitney,* Justices Brandeis and Holmes enunciated views and principles of free expression which set the stage for Supreme Court decisions from 1940 onward. Meaning and interpretation were added to the blunt admonishment that "Congress shall make no law . . . abridging freedom of speech, or of the press."

SCHENCK V. UNITED STATES, 249 U.S. 47 (1919)

*Charles T. Schenck, general secretary of the Socialist party, sent about 15,000 leaflets to men called to military service in World War I, urging them to oppose the Conscription Act. He was indicted under the Espionage Act of 1917, charged with conspiracy to cause insubordination in the U.S. military service. Although his conviction was upheld, the Supreme Court's decision in this case unanimously approved Justice Holmes's "clear and present danger" test granting enlarged latitude for free speech.*

Mr. Justice HOLMES delivered the opinion of the Court:

The document in question upon its first printed side recited the first section of the Thirteenth Amendment, said that the idea embodied in it was violated by the Conscription Act and that a conscript is little better than a convict. In impassioned language it intimated that conscription was despotism in its worst form and a monstrous wrong against humanity in the interest of Wall Street's chosen few. It said, "Do not submit to intimidation," but in form at least confined itself to peaceful measures such as a petition for the repeal of the act. The other and later printed side of the sheet was headed "Assert Your Rights." It stated reasons for alleging that any one violated the Constitution when he refused to recognize "your right to assert your opposition to the draft," and went on "if you do not assert and support your rights, you are helping to deny or disparage rights which it is the solemn duty of all citizens and residents of the United States to retain." It described the arguments on the other side as coming from cunning politicians and a mercenary capitalist press, and even silent consent to the conscription law as helping to support an infamous conspiracy. It denied the power to send our citizens away to foreign shores to shoot up the people of other lands, and added that words could not express the condemnation such coldblooded ruthlessness deserves, etc., winding up, "You must do your share to maintain, support and uphold the rights of the people of this country." Of course the document would not have been sent unless it had been intended to have some effect, and we do not see what effect it could be expected to have upon persons subject to the draft except to influence them to obstruct the carrying of it out. The defendants do not deny that the jury might find against them on this point.

But it is said, suppose that that was the tendency of this circular, it is protected by the First Amendment to the Constitution. Two of the strongest expressions are said to be quoted respectively from well-known public men. It well may be that the prohibition of laws abridging the freedom of speech is not confined to previous restraints, although to prevent them may have been the main purpose, as intimated in *Patterson v. Colorado*, 205 U.S. 454. We admit that in many places and in ordinary times the defendants in saying all that was said in the circular would have been within their constitutional rights. But the character of every act depends upon the circumstances in which it is done. The most stringent protection of free speech would not protect a man in falsely shouting fire in a theatre and causing a panic. It does not even protect a man from an injunction against uttering words that may have all the effect of force. The question in every case is whether the words used are used in such circumstances and are of such a nature as to create a clear and present danger that they will bring about the substantive evils that Congress has a right to prevent. It is a question of proximity and degree. When a nation is at war many things that might be said in time of peace are such a hindrance to its effort that their utterance will not be endured so long as men fight and that no Court could regard them as protected by any constitutional right. It seems to be admitted that if an actual obstruction of the recruiting service were proved, liability for words that produced that effect might be enforced. The statute of 1917 punishes conspiracies to obstruct as well as actual obstruction. If the act (speaking or circulating a paper), its tendency and the intent with which it is done are the same, we perceive no ground for saying that success alone warrants making the act a crime.

The Sedition Act of 1918 went far beyond the 1917 law under which Schenck was convicted. It made punishable speech critical of the war effort that during the Second World War would have been considered mere political comment. Justice Holmes passionately dissented in *Abrams* to what he considered the deprivation of the defendants' constitutional rights.

ABRAMS V. UNITED STATES, 250 U.S. 616 (1919)

*Jacob Abrams (a young Russian living in New York City) and four other Russian nationals were indicted for conspiring to violate the Sedition Act of 1918. They had published two leaflets denouncing capitalist nations for interfering in the Russian Revolution. President Woodrow Wilson and the "plutocratic gang in Washington" were criticized for sending U.S. troops to Russia and U.S. workers producing munitions were urged "not to betray their Russian comrades." The Supreme Court affirmed the lower court conviction, reasoning that the plain purpose of the defendants' writings was to excite, during wartime, disaffection, sedition, riots, and even revolution. Justices Brandeis and Holmes dissented, arguing that Abrams's activities fell short of a clear and present danger. In so doing, they further defined the new test.*

Mr. Justice HOLMES, with whom Justice BRANDEIS joined, dissenting:

I do not doubt for a moment that by the same reasoning that would justify punishing persuasion to murder, the United States constitutionally may punish speech that produces or is intended to produce a clear and imminent danger that it will bring about forthwith certain substantive evils that the United States constitutionally may seek to prevent: The power undoubtedly is greater in time of war than in time of peace because war opens dangers that do not exist at other times.

But as against dangers peculiar to war, as against others, the principle of the right to free speech is always the same. It is only the present danger of immediate evil or an intent to bring it about that warrants Congress in setting a limit to the expression of opinion where private rights are not concerned. Congress certainly cannot forbid all effort to change the mind of the country. Now nobody can suppose that the surreptitious publishing of a silly leaflet by an unknown man, without more, would present any immediate danger that its opinions would hinder the success of the government arms or have any appreciable tendency to do so.

. . . . . . . . . . . . . . . . . . . .

In this case sentences of twenty years imprisonment have been imposed for the publishing of two leaflets that I believe the defendants had as much right to publish as the Government has to publish the Constitution of the United States now vainly invoked by them. Even if I am technically wrong and enough can be squeezed from these poor and puny anonymities to turn the color of legal litmus paper; I will add, even if what I think the necessary intent were shown; the most nominal punishment seems to me all that possibly could be inflicted, unless the defendants are to be made to suffer not for what the indictment alleges but for the creed that they avow—a creed that I believe to be the creed of ignorance and immaturity when honestly held, as I see no reason to doubt that it was held here, but which, although made the subject of examination at the trial, no one has a right even to consider in dealing with the charges before the Court.

Persecution for the expression of opinions seems to me perfectly logical. If you have no doubt of your premises or your power and want a certain result with all your heart you naturally express your wishes in law and sweep away all opposition. To allow opposition by speech seems to indicate that you think the speech impotent, as when a man says that he had squared the circle, or that you do not care whole heartedly for the result, or that you doubt either your power or your premises. But when men have realized that time has upset many fighting faiths, they may come to believe even more than they believe the very foundations of their own conduct that the ultimate good desired is better reached by free trade in ideas—that the best test of truth is the power of the thought to get itself accepted in the competition of the market, and that truth is the only ground upon which their wishes safely can be carried out. That at any rate is the theory of our Constitution. It is an experiment, as all life is an experiment. Every year, if not every day, we have to wager our salvation upon some prophecy based upon imperfect knowledge. While that experiment is part of our system I think that we should be eternally vigilant against attempts to check the expression of opinions that we loathe and believe to be fraught with death, unless they so imminently threaten immediate interference with the lawful and pressing purposes of the law that an immediate check is required to save the country. I wholly disagree with the argument of the Government that the First Amendment left the common law as to seditious libel in force. History seems to me against the notion. I had conceived that the United States through many years had shown its repentance for the Sedition Act of 1798 . . . by repaying fines that it imposed. Only the emergency that makes it immediately dangerous to leave the correction of evil counsels to time warrants making any exception to the sweeping command, "Congress shall make no law abridging the freedom of speech." Of course, I am speaking only of expressions of opinion and exhortations, which were all that were uttered here, but I regret that I cannot put into more impressive words my belief that in their conviction upon this indictment the defendants were deprived of their rights under the Constitution of the United States.

### EXPANSION OF THE DUE PROCESS CLAUSE

One of the most consequential modern developments in constitutional law has been the Supreme Court's expansion of the due process clause of the Fourteenth Amendment to include the rights of the First Amendment. As a result, virtually all actions in state and local courts involving First Amendment issues are subject to review by the Supreme Court. This has enhanced greatly the Court's role as a protector of civil liberties throughout the land.

Although the Fourteenth Amendment was passed in 1868, this judicial evolution was not completed until 1925 in the *Gitlow* case.

GITLOW V. NEW YORK, 268 U.S. 652 (1925)

*Benjamin Gitlow, business manager of a Socialist party paper called* Revolutionary Age, *was convicted in New York of publishing and circulating pamphlets advocating overthrow of organized government by violent and other unlawful means. Gitlow's defense counsel argued that the New York statute deprived him of liberty without due process of law. Though the Supreme Court ruled that the 1902 New York act did not unduly restrict Gitlow's freedom of speech and press, it did accept the view that freedom of speech and of the press are safeguarded against state actions by the due process clause of the Fourteenth Amendment.*

*In upholding Gitlow's conviction, Justice Edward Sanford's opinion relied on the test of "reasonable tendency" rather than "clear and present danger." To this, Justices Brandeis and Holmes dissented.*

Mr. Justice SANFORD delivered the opinion of the Court:

For present purposes we may and do assume that freedom of speech and of the press—which are protected by the First Amendment from abridgment by Congress—are among the fundamental personal rights and "liberties" protected by the due process clause of the Fourteenth Amendment from impairment by the states.

It is a fundamental principle, long established, that the freedom of speech and of the press which is secured by the Constitution does not confer an absolute right to speak or publish, without responsibility, whatever one may choose, or an unrestricted and unbridled license that gives immunity for every possible use of language and prevents the punishment of those who abuse this freedom.

Reasonably limited, it was said by Story in the passage cited, this freedom is an inestimable privilege in a free government; without such limitation, it might become the scourge of the republic.

That a state in the exercise of its police power may punish those who abuse this freedom by utterances inimical to the public welfare, tending to corrupt public morals, incite to crime, or disturb the public peace, is not open to question.

And, for yet more imperative reasons, a state may punish utterances endangering the foundations of organized government and threatening its overthrow by unlawful means. These imperil its own existence as a constitutional state. Freedom of speech and press, said Story, . . . does not protect disturbances to the public peace or the attempt to subvert the government. It does not protect publications or teachings which tend to subvert or imperil the government or to impede or hinder it in the performance of its governmental duties. . . . It does not protect publications prompting the overthrow of government by force; the punishment of those who publish articles which tend to destroy organized society being essential to the security of freedom and the stability of the state. . . . And a state may penalize utterances which openly advocate the overthrow of the representative and constitutional form of government of the United States and the several states by violence or other unlawful means.

In *Toledo Newspaper Co. v. United States,* 247 U.S. 402, . . . it was said: "The safeguarding and fructification of free and constitutional institutions is the very basis and mainstay upon which the freedom of the press rests, and that freedom, therefore, does not and cannot be held to include the right virtually to destroy such institutions."

The two famous dissenters argued for a broader interpretation of free speech.

Mr. Justice HOLMES, with whom Mr. Justice BRANDEIS joined, dissenting:

Mr. Justice Brandeis and I are of opinion that this judgment should be reversed. The general principle of free speech, it seems to me, must be taken to be included in the Fourteenth Amendment, in view of the scope that has been given to the word "liberty" as there used, although perhaps it may be accepted with a somewhat larger latitude of interpretation than is allowed to Congress by the sweeping language that governs or ought to govern the laws of the United States. If I am right then I think that the criterion sanctioned by the full court in *Schenck v. United States* . . . applies:

"The question in every case is whether the words used are

used in such circumstances and are of such a nature as to create a clear and present danger that they will bring about the substantive evils that (the state) has a right to prevent."

If what I think the correct test is applied it is manifest that there was no present danger of an attempt to overthrow the government by force on the part of the admittedly small minority who shared the defendant's views. It is said that this manifesto was more than a theory, that it was an incitement. Every idea is an incitement. It offers itself for belief and if believed it is acted on unless some other belief outweighs it or some failure of energy stifles the movement at its birth. The only difference between the expression of an opinion and an incitement in the narrower sense is the speaker's enthusiasm for the result. Eloquence may set fire to reason. But whatever may be thought of the redundant discourse before us it had no chance of starting a present conflagration. If in the long run the beliefs expressed in proletarian dictatorship are destined to be accepted by the dominant forces of the community, the only meaning of free speech is that they should be given their chance and have their way.

If the publication of this document had been laid as an attempt to induce an uprising against government at once and not at some indefinite time in the future it would have presented a different question. The object would have been one with which the law might deal, subject to the doubt whether there was any danger that the publication could produce any result, or in other words, whether it was not futile and too remote from possible consequences. But the indictment alleges the publication and nothing more.

### BRANDEIS ELABORATES THE CLEAR AND PRESENT DANGER TEST

The *Gitlow* decision gave rise to the expectation that the Supreme Court, even though it had sustained the New York Anarchy Act, might yet overturn the convictions under the more effectively sweeping criminal syndicalism acts such as California had.

WHITNEY V. CALIFORNIA, 274 U.S. 357 (1927)

*Anita Whitney, a philanthropist and Socialist, was convicted of violating the Criminal Syndicalism Act of California, which disallowed, among other things, advocating and teaching criminal syndicalism, the revolutionary doctrine by which workers seize control of the economy and the government by the general strike and other direct means. The Supreme Court upheld her conviction. In his concurring opinion Justice Brandeis elaborated on the clear and present danger test in eloquent words and explained why government is prohibited from restricting freedom of expression.*

Mr. Justice BRANDEIS joined by Mr. Justice HOLMES, concurring:

This court has not yet fixed the standard by which to determine when a danger shall be deemed clear; how remote the danger may be and yet be deemed present; and what degree of evil shall be deemed sufficiently substantial to justify resort to abridgment of free speech and assembly as the means of protection. To reach sound conclusions on these matters, we must bear in mind why a state is, ordinarily, denied the power to prohibit dissemination of social, economic and political doctrine which a vast majority of its citizens believes to be false and fraught with evil consequence.

Those who won our independence believed that the final end of the state was to make men free to develop their faculties, and that in its government the deliberative forces should prevail over the arbitrary. They valued liberty both as an end and as a means. They believed liberty to be the secret of happiness and courage to be the secret of liberty. They believed that freedom to think as you will and to speak as you think are means indispensable to the discovery and spread of political truth; that without free speech and assembly discussion would be futile; that with them, discussion affords ordinarily adequate protection against the dissemination of noxious doctrine; that the greatest menace to freedom is an inert people; that public discussion is a political duty; and that this should be a fundamental principle of the American government. They recognized the risks to which all human institutions are subject. But they knew that order cannot be secured merely through fear of punishment for its infraction; that it is hazardous to discourage thought, hope and imagination; that fear breeds repression; that repression breeds hate; that hate menaces stable government; that the path of safety lies in the opportunity to discuss freely supposed grievances and proposed remedies; and that the fitting remedy for evil counsels is good ones. Believing in the power of reason as applied through public discussion, they eschewed silence coerced by law—the argument of force in its worst form. Recognizing the occasional tyrannies of governing majorities, they amended the Constitution so that free speech and assembly should be guaranteed.

Fear of serious injury cannot alone justify suppression of free speech and assembly. Men feared witches and burnt women. It is the function of speech to free men from the bondage of irrational fears. To justify suppression of free speech there must be reasonable ground to fear that serious evil will result if free speech is practiced. There must be reasonable ground to believe that the danger apprehended is imminent. There must be reasonable ground to believe that the evil to be prevented is a serious one. Every denunciation of existing law tends in some measure to increase the probability that there will be violation of it. Condonation of a breach enhances the probability. Expressions of approval add to the probability. Propagation of the criminal state of mind by teaching syndicalism increases it. Advocacy of law-breaking heightens it still further. But even advocacy of violation, however reprehensible morally, is not a justification for denying free speech where the advocacy falls short of incitement and there is nothing to indicate that the advocacy would be immediately acted on. The wide difference between advocacy and incitement, between preparation and attempt, between assembling and conspiracy, must be borne in mind. In order to support a finding of clear and present danger it must be shown either that immediate serious violence was to be expected or was advocated, or that the past conduct furnished reason to believe that such advocacy was then contemplated.

Those who won our independence by revolution were not cowards. They did not fear political change. They did not exalt order at the cost of liberty. To courageous, self-reliant men, with confidence in the power of free and fearless reasoning applied through the processes of popular government, no danger flowing from speech can be deemed clear and present, unless the incidence of the evil apprehended is so imminent that it may befall before there is opportunity for full discussion. If there be time to expose through discussion the falsehood and fallacies, to avert the evil by the process of education, the remedy to be applied is more speech, not enforced silence. Only an emergency can justify repression. Such must be the rule if authority is to be reconciled with freedom. Such, in my opinion, is the command of the Constitution. It is therefore always open to Americans to challenge a law abridging free speech and assembly by showing that there was no emergency justifying it. . . .

The fact that speech is likely to result in some violence or in destruction of property is not enough to justify its suppression. There must be the probability of serious injury to the state. Among free men, the deterrents ordinarily to be applied to prevent crime are education and punishment for violations of the law, not abridgment of the rights of free speech and assembly.

In the ensuing years, views similar to these of Justice Brandeis have often been expressed in Supreme Court rulings on freedom of expression. Some legal authorities still consider valid the essential elements of the clear and present danger test as enunciated in Justice Brandeis's distinctions between advocacy and incitement, between preparation and attempt, between assembly and conspiracy.

After the Court revolution of 1937, and the subsequent appointments of Justices Hugo L. Black and William O. Douglas, the First Amendment became the focal point of our constitutional law. While the *Gitlow* case has never been explicitly overruled, later cases have relied on Justices Holmes and Brandeis's version of the test. It is still the standard by which the Court judges restrictions on free expression, although the "case-to-case approach" has been enlarged to the "constitutionality of the law" approach of Holmes and the Justices have often disagreed as to when a danger is "clear" or when it is "present" or when the evil involved is "substantial."

## THE "CLEAR AND PRESENT DANGER" TEST REDEFINED

The challenges to free and open government from real or imagined dangers of a Communist conspiracy reached the courts again during the Cold War following World War II. The legal apex came in the *Dennis* case, in which the Holmes and Brandeis doctrine was stretched until it was almost unrecognizable.

This important decision was decided by 6-to-2 margin, as Justice Tom C. Clark, a former attorney general, did not participate. Seven of the justices agreed that "clear and present danger" was the standard to be used, but the eighth, Justice Robert H. Jackson, who concurred with the majority, insisted that in a criminal conspiracy case such as this, the defendants could be convicted even if there were no clear and present danger. In actuality, the Court adopted a new definition of clear and present danger in reaching its decision.

DENNIS V. UNITED STATES, 341 U.S. 494 (1951)

*Eugene Dennis and ten other top leaders of the U.S. Communist party were convicted of violating the 1940 Smith Act which provided for the registration and fingerprinting of aliens and declared it unlawful to advocate or teach the forceful overthrow of any government in the United States or to belong to any group advocating such action. A U.S. court in New York decided that the national leadership of the Communist party had conspired to organize the Communist party to teach and advocate the overthrow and destruction of the U.S. government*

*by force and violence. In upholding the convictions, the Su-
preme Court applied a test suggested by the lower court judge,
Learned Hand, who wrote: "In each case Courts must ask
whether the gravity of the 'evil,' discounted by its improbability, justified such invasion of free speech as is necessary to avoid
the danger." To Chief Justice Fred Vinson the clear and present danger test, while applicable to the isolated speech of individuals or small groups, was inappropriate for testing such a
large-scale conspiratorial movement as the Communist party.
In this important decision, the excerpts included here focus on
the problem of free expression vis-a-vis a domestic Communist
threat.*

Mr. Chief Justice Fred VINSON announced the judgment of the Court and
an opinion in which Mr. Justice Stanley REED, Mr. Justice Harold BURTON,
and Mr. Justice Sherman MINTON joined:

. . . The basis of the First Amendment is the hypothesis that
speech can rebut speech, propaganda will answer propaganda, free
debate of ideas will result in the wisest governmental policies. It
is for this reason that this Court has recognized the inherent value
of free discourse. An analysis of the leading cases in this Court
which have involved direct limitations on speech, however, will
demonstrate that both the majority of the Court and the dissenters
in particular cases have recognized that this is not an unlimited,
unqualified right, but that the societal value of speech, must on
occasion, be subordinated to other values and considerations.

. . . . . . . . . . . . . . . . . . .

The rule we deduce from these cases is that where an offense is
specified by a statute in nonspeech or nonpress terms, a conviction
relying upon speech or press as evidence of violation may be sustained only when the speech or publication created a "clear and
present danger," of attempting or accomplishing the prohibited
crime, e.g. interference with enlistment.

. . . . . . . . . . . . . . . . . . .

Neither Justice Holmes nor Justice Brandeis ever envisioned
that a shorthand phrase should be crystallized into a rigid rule to
be applied inflexibly without regard to the circumstances of each
case. Speech is not an absolute, above and beyond control by the
legislature when its judgment, subject to review here, is that certain
kinds of speech are so undesirable as to warrant criminal sanction.
Nothing is more certain in modern society than the principle that
there are no absolutes, that a name, a phrase, a standard has meaning only when associated with the considerations which gave birth
to the nomenclature. . . . To those who would paralyze our Gov-

ernment in the face of impending threat by encasing it in a semantic straitjacket we must reply that all concepts are relative. . . . Overthrow of the Government by force and violence is certainly a substantial enough interest for the Government to limit speech. Indeed, this is the ultimate value of any society, for if a society cannot protect its very structure from armed internal attack, it must follow that no subordinate value can be protected. If, then, this interest may be protected, the literal problem which is presented is what has been meant by the use of the phrase "clear and present danger" of the utterances bringing about the evil within the power of Congress to punish.

Obviously, the words cannot mean that before the Government may act, it must wait until the *putsch* is about to be executed, the plans have been laid, and the signal is awaited. If Government is aware that a group aiming at its overthrow is attempting to indoctrinate its members and to commit them to a course whereby they will strike when the leaders feel the circumstances permit, action by the Government is required. The argument that there is no need for Government to concern itself, for Government is strong, it possesses ample powers to put down a rebellion, it may defeat the revolution with ease, needs no answer. For that is not the question. Certainly an attempt to overthrow the Government by force, even though doomed from the outset because of inadequate numbers or power of the revolutionists, is a sufficient evil for Congress to prevent. The damage which such attempts create both physically and politically to a nation makes it impossible to measure the validity in terms of the probability of success, or the immediacy of a successful attempt. In the instant case the trial judge charged the jury that they could not convict unless they found that petitioners intended to overthrow the Government "as speedily as circumstances would permit." This does not mean, and could not properly mean, that they would not strike until there was certainty of success. What was meant was that the revolutionists would strike when they thought the time was ripe. We must therefore reject the contention that success or probability of success is the criterion.

.  .  .  .  .  .  .  .  .  .  .  .  .  .  .  .  .  .

Chief Judge Learned Hand, writing for the [lower court] below interpreted the phrase as follows: "In each case courts must ask whether the gravity of the 'evil,' discounted by its improbability, justifies such invasion of free speech as is necessary to avoid the danger." . . . We adopt this statement of the rule. As articulated by Chief Judge Hand, it is as succinct and inclusive as any other we might devise at this time. It takes into consideration those factors which we deem relevant, and relates their significances. More we cannot expect from words.

In concurring, Justice Felix Frankfurter argued that the First Amendment does not provide absolute immunity to all speech. Free speech, he said, must be balanced with other competing interests.

Mr. Justice FRANKFURTER concurring:

But even the all-embracing power and duty of self-preservation are not absolute. Like the war power, which is indeed an aspect of the power of self-preservation, it is subject to applicable constitutional limitations. Our Constitution has no provision lifting restrictions upon governmental authority during periods of emergency, although the scope of a restriction may depend on the circumstances in which it is invoked.

The First Amendment is such a restriction. It exacts obedience even during periods of war; it is applicable when war clouds are not figments of the imagination no less than when they make no law respecting an establishment of religion, or prohibiting the free exercise thereof; or abridging the freedom of speech, or of the press; or the right of the people peaceably to assemble, and to petition the Government for a redress of grievances." The right of a man to think what he pleases, to write what he thinks, and to have his thoughts made available for others to hear or read has an engaging ring of universality. The Smith Act and this conviction under it no doubt restrict the exercise of free speech and assembly. Does that, without more, dispose of the matter?

Just as there are those who regard as invulnerable every measure for which the claim of national survival is invoked, there are those who find in the Constitution a wholly unfettered right of expression. Such literalness treats the words of the Constitution as though they were found on a piece of outworn parchment instead of being words that have called into being a nation with a past to be preserved for the future. The soil in which the Bill of Rights grew was not a soil of arid pedantry. The historic antecedents of the First Amendment preclude the notion that its purpose was to give unqualified immunity to every expression that touched on matters within the range of political interest. The Massachusetts Constitution of 1780 guaranteed free speech; yet there are records of at least three convictions for political libels obtained between 1799 and 1803. The Pennsylvania Constitution of 1790 and the Delaware Constitution of 1792 expressly imposed liability for abuse of the right of free speech. Madison's own State put on its books in 1792 a statute confining the abusive exercise of the right of utterance. And it deserves to be noted that in writing to John Adams's wife, Jefferson did not rest his condemnation of the Sedition Act of 1798 on his belief in unrestrained utterance as to political matter. The

First Amendment, he argued, reflected a limitation upon Federal power, leaving the right to enforce restrictions on speech to the States.

The language of the First Amendment is to be read not as barren words found in a dictionary but as symbols of historic experience illumined by the presuppositions of those who employed them. Not what words did Madison and Hamilton use, but what was it in their minds which they conveyed? Free speech is subject to prohibition of those abuses of expression which a civilized society may forbid. As in the case of every other provision of the Constitution that is not crystallized by the nature of its technical concepts, the fact that the First Amendment is not self-defining and self-enforcing neither impairs its usefulness nor compels its paralysis as a living instrument.

The demands of free speech in a democratic society as well as the interest in national security are better served by candid and informed weighing of the competing interests, within the confines of the judicial process, than by announcing dogmas too inflexible for the non-Euclidian problems to be solved.

But how are competing interests to be assessed? Since they are not subject to quantitative ascertainment, the issue necessarily resolves itself into asking who is to make the adjustment—who is to balance the relevant factors and ascertain which interest is in the circumstances to prevail? Full responsibility for the choice cannot be given to the courts. Courts are not representative bodies. They are not designed to be a good reflex of a democratic society. Their judgment is best informed, and therefore most dependable, within narrow limits. Their essential quality is detachment, founded on independence. History teaches that the independence of the judiciary is jeopardized when courts become embroiled in the passions of the day and assume primary responsibility in choosing between competing political, economic and social pressures.

We must not overlook the value of that interchange. Freedom of expression is the well-spring of our civilization—the civilization we seek to maintain and further by recognizing the right of Congress to put some limitation upon expression. Such are the paradoxes of life. For social development of trial and error, the fullest possible opportunity for the free play of the human mind is an indispensable prerequisite. The history of civilization is in considerable measure the displacement of error which once held sway as official truth by beliefs which in turn have yielded to other truths. Therefore, the liberty of man to search for truth ought not be fettered, no matter what orthodoxies he may challenge. Liberty of thought soon shrivels without freedom of expression. Nor can truth be pursued in an atmosphere hostile to the endeavor or under dangers which are hazarded only by heroes.

Much that should be rejected as illiberal, because repressive and envenoming, may well be not unconstitutional. The ultimate reliance for the deepest needs of civilization must be found outside their vindication in courts of law; apart from all else, judges, howsoever they may conscientiously seek to discipline themselves against it, unconsciously are too apt to be moved by the deep undercurrents of public feeling. A persistent, positive translation of the liberating faith into the feelings and thoughts and actions of men and women is the real protection against attempts to strait-jacket the human mind. Such temptations will have their way, if fear and hatred are not exorcized. The mark of a truly civilized man is confidence in the strength and security derived from the inquiring mind. We may be grateful for such honest comforts as it supports, but we must be unafraid of its incertitudes. Without open minds there can be no open society. And if society be not open the spirit of man is mutilated and becomes enslaved.

. . . . . . . . . . . . . . . . . . .

On the other hand is the interest in free speech. The right to exert all governmental powers in aid of maintaining our institutions and resisting their physical overthrow does not include intolerance of opinions and speech that cannot do harm although opposed and perhaps alien to dominant, traditional opinion. The treatment of its minorities, especially their legal position, is among the most searching tests of the level of civilization attained by a society. It is better for those who have almost unlimited power of government in their hands to err on the side of freedom. We have enjoyed so much freedom for so long that we are perhaps in danger of forgetting how much blood it cost to establish the Bill of Rights.

Of course no government can recognize a "right" of revolution, or a "right" to incite revolution if the incitement has no other purpose or effect. But a speech is seldom restricted to a single purpose, and its effects may be manifold. A public interest is not wanting in granting freedom to speak their minds even to those who advocate the overthrow of the Government by force. For, as the evidence in this case abundantly illustrates, coupled with such advocacy is criticism of defects in our society. Criticism is the spur to reform; and Burke's admonition that a healthy society must reform in order to conserve has not lost its force. Astute observers have remarked that one of the characteristics of the American Republic is indifference to fundamental criticism. Bryce, the American Commonwealth, c. 84. It is a commonplace that there may be a grain of truth in the most uncouth doctrine, however false and repellent the balance may be. Suppressing advocates of overthrow inevitably will also silence critics who do not advocate overthrow but fear that their criticism may be so construed. No matter how clear we may be that the defendants now before us are preparing to overthrow our Government at the propitious moment, it is self-delusion to think that we can punish them for their advocacy without adding to the risks run by loyal citizens who honestly believe in some of the reforms these defendants advance. It is a sobering fact that in sustaining the convictions before us we can hardly escape restriction on the interchange of ideas.

.  .  .  .  .  .  .  .  .  .  .  .  .  .  .  .  .  .  .

"The interest, which [the First Amendment] guards, and which gives it importance, presupposes that there are no orthodoxies—religious, political, economic, or scientific—which are immune from debate and dispute. Back of that is the assumption—itself an orthodoxy, and the one permissible exception—that truth will be most likely to emerge, if no limitations are imposed upon utterances that can with any plausibility be regarded as efforts to present grounds for accepting or rejecting propositions whose truth the utterer asserts, or denies.". . . In the last analysis it is on the validity of this faith that our national security is staked.

It is not for us to decide how we would adjust the clash of interests which this case presents were the primary responsibility for reconciling it ours. Congress has determined that the danger created by advocacy of overthrow justifies the ensuring restriction on freedom of speech. . . . Can we establish a constitutional doctrine which forbids the elected representatives of the people to make this choice? Can we hold that the First Amendment deprives Congress of what it deemed necessary for the Government's protection?

Justices Black and Douglas disagreed. They argued that there are no exceptions to the rule of free speech for all—not even for members of a Communist conspiracy. Douglas emphasized that speech must remain uncontrolled and that government can intervene only when opponents of the state move from words to illegal acts.

Mr. Justice BLACK dissenting:

Undoubtedly, a governmental policy of unfettered communication of ideas does entail dangers. To the Founders of this nation, however, the benefits derived from free expression were worth the risk. They embodied this philosophy in the First Amendment's command that "Congress shall make no law . . . abridging the freedom of speech, or of the press. . . ." I have always believed that the First Amendment is the keystone of our government, that the freedoms it guarantees provide the best insurance against destruction of all freedom.

Mr. Justice DOUGLAS dissenting:

Free speech has occupied an exalted position because of the high service it has given society. Its protection is essential to the very existence of a democracy. The airing of ideas releases pressures which otherwise might become destructive. When ideas compete in the market for acceptance, full and free discussion exposes the false and they gain few adherents. Full and free discussion even of ideas we hate encourages the testing of our own prejudices and preconceptions. Full and free discussion keeps a society from becoming stagnant and unprepared for the stresses and strains that work to tear all civilizations apart.

Full and free discussion has indeed been the first article of our faith. We have founded our political system on it. It has been the safeguard of every religious, political, philosophical, economic, and racial group amongst us. We have counted on it to keep us from embracing what is cheap and false; we have trusted the common sense of our people to choose the doctrine true to our genius and to reject the rest. This has been the one single outstanding tenet that has made our institutions the symbol of freedom and equality. We have deemed it more costly to liberty to suppress a despised minority than to let them vent their spleen. We have above all else feared the political censor. We have wanted a land where our people can be exposed to all the diverse creeds and cultures of the world.

There comes a time when even speech loses its constitutional immunity. Speech innocuous one year may at another time fan such destructive flames that it must be halted in the interests of the safety of the Republic. That is the meaning of the clear and present danger test. When conditions are so critical that there will be no time to avoid the evil that the speech threatens, it is time to call a halt. Otherwise, free speech which is the strength of the Nation will be the cause of its destruction.

Yet free speech is the rule, not the exception. The restraint to be constitutional must be based on more than fear, on more than passionate opposition against the speech, on more than a revolted dislike for its contents. There must be some immediate injury to society that is likely if speech is allowed.

. . . . . . . . . . . . . . . . . . .

The First Amendment provides that "Congress shall make no law . . . abridging the freedom of speech." The Constitution provides no exception. This does not mean, however, that the Nation need hold its hand until it is in such weakened condition that there is no time to protect itself from incitement to revolution. Seditious conduct can always be punished. But the command of the First Amendment is so clear that we should not allow Congress to call a halt to free speech except in the extreme case of peril from the speech itself. The First Amendment makes confidence in the common sense of our people and in their maturity of judgment the great postulate of our democracy. Its philosophy is that violence is rarely, if ever, stopped by denying civil liberties to those advocating resort to force. The First Amendment reflects the philosophy of Jefferson "that it is time enough for the rightful purposes of civil government, for its officers to interfere when principles break out into overt acts against peace and good order." The political censor has no place in our public debates. Unless and until extreme and necessitous circumstances are shown, our aim should be to keep speech unfettered and to allow the processes of law to be invoked only when the provocateurs among us move from speech to action.

Vishinsky wrote in 1938 in *The Law of the Soviet State,* "In our State, naturally, there is and can be no place for freedom of speech, press and so on for the foes of socialism."

Our concern should be that we accept no such standard for the United States. Our faith should be that our people will never give support to these advocates of revolution, so long as we remain loyal to the purposes for which our Nation was founded.

Six years later, other Communist leaders at the state, local, as well as national levels were convicted under the same Smith Act. It should be remembered that these cases, unlike most other free expression cases, involved a criminal conspiracy by a disciplined party apparatus influenced from abroad. A lone individual exercising his freedom of expression was not being restrained by government. Despite *Dennis,* the Holmes-Brandeis version of the test still would apply for individual speakers and writers.

### TOLERANCE URGED FOR ALL POLITICAL VIEWS

The efforts of the U.S. government to convict still more Communist party leaders were checked a few years later in *Yates.* In this case, Justice Black argued that the best insurance for freedom and security of all is the widest tolerance of all ideas and views.

YATES V. UNITED STATES, 354 U.S. 298 (1957)

*Six years after the Dennis case, fourteen "second string" Communist party leaders were convicted under the Smith Act. But here the Supreme Court found two decisive differences between this and the Dennis case and set aside the convictions.*

Mr. Justice BLACK, concurring in part and dissenting in part, wrote:

In essence, petitioners were tried upon the charge that they believe in and want to foist upon this country a different and to us a despicable form of authoritarian government in which voices criticizing the existing order are summarily silenced. I fear that the present type of prosecutions are more in line with authoritarian government than with that expressed by our First Amendment.

Doubtlessly, dictators have to stamp out causes and beliefs which they deem subversive to their evil regimes. But governmental suppression of causes and beliefs seems to me to be the very antithesis of what our Constitution stands for. The choice expressed in the First Amendment in favor of free expression was made against a turbulent background by men such as Jefferson, Madison and Mason—men who believed that loyalty to the provisions of this Amendment was the best way to assure a long life for this new nation and its Government. Unless there is complete freedom of expression of all ideas, whether we like them or not, concerning the way government should be run and who shall run it, I doubt if any views in the long run can be secured against the censor. The First Amendment provides the only kind of security system that can preserve a free government—one that leaves the way open for people to favor, discuss, advocate, or incite causes and doctrines however obnoxious and antagonistic such views may be to the rest of us.

In another Communism case, *Barenblatt,* Justice Black again opposed what he considered attempts by the Court to water down the meaning of the First Amendment. The special target of his dissent was the Court's "balancing test," which he felt runs counter to the original intent of the Bill of Rights.

BARENBLATT V. UNITED STATES, 360 U.S. 109 (1959)

*Lloyd Barenblatt, a former psychology teacher at Vassar, refused to answer questions before the House Committee on Un-American Activities concerning his alleged past membership in the Communist party. Although he based his silence on his First Amendment rights, he was cited for contempt of Congress. The citation was upheld by the Supreme Court.*

Mr. Justice BLACK, with whom Justices Earl WARREN and DOUGLAS joined, dissenting:

The First Amendment says in no equivocal language that Congress shall pass no law abridging freedom of speech, press, assembly or petition. The activities of this Committee, authorized by Con-

gress, do precisely that, through exposure, obloquy and public scorn.
. . . The Court does not really deny this fact but relies on a combination of three reasons for permitting the infringement: (A) The
notion that despite the First Amendment's command Congress can
abridge speech and association if this Court decides that the governmental interest in abridging speech is greater than an individual's interest in exercising that freedom, (B) the Government's right
to "preserve itself," (C) the fact that the Committee is only after
Communists or suspected Communists in this investigation.

. . . . . . . . . . . . . . . . . . . .

To apply the Court's balancing test under such circumstances
is to read the First Amendment to say "Congress shall pass no law
abridging freedom of speech, press, assembly and petition, unless
Congress and the Supreme Court reach the joint conclusion that on
balance the interest of the Government in stifling these freedoms is
greater than the interest of the people in having them exercised."
This is closely akin to the notion that neither the First Amendment
nor any other provision of the Bill of Rights should be enforced
unless the Court believes it is reasonable to do so. Not only does
this violate the genius of our written Constitution, but it runs expressly counter to the injunction to Court and Congress made by
Madison when he introduced the Bill of Rights. "If they (the first
ten amendments) are incorporated into the Constitution, independent tribunals of justice will consider themselves in a peculiar manner the guardians of those rights; they will be an impenetrable bulwark against every assumption of power in the Legislative or
Executive; they will be naturally led to resist every encroachment
upon rights expressly stipulated for in the Constitution by the
declaration of rights." Unless we return to this view of our judicial
function, unless we once again accept the notion that the Bill of
Rights means what it says and that this Court must enforce that
meaning, I am of the opinion that our great charter of liberty will
be more honored in the breach than in the observance.

. . . . . . . . . . . . . . . . . . .

(B) Moreover, I cannot agree with the Court's notion that First
Amendment freedoms must be abridged in order to "preserve" our
country. That notion rests on the unarticulated premise that this
Nation's security hangs upon its power to punish people because of
what they think, speak or write about, or because of those with
whom they associate for political purposes. The Government in its
brief, virtually admits this position when it speaks of the "communication of unlawful ideas." I challenge this premise, and deny that
ideas can be proscribed under our Constitution. I agree that
despotic governments cannot exist without stifling the voice of
opposition to their oppressive practices. The First Amendment
means to me, however, that the only constitutional way our Govern-

ment can preserve itself is to leave its people the fullest possible freedom to praise, criticize or discuss, as they see fit, all governmental policies and to suggest, if they desire, that even its most fundamental postulates are bad and should be changed; "Therein lies the security of the Republic, the very foundation of constitutional government." On that premise this land was created, and on that premise it has grown to greatness. Our Constitution assumes that the common sense of the people and their attachment to our country will enable them, after free discussion, to withstand ideas that are wrong. To say that our patriotism must be protected against false ideas by means other than these is, I think, to make a baseless charge. Unless we can rely on these qualities—if, in short, we begin to punish speech—we cannot honestly proclaim ourselves to be a free nation and we have lost what the Founders of this land risked their lives and their sacred honor to defend.

## ABSOLUTIST VIEW OF INDIVIDUAL FREEDOM

In *Braden,* a case similar to *Barenblatt,* Justice Black, supported in his dissent by Chief Justice Warren and Justice Douglas, made another strong plea for unrestricted freedom of expression. His absolutist position would require that government follow the literal dictates of the First Amendment.

### BRADEN V. UNITED STATES, 365 U.S. 431 (1961)

*Carl Braden, an opponent of segregation was brought before a U.S. district court in Georgia after refusing to answer questions of a sub-committee of the House Un-American Activities Committee investigating Communist infiltration in the South. By a 5-to-4 vote the Supreme Court upheld his conviction of contempt of Congress.*

Mr. Justice BLACK, with whom Justices WARREN and DOUGLAS joined, disssenting:

Both *Barenblatt* and *Beauharnais* are offspring of a constitutional doctrine that is steadily sacrificing individual freedom of religion, speech, press, assembly and petition to governmental control. There have been many other such decisions and the indications are that this number will continue to grow at an alarming rate. For the presently prevailing constitutional doctrine, which treats the First Amendment as a mere admonition, leaves the liberty-giving freedoms which were intended to be protected by that Amendment completely at the mercy of Congress and this Court whenever a majority of this Court concludes, on the basis of any of the several judicially created "tests" now in vogue, that abridgement of these freedoms is more desirable than freedom itself. Only a few days ago, the application of this constitutional doctrine wiped out the rule forbidding prior censorship of movies in an opinion that leaves the door wide open to, if indeed it does not actually invite, prior censorship of other means of publication. And the Blackstonian condemnation of prior censorship had long been thought, even by those whose ideas of First Amendment liberties had been most restricted, to be the absolute minimum of the protection demanded by that Amendment.

I once more deny, as I have found it repeatedly necessary to do in other cases, that this Nation's ability to preserve itself depends upon suppression of the freedoms of religion, speech, press, assembly and petition. But I do believe that the noble-sounding slogan of "self-preservation" rests upon a premise that can itself destroy any democratic nation by a slow process of eating away at the liberties that are indispensable to its healthy growth. The very foundation of a true democracy and the foundation upon which this Nation was built is the fact that government is responsive to the views of its citizens, and no nation can continue to exist on such a foundation unless its citizens are wholly free to speak out fearlessly for or against their officials and their laws. When it begins to send its dissenters, such as Barenblatt, Uphaus, Wilkinson, and now Braden, to jail, the liberties indispensable to its existence must be fast disappearing. If self-preservation is to be the issue that decides these cases, I firmly believe they must be decided the other way. Only by a dedicated preservation of the freedoms of the First Amendment can we hope to preserve our Nation and its traditional way of life.

It is already past the time when people who recognize and cherish the life-giving and life-preserving qualities of the freedoms protected by the Bill of Rights can afford to sit complacently by while those freedoms are being destroyed by sophistry and dialectics. For at least 11 years, since the decision of this Court in *American Communications Ass'n, C.I.O. v. Douds,* the forces of destruction have been hard at work. Much damage had already been done. If this dangerous trend is not stopped now, it may be an impossible task to stop it at all. The area set off for individual freedom by the Bill of Rights was marked by boundaries precisely defined. It is my belief that the area so set off provides an adequate minimum protection for the freedoms indispensable to individual liberty. Thus we have only to observe faithfully the boundaries already marked for us. For the present, however, the two cases decided by this Court today and the many others like them that have been decided in the past 11 years have all but obliterated those boundaries. There are now no limits to congressional encroachment in this field except such as a majority of this Court may choose to set by a value-weighing process on a case-by-case basis.

I cannot accept such a process. As I understand it, this Court's duty to guard constitutional liberties is to guard those liberties the Constitution defined, not those that may be defined from case to case on the basis of this Court's judgment as to the relative importance of individual liberty and governmental power. The majority's approach makes the First Amendment, not the rigid protection of liberty its language imports, but a poor flexible imitation. This weak substitute for the First Amendment is, to my mind, totally unacceptable for I believe that Amendment forbids, among other things, any agency of the Federal Government—be it legislative, executive or judicial—to harass or punish people for their beliefs, or for their speech about, or public criticism of, laws and public officials. The Founders of this Nation were not then willing to trust the definition of First Amendment freedoms to Congress or this Court, nor am I now. History and the affairs of the present day show that the Founders were right. There are grim reminders all around this world that the distance between individual liberty and firing squads is not always as far as it seems. I would overrule *Barenblatt*, its forerunners and its progeny, and return to the language of the Bill of Rights. The new and different course the Court is following is too dangerous.

WILKINSON V. UNITED STATES, 365 U.S. 399 (1961)

*In another contempt of Congress case, Frank Wilkinson, an outspoken critic of HUAC, was convicted of unlawfully refusing to answer questions before a sub-committee of the House Un-American Activities Committee. Again by 5-to-4, the Supreme Court upheld the conviction.*

Mr. Justice DOUGLAS, with whom Justices WARREN and BLACK joined, dissenting:

Criticism of government finds sanctuary in several portions of the First Amendment. It is part of the right of free speech. It embraces freedom of the press. Can editors be summoned before the Committee and be made to account for their editorials denouncing the Committee, its tactics, its practices, its policies? If petitioner can be questioned concerning his opposition to the Committee, then I see no reason why editors are immune. The list of editors will be long as is evident from the editorial protests against the Committee's activities, including its recent film, Operation Abolition.

It is not surprising that the opinions concerning free expression given by the United States Supreme Court in the fifties and sixties have been rooted in the same Court's definitions in such decisions as *Schenck, Abrams, Gitlow,* and *Whitney.* In the "clear and present danger" test Justices Holmes and Brandeis tried to draw a line between expression that is constitutionally protected and that which is illegal. In their eloquent arguments for the rights of unpopular minorities or political pariahs to speak, they pointed out the tangible benefits that accrue to all from the free and open marketplace of ideas advocated by this nation's founders. Though in *Dennis* their test was fundamentally revised, the principles of unfettered expression were retained.

Printed or spoken expression that is somehow deemed a threat to the security of the nation is often most vulnerable to suppression by government in time of war or when political and social tensions run high. During the 1960's as concern over an internal Communist menace has again receded, cases involving loyalty and security issues have declined in number on the Supreme Court docket. But though in this nation such times of tension have produced suppression they have also produced greater freedom of expression, thanks in large measure to the decisions of the Supreme Court from 1919 on. The ideas and statements on the permissible limits of free expression enunciated by Justices Holmes, Brandeis, Douglas, and Black will undoubtedly continue to influence the Court in its rulings on similar decisions in the future. Nonetheless, the series of decisions quoted in this chapter are sobering reminders that in twentieth-century America, unpopular political expression is more likely to be suppressed if the speaker, writer, or publisher happens to be a Communist or is accused of being one.

# Chapter Three

✿

# FREEDOM FROM PRIOR RESTRAINT:
## CENSORSHIP

✿

Much of the early struggle for freedom of the press in England centered around the problems of prior restraint and censorship. In an effort to control the press, the English kings, through the Licensing Act of 1662, had decreed that no pamphlet or book could be printed unless it first had been submitted to a governmental censor or licensing official and his approval obtained. Publication without a license was a criminal offense.

John Milton's *Areopagitica* (1644) was primarily an attack on such governmental power. Milton understood and even shared the concern that the printing press might be used to question the validity of state religious views and the divine right of kings, but he condemned licensing as a device for repressing free men's thoughts. His famed treatise had little impact at the time of its writing, however, and it was not until 1695 when the English House of Commons refused to extend the Licensing Act, that press freedom from prior restraint received its necessary legislative support. Gradually—and only gradually—did freedom from licensing enter the English Common Law which Blackstone summarized in his famous statement of the eighteenth-century concept of freedom of the press:

The liberty of the press is indeed essential to the nature of a free state; but this consists in laying no previous restraints upon publication, and not in freedom from censure for criminal matter when published. Every freeman has an undoubted right to lay what sentiments he pleases before the public; to forbid this is to destroy the freedom of the press, but if he publishes what is improper, mischievous, or illegal, he must take the consequences of his own temerity.

Blackstone's words have long had relevance for freedom of the press in America. As Justice Oliver Wendell Holmes wrote in *Patterson v. Colorado*,[1] freedom from preliminary restraint "extends as well to the false as to the true; the subsequent punishment may extend as well to the true as to the false."

Professor Paul Freund pointed out that in 1913:

an able historian searching classical legal authorities was able to assert flatly that prior restraints are illegitimate and subsequent punishment is freely available. Chief Justice [Charles Evans] Hughes in the *Near* case gave the *coup de grâce* to the latter part of this proposition while maintaining there are special objections to prior restraint. It is now clear that if subsequent penalties may constitute abridgements under the First Amendment, it is also true that some forms of prior restraint may be perfectly proper. Both terms of the Blackstonian formula have been qualified.[2]

The decisions cited in this chapter and in Chapter 12, "Freedom of Motion Pictures," illustrate how the modern Supreme Court, beginning with *Near*, has dealt with problems of prior restraint. They show, too, how far the Court has moved away from the simplistic view of press freedom provided by Blackstone.

The Court's current position on Blackstone's prior restraint dictum was well expressed by Chief Justice Earl Warren in the *Times Film Corp. v. Chicago:*

There has been general criticism of the theory that Blackstone's statement was embodied in the First Amendment, the objection being "that the mere exception from previous restraints cannot be all that is secured by the constitutional provisions"; and that "the liberty of the press might be rendered a mockery and a delusion, and the phrase itself a by-word, if, while every man was at liberty to publish what he pleased, the public authorities might nevertheless punish him for harmless publications." The objection has been that Blackstone's definition is too narrow; it had been generally

[1] 205 U.S. 454 (1907).

[2] Freund, *The Supreme Court of the United States* (New York: Merdian Books, 1961), p. 63.

conceded that the protection of the First Amendment extends *at least* to the interdiction of licensing and censorship and to the previous restraint of free speech.[3]

### THE "MINNESOTA GAG LAW" DECISION

Although in principle all mass media enjoy the same basic protection of the First Amendment, books and motion pictures seem to be more susceptible to prior restraint by government while newspapers remain fairly immune. This may be due in large part to the impact of the *Near* case, regarded as the most important Supreme Court decision to date in its protection of a free and unfettered newspaper press. In this first Supreme Court case of a state law infringing on a newspaper's press freedom, Chief Justice Hughes incisively outlined the reasons why the press must be free to report on and to criticize government without fear of prior restraint.

Chief Justice Hughes pointedly did not rely on the "clear and present danger" test but instead advanced a qualified interpretation of the Blackstonian concept: "The protection even as to previous restraint is not absolutely unlimited. But the limitation has been recognized only in exceptional cases." The exceptional cases which in Justice Hughes's view forfeited freedom from prior restraint included matters involving obscenity; acts obstructing the government's wartime efforts; and incitements to violence and forceful overthrow of government. These exceptions did not extend to the criticism of public officials, a key element in the *Near* case.

In the sixties prior restraint came to the fore again in connection with the efforts of communities to control commercialized obscenity in books and magazines. This is illustrated in the *Roth, Kingsley,* and *Ginzburg* cases.

### NEAR V. MINNESOTA, 283 U.S. 697 (1931)

*The "Minnesota gag law" case (as it was called), followed on the 1925 Gitlow decision. It was the first newspaper case which applied against the states the provisions of the First Amendment through the Fourteenth Amendment. The decision struck down a state statute which had authorized prior restraint of publications considered undesirable by Minnesota courts. This law provided that anyone in the business of regularly publishing a "malicious, scandalous and defamatory news-*

[3] 365 U.S. 43 (1961).

*paper, magazine, or other periodical" was guilty of a nuisance;
suits by the state were authorized to abate the nuisance and
enjoin the publishers from future violations.*

*The statute was designed to stop a local "smear sheet"
called* The Saturday Press, *which had been highly critical of
government officials. The publisher, H. M. Near, was cited and
brought into court under a show-cause order backed by a temporary injunction which stopped all activity of the paper. At
the end of the hearing, the injunction was made permanent,
with the proviso that Near could resume publishing if he could
convince the court that he would operate a newspaper free of
the objectionable features mentioned in the statute.*

*Significantly, the Supreme Court found the statute to be
almost the only one in American history which imposed prior
censorship on comment about alleged wrongdoing of public
officials.*

Mr. Chief Justice HUGHES delivered the opinion of the Court:

This statute, for the suppression as a public nuisance of a newspaper or periodical, is unusual, if not unique, and raises questions
of grave importance transcending the local interests involved in the
particular action. It is no longer open to doubt that the liberty of
the press and of speech is within the liberty safeguarded by the due
process clause of the Fourteenth Amendment from invasion by state
action. It was found impossible to conclude that this essential personal liberty of the citizen was left unprotected by the general
guaranty of fundamental rights of person and property.

. . . . . . . . . . . . . . . . .

If we cut through mere details of procedure, the operation and
effect of the statute in substance is that public authorities may bring
the owner or publisher of a newspaper or periodical before a judge
upon a charge of conducting a business of publishing scandalous
and defamatory matter—in particular that the matter consists of
charges against public officers of official dereliction—and, unless the
owner or publisher is able and disposed to bring competent evidence
to satisfy the judge that the charges are true and are published with
good motives and for justifiable ends, his newspaper or periodical
is suppressed and further publication is made punishable as a
contempt. This is of the essence of censorship.

The question is whether a statute authorizing such proceedings
in restraint of publication is consistent with the conception of the
liberty of the press as historically conceived and guaranteed. In
determining the extent of the constitutional protection, it has been
generally, if not universally, considered that it is the chief purpose

of the guaranty to prevent previous restraints upon publication. The struggle in England, directed against the legislative power of the licenser, resulted in renunciation of the censorship of the press. The liberty deemed to be established was thus described by Blackstone: "The liberty of the press is indeed essential to the nature of a free state; but this consists in laying no previous restraints upon publications, and not in freedom from censure for criminal matter when published. Every freeman has an undoubted right to lay what sentiments he pleases before the public; to forbid this, is to destroy the freedom of the press; but if he publishes what is improper, mischievous or illegal, he must take the consequence of his own temerity."

.    .    .    .    .    .    .    .    .    .    .    .    .    .    .    .    .    .    .    .

In the present case, we have no occasion to inquire as to the permissible scope of subsequent punishment. For whatever wrong the appellant has committed or may commit, by his publications, the state appropriately affords both public and private redress by its libel laws. As has been noted, the statute in question does not deal with punishments; it provides for no punishment, except in case of contempt for violation of the court's order, but for suppression and injunction—that is, for restraint upon publication.

The objection has also been made that the principle as to immunity from previous restraint is stated too broadly, if every such restraint is deemed to be prohibited. That is undoubtedly true; the protection even as to previous restraint is not absolutely unlimited. But the limitation has been recognized only in exceptional cases. "When a nation is at war many things that might be said in time of peace are such a hindrance to its effort that their utterance will not be endured so long as men fight and that no Court could regard them as protected by any constitutional right." *Schenck v. United States*, 249 U.S. 47. No one would question but that a government might prevent actual obstruction to its recruiting service or the publication of the sailing dates of transports or the number and location of troops. On similar grounds, the primary requirements of decency may be enforced against obscene publications. The security of the community life may be protected against incitements to acts of violence and the overthrow by force of orderly government. The constitutional guaranty of free speech does not protect a man from an injunction against uttering words that may have all the effect of force. These limitations are not applicable here. . . .

The exceptional nature of its limitations places in a strong light the general conception that liberty of the press, historically considered and taken up by the Federal Constitution, has meant, principally although not exclusively, immunity from previous restraints or censorship.

Madison, who was the leading spirit in the preparation of the First Amendment of the Federal Constitution, thus described the practice and sentiment which led to the guaranties of liberty of the press in State Constitutions:

"In every State, probably, in the Union, the press has exerted a freedom in canvassing the merits and measures of public men of every description which has not been confined to the strict limits of the common law. On this footing the freedom of the press has stood; on this footing it yet stands. . . . Some degree of abuse is inseparable from the proper use of everything, and in no instance is this more true than in that of the press. It has accordingly been decided by the practice of the States, that it is better to leave a few of its noxious branches to their luxuriant growth, than, by pruning them away, to injure the vigour of those yielding the proper fruits. And can the wisdom of this policy be doubted by any who reflect that to the press alone, chequered as it is with abuses, the world is indebted for all the triumphs which have been gained by reason and humanity over error and oppression; who reflect that to the same beneficent source the United States owe much of the lights which conducted them to the ranks of a free and independent nation, and which have improved their political system into a shape so auspicious to their happiness? Had 'Sedition Acts,' forbidding every publication that might bring the constituted agents into contempt or disrepute, or that might excite the hatred of the people against the authors of unjust or pernicious measures, been uniformly enforced against the press, might not the United States have been languishing at this day under the infirmities of a sickly Confederation? Might they not, possibly, be miserable colonies, groaning under a foreign yoke?"

The fact that for approximately one hundred and fifty years there has been almost an entire absence of attempts to impose previous restraints upon publications relating to the malfeasance of public officers is significant of the deep-seated conviction that such restraints would violate constitutional right. Public officers, whose character and conduct remain open to debate and free discussion in the press, find their remedies for false accusations in actions under libel laws providing for redress and punishment, and not in proceedings to restrain the publication of newspapers and periodicals. The general principle that the constitutional guaranty of the liberty of the press gives immunity from previous restraints has been approved in many decisions under the provisions of state constitutions.

The importance of this immunity has not lessened. While reckless assaults upon public men, and efforts to bring obloquy upon those who are endeavoring faithfully to discharge official duties, exert a baleful influence and deserve the severest condemnation in public opinion, it cannot be said that this abuse is greater, and it is believed to be less, than that which characterized the period in which our institutions took shape. Meanwhile, the administration of government has become more complex, the opportunities for malfeasance and corruption have multiplied, crime has grown to most serious proportions, and the danger of its protection by unfaithful officials and of the impairment of the fundamental security of life and property of criminal alliances and official neglect, emphasizes the primary need of a vigilant and courageous press, especially in great cities. The fact that the liberty of the press may be abused by miscreant purveyors of scandal does not make any the less necessary the immunity of the press from previous restraint in dealing with official misconduct. Subsequent punishment for such abuses as may exist is the appropriate remedy, consistent with constitutional privilege.

The freedom of the press from previous restraint has never been regarded as limited to such animadversions as lay outside the range of penal enactments. Historically, there is no such limitation; it is inconsistent with the reason which underlies the privilege, as the privilege so limited would be of slight value for the purposes for which it came to be established.

The statute in question cannot be justified by reason of the fact that the publisher is permitted to show, before injunction issues, that the matter published is true and is published with good motives and for justifiable ends. If such a statute, authorizing suppression and injunction on such a basis, is constitutionally valid, it would be equally permissible for the Legislature to provide that at any time the publisher of any newspaper could be brought before a court, or even an administrative officer (as the constitutional protection may not be regarded as resting on mere procedural details), and required to produce proof of the truth of his publication, or of what he intended to publish and of his motives, or stand enjoined. If this can be done, the Legislature may provide machinery for determining in the complete exercise of its discretion what are justifiable ends and restraining publication accordingly. And it would be but a step to a complete system of censorship. The recognition of authority to impose previous restraint upon publication in order to protect the community against the circulation of charges of misconduct, and especially of official misconduct, necessarily would carry with it the admission of the authority of the censor against which the constitutional barrier was erected. The preliminary freedom, by virute of the very reason for its existence, does not depend, as this court has said, on proof of truth. . . .

Equally unavailing is the insistence that the statute is designed to prevent the circulation of scandal which tends to disturb the public peace and to provoke assaults and the commission of crime.

Charges of reprehensible conduct, and in particular of official mal-feasance, unquestionably create a public scandal, but the theory of the constitutional guaranty is that even a more serious public evil would be caused by authority to prevent publication. "To prohibit the intent to excite those unfavorable sentiments against those who administer the Government, is equivalent, to a prohibition of the actual excitement of them; and to prohibit the actual excitement of them is equivalent to a prohibition of discussions having that tend-ency and effect; which, again, is equivalent to a protection of those who administer the Government, if they should at any time deserve the contempt or hatred of the people, against being exposed to it by free animadversions on their characters and conduct." There is nothing new in the fact that charges of reprehensible conduct may create resentment and the disposition to resort to violent means of redress, but this well-understood tendency did not alter the deter-mination to protect the press against censorship and restraint upon publication. As was said in *New Yorker Staats-Zeitung v. Nolan* . . . : "If the township may prevent the circulation by resorting to physical violence, there is no limit to what may be prohibited." The danger of violent reactions becomes greater with effective organiza-tion of defiant groups resenting exposure, and, if this consideration warranted legislative interference with the initial freedom of publi-cation, the constitutional protection would be reduced to a mere form of words.

### OBSCENITY NOT PROTECTED BY FIRST AMENDMENT

The *Near* case's exclusion of obscenity from protection against prior restraint or censorship provided a logical as well as legal precedent for the important 1957 *Roth* case. If free-dom from prior restraint, as Chief Justice Hughes said, does not extend to obscenity, then is obscenity entirely outside the protection of the First Amendment? In *Roth,* the Court held that it was.

In upholding the censorious aspects of the federal obscen-ity statute as well as a similar California law, the Supreme Court for the first time explicitly placed obscenity beyond the protection of the Constitution. And for the first time, the Court provided a standard for determining obscenity: "Whether to the average person, applying contemporary com-munity standards, the dominant theme of the material taken as a whole appeals to prurient interest." In his dissent, Justice William O. Douglas pointed out some of the inherent problems of the *Roth* test for obscenity.

ROTH V. UNITED STATES, ALBERTS V. CALIFORNIA, 354 U.S. 476 (1957)

*Samuel Roth was a New York seller of books, photographs, and magazines. He employed circulars and advertising matter to solicit sales. He was convicted in a U.S. district court in New York of mailing an obscene book in violation of the federal obscenity statute. In the companion case, David S. Alberts, who conducted a mail order business from Los Angeles, was charged with keeping obscene and indecent books for sale and with writing and publishing an obscene advertisement in violation of the California penal code. The Supreme Court upheld the convictions in both cases.*

Mr. Justice William J. BRENNAN delivered the opinion of the Court:

The dispositive question is whether obscenity is utterance within the area of protected speech and press. Although this is the first time this question has been squarely presented to this court, either under the First Amendment or under the Fourteenth Amendment, expressions found in numerous opinions indicate that this court has always assumed that obscenity is not protected by the freedoms of speech and press. . . .

The guaranties of freedom of expression in effect in 10 of the 14 states which by 1792 had ratified the Constitution, gave no absolute protection for every utterance. Thirteen of the 14 states provided for the prosecution of libel, and all of those states made either blasphemy or profanity, or both, statutory crimes. As early as 1712, Massachusetts made it criminal to publish "any filthy, obscene or profane song, pamphlet, libel or mock sermon in imitation or mimicking of religious services. . . ." Thus, profanity and obscenity were related offenses.

In light of this history, it is apparent that the unconditional phrasing of the First Amendment was not intended to protect every utterance. This phrasing did not prevent this Court from concluding that libelous utterances are not within the area of constitutionally protected speech. . . . At the time of the adoption of the First Amendment, obscenity law was not as fully developed as libel law, but there is sufficiently contemporaneous evidence to show that obscenity, too, was outside the protection intended for speech and press.

. . . . . . . . . . . . . . . . . . . .

All ideas having even the slightest redeeming social importance—unorthodox ideas, controversial ideas, even ideas hateful to the prevailing climate of opinion—have the full protection of the guaranties, unless excludable because they encroach upon the limited area of more important interests. But implicit in the history of the First Amendment is the rejection of obscenity as utterly without redeeming social importance. . . . We hold that obscenity is not within the area of constitutionally protected speech or press.

. . . . . . . . . . . . . . . . . . . .

However, sex and obscenity are not synonymous. Obscene material is material which deals with sex in a manner appealing to prurient interest. The portrayal of sex, e.g., in art, literature and scientific works, is not itself sufficient reason to deny material the constitutional protection of freedom of speech and press. Sex, a great and mysterious motive force in human life, has indisputably been a subject of absorbing interest to mankind through the ages; it is one of the vital problems of human interest and public concern.

The fundamental freedoms of speech and press have contributed greatly to the development and well-being of our free society and are indispensable to its continued growth. Ceaseless vigilance is the watchword to prevent their erosion by Congress or by the States. The door barring federal and state intrusion into this area cannot be left ajar; it must be kept tightly closed and opened only the slightest crack necessary to prevent encroachment upon more important interests. It is therefore vital that the standards for judging obscenity safeguard the protection of freedom of speech and press for material which does not treat sex in a manner appealing to prurient interest.

. . . . . . . . . . . . . . . . . . . .

Some courts now apply this obscenity test: "Whether to the average person, applying contemporary community standards, the dominant theme of the material taken as a whole appeals to prurient interest."

Justice Douglas, in dissent, touched on some of the implications of the majority decision—the exalting of the role of the censor and the effect on literary standards, to mention two. He also felt the Court profoundly curtailed the First Amendment by allowing punishment of mere speech or publication which is not itself a part of an unlawful action.

Mr. Justice DOUGLAS, with whom Mr. Justice Hugo BLACK joined, dissenting:

The test of obscenity the court endorses today gives the censor free range over a vast domain. To allow the state to step in and punish mere speech or publication that the judge or the jury thinks has an *undesirable* impact on thoughts but that is not shown to be a part of unlawful action is drastically to curtail the First Amendment.

. . . . . . . . . . . . . . . . . .

I assume there is nothing in the Constitution which forbids Congress from using its power over the mails to proscribe *conduct* on the grounds of good morals. No one would suggest that the First Amendment permits nudity in public places, adultery, and other phases of sexual misconduct.

I can understand (and at times even sympathize with) programs of civic groups and church groups to protect and defend the existing moral standards of the community. I can understand the motives of the Anthony Comstocks who would impose Victorian standards on the community. When speech alone is involved, I do not think that government, consistently with the First Amendment, can become the sponsor of any of these movements. I do not think that government, consistently with the First Amendment, can throw its weight behind one school or another. Government should be concerned with antisocial conduct, not with utterances. Thus, if the First Amendment guarantee of freedom of speech and press is to mean anything in this field, it must allow protests even against the moral code that the standard of the day sets for the community. In other words, literature should not be suppressed merely because it offends the moral code of the censor.

The legality of a publication in this country should never be allowed to turn either on the purity of thought which it instills in the mind of the reader or on the degree to which it offends the community conscience. By either test the role of the censor is exalted, and society's values in literary freedom are sacrificed.

Freedom of expression can be suppressed if, and to the extent that, it is so closely brigaded with illegal action as to be an inseparable part of it. . . . As a people, we cannot afford to relax that standard. For the test that suppresses a cheap tract today can suppress a literary gem tomorrow. All it need do is to incite a lascivious thought or arouse a lustful desire. The list of books that judges or juries can place in that category is endless.

I would give the broad sweep of the First Amendment full support. I have the same confidence in the ability of our people to reject noxious literature as I have in their capacity to sort out the true from the false in theology, economics, politics, or any other field.

### "PRIOR RESTRAINT" MORE SHARPLY DEFINED

In the same year as *Roth* (1957), a case involving a New York statute controlling pornography again raised the issue of how much, if any, prior restraint is permitted under the First Amendment. Justice Felix Frankfurter, in the Court opinion, cited *Near* in upholding this law and urged that the Court assess particular cases more pragmatically when dealing with situations of prior restraint.

## KINGSLEY BOOKS V. BROWN, 354 U.S. 436 (1957)

*This case grew out of a proceeding to enjoin the distribution of certain booklets and to direct that the booklets be surrendered to the sheriff of New York County. The case provided a test of the New York statute which provided that a municipality could seek an injunction prohibiting the sale of any indecent printed matter; the seller had the right to trial of the issues within one day and a decision within two days after the end of the trial. The Supreme Court of New York County held this does not constitute prior censorship of literary products and does not violate freedom of the press. The Supreme Court affirmed the lower court judgment.*

Mr. Justice FRANKFURTER delivered the opinion of the Court:

If New York chooses to subject persons who disseminate obscene "literature" to criminal prosecution and also to deal with such books as deodands of old, or both, with due regard, of course, to appropriate opportunities for the trial of the underlying issue, it is not for us to gainsay its selection of remedies. Just as *Near v. Minnesota,* one of the landmark opinions in shaping the constitutional protection of freedom of speech and of the press, left no doubts that "Liberty of speech, and of the press, is also not an absolute right," . . . it likewise made clear that "the protection even as to previous restraint is not absolutely unlimited."

.   .   .   .   .   .   .   .   .   .   .   .   .   .   .   .   .   .

The phrase "prior restraint" is not a self-wielding sword. Nor can it serve as a talismanic test. The duty of closer analysis and critical judgement in applying the thought behind the phrase has thus been authoritatively put by one who brings weighty learning to his support of constitutionally protected liberties. "What is needed," writes Professor Paul Freund, "is a pragmatic assessment of its operation in the particular circumstances. The generalization that prior restraint is particularly obnoxious in civil liberties cases must yield to more particularistic analysis." The Supreme Court and Civil Liberties, 4 *Vand. Law Review,* 533, 539.

.   .   .   .   .   .   .   .   .   .   .   .   .   .   .   .   .   .

Unlike *Near,* paragraph 22-a (of the contested statute) is concerned solely with obscenity and, as authoritatively construed, it studiously withholds restraint upon matters not already published and not yet found to be offensive.

The four dissenters would give the First Amendment a broader sweep, and warn against increasing the powers of the official censor.

Mr. Chief Justice Earl WARREN dissenting:

It is the manner of use that should determine obscenity. It is the conduct of the individual that should be judged, not the quality of art or literature. To do otherwise is to impose a prior restraint and hence to violate the Constitution. Certainly in the absence of a prior judicial determination of illegal use, books, pictures, and other objects of expression should not be destroyed. It savors too much of book burning.

Mr. Justice DOUGLAS, with whom Justices BLACK and BRENNAN joined, dissented:

There are two reasons why I think this restraining order should be dissolved.

First, the provision for an injunction *pendente lite* [while litigation continues] gives the State the paralyzing power of a censor. A decree can issue ex parte—without a hearing and without any ruling or finding on the issue of obscenity. This provision is defended on the ground that it is only a little encroachment, that a hearing must be promptly given and a finding of obscenity promptly made. But every publisher knows what awful effect a decree issued in secret can have. We tread here on First Amendment grounds. And nothing is more devastating to the rights that it guarantees than the power to restrain publication before even a hearing is held. This is prior restraint and censorship at its worst.

Second, the procedure for restraining by equity decree the distribution of all the condemned literature does violence to the First Amendment. The judge or jury which finds the publisher guilty in New York City acts on evidence that may be quite different from evidence before the judge or jury that finds the publisher not guilty in Rochester. In New York City the publisher may have been selling his tracts to juveniles, while in Rochester he may have sold to professional people. The nature of the group among whom the tracts are distributed may have an important bearing on the issue of guilt in any obscenity prosecution. Yet the present statute makes one criminal conviction conclusive and authorizes a statewide decree that subjects the distributor to the contempt power. I think every publication is a separate offense which entitles the accused to a separate trial. Juries or judges may differ in their opinions, community by community, case by case. The publisher is entitled to that leeway under our constitutional system. One is entitled to defend every utterance on its merits and not to suffer today for what he uttered yesterday. Free speech is not to be regulated like diseased cattle and impure butter. The audience (in this case the judge or the jury) that hissed yesterday may applaud today, even for the same performance.

The regime approved by the Court goes far toward making the censor supreme. It also substitutes punishment by contempt for punishment by jury trial. In both respects it transgresses constitutional guarantees.

I would reverse this judgment and direct the restraining order to be dissolved.

### DANGERS OF BOOK CENSORSHIP

Another censorship case, *Smith v. California,* this time won by the bookseller, gave Justices Black and Douglas an opportunity to expound on the dangers they believed to be implicit in censorship.

They felt that in any conflict between freedom of expression and government efforts to suppress objectionable matter, free expression should have the widest possible scope.

SMITH V. CALIFORNIA, 361 U.S. 147 (1959)

*Eleasar Smith, proprietor of a book store, was convicted in a Los Angeles municipal court of violating an ordinance dealing with obscene materials and he appealed. At the U.S. Supreme Court, the judgment was reversed. Justice Brennan's Court opinion held that the Los Angeles ordinance, which dispensed with the element of scienter (knowledge by the bookseller of the contents of the book) and imposed strict criminal liability on a bookseller possessing obscene material, inhibited constitutionally protected expression to such an extent that it could not stand.*

Mr. Justice BLACK concurring:

What are the "more important" interests for the protection of which constitutional freedom of speech and press must be given second place? What is the standard by which one can determine when abridgment of speech and press goes "too far" and when it is slight enough to be constitutionally allowable? Is this momentous decision to be left to a majority of this court on a case-by-case basis?

What express provision or provisions of the Constitution put freedom of speech and press in this precarious position of subordination and insecurity?

Certainly the First Amendment's language leaves no room for inference that abridgments of speech and press can be made just because they are slight. That Amendment provides, in simple words, that "Congress shall make no law . . . abridging the freedom of speech, or of the press." I read "no law . . . abridging" to mean no law abridging. The First Amendment, which is the supreme law of the land, has thus fixed its own value on freedom of speech and press by putting these freedoms wholly "beyond the reach" of federal power to abridge. No other provision of the Constitution purports to dilute the scope of these unequivocal commands of the First Amendment. Consequently, I do not believe that any federal agencies, including Congress and this Court, have power or authority to subordinate speech and press to what they think are "more important interests." The contrary notion is, in my judgment, court-made not Constitution-made.

. . . . . . . . . . . . . . . . . .

If, as it seems, we are on the way to national censorship, I think it is timely to suggest again that there are grave doubts in my mind as to the desirability or constitutionality of this Court's becoming a Supreme Board of Censors—reading books and reviewing television performances to determine whether, if permitted, they might adversely affect the morals of the people throughout the many diversified local communities in this vast country. It is true that the ordinance here is on its face only applicable to "obscene or indecent writing." It is also true that this particular kind of censorship is considered by many to be "the obnoxious thing in its mildest and least repulsive form. . . ." But "illegitimate and unconstitutional practices get their first footing in that way. . . . It is the duty of courts to be watchful for the constitutional rights of the citizen, and against any stealthy encroachments thereon." *Boyd v. United States,* 116 U.S. 616. While it is "obscenity and indecency" before us today, the experience of mankind—both ancient and modern—shows that this type of elastic phrase can, and most likely will, be synonymous with the political and maybe with the religious unorthodoxy of tomorrow.

Censorship is the deadly enemy of freedom and progress. The plain language of the Constitution forbids it. I protest against the Judiciary giving it a foothold here.

Mr. Justice DOUGLAS concurring:

I need not repeat here all I said in my dissent in *Roth v. United States,* . . . to underline my conviction that neither the author nor the distributor of this book can be punished under our Bill of Rights for publishing or distributing it. The notion that obscene publications or utterances were not included in free speech developed in this country much later than the adoption of the First Amendment, as the judicial and legislative developments in this country show. Our leading authorities on the subject have summarized the matter as follows:

"In the United States before the Civil War there were few reported decisions involving obscene literature. This of course is no indication that such literature was not in circulation at that time; the persistence of pornography is entirely too strong to warrant such an inference. Nor is it an indication that the people of the time were totally indifferent to the proprieties of the literature they read. In 1851, Nathaniel Hawthorne's *The Scarlet Letter* was bitterly attacked as an immoral book that degraded literature and encouraged social licentiousness. The lack of cases merely means that the problem of obscene literature was not thought to be of sufficient importance to justify arousing the forces of the state of censorship." Lockhart and McClure, "Literature, The Law of Obscenity, and the Constitution," 38 *Minn. L. Rev.* 295, 324–325.

Neither we nor legislatures have power, as I see it, to weigh the values of speech or utterance against silence. The only grounds for suppressing this book are very narrow. I have read it; and while it is repulsive to me, its publication or distribution can be constitutionally punished only on a showing not attempted here. My view was stated in the Roth case. . . .

Yet my view is in the minority; and rather fluid tests of obscenity prevail which require judges to read condemned literature and pass judgment on it. This role of censor in which we find ourselves is not an edifying one. But since by the prevailing school of thought we must perform it, I see no harm, and perhaps some good, in the rule fashioned by the Court which requires a showing of scienter. For it recognizes implicitly that these First Amendment rights, by reason of the strict command in that Amendment—a command that carries over to the States by reason of the Due Process Clause of the Fourteenth Amendment—are preferred rights. What the Court does today may possibly provide some small degree of safeguard to booksellers by making those who patrol bookstalls proceed less high handedly than has been their custom.

## "CENSOR AND FIRST AMENDMENT ARE INCOMPATIBLE"

Attempts to censor books and magazines have often been conducted in informal or extralegal ways. One such effort in Rhode Island was overturned by the Supreme Court. The facts of the case are given in detail in the excerpt because they illustrate the way such informal censorship operates.

BANTAM BOOKS V. SULLIVAN, 372 U.S. 58 (1963)

> *The Rhode Island legislature created a commission to "educate the public about obscene literature and material manifestly tending to corrupt youth." The commission notified distributors of magazines and books in the state that certain publications were considered objectionable for persons under eighteen years of age. These notices had the effect of stopping all sale of the books on the list. By an 8-to-1 decision, the Supreme Court held that the commission's methods constituted informal censorship which violated the First Amendment.*

Mr. Justice BRENNAN delivered the opinion of the Court:

Appellants are four New York publishers of paperback books which have for some time been widely distributed in Rhode Island. Max Silverstein & Sons is the exclusive wholesale distributor of appellants' publications throughout most of the State. The Commission's practice has been to notify a distributor on official Commission stationery that certain designated books or magazines distributed by him had been reviewed by the Commission and had been declared by a majority of its members to be objectionable for sale, distribution or display to youths under 18 years of age. Silverstein had received at least 35 such notices at the time this suit was brought. Among the paperback books listed by the Commission as "objectionable" were one published by appellant Dell Publishing Co. (*Peyton Place* by Grace Metalious) and another published by appellant Bantam Books, Inc. (*The Bramble Bush* by Charles Mergendahl).

The typical notice to Silverstein either elicited or thanked Silverstein, in advance, for his "cooperation" with the Commission, usually reminding Silverstein of the Commission's duty to recommend to the Attorney General prosecution of purveyors of obscenity. Copies of the lists of "objectionable" publications were circulated to local police departments, and Silverstein was so informed in the notices.

Silverstein's reaction on receipt of a notice was to take steps to stop further circulation of copies of the listed publications. He would not fill pending orders for such publications and would refuse new orders. He instructed his field men to visit his retailers and to pick up all unsold copies, and would then promptly return them to the publishers. A local police officer usually visited Silverstein shortly after Silverstein's receipt of a notice to learn what action he had taken. Silverstein was usually able to inform the officer that a specified number of the total copies received from a publisher had been returned. According to the testimony, Silverstein acted as he did on receipt of the notice "rather than face the possibility of some sort of a court action against ourselves, as well as the people we supply."

. . . . . . . . . . . . . . . . . . . . . . .

Appellants argue that the Commission's activities . . . amount to a scheme of governmental censorship devoid of the constitutionally required safeguards for state regulation of obscenity, and thus abridge First Amendment liberties, protected by the Fourteenth Amendment from infringement by the States. We agree that the activities of the Commission are unconstitutional and therefore reverse the Rhode Island Supreme Court's judgment.

. . . . . . . . . . . . . . . . . . . . . . .

Thus, the Fourteenth Amendment requires that regulation by the States of obscenity conform to procedures that will ensure against the curtailment of constitutionally protected expression, which is often separated from obscenity only by a dim and uncertain line. It is characteristic of the freedoms of expression in general that they are vulnerable to gravely damaging yet barely visible encroachments. Our insistence that regulations of obscenity scrupulously embody the most rigorous procedural safeguards, *Smith v. California*, . . . is therefore but a special instance of the larger principle that the freedoms of expression must be ringed about with adequate bulwarks. . . .

But, it is contended, these salutary principles have no application to the activities of the Rhode Island Commission because it does not regulate or suppress obscenity but simply exhorts booksellers and advises them of their legal rights. This contention, premised on the Commission's want of power to apply formal legal sanctions, is untenable. It is true that appellants' books have not been seized or banned by the State, and that no one has been prosecuted for their possession or sale. But though the Commission is limited to informal sanctions—the threat of invoking legal sanctions and other means of coercion, persuasion, and intimidation—the record amply demonstrates that the Commission deliberately set about to achieve the suppression of publications deemed "objectionable" and succeeded in its aim. We are not the first to look through forms to the substance and recognize that informal censorship may sufficiently inhibit the circulation of publications to warrant injunctive relief.

. . . . . . . . . . . . . . . . . . . . . .

What Rhode Island has done, in fact, has been to subject the distribution of publications to a system of prior administrative restraints, since the Commission is not a judicial body and its decisions to list particular publications as objectionable do not follow judicial determinations that such publications may lawfully be banned. Any system of prior restraints of expression comes to this Court bearing a heavy presumption against its constitutional validity.

Justice Douglas, in concurring, went further. Restating his view that the censor and free expression cannot exist together, he reminds us that extralegal censorship, that vague but constant fear of arbitrary government suppression, is widespread throughout the world today as indeed it has been since the invention of the printing press.

Mr. Justice DOUGLAS concurring:

While I join the opinion of the Court, I adhere to the views I expressed in *Roth v. United States,* 354 U.S. 476, respecting the very narrow scope of governmental authority to suppress publications on the grounds of obscenity. Yet, as my Brother Brennan makes clear, the vice of Rhode Island's system is apparent whatever one's view of the constitutional status of "obscene" literature. This is censorship in the raw; and in my view the censor and the First Amendment are incompatible. If a valid law has been violated, authors and publishers and vendors can be made to account. But they would then have on their side all the procedural safeguards of the Bill of Rights, including trial by jury. From the viewpoint of the State that is a more cumbersome procedure, action on the majority vote of the censors being far easier. But the Bill of Rights was designed to fence in the Government and makes its intrusions on liberty difficult and its interference with freedom of expression well-nigh impossible.

All nations have tried censorship and only a few have rejected it. Its abuses mount high. Today Iran censors news stories in such a way as to make false or misleading some reports of reputable news agencies. For the Iranian who writes the stories and lives in Teheran goes to jail if he tells the truth. Thus censorship in Teheran has as powerful extralegal sanctions as censorship in Providence.

## A NEW TEST FOR OBSCENITY

When it decided the 1957 *Roth* case, the Supreme Court hoped that it had constructed a standard for obscenity that could be applied by trial judges without constant appeals to the high court. It also hoped to shield non-obscene expression from overzealous censorship. The *Roth* standard was: "Whether to the average person, applying contemporary community standards, the dominant theme of the material taken as a whole appeals to prurient interest."

But obscenity cases have kept coming to the Supreme Court, and in 1966 a highly subjective element was grafted onto the *Roth* test which some observers believe might even further increase the number of censorship cases the Court will feel impelled to adjudicate.

In its rulings on three related censorship cases, a divided Court issued fourteen separate opinions by seven justices. This splintering of opinion disappointed those observers who had hoped for a more definitive standard on obscenity.

In *A Book Named "John Cleland's Memoirs of a Woman of Pleasure" v. Massachusetts,* the Court reversed a Massachusetts finding that the eighteenth-century novel *Fanny Hill* was obscene and held that a publication is not obscene unless three elements "coalesce"; the work must "appeal to prurient interest"; it must be "patently offensive"; and it must be "utterly without redeeming social value."[4]

In another case, *Mishkin v. New York,*[5] the Court affirmed the New York state conviction of Edward Mishkin, who published admittedly "sadistic and masochistic" tracts. The decision rejected Mishkin's claim that material is not obscene if it leaves the "average person" cold and appeals only to the prurient interest of perverted people. The Court said that if a publication is intended for deviant sexual groups it is obscene if it appeals to the pruient interests of these groups.

In the third and best-known case, the Court affirmed the conviction of publisher Ralph Ginzburg for sending *Eros* and other erotic publications through the mails. The Court ruled that when an objective examination fails to establish whether an item is obscene, the courts may look to the publisher's intent. If he tried to "titillate the public's sexual interest" in marketing his product, then the courts may take his advertising "at its face value" and declare the book obscene.

This new element—the "publisher's intent" as demonstrated by the way the book is marketed—has obvious implications for advertising and promotion and may have far-reaching

⁴ 383 U.S. 413 (1966).
⁵ 383 U.S. 502 (1966).

implications for both the retailing of printed erotica and for advertising techniques in general.

Justice Douglas in dissenting said the ruling condemned the ancient techniques of sex-appeal in advertising. The dissenters also argued that the five-year jail sentence and $28,000 fine imposed on Ginzburg were much too harsh for any activity involving printed expression.

GINZBURG V. UNITED STATES, 383 U.S. 463 (1966)

Mr. Justice BRENNAN delivered the opinion of the Court:

A judge sitting without a jury in the District Court for the Eastern District of Pennsylvania convicted petitioner Ginzburg and three corporations controlled by him upon all 28 counts of an indictment charging violation of the federal obscenity statute. . . . Each count alleged that a resident of the Eastern District received mailed matter, either one of three publications challenged as obscene, or advertising telling how and where the publications might be obtained. The Court of Appeals for the Third Circuit affirmed. . . . We granted certiorari. . . . We affirm. Since petitioners do not argue that the trial judge misconceived or failed to apply the standards we first enunciated in *Roth v. United States,* . . . the only serious question is whether those standards were correctly applied.

In the cases in which this Court has decided obscenity questions since *Roth,* it has regarded the materials as sufficient in themselves for the determination of the question. In the present case, however, the prosecution charged the offense in the context of the circumstances of production, sale, and publicity and assumed that, standing alone, the publications themselves might not be obscene. We agree that the question of obscenity may include consideration of the setting in which the publications were presented as an aid to determining the question of obscenity, and assume without deciding that the prosecution could not have succeeded otherwise. As in *Mishkin v. New York,* . . . and as did the courts below, . . . we view the publications against a background of commercial exploitation of erotica solely for the sake of their prurient appeal. The record in that regard amply supports the decision of the trial judge that the mailing of all three publications offended the statute.

The three publications were *Eros,* a hard-cover magazine of expensive format; *Liaison,* a bi-weekly newsletter; and *The Housewife's Handbook on Selective Promiscuity* (hereinafter the *Handbook*), a short book. The issue of *Eros* specified in the indictment, Vol. 1, No. 4, contains 15 articles and photo-essays on the subject of love, sex, and sexual relations. The specified issue of *Liaison,* Vol.

1, No. 1, contains a prefatory "Letter from the Editors" announcing
its dedication to "keeping sex an art and preventing it from becoming a science." The remainder of the issue consists of digests of
two articles concerning sex and sexual relations which had earlier
appeared in professional journals and a report of an interview with
a psychotherapist who favors the broadest license in sexual relationships. As the trial judge noted, "[w]hile the treatment is largely
superficial, it is presented entirely without restraint of any kind.
According to defendants' own expert, it is entirely without literary
merit, . . . the *Handbook* purports to be sexual autobiography
detailing with complete candor the author's sexual experiences
from age 3 to age 36. The text includes, and prefatory and concluding sections of the book elaborate, her views on such subjects
as sex education of children, laws regulating private consensual
adult sexual practices, and the equality of women in sexual relationships. It was claimed at trial that women would find the book
valuable, for example as a marriage manual or as an aid to the sex
education of their children.

Besides testimony as to the merit of the material, there was
abundant evidence to show that each of the accused publications
was originated or sold as stock in trade of the sordid business of
pandering—"the business of purveying textual or graphic matter
openly advertised to appeal to the erotic interest of their customers."
*Eros* early sought mailing privilege from the postmasters of Intercourse and Blue Ball, Pennsylvania. The trial court found the obvious, that these hamlets were chosen only for the value their names
would have in furthering petitioners' efforts to sell their publications on the basis of salacious appeal; the facilities of the post offices were inadequate to handle the anticipated volume of mail,
and the privileges were denied. Mailing privileges were then obtained from the postmaster of Middlesex, New Jersey. *Eros* and
*Liaison* thereafter mailed several million circulars soliciting subscriptions from that post office; over 5,500 copies of the *Handbook*
were mailed.

The "leer of the sensualist" also permeates the advertising for
the three publications. The circulars sent for *Eros* and *Liaison*
stressed the sexual candor of the respective publications, and
openly boasted that the publishers would take full advantage of
what they regarded an unrestricted license allowed by law in the
expression of sex and sexual matters. The advertising for the *Handbook*, apparently mailed from New York, consisted almost entirely
of a reproduction of the introduction of the book, written by one
Dr. Albert Ellis. Although he alludes to the book's informational
value and its putative therapeutic usefulness, his remarks are preoccupied with the book's sexual imagery. The solicitation was in-
discriminate, not limited to those, such as physicians or psychiatrists,

who might independently discern the book's therapeutic worth. Inserted in each advertisement was a slip labeled "GUARANTEE" and reading, "Documentary Books, Inc., unconditionally guarantees full refund on the price of *The Housewife's Handbook on Selective Promiscuity* if the book fails to reach you because of U.S. Post Office censorship interference." Similar slips appeared in the advertising for *Eros* and *Liaison;* they highlighted the gloss petitioners put on the publications, eliminating any doubt what the purchaser was being asked to buy.

This evidence, in our view, was relevant in determining the ultimate question of "obscenity" and, in the context of this record, serves to resolve all ambiguity and doubt. The deliberate representation of petitioners' publications as erotically arousing, for example, stimulated the reader to accept them as prurient; he looks for titillation, not for saving intellectual content. Similarly, such representation would tend to force public confrontation with the potentially offensive aspects of the work; the brazenness of such an appeal heightens the offensiveness of the publications to those who are offended by such material. And the circumstances of presentation and dissemination of material are equally relevant to determining whether social importance claimed for material in the courtroom was, in the circumstances, pretense or reality—whether it was the basis upon which it was traded in the marketplace or a spurious claim for litigation purposes. Where the purveyor's sole emphasis is on the sexually provocative aspects of his publications, that fact may be decisive in the determination of obscenity. Certainly in a prosecution which, as here, does not necessarily imply suppression of the materials involved, the fact that they originate or are used as a subject of pandering is relevant to the application of the *Roth* test.

A proposition argued as to *Eros,* for example, is that the trial judge improperly found the magazine to be obscene as a whole, since he concluded that only four of the 15 articles predominately appealed to prurient interest and substantially exceeded community standards of candor, while the other articles were admittedly non-offensive. But the trial judge found that "[t]he deliberate and studied arrangement of *Eros* is editorialized for the purpose of appealing predominantly to prurient interest and to insulate through the inclusion of non-offensive material." However erroneous such a conclusion might be if unsupported by the evidence of pandering, the record here supports it. *Eros* was created, represented and sold solely as a claimed instrument of the sexual stimulation it would bring. Like the other publications, its pervasive treatment of sex and sexual matters rendered it available to exploitation by those who would make a business of pandering to "the widespread weakness for titillation by pornography." Petitioners' own expert agreed, correctly we think, that "[i]f the object [of a work] is material gain for the creator through an appeal to the sexual curiosity and appetite," the work is pornographic. In other words, by animating sensual detail to give the publication a salacious cast, petitioners reinforced what is conceded by the Government to be an otherwise debatable conclusion.

A similar analysis applied to the judgment regarding the *Handbook*. The bulk of the proofs directed to social importance concerned this publication. Before selling publication rights to petitioners, its author had printed it privately; she sent circulars to persons whose names appeared on membership lists of medical and psychiatric associations, asserting its value as an adjunct in therapy. Over 12,000 sales resulted from this solicitation, and a number of witnesses testified that they found the work useful in their professional practice. The Government does not seriously contest the claim that the book has worth in such a controlled, or even neutral, environment. Petitioners, however, did not sell the book to such a limited audience, or focus their claims for it on its supposed therapeutic or educational value; rather, they deliberately emphasized the sexually provocative aspects of the work, in order to catch the salaciously disposed. They proclaimed its obscenity; and we cannot conclude that the court below erred in taking their own evaluation at its face value and declaring the book as a whole obscene despite the other evidence.

. . . . . . . . . . . . . . . . .

We perceive no threat to First Amendment guarantees in thus holding that in close cases evidence of pandering may be probative with respect to the nature of the material in question and thus satisfy the *Roth* test. No weight is ascribed to the fact that petitioners have profited from the sale of publications which we have assumed but do not hold cannot themselves be adjudged obscene in the abstract; to sanction consideration of this fact might indeed induce self-censorship, and offend the frequently stated principles that commercial activity, in itself, is no justification for narrowing the protection of expression secured by the First Amendment. Rather, the fact that each of these publications was created or exploited entirely on the basis of its appeal to prurient interests strengthens the conclusion that the transactions here were sales of illicit merchandise, not sales of constitutionally protected matter. A conviction for mailing obscene publications, but explained in part by the presence of this element, does not necessarily suppress the materials in question, nor chill their proper distribution for a proper use. Nor should it inhibit the enterprise of others seeking through serious endeavor to advance human knowledge or understanding in science, literature, or art. All that will have been determined is that questionable publications are obscene in a context which brands them as obscene as that term is defined in *Roth*—a use inconsistent with any claim to the shelter of the First Amendment. "The nature of the materials is, of course, relevant as an attribute of the defendant's conduct, but the materials are thus placed in context from which they draw color and character. A wholly different result might be reached in a different setting." *Roth v. United States,* . . . (Warren, C.J., concurring).

It is important to stress that this analysis simply elaborates the test by which the obscenity *vel non* of the material must be judged. Where an exploitation of interests in titillation by pornography is shown with respect to material lending itself to such exploitation through pervasive treatment or description of sexual matters, such evidence may support the determination that the material is obscene even though in other contexts the material would escape such condemnation. . . .

Long a consistent foe of all censorship, Justice Black felt that a man should not be sent to prison for the discussion of a subject that is as much a part of our lives as is sex.

Mr. Justice BLACK, dissenting:

Only one stark fact emerges with clarity out of the confusing welter of opinions and thousands of words written in this and two other cases today. That fact is that Ginzburg, petitioner here, is now finally and authoritatively condemned to serve five years in prison for distributing printed matter about sex which neither Ginzburg nor anyone else could possibly have known to be criminal. Since, as I have said many times, I believe the Federal Government is without any power whatever under the Constitution to put any type of burden on speech and expression of ideas of any kind (as distinguished from conduct), I agreed with Part II of the dissent of my Brother Douglas in this case, and I would reverse Ginzburg's conviction on this ground alone. Even assuming, however, that the Court is correct in holding today that Congress does have power to clamp official censorship on some subjects selected by the Court in some ways approved by it, I believe that the federal obscenity statute as enacted by Congress and as enforced by the Court against Ginzburg in this case should be held invalid on two other grounds.

. . . . . . . . . . . . . . . . . . .

It is obvious that the effect of the Court's decisions in the three obscenity cases handed down today is to make it exceedingly dangerous for people to discuss either orally or in writing anything about sex. Sex is a fact of life. Its pervasive influence is felt throughout the world and it cannot be ignored. Like all other facts of life it can lead to difficulty and trouble and sorrow and pain. But while it may lead to abuses, and has in many instances, no words need be spoken in order for people to know that the subject is one pleasantly interwoven in all human activities and involves the very substance of the creation of life itself. It is a subject which people are bound to consider and discuss whatever laws are passed by any government to try to suppress it. Though I do not suggest any way to solve the problems that may arise from sex or discussions about sex, of one thing I am confident, and that is that federal censorship is not the answer to these problems. I find it difficult to see how talk about sex can be placed under the kind of censorship the Court here approves without subjecting our society to more dangers than we can anticipate at the moment. It was to avoid exactly such dangers that the First Amendment was written and adopted. For myself I would follow the course which I believe is required by the First Amendment, that is, recognize that sex at least as much as any other aspect of life is so much a part of our society that its discussions should not be made a crime.

I would reverse this case.

Another dissenter, Justice Potter Stewart, argued that the Court must apply First Amendment protection fairly to all and should not discriminate against Ginzburg because it disapproved of his "sorbid business."

Mr. Justice STEWART, dissenting:

Ralph Ginzburg has been sentenced to five years in prison for sending through the mail copies of a magazine, a pamphlet, and a book. There was testimony at his trial that these publications possess artistic and social merit. Personally, I have a hard time discerning any. Most of the material strikes me as both vulgar and unedifying. But if the First Amendment means anything, it means that a man cannot be sent to prison merely for distributing publications which offend a judge's esthetic sensibilities, mine or any other's.

Censorship reflects a society's lack of confidence in itself. It is a hallmark of an authoritarian regime. Long ago those who wrote our First Amendment charted a different course. They believed a society can be truly strong only when it is truly free. In the realm of expression they put their faith, for better or for worse, in the enlightened choice of the people, free from the interference of a policeman's intrusive thumb or a judge's heavy hand. So it is that the Constitution protects coarse expression as well as refined, and vulgarity no less than elegance. A book worthless to me may convey something of value to my neighbor. In the free society to which our Constitution has committed us, it is for each to choose for himself.

Because such is the mandate of our Constitution, there is room for only the most restricted view of this Court's decision in *Roth v. United States*. . . .

There does exist a distinct and easily identifiable class of material in which all of these elements coalesce. It is that, and that alone, which I think government may constitutionally suppress, whether by criminal or civil sanctions. I have referred to such material before as hardcore pornography, without trying further to define it. . . . In order to prevent any possible misunderstanding, I have set out in the margin a description, borrowed from the Solicitor General's brief, of the kind of thing to which I have reference.[6]

Although arguments can be made to the contrary, I accept the proposition that the general dissemination of matter of this description may be suppressed under valid laws. That has long been the almost universal judgment of our society. But material of this sort is wholly different from the publications mailed by the petitioner in the present case, and different not in degree but in kind.

The Court today appears to concede that the materials Ginzburg mailed were themselves protected by the First Amendment. But, the Court says, Ginzburg can still be sentenced five years in prison for mailing them. Why? Because, says the Court, he was guilty of "commercial exploitation," of "pandering," and of "titillation." But Ginzburg was not charged with "commercial exploitation"; he was not charged with "pandering"; he was not charged with "titillation." Therefore, to affirm his conviction now on any of those grounds, even if otherwise valid, is to deny him due process of law. But those grounds are *not*, of course, otherwise valid. Neither the statute under which Ginzburg was convicted nor any other federal statute I know of makes "commercial exploitation" or "pandering" or "titillation" a criminal offense. And any criminal law that sought to do so in the terms so elusively defined by the Court would, of course, be unconstitutionally vague and therefore void. All of these matters are developed in the dissenting opinions of my Brethern, and I simply note here that I fully agree with them.

For me, however, there is another aspect of the Court's opinion in this case that is even more regrettable. Today the Court assumes the power to deny Ralph Ginzburg the protection of the First

[6] ". . . Such materials include photographs, both still and motion pictures, with no pretense of artistic value, graphically depicting acts of sexual intercourse, including various acts of sodomy and sadism, and sometimes involving several participants in scenes of orgy-like character. They also include strips of drawings in comic-book format grossly depicting similar activities in an exaggerated fashion. There are, in addition, pamphlets and booklets, sometimes with photographic illustrations, verbally describing such activities in a bizarre manner with no attempt whatsoever to afford portrayals of character or situation and with no pretense to literary value. All of this material . . . cannot conceivably be characterized as embodying communication of ideas or artistic values inviolate under the First Amendment. . . ."

Amendment because it disapproves of his "sordid business." That is a power the Court does not possess. For the First Amendment protects us all with an even hand. It applies to Ralph Ginzburg with no less completeness and force than to G. P. Putnam Sons. In upholding and enforcing the Bill of Rights, this Court has no power to pick or to choose. When we lose sight of that fixed star of constitutional adjudication, we lose our way. For then we forsake a government of law and are left with government by Big Brother.

I dissent.

Mr. Justice DOUGLAS dissenting (in *Mishkin* as well as in *Ginzburg*):

The use of sex symbols to sell literature, today condemned by the Court, engrafts another exception on First Amendment rights that is as unwarranted as the judge-made exception concerning obscenity. This new exception condemns an advertising technique as old as history. The advertisements of our best magazines are chock-full of thighs, ankles, calves, bosoms, eyes, and hair, to draw the potential buyers' attention to lotions, tires, food, liquor, clothing, autos, and even insurance policies. The sexy advertisement neither adds to nor detracts from the quality of the merchandise being offered for sale. And I do not see how it adds to or detracts one whit from the legality of the book being distributed. A book should stand on its own, irrespective of the reasons why it was written or the wiles used in selling it. I cannot imagine any promotional effort that would make chapters 7 and 8 of the Song of Solomon any the less or any more worthy of First Amendment protection than does its unostentatious inclusion in the average edition of the Bible.

## ELECTION DAY EDITORIAL CASE

The right of the press freely to report and comment upon public affairs and government officials was resoundingly upheld in the landmark *Near* decision. It stands today as a firm bulwark of press freedom despite the fact that Chief Justice Hughes's views were accepted by only a 5-to-4 majority. It was reaffirmed when another state law that stifled newspaper criticism of public affairs—this time a corrupt practices law in Alabama—was overturned by the Supreme Court in 1966.

MILLS V. ALABAMA, 384 U.S. 214 (1966)

*Although the words "prior restraint" appear nowhere in the decision, there is little question but that the Alabama act had just that effect. The Alabama Press Association and the*

*Southern Newspaper Publishers Association, appearing as*
Amici Curiae *(friends of the court), reported that since Novem-*
*ber 1962, editorial comment on election day had been non-*
*existent in Alabama because of the law.*

Mr. Justice BLACK delivered the opinion of the Court:

The question squarely presented here is whether a State, consistently with the United States Constitution, can make it a crime
for the editor of a daily newspaper to write and publish an editorial
on election day urging people to vote a certain way on issues submitted to them.

On November 6, 1962, Birmingham, Alabama, held an election
for the people to decide whether they preferred to keep their existing city commission form of government or replace it with a
mayor-council government. On election day the *Birmingham Post
Herald,* a daily newspaper, carried an editorial written by its editor,
appellant James E. Mills, in which it strongly urged the people to
adopt the mayor-council form of government. Mills was later arrested on a complaint charging that by publishing the editorial on
election day he had violated Section 285 of the Alabama Corrupt
Practices Act, Ala. Code, 1940, Tit. 17, Section 268–286, which
makes it a crime "to do any electioneering or to solicit any votes in
support of or in opposition to any proposition that is being voted on
on the day on which the election affecting such candidates or propositions is being held." The trial court sustained demurrers to the
complaint on the grounds that the state statute abridged freedom of
speech and press in violation of the Alabama Constitution and the
First and Fourteenth Amendments to the United States Constitution. On appeal by the State, the Alabama Supreme Court held that
publication of the editorial on election day undoubtedly violated
the state law and then went on to reverse the trial court by holding
that the state statute as applied did not unconstitutionally abridge
freedom of speech or press. Recognizing that the state law did limit
and restrict both speech and press, the State Supreme Court nevertheless sustained it was a valid exercise of the State's police power
chiefly because, as that court said, the press "restriction, everything
considered, is within the field of reasonableness" and "not an unreasonable limitation upon free speech, which includes free press."
The case is here on appeal under 28 U.S.C. Section 1257 (1964 ed.).

We come now to the merits. The First Amendment, which applies to the States through the Fourteenth, prohibits laws "abridging
the freedom of speech, or of the press." The question here is
whether it abridges freedom of the press for a State to punish a
newspaper editor for doing no more than publishing an editorial
on election day urging people to vote a particular way in the elec-

tion. We should point out at once that this question in no way involves the extent of a State's power to regulate conduct in and around the polls in order to maintain peace, order, and decorum there. The sole reason for the charge that Mills violated the law is that he wrote and published an editorial on election day which urged Birmingham voters to cast their votes in favor of changing their form of government.

Whatever differences may exist about interpretations of the First Amendment, there is practically universal agreement that a major purpose of that Amendment was to protect the free discussion of governmental affairs. This of course includes discussions of candidates, structures and forms of government, the manner in which government is operated or should be operated, and all such matters relating to political processes. The Constitution specifically selected the press, which includes not only newspapers, books, and magazines, but also humble leaflets and circulars, see *Lovell v. Griffin*, . . . to play an important role in the discussion of public affairs. Thus the press serves and was designed to serve as a powerful antidote to any abuses of power by governmental officials and as a constitutionally chosen means for keeping officials elected by the people responsible to all the people whom they were selected to serve. Suppression of the right of the press to praise or criticize governmental agents and to clamor and contend for or against change, which is all that this editorial did, muzzles one of the very agencies the Framers of our Constitution thoughtfully and deliberately selected to improve our society and keep it free. The Alabama Corrupt Practices Act by providing criminal penalties for publishing editorials such as the one here silences the press at a time when it can be most effective. It is difficult to conceive of a more obvious and flagrant abridgment of the constitutionally guaranteed freedom of the press.

Admitting that the state law restricted a newspaper editor's freedom to publish editorials on election day, the Alabama Supreme Court nevertheless sustained the constitutionality of the law on the ground that the restrictions on the press were only "reasonable restrictions" or at least "within the field of reasonableness." The Court reached this conclusion because it thought the law imposed only a minor limitation on the press—restricting it only on election days—and because the Court thought the law served a good purpose. It said: "It is a salutary legislative enactment that protects the public from confusive last-minute charges and countercharges and the distribution of propaganda in an effort to influence voters on an election day; when as a practical matter, because of lack of time, such matters cannot be answered or their truth determined until after the election is over." . . .

This argument, even if it were relevant to the constitutionality of the law, has a fatal flaw. The state statute leaves people free to hurl their campaign charges up to the last minute of the day before election. The law held valid by the Alabama Supreme Court then goes on to make it a crime to answer those "last-minute" charges on election day, the only time they can be effectively answered. Because the law prevents any adequate reply to these charges, it is wholly ineffective in protecting the electorate "from confusive last-minute charges and countercharges." We hold that no test of reasonableness can save a state law from invalidation as a violation of the First Amendment when that law makes it a crime for a newspaper editor to do no more than urge people to vote one way or another in a publicly held election.

The judgment of the Supreme Court of Alabama is reversed and the case is remanded for further proceedings not inconsistent with this opinion.

Clearly, censorship and prior restraint of the printed word are repugnant under our Constitution. The problem for the Supreme Court is how to maintain this principle while doing justice to the other legitimate needs of government. The decisions covered in this chapter illustrate the variety of situations in which censorship and prior restraint, often complicated by obscenity issues, can be crucial factors in a freedom of the press decision.

Blackstone's classic injunction against "no previous restraints" has yielded to what Professor Freund has called "more particularistic analysis." In the process, the Supreme Court of the United States has made it increasingly difficult for the official censor to ply his trade. In newspapers, books, or magazines, there is today a greatly increased freedom to publish without fear that government will intervene before the public is reached.

However, as its fourteen separate opinions in the 1966 *Mishkin, Ginzburg,* and *Fanny Hill* decisions indicate, the Court has not yet agreed on a workable standard to define and deal with the thorny and recurring problem of obscenity.

*Chapter Four*

FREEDOM FROM PRIOR RESTRAINT:
LICENSING AND DISCRIMINATORY TAXATION

As we have seen, an essential element of freedom of the press is the concept that a citizen does not require a government license to publish any printed material. This right to publish is the same whether it involves a giant corporation launching yet another mass magazine or an individual citizen producing a mimeographed handout. Both are exercising a right that belongs to all Americans.

The authoritarian English licensing system ended in 1695. Since then, both the English and American press have been leery of any government efforts to revive practices that smack of licensing. American courts have become more intolerant of licensing than any other restrictive device. (A major exception to freedom from licensing today is in broadcasting, which requires regulation and licensing for the technical reason of preventing one broadcaster from interfering with the signal of another. The licensing of broadcasting is discussed in Chapter 13, "Freedom of Broadcasting.")

State and local governments ordinarily require licenses for most business enterprises; such a license tax has been so long accepted that few understand the censorship potential in the discretion the official has to issue or withhold the license.

THE LONG STRUGGLE AGAINST THE LICENSOR

Curiously the major cases that enabled the Supreme Court to define the modern limits of licensing or license taxes as applied to the press came not from newspapers or broadcasters but from Jehovah's Witnesses, the religious sect which fought its many battles against religious persecution all the way to the Supreme Court during the 1930's and 1940's.

The participants in civil liberties contests have changed in this generation so it is easy to forget the tribulations that this sect has suffered. According to the American Civil Liberties Union, in six months of 1940 alone, 1,488 men, women, and children of the sect were victims of mob violence in 355 communities in 44 states.

The sect's numerous legal battles and the resultant Supreme Court decisions have added a good deal of meaning to the first part of the First Amendment, "Congress shall make no law respecting an establishment of religion, or prohibiting the free exercise thereof." But because one phase of the Witnesses' practice of their religion involves the printing and selling of religious tracts from door to door and on street corners, they also added important meaning and definition to the middle clause of the Amendment, "or abridging the freedom of speech, or of the press." As a persecuted minority, they came before the Court claiming a right that belongs to all—the right of free expression.

LOVELL V. GRIFFIN, 303 U.S. 444 (1938)

*Alma Lovell, a member of Jehovah's Witnesses, was convicted in the recorder's court of Griffin, Georgia, for violating a city ordinance and was sentenced to fifty days in jail when she refused to pay a $50 fine. The ordinance read:*

*"That the practice of distributing, either by hand or otherwise, circulars, hand books, advertising, or literature of any kind, whether said articles are being delivered free or whether same are being sold, within the limits of the city of Griffin without first obtaining written permission from the city manager of the city of Griffin, such practice shall be deemed a nuisance and punishable as an offense against the city of Griffin."*

*Although Alma Lovell was distributing Jehovah's Witness literature she was also engaged in a press activity in selling her printed tracts on street corners and from door to door. On an appeal to the Supreme Court, she won her case.*

*Chief Justice Charles Evans Hughes, in the Court opinion,*

*reviewed the historic struggle that the small printer and pamphleteer had waged against the licensor. And licensing, at least as practiced in Griffin, Georgia, amounted to prior restraint because it controlled circulation and "indeed, without circulation, the publication would be of little value."*

Mr. Chief Justice HUGHES delivered the opinion of the Court:

We think that the ordinance is invalid on its face. Whatever the motive which induced its adoption, its character is such that it strikes at the very foundation of the freedom of the press by subjecting it to license and censorship. The struggle for the freedom of the press was primarily directed against the power of the licensor. It was against that power that John Milton directed his assault by his "Appeal for the Liberty of Unlicensed Printing." And the liberty of the press became initially a right to publish "without a license what formerly could be published only with one." While this freedom from previous restraint upon publication cannot be regarded as exhausting the guaranty of liberty, the prevention of that restraint was a leading purpose in the adoption of the constitutional provision.

Legislation of the type of ordinance in question would restore the system of license and censorship in its baldest form.

The liberty of the press is not confined to newspapers and periodicals. It necessarily embraces pamphlets and leaflets. These indeed have been historic weapons in the defense of liberty, as the pamphlets of Thomas Paine and others in our own history abundantly attest. The press in its historic connotation comprehends every sort of publication which affords a vehicle of information and opinion.

The ordinance cannot be saved because it relates to distribution and not to publication. "Liberty of circulating is as essential to that freedom as liberty of publishing; indeed, without the circulation, the publication would be of little value." *Ex parte Jackson.* . . .

This decision is of major importance because it explicitly provides the same constitutional protection to distribution of literature that it does to publication.

## LOCAL REGULATIONS MUST NOT RESTRICT THE PRESS

The restrictive licensing that the Witnesses faced in *Griffin* was part of a nationwide pattern of municipal efforts to curb their religious press activities. As Justice Owen J. Roberts said in *Schneider*, cities may enact ordinances to regulate the distribution of printed matter, but these regulations must not abridge the individual's freedom of expression; to do so "strikes at the very heart of the constitutional guarantees."

SCHNEIDER V. NEW JERSEY, 308 U.S. 147 (1939)

*A year after* Lovell, *the Supreme Court reviewed four more ordinances enacted in various parts of the country. All were directed at the pamphleteering of religious sects whether they were selling or giving away their literature. The ordinances permitted the use of city government regulatory power to prevent pamphlets from littering the streets. Though upheld by state courts, the Supreme Court reversed the rulings and expanded on the* Lovell *case.*

Mr. Justice ROBERTS delivered the opinion of the Court:

Although a municipality may enact regulations in the interest of the public safety, health, welfare or convenience, these may not abridge the individual liberties secured by the Constitution to those who wish to speak, write, print or circulate information or opinion.

Municipal authorities, as trustees for the public, have the duty to keep their communities' streets open and available for movement of people and property, the primary purpose to which the streets are dedicated. So long as legislation to this end does not abridge the constitutional liberty of one rightfully upon the street to impart information through speech or the distribution of literature, it may lawfully regulate the conduct of those using the streets. For example, a person could not exercise this liberty by taking his stand in the middle of a crowded street, contrary to traffic regulations, and maintain his position to the stoppage of all traffic; a group of distributors could not insist upon a constitutional right to form a cordon across the street and to allow no pedestrian to pass who did not accept a tendered leaflet; nor does the guarantee of freedom of speech or of the press deprive a municipality of power to enact regulations against throwing literature broadcast in the streets. Prohibition of such conduct would not abridge the constitutional liberty since such activity bears no necessary relationship to the freedom to speak, write, print or distribute information or opinion.

This court has characterized the freedom of speech and that of the press as fundamental personal rights and liberties. The phrase is not an empty one and was not lightly used. It reflects the belief of the framers of the Constitution that exercise of the rights lies at the foundation of free government by free men. It stresses, as do many opinions of this Court, the importance of preventing the restriction of enjoyment of these liberties.

As was pointed out in the *Lovell v. Griffin* case, pamphlets have proved most effective instruments in the dissemination of opinion. And perhaps the most effective way of bringing them to the notice of individuals is their distribution at the homes of the people. On this method of communication the ordinance imposes censorship, abuse of which engendered the struggle in England which eventuated in the establishment of the doctrine of the freedom of the press embodied in our Constitution. To require a censorship through license which makes impossible the free and unhampered distribution of pamphlets strikes at the very heart of the constitutional guarantees.

When a local government requires a license there is usually a tax that goes along with it. In several cases involving licensing of the press, the Court was mainly concerned with the taxation issue.

## TAXES CAN SUPPRESS

Because it is a business enterprise, the press, of course, is not immune from taxation. Anyone who prints something to sell can expect to pay some kind of non-discriminatory license tax, or a tax on his earnings.

There have been times, however, when the nature and extent of a particular tax served to restrict the right of publication. The British Parliament in 1712 taxed pamphlets, printed papers, and advertisements, and required that a stamp be placed on every newspaper. These levies came to be known as "taxes on knowledge," and one effect was to keep the selling price high enough to restrict circulation of newspapers, especially to relatively poor people. In England the tax on pamphlets ended in 1833 and the stamp requirement on newspapers ended in 1855. The landmark case in U.S. constitutional law concerning discriminatory taxation of the press involved the daily newspapers of Louisiana and that state's controversial political figure, Huey Long. Political leaders have sometimes employed the power of government in reprisals against their press critics, and sometimes, as in *Grosjean v. American Press Co.*, the Constitution and the Supreme Court are freedom's last line of defense. This case also illustrates that freedom of the press, to be meaningful, encompasses more than freedom from prior restraint or censorship.

GROSJEAN V. AMERICAN PRESS CO., 297 U.S. 233 (1936)

*During the 1930's, Huey Long's dictatorial state political machine encountered increased opposition from the larger daily newspapers in Louisiana. In retaliation, the legislature, controlled by Long and his followers, passed a special 2 per cent tax on the gross advertising income of papers with 20,000 or more circulation weekly. Only thirteen out of 163 newspapers in the state qualified for this tax, but twelve of the thirteen were outspoken critics of Long. It was an obvious attempt to gag press critics. Challenged by nine daily newspaper publishers, the Louisiana law was overturned by the Supreme Court, which ruled that the law violated freedom of the press.*

*In this significant decision, a noted conservative, Justice George Sutherland, summarized the historical reasons why newspaper publishers dread special taxes. Such taxes were forbidden, he said, to "preserve an untrammeled press as a vital source of public information." The opinion adopted the test of Judge Thomas Cooley, the great nineteenth-century constitutional authority, that the evils to be avoided were not merely those of prior restraint or censorship but any "action of the government which might prevent such free and general discussion of public matters as seems absolutely essential to prepare the public for an intelligent exercise of their rights as citizens." Huey Long's special tax on Louisiana newspapers was unconstitutional because it was a deliberate device to limit the flow of information that free people need to govern themselves.*

Mr. Justice George SUTHERLAND delivered the opinion of the Court:

A determination of the question whether the tax is valid in respect of the point now under review requires an examination of the history and circumstances which antedated and attended the adoption of the abridgment clause of the First Amendment, since that clause expresses one of those "fundamental principles of liberty and justice which lie at the base of all our civil and political institutions." . . . The history is a long one; but for present purposes it may be greatly abbreviated.

For more than a century prior to the adoption of the amendment—and, indeed, for many years thereafter—history discloses a persistent effort on the part of the British government to prevent or abridge the free expression of any opinion which seemed to criticize or exhibit in an unfavorable light, however truly, the agencies and operations of the government. The struggle between the proponents of measures to that end and those who asserted the right of free expression was continuous and unceasing. As early as 1644, John Milton, in an "Appeal for the Liberty of Unlicensed Printing," assailed an act of Parliament which had just been passed providing for censorship of the press previous to publication. He vigorously defended the right of every man to make public his honest views "without previous censure"; and declared the impossibility of finding any man base enough to accept the office of censor and at the same time good enough to be allowed to perform its duties. Collett, *History of the Taxes on Knowledge,* vol. I, pp. 4–6. The act expired by its own terms in 1695. It was never renewed; and the liberty of the press thus became, as pointed out by Wickwar *(The Struggle for the Freedom of the Press)* merely "a right or liberty to publish without a license what formerly could be published only with one." But mere exemption from previous censorship was soon recognized as too narrow a view of the liberty of the press.

In 1712, in response to a message from Queen Anne (Hansard's *Parliamentary History of England,* vol. 6, pp. 1063), Parliament imposed a tax upon all newspapers and upon advertisements. Collett, vol. I, pp. 8–10. That the main purpose of these taxes was to suppress the publication of comments and criticisms objectionable to the Crown does not admit of doubt. Stewart, "Lennox and the Taxes on Knowledge," 15 *Scottish Historical Review,* 322–327. There followed more than a century of resistance to, and evasion of, the taxes, and of agitation for their repeal. In the article last referred to (p. 326), which was written in 1918, it was pointed out that these taxes constituted one of the factors that aroused the American colonists to protest against taxation for the purposes of the home government; and that the revolution really began when, in 1765, that government sent stamps for newspaper duties to the American colonies.

These duties were quite commonly characterized as "taxes on knowledge," a phrase used for the purpose of describing the effect of the exactions and at the same time condemning them. That the taxes had, and were intended to have, the effect of curtailing the circulation of newspapers, and particularly the cheaper ones whose readers were generally found among the masses of the people, went almost without question, even on the part of those who defended the act. May *(Constitutional History of England,* 7th Ed., vol. 2, p. 245), after discussing the control by "previous censure," says: ". . . a new restraint was devised in the form of a stamp duty on newspapers and advertisements—avowedly for the purpose of repressing libels. This policy, being found effectual in limiting the circulation of cheap papers, was improved upon in the two following reigns, and continued in high esteem until our own time." Collett (vol. I, p. 14), says: "Any man who carried on printing or publishing for a livelihood was actually at the mercy of the Commissioners of Stamps, when they chose to exert their powers."

Citations of similar import might be multiplied many times; but the foregoing is enough to demonstrate beyond peradventure that in the adoption of the English newspaper stamp tax and the tax on advertisements, revenue was of subordinate concern; and that the dominant and controlling aim was to prevent, or curtail the opportunity for, the acquisition of knowledge by the people in respect of their governmental affairs. It is idle to suppose that so many of the best men of England would for a century of time have waged, as they did, stubborn and often precarious warfare against these taxes if a mere matter of taxation had been involved. The aim of the struggle was not to relieve taxpayers from a burden, but to establish and preserve the right of the English people to full information in respect of the doings or misdoings of their government. Upon the correctness of this conclusion the very characterization of the exactions as "taxes on knowledge" sheds a flood of corroborative light. In the ultimate, an informed and enlightened public opinion was the thing at stake; for, as Erskine, in his great speech in defense of Paine, has said, "The liberty of opinion keeps governments themselves in due subjection to their duties." *Erskine's Speeches*, High's Ed., vol. I, p. 525. . . .

In 1785, only four years before Congress had proposed the First Amendment, the Massachusetts Legislature, following the English example, imposed a stamp tax on all newspapers and magazines. The following year an advertisement tax was imposed. Both taxes met with such violent opposition that the former was repealed in 1786, and the latter in 1788. Duniway, *Freedom of the Press in Massachusetts*, pp. 136, 137. . . .

The framers of the First Amendment were familiar with the English struggle, which then had continued for nearly eighty years and was destined to go on for another sixty-five years, at the end of which time it culminated in a lasting abandonment of the obnoxious taxes. The framers were likewise familiar with the then recent Massachusetts episode; and while that occurrence did much to bring about the adoption of the amendment, the predominant influence must have come from the English experience. It is impossible to concede that by the words "freedom of the press" the framers of the amendment intended to adopt merely the narrow view then reflected by the law of England that such freedom consisted only in immunity from previous censorship; for this abuse had then permanently disappeared from English practice. It is equally impossible to believe that it was not intended to bring within the reach of these words such modes of restraint as were embodied in the two forms of taxation already described. Such belief must be rejected in the face of the then well-known purpose of the exactions and the general adverse sentiment of the colonies in respect of them. Undoubtedly, the range of a constitutional provision phrased in terms of the common law sometimes may be fixed by recourse to the applicable rules of that law. But the doctrine which justifies such re-

course, like other canons of construction, must yield to more compelling reasons whenever they exist. And, obviously, it is subject
to the qualification that the common law rule invoked shall be one
not rejected by our ancestors as unsuited to their civil or political
conditions.

In the light of all that has now been said, it is evident that the
restricted rules of the English law in respect of the freedom of the
press in force when the Constitution was adopted were never accepted by the American colonists, and that by the First Amendment
it was meant to preclude the national government, and by the
Fourteenth Amendment to preclude the states, from adopting any
form of previous restraint upon printed publications, or their circulation, including that which had theretofore been effected by
these two well-known and odious methods.

Judge Cooley has laid down the test to be applied: "The evils
to be prevented were not the censorship of the press merely, but any
action of the government by means of which it might prevent such
free and general discussion of public matters as seems absolutely
essential to prepare the people for an intelligent exercise of their
rights as citizens." 2 Cooley's *Constitutional Limitations* (8th Ed.)
p. 886.

It is not intended by anything we have said to suggest that
the owners of newspapers are immune from any of the ordinary
forms of taxation for support of the government. But this is not an
ordinary form of tax, but one single in kind, with a long history of
hostile misuse against the freedom of the press.

The predominant purpose of the grant of immunity here invoked was to preserve an untrammeled press as a vital source of
public information. The newspapers, magazines and other journals
of the country, it is safe to say, have shed and continue to shed, more
light on the public and business affairs of the nation than any other
instrumentality of publicity; and since informed public opinion is
the most potent of all restraints upon misgovernment, the suppression or abridgment of the publicity afforded by a free press cannot
be regarded otherwise than with grave concern. The tax here
involved is bad not because it takes money from the pockets of the
appellees. If that were all, a wholly different question would be
presented. It is bad because, in the light of its history and of its
present setting, it is seen to be a deliberate and calculated device in
the guise of a tax to limit the circulation of information to which
the public is entitled in virtue of the constitutional guaranties. A
free press stands as one of the great interpreters between the government and the people. To allow it to be fettered is to fetter
ourselves.

In view of the persistent search for new subjects of taxation, it
is not without significance that, with the single exception of the

Louisiana statute, so far as we can discover, no state during the one hundred fifty years of our national existence has undertaken to impose a tax like that now in question.

The form in which the tax is imposed is in itself suspicious. It is not measured or limited by the volume of advertisements. It is measured alone by the extent of the circulation of the publication in which the advertisements are carried, with the plain purpose of penalizing the publishers and curtailing the circulation of a selected group of newspapers.

Citing Chief Justice Stone as his authority, Irving Brant said that Justice Sutherland's famous opinion in *Grosjean* actually included an earlier concurring opinion by Justice Benjamin Cardozo, which the Court adopted and agreed to incorporate into Justice Sutherland's Court opinion.[1] So, many of the eloquent words in the above quotation may be those of Justice Cardozo. In any event, the Court unanimously condemned this Louisiana "tax on knowledge" and the rule was later applied to the license taxes imposed on the Jehovah's Witnesses who practiced their religion in part by distributing and selling religious tracts.

### RESTRICTIVE TAXES STRUCK DOWN AGAIN

During the 1930's and 1940's some communities resorted to the device of the license tax to curb the activities of the Jehovah's Witnesses. The judicial question that arose was whether such a tax impeded freedom of expression.

JONES V. OPELIKA, 316 U.S. 584 (1942)

(vacated and new opinion adopted, 319 U.S. 103 [1943])

*The Court twice considered this issue in* Jones v. Opelika *and reversed itself once.* Jones, *an ordained minister of Jehovah's Witnesses, was convicted of violating an Opelika, Alabama, ordinance requiring that a license be bought from the city council before books could be sold or distributed. As in other Jehovah's Witnesses cases, Jones was involved in a press as well as religious activity. In the 1942 decision, his conviction was upheld by the Supreme Court with four justices dissenting. Justice Stanley Reed in the 1942 Court opinion saw*

---

[1] Brant, *The Bill of Rights: Its Origin and Meaning* (New York: Bobbs-Merrill, 1965), pp. 403–4.

*the tax as a reasonable adjustment of interests and not as a
threat to freedom of the press. However, in 1943, the Court
reconsidered the case and adopted the 1942 minority opinion
of Chief Justice Harlan F. Stone as the ruling view. Arguing
for a broad scope for speech and press, Chief Justice Stone had
said the Constitution has put these freedoms in a "preferred
position."*

Mr. Justice REED delivered the opinion of the Court in 1942:

If all expression of religion or opinion, however, were subject
to the discretion of authority, our unfettered dynamic thoughts or
moral impulses might be made only colorless and sterile ideas. To
give them life and force, the Constitution protects their use. No
difference of view as to the importance of the freedoms of press or
religion exists. They are "fundamental personal rights and liberties." *Schneider v. New Jersey.* . . . To proscribe the dissemination
of doctrines or arguments which do not transgress military or moral
limits is to destroy the principal bases of democracy—knowledge and
discussion. One man, with views contrary to the rest of his com-
patriots, is entitled to the privilege of expressing his ideas by speech
or broadside to anyone willing to listen or to read. Too many settled beliefs have in time been rejected to justify this generation in
refusing a hearing to its own dissentients. But that hearing may be
limited by action of the proper legislative body to times, places and
methods for the enlightenment of the community which, in view of
existing social and economic conditions, are not at odds with the
preservation of peace and good order.

This means that the proponents of ideas cannot determine entirely for themselves the time and place and manner for the diffu-
sion of knowledge or for their evangelism, any more than the civil
authorities may hamper or suppress the public dissemination of
facts and principles by the people. The ordinary requirements of
civilized life compel this adjustment of interests. The task of
reconcilement is made harder by the tendency to accept as dominant
any contention supported by a claim of interference with the practice of religion or the spread of ideas. Believing as this nation has
from the first that the freedoms of worship and expression are closely
akin to the illimitable privileges of thought itself, any legislation
affecting those freedoms is scrutinized to see that the interferences
allowed are only those appropriate to the maintenance of a civilized
society. The determination of what limitation may be permitted
under such an abstract test rests with the legislative bodies, the
courts, the executive and the people themselves guided by the experience of the past, the needs of revenue for law enforcement, the

requirements and capacities of police protection, the dangers of disorder and other pertinent factors.

Upon the courts falls the duty of determining the validity of such enactments as may be challenged as unconstitutional by litigants. In dealing with these delicate adjustments this Court denies any place to administrative censorship of ideas or capricious approval of distributors.

Chief Justice Stone's strong dissent to this 1942 decision became the basis of the Court opinion a year later. In his dissent he compared the Opelika tax to the eighteenth-century British stamp taxes which were a moving cause of the American Revolution. He said the flat license tax "falls short only of outright censorship or suppression." The First Amendment was seen as a "preferred freedom."

Mr. Chief Justice STONE, with whom Justices Frank MURPHY, William O. DOUGLAS, and Hugo BLACK joined, dissenting:

No one could doubt that taxation which may be freely laid upon activities not within the protection of the Bill of Rights could—when applied to the dissemination of ideas—be made the ready instrument for destruction of that right. Few would deny that a license tax laid specifically on the privilege of disseminating ideas would infringe the right of free speech. For one reason among others, if the state may tax the privilege it may fix the rate of tax and, through the tax, control or suppress the activity which it taxes.

. . . . . . . . . . . . . . . . .

The First Amendment is not confined to safeguarding freedom of speech and freedom of religion against discriminatory attempts to wipe them out. On the contrary, the Constitution by virtue of the First and Fourteenth Amendments, has put those freedoms in a preferred position. Their commands are not restricted to cases where the protected privilege is sought out for attack. They extend at least to every form of taxation which, because it is a condition of the exercise of the privilege, is capable of being used to control or suppress it.

. . . . . . . . . . . . . . . . .

The First Amendment prohibits all laws abridging freedom of press and religion, not merely some laws or all except tax laws. It is true that the constitutional guaranties of freedom of press and religion, like the commerce clause, make no distinction between fixed-sum taxes and other kinds. But that fact affords no excuse to courts, whose duty it is to enforce those guaranties, to close their eyes to the characteristics of a tax which render it destructive of freedom of press and religion.

We may lay to one side the Court's suggestion that a tax otherwise unconstitutional is to be deemed valid unless it is shown that there are none who, for religion's sake, will come forward to pay the unlawful exaction. The defendants to whom the ordinances have been applied have not paid it and there is nothing in the Constitution to compel them to seek the charity of others to pay it before protesting the tax. It seems fairly obvious that if the present taxes, laid in small communities upon peripatetic religious propagandists, are to be sustained, a way has been found for the effective suppression of speech and press and religion despite constitutional guaranties. The very taxes now before us are better adapted to that end than were the stamp taxes which so successfully curtailed the dissemination of ideas by eighteenth century newspapers and pamphleteers, and which were a moving cause of the American Revolution. . . . Vivid recollections of the effect of those taxes on the freedom of the press survived to inspire the adoption of the First Amendment.

.   .   .   .   .   .   .   .   .   .   .   .   .   .   .   .   .   .

In its potency as a prior restraint on publication the flat license tax falls short only of outright censorship or suppression.

Also in dissent in 1942, Justice Murphy argued that if free speech and press are to be preserved, municipalities should not be free to raise general revenue by taxes on the circulation of information and opinion in non-commercial causes.

Mr. Justice MURPHY, with whom Justices STONE, BLACK, and DOUGLAS joined, dissenting:

Freedom of speech, freedom of the press, and freedom of religion all have a double aspect—freedom of thought and freedom of action. Freedom to think is absolute of its own nature; the most tyrannical government is powerless to control the inward workings of the mind. But even an aggressive mind is of no missionary value unless there is freedom of action, freedom to communicate its message to others by speech and writing. Since in any form of action there is a possibility of collision with the rights of others, there can be no doubt that this freedom to act is not absolute but qualified, being subject to regulation in the public interest which does not unduly infringe the right.

It matters not that petitioners asked contributions for their literature. Freedom of speech and freedom of the press cannot and must not mean freedom only for those who can distribute their broadsides without charge. There may be others with messages more vital but purses less full, who must seek some reimbursement for their outlay or else forego passing on their ideas. The pamphlet, an historic weapon against oppression, *Lovell v. Griffin,* . . . is today the convenient vehicle of those with limited resources because newspaper space and radio time are expensive and the cost of establishing such enterprises great. If freedom of speech and freedom of the press are to have any concrete meaning, people seeking to distribute information and opinion, to the end only that others shall have the benefit thereof, should not be taxed for circulating such matter. It is unnecessary to consider now the validity of such taxes on commercial enterprises engaged in the dissemination of ideas. . . . Petitioners were not engaged in a traffic for profit. While the courts below held their activities were covered by the ordinances, it is clear that they were seeking only to further their religious convictions by preaching the gospel to others.

The exercise, without commercial motives, of freedom of speech, freedom of the press, or freedom of worship are not proper sources of taxation for general revenue purposes. In dealing with a permissible regulation of these freedoms and the fee charged in connection therewith, we emphasized the fact that the fee was "not a revenue tax, but one to meet the expense incident to the administration of the act and to the maintenance of public order," and stated only that, "There is nothing contrary to the Constitution in the charge of a fee limited to the purpose stated." *Cox v. New Hampshire,* 312 U.S. 569. . . . The taxes here involved are ostensibly for revenue purposes; they are not regulatory fees. Respondents do not show that the instant activities of Jehovah's Witnesses create special problems causing a drain on the municipal coffers, or that these taxes are commensurate with any expenses entailed by the presence of the Witnesses. In the absence of such a showing I think no tax whatever can be levied on petitioners' activities in distributing their literature or disseminating their ideas. If the guaranties of freedom of speech and freedom of the press are to be preserved, municipalities should not be free to raise general revenue by taxes on the circulation of information and opinion in non-commercial causes; other sources can be found, the taxation of which will not choke off ideas. Taxes such as the instant ones violate petitioners' right to freedom of speech and freedom of the press, protected against state invasion by the Fourteenth Amendment.

Liberty of conscience is too full of meaning for the individuals in this nation to permit taxation to prohibit or substantially impair the spread of religious ideas, even though they are controversial and run counter to the established notions of a community. If this court is to err in evaluating claims that freedom of speech, freedom of the press, and freedom of religion have been invaded, far better that it err in being overprotective of these precious rights.

Licensing and unjust taxes were methods used by authoritarian governments to restrict or control the printed word. Such long-repudiated restraints on a free press can and do reappear in contemporary times, as the *Lovell, Schneider, Grosjean,* and *Jones* decisions remind us. But, in each case, the Supreme Court has reaffirmed time-honored principles of press freedom and held that the licensing and taxing powers of government, as essential and legitimate as they may be, cannot be used to restrict or diminish in any way the freedom of the press. To fetter the press is to fetter the people. The threats of discriminatory licenses and taxes ("the power to tax is the power to destroy") have come from the legislative and executive branches of government. From the third branch of government, the judiciary, has come another sort of limitation of press freedom—the contempt power of courts.

*Chapter Five*

# PRESS FREEDOM AND THE ADMINISTRATION OF JUSTICE: CONTEMPT OF COURT

IT IS ESSENTIAL to a free and independent judiciary that the "calm course of justice" be maintained so that the minds of jurors and judges are not "distorted by extra-judicial considerations."

To function properly, "courts must have the authority 'necessary in a strict sense' to enable them to go on with their work. In doing their work, courts, like others, may encounter obstructions. They must, therefore, be invested with incidental powers of self-protection. A clamor in a courtroom may interrupt proceedings; a contumacious witness may halt a trial. . . ."[1]

A disruptive clamor can take many forms. In some situations, newspaper or broadcasting reports, pictures, and editorials on approaching or pending trials may have an inflammatory effect and consequently obstruct the fair administration of justice.

To maintain the required courtroom calm, judges have the contempt power. Any disobedience of constituted legal authority or disrespect may constitute contempt. The power to enforce legal judgments, decrees, and orders is, of course, inherent in the administration of justice. Without it, courts would be ineffectual.

But how far does the contempt power extend? It certainly encompasses disturbances within the court itself, but does it

[1] Felix Frankfurter and James M. Landis, "Power of Congress Over Procedure in Criminal Contempts," 37 *Harv. L. Rev.* 1010, 1022 (1924).

reach out onto the street and to newspaper and broadcasting critics who comment on approaching or pending cases but who are physically not near the courtroom at all?

In times past the contempt power has collided with freedom of the press and the right of the public to full information about the courts so that "the public may judge whether our system is fair and right."

## DIFFERENCE IN PRACTICES, GREAT BRITAIN AND THE UNITED STATES

Marked differences in practice exist between Great Britain and the United States in this area. In England, no constitutional, judicial, or legislative processes stricture the contempt power which is often harshly employed by judges against newspapers publishing any information considered disruptive of the processes of justice.

British courts permit no newspaper comment on current or pending criminal proceedings beyond the barest recital of the procedural steps. In an appendix to Justice Felix Frankfurter's opinion in *Maryland v. Baltimore Radio Show*,[2] a summary of British experience notes that between 1902 and 1949, thirteen editors or newspaper publishers were convicted of contempt. And, in 1949, the Lord Chief Justice fined the London *Daily Mirror* £10,000 and sent its editor to jail for three months for its sensational reporting of the crimes of the "English Bluebeard" then on trial.

In the United States, on the other hand, the press has so much leeway in pre-trial publicity that the system often seems to protect the irresponsible individual journalist. Congress, in the Federal Contempt Act in 1831 attempted to define the contempt power of federal courts. This was after a notorious political dispute in which Federal District Judge James H. Peck used contempt to punish a distant critic of his decision in a federal lands case. In 1831 Judge Peck was impeached and tried in the U.S. Senate. The impeachment failed by one vote but within nine days Congress had passed the new contempt act. The key provision limited contempt to misbehavior in the courtroom or "so near thereto as to obstruct the administration of justice."[3] Most of the state courts (in which the

[2] 338 U.S. 912 (1950).
[3] Act of Mar. 2, 1831, c. 99, 4 Stat. 487.

majority of newspaper contempt cases has been tried) long refused to recognize that the words "so near thereto" actually drew a geographical line or established any kind of limit on the judicial contempt power. Zechariah Chafee said they had construed "so near thereto" in a casual sense as meaning "in close relationship thereto" and then allowed closeness to include almost any tendency to obstruct the administration of justice.[4]

The Supreme Court interpreted the 1831 act the same way until the *Nye* case in 1941. In *Toledo Newspaper Co. v. United States,*[5] the Court upheld a contempt conviction against the *Toledo News-Bee*. It affirmed the lower court's finding that the *News-Bee's* articles "manifestly tended to interfere with and obstruct the court in the discharge of its duty in a matter pending before it." The Supreme Court decided that the 1831 act did not prohibit the judge's summary action even though the only physical nearness to the court was that the judge was a daily reader of the *News-Bee*.

Dissenting in *Toledo,* Justice Oliver Wendell Holmes said:

When it is considered how contrary it is to our practice and ways of thinking for the same person to be accuser and sole judge in a matter which, if he be sensitive, may involve strong personal feeling, I should expect the power to be limited by the necessities of the case "to insure order and decorum in their presence," as is stated in *Ex parte Robinson,* 19 Wall. 505. . . . And when the words of the statute (of 1831) are read it seems to me that the limit is too plain to be construed away.

In *Nye v. United States,* however, the Court specifically overruled the *Toledo* finding. The Court majority established the doctrine that the words "so near thereto" in the 1831 act of Congress were to be considered "geographical terms."[6] By so doing, the Court restricted the power of the judges to punish press or broadcasting critics for "constructive" or "indirect" contempt, i.e., press acts committed away from the courtroom. This, of course, protects news media from contempt charges in matters of pre-trial publicity. The *Nye* case was but a prelude to a landmark decision on contempt.

[4] Chafee, *Government and Mass Communications* (Chicago: University of Chicago Press, 1947), p. 391.
[5] 247 U.S. 402 (1918).
[6] 313 U.S. 33 (1941).

### GREATER FREEDOM TO JUDGE THE JUDGES

For freedom of the press in the United States, the most dramatic change in the long struggle over contempt occurred in the 1941 *Bridges* case. This decision manifestly enlarged the right of the American press to comment on pending cases and, at the same time, moved U.S. practices even more markedly away from those of Britain. It gave the American press possibly the greatest freedom of any in the world to report and comment on judicial activities.

BRIDGES V. CALIFORNIA
TIMES-MIRROR CO. V. SUPERIOR COURT, 314 U.S. 252 (1941)

*In these two similar cases, the labor leader, Harry Bridges, and the Los Angeles* Times, *were found guilty and fined for contempt of court for commenting on pending litigation.*

*The circumstances were these:*

*In 1937 and 1938, the* Times *published a series of editorials. One titled "Sit Strikers Convicted," approved the conviction of twenty-two sitdown strikers, and appeared in print after the verdict but before the sentencing. Another, "Probation for Gorillas?" spoke approvingly of the conviction of two labor leaders for assault, and urged the court to make "examples" of the defendants.*

*In* Bridges, *the well-known longshoremen labor leader sent a telegram to the U.S. Secretary of Labor which referred to a judge's decision in a labor case (then pending a new trial), as "outrageous," and threatened a major labor tie-up as a result.*

*In a far-reaching decision in favor of Bridges and the* Times, *Justice Hugo Black argued for greater freedom to comment on pending cases and ruled that the "clear and present danger" test, not the "bad tendency" test as in the* Gitlow *case, should be applied to cases before a court. Noting the difference from British practice, he said it was the clear purpose of the Bill of Rights to give Americans greater freedom of expression than Englishmen enjoyed. In his view, while controversial cases are before a court, there are greater benefits in public discussion than in enforced silence.*

Mr. Justice BLACK delivered the opinion of the Court:

. . . Moreover, the likelihood, however great, that a substantive evil would result cannot alone justify a restriction upon freedom of speech or the press. The evil itself must be "substantial," Brandeis, J., concurring in *Whitney v. California* . . .; it must be "serious," . . . and even the expression of "legislative preferences or beliefs" cannot transform minor matters of public inconvenience or annoyance into substantive evils of sufficient weight to warrant the curtailment of liberty of expression. *Schneider v. New Jersey.* . . .

What finally emerges from the "clear and present danger" cases is a working principle that the substantive evil must be extremely serious and the degree of imminence extremely high before utterances can be punished. These cases do not purport to mark the furthermost constitutional boundaries of protected expression, nor do we here. They do no more than recognize a minimum compulsion of the Bill of Rights. For the "First Amendment does not speak equivocally. It prohibits any law abridging the freedom of speech, or of the press." It must be taken as a command of the broadest scope that explicit language, read in the context of a liberty-loving society, will allow.

.   .   .   .   .   .   .   .   .   .   .   .   .   .   .   .   .   .

No purpose in ratifying the Bill of Rights was clearer than that of securing for the people of the United States much greater freedom of religion, expression, assembly, and petition than the people of Great Britain ever enjoyed. . . .

Ratified as it was while the memory of many oppressive English restrictions on the enumerated liberties was still fresh, the First Amendment cannot reasonably be taken as approving prevalent English practices. On the contrary, the only conclusion supported by history is that the unqualified prohibitions laid down by the framers were intended to give to liberty of the press, as to other liberties, the broadest scope that could be countenanced in an orderly society.

.   .   .   .   .   .   .   .   .   .   .   .   .   .   .   .   .   .

We may appropriately begin our discussion of the judgments below by considering how much, as a practical matter, they would affect liberty of expression. It must be recognized that public interest is much more likely to be kindled by a controversial event of the day than by a generalization, however penetrating, of the historian or scientist. Since they punish utterances made during the pendency of a case, the judgments below therefore produce their restrictive results at the precise time when public interest in the matters discussed would naturally be at its height. Moreover, the ban is likely to fall not only at a crucial time but upon the most important topics of discussion. Here, for example, labor controversies were the topics of some of the publications. Experience shows that the more acute labor controversies are, the more likely it is that in some aspect they will get into court. It is therefore the controversies that command most interest that the decision below would remove from the arena of public discussion.

No suggestion can be found in the Constitution that the freedom there guaranteed for speech and the press bears an inverse ratio to the timeliness and importance of the ideas seeking expression. Yet, it would follow as a practical result of the decisions below that anyone who might wish to give public expression to his views on a pending case involving no matter what problem of public interest, just at the time his audience would be most receptive, would be as effectively discouraged as if a deliberate statutory scheme of censorship had been adopted. Indeed, perhaps more so, because under a legislative specification of the particular kinds of expressions prohibited and the circumstances under which the prohibitions are to operate, the speaker or publisher might at least have an authoritative guide to the permissible scope of comment, instead of being compelled to act at the peril that judges might find in the utterance a "reasonable tendency" to obstruct justice in a pending case.

This unfocussed threat is, to be sure, limited in time, terminating as it does upon final disposition of the case. But this does not change its censorial quality. An endless series of moratoria on public discussion, even if each were very short, could hardly be dismissed as an insignificant abridgment of freedom of expression. And to assume that each would be short is to overlook the fact that the "pendency" of a case is frequently a matter of months or even years rather than days or weeks.

For these reasons we are convinced that the judgments below result in a curtailment of expression that cannot be dismissed as insignificant. If they can be justified at all, it must be in terms of some serious substantive evil which they are designed to avert. The substantive evil here sought to be averted has been variously described below. It appears to be double: disrespect for the judiciary; and disorderly and unfair administration of justice. The assumption that respect for the judiciary can be won by shielding judges from published criticism wrongly appraises the character of American public opinion. For it is a prized American privilege to speak one's mind, although not always with perfect good taste, on all public institutions. And an enforced silence, however limited, solely in the name of preserving the dignity of the bench, would probably engender resentment, suspicion, and contempt much more than it would enhance respect.

The other evil feared, disorderly and unfair administration of justice, is more plausibly associated with restricting publications which touch upon pending litigation. The very word "trial" connotes decisions on the evidence and arguments properly advanced in open court. Legal trials are not like elections, to be won through the use of the meeting-hall, the radio, and the newspaper. But we cannot start with the assumption that publications of the kind here involved actually do threaten to change the nature of legal trials, and that to preserve judicial impartiality, it is necessary for judges to have a contempt power by which they can close all channels of public expression to all matters which touch upon pending cases.

Dissenting to Justice Black's assertion that freedom of speech and press are "preferred freedoms" which should be given the widest possible latitude, Justice Frankfurter argued for a "balancing of interests." While recognizing the importance of free expression, Justice Frankfurter said that it must be measured here against an equally important claim—the right of California to act to safeguard its system of justice.

Mr. Justice FRANKFURTER, with whom Justices Owen ROBERTS and James BYRNES joined, dissenting:

Our whole history repels the view that it is an exercise of one of the civil liberties secured by the Bill of Rights for a leader of a large following or for a powerful metropolitan newspaper to attempt to overawe a judge in a matter immediately pending before him. The view of the majority deprives California of means for securing to its citizens justice according to law—means which, since the Union was founded, have been the possession, hitherto unchallenged, of all the states. This sudden break with the uninterrupted course of constitutional history has no constitutional warrant. To find justification for such deprivation of historic powers of the states is to misconceive the idea of freedom of thought and speech as guaranteed by the Constitution.

. . . . . . . . . . . . . . . . . . . .

Free speech is not so absolute or irrational a conception as to imply paralysis of the means for effective protection of all the freedoms secured by the Bill of Rights. . . . In the cases before us, the claims on behalf of freedom of speech and of the press encounter claims on behalf of liberties no less precious. California asserts her right to do what she had done as a means of safeguarding her system of justice.

The administration of justice by an impartial judiciary had been basic to our conception of freedom ever since Magna Carta. It is the concern not merely of the immediate litigants. Its assurance is everyone's concern, and it is protected by the liberty guaranteed by the Fourteenth Amendment.

. . . . . . . . . . . . . . . . . . . .

A trial is not a "free trade in ideas," nor is the best test of truth

in a courtroom "the power of the thought to get itself accepted in
the competition of the market." . . . A court is a forum with
strictly defined limits for discussion. It is circumscribed in the range
of its inquiry and in its methods by the Constitution, by laws, and
by age-old traditions. Its judges are restrained in their freedom of
expression by historic compulsions resting on no other officials of
government. They are so circumscribed precisely because judges
have in their keeping the enforcement of rights and the protection
of liberties which, according to the wisdom of the ages, can only be
enforced and protected by observing such methods and traditions.

The Constitution was not conceived as a doctrinaire document,
nor was the Bill of Rights intended as a collection of popular slo-
gans. We are dealing with instruments of government. We cannot
read into the Fourteenth Amendment the freedom of speech and of
the press protected by the First Amendment and at the same time
read out age-old means employed by states for securing the calm
course of justice. The Fourteenth Amendment does not forbid a
state to continue the historic process of prohibiting expressions calculated to subvert a specific exercise of judicial power. So to assure
the impartial accomplishment of justice is not an abridgment of
freedom of speech or freedom of the press, as these phases of liberty
have heretofore been conceived even by the stoutest libertarians. In
fact, these liberties themselves depend upon an untrammeled judiciary whose passions are not even unconsciously aroused and
whose minds are not distorted by extra judicial considerations.

Of course freedom of speech and of the press are essential to
the enlightenment of a free people and in restraining those who
wield power. Particularly should this freedom be employed in comment upon the work of courts who are without many influences
ordinarily making for humor and humility, twin antidotes to the
corrosion of power. But the Bill of Rights is not self-destructive.
Freedom of expression can hardly carry implications that nullify
the guarantees of impartial trials. And since courts are the ultimate resorts for vindicating the Bill of Rights, a state may surely
authorize appropriate historic means to assure that the process for
such vindication be not wrenched from its rational tracks into the
more primitive melee of passion and pressure. The need is great
that courts be criticized but just as great that they be allowed to do
their duty.

## THE PRESS IS OBLIGED TO BE RESPONSIBLE

The *Bridges* case still stands, providing wide scope for
public comment on pending court cases. But state courts were
slow to accept the full implications of *Bridges*. In 1946 there
came a case rising out of newspaper editorials which sharply

admonished Florida state courts. *Pennekamp v. Florida* proved important for U.S. journalism because of the comments on press practices in the concurring opinions by Justices Frankfurter, Frank Murphy, and Wiley Rutledge.

PENNEKAMP V. FLORIDA, 328 U.S. 331 (1946)

*The publisher and associate editor of the* Miami Herald *were responsible for the publication of two editorials and a cartoon accusing a Florida trial court in non-jury proceedings of being too lenient to criminals and gambling establishments. Two of the cases had been dismissed. In the third, a rape case, an indictment had been obtained and trial was pending.*

*The newspapermen were cited for contempt on the charge that the publications impugned the integrity of the court, tended to create a distrust for the court, suppressed the truth, and tended to obstruct the impartial administration of justice in pending cases. The contempt citation, upheld by the Florida Supreme Court, was reversed by the U.S. Supreme Court, reaffirming the* Bridges *decision in ringing terms.*

Mr. Justice Stanley REED delivered the opinion of the Court:

Free discussion of the problems of society is a cardinal principle of Americanism—a principle which all are zealous to preserve. Discussion that follows the termination of a case may be inadequate to emphasize the danger to public welfare of supposedly wrongful judicial conduct. It does not follow that public comment of every character upon pending trials or legal proceedings may be as free as a similar comment after complete disposal of the litigation. Between the extremes there are areas of discussion which an understanding writer will appraise in the light of the effect on himself and on the public of creating a clear and present danger to the fair and orderly judicial administration. Courts must have power to protect the interests of prisoners and litigants before them from unseemly efforts to pervert judicial action. In the borderline instances where it is difficult to say upon which side the alleged offense falls, we think the specific freedom of public comment should weigh heavily against a possible tendency to influence pending cases. Freedom of discussion should be given the widest range compatible with the essential requirement of the fair and orderly administration of justice.

Though he concurred, Justice Frankfurter lectured the press on its responsibilities. Returning to his "balancing of interests" view, he said that a free press cannot be given precedence over the claims of an independent judiciary. He insisted that the press must exercise its great freedom with due responsibility. Calling "trial by newspaper" an evil influence upon the administration of criminal justice, he cogently argued in favor of the English law's greater control over pre-trial publicity.

Mr. Justice FRANKFURTER concurring:

. . . Without a free press there can be no free society. Freedom of the press, however, is not an end in itself but a means to the end of a free society. The scope and nature of the constitutional protection of freedom of speech must be viewed in that light and in that light applied. The independence of the judiciary is no less a means to the end of a free society, and the proper functioning of an independent judiciary puts the freedom of the press in its proper perspective. For the judiciary cannot function properly if what the press does is reasonably calculated to disturb the judicial judgment in its duty and capacity to act solely on the basis of what is before the court. A judiciary is not independent unless courts of justice are enabled to administer law by absence of pressure from without, whether exerted through the blandishments of reward or the menace of disfavor. In the noble words, penned by John Adams, of the First Constitution of Massachusetts: "It is essential to the preservation of the rights of every individual, his life, liberty, property, and character, that there be an impartial interpretation of the laws, and administration of justice. It is the right of every citizen to be tried by judges as free, impartial, and independent as the lot of humanity will admit." A free press is not to be preferred to an independent judiciary, nor an independent judiciary to a free press. Neither has primacy over the other; both are indispensable to a free society. The freedom of the press in itself presupposes an independent judiciary through which that freedom may, if necessary, be vindicated. And one of the potent means for assuring judges their independence is a free press.

A free press is vital to a democratic society because its freedom gives it power. Power in a democracy implies responsibility in its exercise. No institution in a democracy, either governmental or private, can have absolute power. Nor can the limits of power which enforce responsibility be finally determined by the limited power itself. See Carl L. Becker, *Freedom and Responsibility in the American Way of Life* (1945). In plain English, freedom carries with it responsibility even for the press; freedom of the press is not a freedom from responsibility for its exercise. Most state constitutions expressly provide for liability for abuse of the press's freedom. That there was such legal liability was so taken for granted by the framers of the First Amendment that it was not spelled out. Responsibility for its abuse was imbedded in the law. The First Amendment safeguarded the right.

These are generalities. But they are generalities of the most practical importance in achieving a proper adjustment between a free press and an independent judiciary.

.   .   .   .   .   .   .   .   .   .   .   .   .   .   .   .   .   .   .

"Trial by newspaper," like all catch phrases, may be loosely used but it summarizes an evil influence upon the administration of criminal justice in this country. Its absence in England, at least its narrow confinement there, furnishes an illuminating commentary. It will hardly be claimed that the press is less free in England than in the United States. Nor will any informed person deny that the administration of criminal justice is more effective there than here. This is so despite the commonly accepted view that English standards of criminal justice are more civilized, or, at the least, that recognized standards of fair conduct in the prosecution of crime are better observed.

Thus, "the third degree" is not unjustly called "the American method." This is not the occasion to enlarge upon the reasons for the greater effectiveness of English criminal justice but it may be confidently asserted that it is more effective partly because its standards are so civilized. There are those who will resent such a statement as praise of another country and dispraise of one's own. What it really means is that one covets for his own country a quality of public conduct not surpassed elsewhere.

Certain features of American criminal justice have long been diagnosed by those best qualified to judge as serious and remediable defects. On the other hand, some mischievous accompaniments of our system have been so pervasive that they are too often regarded as part of the exuberant American spirit. Thus, "trial by newspapers" has sometimes been explained as a concession to our peculiar interest in criminal trials. Such interest might be an innocent enough pastime were it not for the fact that the stimulation of such curiosity by the press and the response to such stimulated interest have not failed to cause grievous tragedies committed under the forms of law. Of course trials must be public and the public have a deep interest in trials. The public's legitimate interest, however, precludes distortion of what goes on inside the courtroom, dissemination of matters that do not come before the court, or other trafficking with truth intended to influence proceedings or inevitably calculated to disturb the course of justice. The atmosphere in a courtroom may be subtly influenced from without. . . . Cases are too often tried in newspapers before they are tried in court, and the cast of characters in the newspaper trial too often differs greatly

from the real persons who appear at the trial in court and who may
have to suffer its distorted consequences.

Newspapers and newspapermen themselves have acknowledged
these practices, deplored their evils, and urged reform. . . . One of
the most zealous claimants of the prerogatives of the press, the
*Chicago Tribune,* has even proposed legal means for the correction
of these inroads upon the province of criminal justice: "The
*Tribune* advocates and will accept drastic restriction of this preliminary publicity. The penetration of the police system and the
courts by journalists must stop. With such a law there would be
no motivation for it. Though such a law will be revolutionary in
American journalism, though it is not financially advisable for
newspapers, it is still necessary. Restrictions must come."

It is not for me to express approval of these views, still less,
judgment on the constitutional issues that would arise if they were
translated into legislation. But they are relevant to an understanding of the nature of our problem. They serve also to emphasize that
the purpose of the Constitution was not to erect the press into a
privileged institution but to protect all persons in their right to
print what they will as well as to utter it. ". . . the liberty of the
press is no greater and no less than the liberty of every subject of
the Queen," *Regina v. Gray,* (1900) 2 Q.B. 36, 40, and in the United
States, it is no greater than the liberty of every citizen of the Republic. The right to undermine the proceedings in court is not a
special prerogative of the press. . . .

The press does have the right, which is its professional function,
to criticize and to advocate. The whole gamut of public affairs is the
domain for fearless and critical comment, and not least the administration of justice. But the public function which belongs to the
press makes it an obligation of honor to exercise this function only
with the fullest sense of responsibility. Without such a lively sense
of responsibility a free press may readily become a powerful
instrument of injustice.

.  .  .  .  .  .  .  .  .  .  .  .  .  .  .  .  .  .  .  .

If men, including judges and journalists, were angels, there
would be no problems of contempt of court. Angelic judges would
be undisturbed by extraneous influences and angelic journalists
would not seek to influence them. The power to punish for contempt, as a means of safeguarding judges in deciding on behalf of
the community as impartially as is given to the lot of men to decide,
is not a privilege accorded to judges. The power to punish for contempt of court is a safeguard not for judges as persons but for the
function which they exercise. It is a condition of that function—
indispensable for a free society—that in a particular controversy
pending before a court and awaiting judgment, human beings,

however strong, should not be torn from their moorings of impartiality by the undertow of extraneous influence. In securing freedom of speech, the Constitution hardly meant to create the right to influence judges or juries. That is no more freedom of speech than stuffing a ballot box is an exercise of the right to vote. . . .

Due regard for these general considerations must dispose of the present controversy. Since at the core of our problem is a proper balance between two basic conditions of our constitutional democracy—freedom of utterance and impartial justice—we cannot escape the exercise of judgment on the particular circumstances of the particular case. And we must always bear in mind that since a judgment from a state court comes here as the voice of the state, it must be accorded every fair intendment that in reason belongs to action by a state.

Justice Frank Murphy, one of the outstanding champions of civil liberties on that Court, took a different tack than Justice Frankfurter. Press criticism of the bench may even be vitriolic, scurrilous, or erroneous without being in contempt, he claimed.

Mr. Justice MURPHY concurring:

Were we to sanction the judgment rendered by the court below we would be approving, in effect, an unwarranted restriction upon the freedom of the press. That freedom covers something more than the right to approve and condone insofar as the judiciary and the judicial process are concerned. It also includes the right to criticize and disparage, even though the terms be vitriolic, scurrilous or erroneous. To talk of a clear and present danger arising out of such criticism is idle unless the criticism makes it impossible in a very real sense for a court to carry on the administration of justice. That situation is not even remotely present in this case.

Judges should be foremost in their vigilance to protect the freedom of others to rebuke and castigate the bench and in their refusal to be influenced by unfair or misinformed censure. Otherwise freedom may rest upon the precarious base of judicial sensitiveness and caprice. And a chain reaction may be set up, resulting in countless restrictions and limitations upon liberty.

Justice Rutledge also felt that leeway must be provided for inaccurate and erroneous reporting of legal events but he lamented, as do many on the bench, that journalistic standards in covering the courts are not higher.

Mr. Justice RUTLEDGE concurring:

One can have no respect for a newspaper which is careless with facts and with insinuations founded in its carelessness. Such a disregard for the truth not only flouts standards of journalistic activity observed too often by breach, but in fact tends to bring the courts and those who administer them into undeserved public obloquy.

But if every newspaper which prints critical comment about courts without justifiable basis in fact, or withholds the full truth in reporting their proceedings or decisions, or goes even further and misstates what they have done, were subject on these accounts to punishment for contempt, there would be few not frequently involved in such proceedings. There is perhaps no area of news more inaccurately reported factually, on the whole, though with some notable exceptions, than legal news.

Some part of this is due to carelessness, often induced by the haste with which news is gathered and published, a smaller portion to bias or more blameworthy causes. But a great deal of it must be attributed, in candor, to ignorance which frequently is not at all blameworthy. For newspapers are conducted by men who are laymen to the law. With too rare exceptions their capacity for misunderstanding the significance of legal events and procedures, not to speak of opinions, is great. But this is neither remarkable nor peculiar to newsmen. For the law, as lawyers best know, is full of perplexities.

In view of these facts any standard which would require strict accuracy in reporting legal events factually or in commenting upon them in the press would be an impossible one. Unless the courts and judges are to be put above criticism, no such rule can obtain. There must be some room for misstatement of fact, as well as for misjudgment, if the press and others are to function as critical agencies in our democracy concerning courts as for all other instruments of government.

## JUDGES MUST NOT RETALIATE AGAINST PUBLIC CRITICISM

Another example of the reluctance of state courts to accept the ruling of the *Bridges* case was provided by *Craig v. Harney.*

CRAIG V. HARNEY, 331 U.S. 367 (1947)

*A Texas newspaper, the Corpus Christi Caller-Times, reported a local trial in which there was much interest. The trial court charged that the news stories distorted the trial by neglecting to bring out an essential point in the argument of one of the parties. The failure to report accurately, the Texas court said, inflamed public opinion against the court and threatened a disturbance in the courtroom as the trial continued. The Texas court concluded that a "clear and present danger" existed and found the paper in contempt.*

*The Supreme Court held that the Texas court became involved in a public controversy because of the nature of the case, the way it was handled, and the public sympathy for a soldier overseas, and not because a newspaper printed a story about it. The decision is significant because it provides the press protection against contempt proceedings when commenting on a trial involving private parties only. The conviction was reversed.*

Mr. Justice William O. DOUGLAS delivered the opinion of the Court:

We start with the news articles. A trial is a public event. What transpires in the court room is public property. If a transcript of the court proceedings had been published, we suppose one would claim that the judge could punish the publisher for contempt. And we can see no difference though the conduct of the attorneys, of the jury, or even of the judge himself, may have reflected on the court. Those who see and hear what transpired can report it with impunity. There is no special requisite of the judiciary which enables it, as distinguished from other institutions of democratic government, to suppress, edit, or censor events which transpire in proceedings before it.

The articles of May 26, 27, and 28 were partial reports of what transpired at the trial. They did not reflect good reporting, for they failed to reveal the precise issue before the judge. They said that Mayes, the tenant, had tendered a rental check. They did not disclose that the rental check was postdated and hence, in the opinion of the judge, not a valid tender. In that sense the news articles were by any standard an unfair report of what transpired. But inaccuracies in reporting are commonplace. Certainly a reporter could not be laid by the heels for contempt because he missed the essential point in a trial or failed to summarize the issues to accord with the views of the judge who sat on the case. Conceivably, a plan of reporting on a case could be so designed and executed as to poison the public mind, to cause a march on the court house, or otherwise so disturb the delicate balance in a highly wrought situation as to imperil the fair and orderly functioning of the judicial process. But it takes more imagination than we possess to find in this rather sketchy and one-sided report of a case any imminent or serious threat to a judge of reasonable fortitude. . . .

The accounts of May 30 and 31 dealt with the news of what certain groups of citizens proposed to do about the judge's ruling in the case. So far as we are advised, it was a fact that they planned to take the proposed action. The episodes were community events of legitimate interest. Whatever might be the responsibility of the group which took the action, those who reported it stand in a different position. Even if the former were guilty of contempt, freedom of the press may not be denied a newspaper which brings their conduct to the public eye.

Justice Murphy seconded the views of Justice Douglas and advised his fellow judges to ignore their critics.

Mr. Justice MURPHY concurring:

A free press lies at the heart of our democracy and its preservation is essential to the survival of liberty. Any inroad made upon the constitutional protection of a free press tends to undermine the freedom of all men to print and to read the truth.

In my view, the Constitution forbids a judge from summarily punishing a newspaper editor for printing an unjust attack upon him or his method of dispensing justice. The only possible exception is in the rare instance where the attack might reasonably cause a real impediment to the administration of justice. Unscrupulous and vindictive criticism of the judiciary is regrettable. But judges must not retaliate by a summary suppression of such criticism for they are bound by the command of the First Amendment. Any summary suppression of unjust criticism carries with it an ominous threat of summary suppression of all criticism. It is to avoid that threat that the First Amendment, as I view it, outlaws the summary contempt methods of suppression.

Silence and a steady devotion to duty are the best answers to irresponsible criticism; and those judges who feel the need for giving a more visible demonstration of their feelings may take advantage of various laws passed for that purpose which do not impinge upon a free press. The liberties guaranteed by the First Amendment, however, are too highly prized to be subjected to the hazards of summary contempt procedure.

## PROTECTION FOR DISCUSSION OF PUBLIC INTEREST

The *Bridges, Pennekamp,* and *Craig* decisions of the 1940's greatly expanded the freedom of the American press to comment on pending cases and on the judges themselves.

In the more recent contempt case, *Wood v. Georgia* (1962),

the Supreme Court upheld the right of the individual to speak his mind, even though he was criticizing a court while doing it.

WOOD V. GEORGIA, 370 U.S. 375 (1962)

*James I. Wood, an elected sheriff, was convicted of contempt in a Bibb County, Georgia, court. The Supreme Court held that out-of-court statements by the sheriff to the press questioning the advisability of a grand jury investigation into block voting by Negroes did not present a clear and present danger to the administration of justice. Therefore, the Georgia court's use of contempt power abridged the sheriff's right of free speech and press.*

Mr. Chief Justice Earl WARREN delivered the opinion of the Court:

Thus we have simply been told, as a matter of law without factual support, that if a State is unable to punish persons for expressing their views on matters of great public importance when those matters are being considered in an investigation by the grand jury, a clear and present danger to the administration of justice will be created. We find no such danger in the record before us. The type of "danger" evidenced by the record is precisely one of the types of activity envisioned by the Founders in presenting the First Amendment for ratification. "Those who won our independence had confidence in the power of free and fearless reasoning and communication of ideas to discover and spread political . . . truth." *Thornhill v. Alabama,* 310 U.S. 88. In *Thornhill* the Court also reiterated the thinking of the Founders when it said that a broad conception of the First Amendment is necessary "to supply the public need for information and education with respect to the significant issues of the times. . . . Freedom of discussion, if it would fulfill its historic function in this nation, must embrace all issues about which information is needed or appropriate to enable the members of society to cope with the exigencies of their period." Men are entitled to speak as they please on matters vital to them; errors in judgment or unsubstantiated opinions may be exposed, of course, but not through punishment for contempt for the expression. Under our system of government, counter-argument and education are the weapons available to expose these matters, not abridgment of the rights of free speech and assembly. . . . Hence, in the absence of some other showing of a substantive evil actually designed to impede the course of justice in justification of the exercise of the contempt power to silence the petitioner, his utterances are entitled to be protected.

. . . . . . . . . . . . . . . . .

The First Amendment envisions that persons be given the opportunity to inform the community of both sides of the issue under such circumstances. That this privilege should not lightly be curtailed is ably expressed in a passage from Judge Cooley's 2 *Constitutional Limitations* (8th ed. 1927) 885, where he stated that the purpose of the First Amendment includes the need: ". . . to protect parties in the free publication of matters of public concern, to secure their right to a free discussion of public events and public measures, and to enable every citizen at any time to bring the government and any person in authority to the bar of public opinion by any just criticism upon their conduct in the exercise of the authority which people conferred upon them."

The *Bridges v. California* decision was a major turning point in the long history of contempt. It is a great bulwark protecting the right of the American press, and of American citizens, to comment on pending court cases, to scrutinize legal processes, and even to criticize harshly the conduct of judges on the bench. Many persons in the journalism profession (and many outside as well) do not fully appreciate how pervasive this right to "judge the judges" is. The contempt power remains, but it is strictly confined to affairs in the courtroom or "so near thereto." A judge may no longer reach out beyond the courthouse to punish outspoken critics by contempt actions. Some lower court judges occasionally try, but they are invariably overruled by higher authority.

*Chapter Six*

❈

# PRESS FREEDOM
# AND THE ADMINISTRATION OF JUSTICE:
# PRE-TRIAL PUBLICITY
# AND DEFENDANTS' RIGHTS

❈

THE THREE major contempt decisions of the 1940s—*Bridges, Pennekamp,* and *Craig*—greatly expanded the freedom of the press to report and comment on matters before the courts; but the contempt charges in these cases did not involve the jeopardizing of an individual's right to a fair trial.

A cornerstone of our form of justice is that any defendant is entitled to a "fair and public trial." A free press helps protect that right by its scrutiny of events before and during the trial. But an overzealous press, by irresponsible coverage of a particularly sensational criminal case, can create an atmosphere in which a defendant is unable to receive a fair hearing: it becomes difficult to select a jury which has not already made up its mind as to the defendant's guilt or innocence. This has been called "trial by newspaper."

The issue of "trial by newspaper"—more properly "trial by mass media," since television has now become a major medium in news dissemination—was brought dramatically to public attention by the media coverage of the assassination of President John F. Kennedy in 1963. In its report the Warren Commmission was critical of both the Dallas police and the news media for their handling of the news of that tragic event. The American Bar Association declared in December, 1963, that "widespread publicizing of [alleged assassin Lee Harvey] Oswald's alleged guilt, involving statements by officials and public disclosures of the details of 'evidence' would have made it extremely difficult to impanel an unprejudiced jury and afford the accused a fair trial." Ironically, had he lived, Oswald may not have been convicted of the crime the Warren Commission said he committed. This is because, under American judicial procedures, he could not have received a fair and impartial trial; a conviction, therefore, probably would have been overturned by a higher court.

The unprecedented events in Dallas have underlined the fact that the Supreme Court in recent years has shown an increasing annoyance with the press coverage of certain sensational crimes in which the defendant's rights appear to have been jeopardized by pre-trial publicity. On several occasions, it has ordered new trials.

But it is well to note that the Supreme Court has not ruled any news medium in contempt for so doing. In a significant 1950 ruling, it refused to consider a case involving a contempt conviction for pre-trial publicity that may have jeopardized a criminal defendant's rights.

MARYLAND V. BALTIMORE RADIO SHOW, 338 U.S. 912 (1950)

*The Baltimore Radio Show, Inc., WFBR; the Baltimore Radio Broadcasting Corporation, WCBM; and the Maryland Broadcasting Company were found guilty of contempt for broadcasting over local radio stations news dispatches about a person in custody on a charge of murder. The trial court sought to punish the broadcasting companies for an inflammatory report that the man arrested for a brutal murder had confessed, had a long criminal record, and upon being taken to the scene of the crime, had re-enacted it. The Court of Appeals of Maryland reversed the contempt conviction on the basis of the Supreme Court's liberal doctrine of contempt in* Bridges, Pennekamp, *and* Craig. *Then the State of Maryland appealed the case to the Supreme Court.*

*Denial of the petition for writ of certiorari meant only that fewer than four members of the Supreme Court thought that certiorari should be granted. The Court never says why it has refused to review a case and such a denial carries with it no sure implication regarding the views of the Court on the merits of the case.*

*The Maryland Court of Appeals' reversal stood, and the effect was to expand upon the* Bridges, Pennekamp, *and* Craig *decisions.*

*Justice Felix Frankfurter, who obviously wanted to review the decision, filed an opinion about the denial of the certiorari petition in which he quoted at length from the record of the trial court describing the facts of the case. He appended to his decision a list of English cases "dealing with situations in which publications were claimed to have injuriously affected the prosecutions for crimes awaiting jury determination." He listed thirteen cases in which contempt was found and four in which it was not. He mentioned, incidentally, no American cases. In addition, he enunciated his own views on "trial by mass media."*

Mr. Justice FRANKFURTER said:

The issues considered by the Court of Appeals bear on some of the basic problems of a democratic society. Freedom of the press, properly conceived, is basic to our constitutional system. Safeguards for the fair administration of criminal justice are enshrined in our Bill of Rights. Respect for both of these indispensable elements of our constitutional systems presents some of the most difficult and delicate problems for adjudication. It has taken centuries of struggle to evolve our system for bringing the guilty to book, protecting the innocent, and maintaining the interests of society consonant with our democratic professions. One of the demands of a democratic society is that the public should know what goes on in courts by being told by the press what happens there, to the end that the public may judge whether our system of criminal justice is fair and right. On the other hand our society has set apart court and jury as the tribunal for determining guilt or innocence on the basis of evidence adduced in court, so far as is humanly possible. It would be the grossest perversion of all that Mr. Justice Holmes represents to suggest that it is also true of the thought behind a criminal charge " . . . that the best test of truth is the power of the thought to get itself accepted in the competition of the market." *Abrams v. United States.* Proceedings for the determination of guilt or innocence in open court before a jury are not in competition with any other means for establishing the charge.

I have set forth in an appendix the course of recent English decisions dealing with situations . . . in which publications were claimed to have injuriously affected the prosecutions for crimes awaiting jury determination.

Reference is made to this body of experiences merely for the purpose of the kind of questions that would have to be faced were we called upon to pass on the limits that the 14th Amendment places upon the power of states to safeguard the fair administration of criminal justice by jury trial from mutilation of or distortion by extraneous influences. These are issues that this court has not yet adjudicated. It is not to be supposed that by implication it means to adjudicate them by refusing to adjudicate.

More recently, the Supreme Court has become increasingly concerned about the rights of defendants in criminal trials. *Irvin v. Dowd* involved the rights of a man accused of murder; here the Court reacted against the sensational and excessive pre-trial publicity sometimes given to cases of considerable public interest. Although the large majority of criminal trials, particularly in the large cities, are given little press coverage, there is the occasional one during which an otherwise responsible press seems to ignore its own standards.

IRVIN V. DOWD, 366 U.S. 716 (1961)

*Leslie Irvin, who was called by newspapers a "mad dog killer," was convicted of murder and sentenced to death in Indiana. In appealing to the Supreme Court, Irvin maintained that he had not received a fair trial because his jurors were influenced by the wide publicity the mass media had given the case. The publicity had been mostly and vehemently anti-Irvin. The Supreme Court found that Irvin's jurors could not have been impartial in this case, overturned his conviction, and remanded the case for retrial. The growing irritation of some Justices with "trial by mass media" is sharply reflected in the views of Justices Tom C. Clark and Frankfurter.*

Mr. Justice CLARK delivered the opinion of the Court:

. . . It is not required, however, that the jurors be totally ignorant of the facts and issues involved. In these days of swift, widespread and diverse methods of communication, an important case can be expected to arouse the interest of the public in the vicinity, and scarcely any of those best qualified to serve as jurors will not have formed some impression or opinion as to the merits of the case. This is particularly true in criminal cases. To hold that the mere existence of any preconceived notion as to the guilt or innocence of an accused, without more, is sufficient to rebut the presumption of a prospective juror's impartiality, would be to establish an impossible standard. It is sufficient if the juror can lay aside his impression or opinion and render a verdict based on the evidence presented in court.

. . . . . . . . . . . . . . . . . .

Here the buildup of prejudice is clear and convincing. An examination of the then current community pattern of thought as indicated by the popular news media is singularly revealing. For example, petitioner's first motion for a change of venue from Gibson County alleged that the awaited trial of petitioner had become the cause celebre of this small community—so much so that curbstone opinions, not only as to petitioner's guilt but even as to what punishment he should receive, were solicited and recorded on the public streets by a roving reporter, and later were broadcast over the local stations. A reading of the 46 exhibits which petitioner attached to his motion indicates that a barrage of newspaper headlines, articles, cartoons and pictures was unleashed against him during the six or seven months preceding his trial. The motion further alleged that the newspapers in which the stories appeared were delivered regularly to approximately 95% of the dwellings in Gibson County and that, in addition, the Evansville radio and TV stations, which likewise blanketed that county, also carried extensive newscasts covering the same incidents. These stories revealed the details of his background, including a reference to crimes committed when a juvenile, his convictions for arson almost 20 years previously, for burglary and by a court-martial on AWOL charges during the war. He was accused of being a parole violator. The headlines announced his police line-up identification, that he faced a lie detector test, had been placed at the scene of the crime and that the six murders were solved but the petitioner refused to confess. Finally, they announced his confession to the six murders and the fact of his indictment for four of them in Indiana. They reported petitioner's offer to plead guilty if promised a 99-year sentence, but also the determination, on the other hand, of the prosecutor to secure the death penalty, and that petitioner had confessed to 24 burglaries (the modus operandi of these robberies was compared to that of the murders and the similarity noted). One story dramatically relayed the promise of a sheriff to devote his life to securing petitioner's execution by the State of Kentucky, where petitioner is alleged to have committed one of the six murders, if Indiana failed to do so. Another characterized petitioner as remorseless and without conscience but also as having been found sane by a court-appointed panel of doctors. In many of the stories petitioner was described as the "confessed slayer of six," a parole violator and fraudulent-check artist. Petitioner's court-appointed counsel was quoted as having received "much criticism over being Irvin's counsel" and it was pointed out by way of excusing the attorney, that he would be subject to disbarment should he refuse to represent Irvin. On the day before the trial the newspapers carried the story that Irvin had orally admitted the murder of Kerr (the victim in this case) as well as "the robbery-murder of Mrs. Mary Holland; the murder of Mrs. Wilhelmina Sailer in Posey County, and the slaughter of three members of the Duncan family in Henderson County, Kentucky."

It cannot be gainsaid that the force of this continued adverse publicity caused a sustained excitement and fostered a strong prejudice among the people of Gibson County. In fact, on the second day devoted to the selection of the jury, the newspapers reported that "strong feelings, often bitter and angry, rumbled to the surface," and that "the extent to which the multiple murders—three in one family—have aroused feelings throughout the area was emphasized Friday when 27 of the 35 prospective jurors questioned were excused for holding biased pretrial opinions." . . . A few days later the feeling was described as "a pattern of deep and bitter prejudice against the former pipe-fitter." Spectator comments, as printed by the newspapers, were "my mind is made up"; "I think he is guilty"; and "he should be hanged."

Finally, and with remarkable understatement, the headlines reported that "impartial jurors are hard to find." . . .

Here the "pattern of deep and bitter prejudice" shown to be present throughout the community, cf. *Stroble v. California*, 343 U.S. 181, was clearly reflected in the sum total of the *voir dire* examination of a majority of the jurors finally placed in the jury box. Eight out of the 12 thought petitioner was guilty. With such an opinion permeating their minds, it would be difficult to say that each could exclude this preconception of guilt from his deliberations. The influence that lurks in an opinion once formed is so persistent that it unconsciously fights detachment from the mental processes of the average man. . . . Where one's life is at stake—and accounting for the frailties of human nature—we can only say that in the light of the circumstances here the finding of impartiality does not meet constitutional standards. Two-thirds of the jurors had an opinion that petitioner was guilty and were familiar with the material facts and circumstances involved, including the fact that other murders were attributed to him, some going so far as to say that it would take evidence to overcome their belief.

Long a vocal critic of trial by mass media, Justice Frankfurter here reiterated that the fair administration of justice must not be subordinated to freedom of the press. And he hinted at the possibility of future legal restrictions on pre-trial coverage, when he said: "The Court has not yet decided that . . . the poisoner (of jurors' minds) is constitutionally protected in plying his trade."

Mr. Justice FRANKFURTER concurring:

. . . One of the rightful boasts of Western civilization is that the State has the burden of establishing guilt solely on the basis of evidence produced in court and under circumstances assuring an accused all the safeguards of a fair procedure. These rudimentary conditions for determining guilt are inevitably wanting if the jury which is to sit in judgment on a fellow human being comes to its task with its mind ineradicably poisoned against him. How can fallible men and women reach a disinterested verdict based exclusively on what they heard in court when, before they entered the jury box, their minds were saturated by press and radio for months preceding by matter designed to establish the guilt of the accused. A conviction so secured obviously constitutes a denial of due process of law in its most rudimentary conception.

Not a Term passes without this Court being importuned to review convictions, had in States throughout the country, in which substantial claims are made that a jury trial has been distorted because of inflammatory newspaper accounts—too often, as in this case, with the prosecutor's collaboration—exerting pressures upon potential jurors before trial and even during the course of trial, thereby making it extremely difficult, if not impossible, to secure a jury capable of taking in, free of prepossessions, evidence submitted in open court. Indeed such extraneous influences, in violation of the decencies guaranteed by our Constitution, are sometimes so powerful that an accused is forced, as a practical matter, to forego trial by jury. . . .

This Court has not yet decided that the fair administration of criminal justice must be subordinated to another safeguard of our Constitutional system—freedom of the press, properly conceived. The Court has not yet decided, that, while convictions must be reversed and miscarriages of justice result because the minds of jurors or potential jurors were poisoned, the poisoner is constitutionally protected in plying his trade.

## THE DANGERS OF "TRIAL BY TELEVISION"

Not long after the *Irvin* decision, a similar case came up to the Supreme Court. This time it was television, not newspapers, that created a situation which made a fair trial difficult, if not impossible.

RIDEAU V. LOUISIANA, 373 U.S. 723 (1963)

*The defendant, Wilbert Rideau, was convicted of murder in a Louisiana court. But the circumstances suggest that Rideau*

*was convicted on television before the case ever came to court.
The Court opinion, by Justice Potter Stewart, reviewed the
pertinent facts and reflected the Court's increasing concern for
the rights of defendants in criminal trials. The Court reversed
his conviction. He was later retried and convicted in Louisiana.*

Mr. Justice STEWART delivered the opinion of the Court:

On the evening of February 16, 1961, a man robbed a bank in
Lake Charles, Louisiana, kidnapped three of the bank's employees,
and killed one of them. A few hours later the petitioner, Wilbert
Rideau, was apprehended by the police and lodged in the Calcasieu
Parish jail in Lake Charles. The next morning a moving picture
film with a sound track was made of an "interview" in the jail between Rideau and the sheriff of Calcasieu Parish. This "interview"
lasted approximately 20 minutes. It consisted of interrogation by
the sheriff and admissions by Rideau that he had perpetrated the
bank robbery, kidnapping, and murder. Later the same day the
filmed "interview" was broadcast over a television station in Lake
Charles, and some 24,000 people in the community saw and heard it
on television. The sound film was again shown on television the
next day to an estimated audience of 53,000 people. The following
day the film was again broadcast by the same television station, and
this time approximately 20,000 people saw and heard the "interview" on their television sets. Calcasieu Parish has a population of
approximately 150,000 people.

Some two weeks later, Rideau was arraigned on charges of
armed robbery, kidnapping, and murder, and two lawyers were ap-
pointed to represent him. His lawyers promptly filed a motion for a
change of venue, on the ground that it would deprive Rideau of
rights guaranteed to him by the United States Constitution to force
him to trial in Calcasieu Parish after the three television broadcasts
there of his "interview" with the sheriff. After a hearing, the motion for change of venue was denied, and Rideau was accordingly
convicted and sentenced to death on the murder charge in the
Calcasieu Parish trial court.

Three members of the jury which convicted him had stated
on *voir dire* that they had seen and heard Rideau's televised "interview" with the sheriff on at least one occasion. Two members
of the jury were deputy sheriffs of Calcasieu Parish. Rideau's
counsel had requested that these jurors be excused for cause, having
exhausted all of their peremptory challenges, but these challenges
for cause had been denied by the trial judge. The judgment of conviction was affirmed by the Supreme Court of Louisiana, and the
case is here on a petition for a writ of certiorari.

The record in this case contains as an exhibit the sound film which was broadcast. What the people of Calcasieu Parish saw on their television sets was Rideau, in jail, flanked by the sheriff and two state troopers, admitting in detail the commission of the robbery, kidnapping, and murder, in response to leading questions by the sheriff. The record fails to show whose idea it was to make the sound film, and broadcast it over the local television station, but we know from the conceded circumstances that the plan was carried out with the active cooperation and participation of the local law enforcement officers. And certainly no one has suggested that it was Rideau's idea, or even that he was aware of what was going on when the sound film was being made.

In the view we take of this case, the question of who originally initiated the idea of the televised interview is, in any event, a basically irrelevant detail. For we hold that it was a denial of due process of law to refuse the request for a change of venue, after the people of Calcasieu Parish had been exposed repeatedly and in depth to the spectacle of Rideau personally confessing in detail to the crimes with which he was later to be charged. For anyone who has ever watched television the conclusion cannot be avoided that this spectacle, to the tens of thousands of people who saw and heard it, in a very real sense *was* Rideau's trial—at which he pleaded guilty to murder. Any subsequent court proceedings in a community so pervasively exposed to such a spectacle could be but a hollow formality.

. . . . . . . . . . . . . . . . . . . .

The case now before us does not involve physical brutality. The kangaroo court proceedings in this case involved a more subtle but no less real deprivation of due process of law. Under our Constitution's guarantee of due process, a person accused of committing a crime is vouchsafed basic minimal rights. Among these are the right to counsel, the right to plead not guilty, and the right to be tried in a courtroom presided over by a judge. Yet in this case the people of Calcasieu Parish saw and heard, not once but three times, a "trial" of Rideau in a jail, presided over by a sheriff, where there was no lawyer to advise Rideau of his right to stand mute.

The record shows that such a thing as this never took place before in Calcasieu Parish, Louisiana. Whether it has occurred elsewhere, we do not know. But we do not hesitate to hold, without pausing to examine a particularized transcript of the *voir dire* examination of the members of the jury, that due process of law in this case required a trial before a jury drawn from a community of people who had not seen and heard Rideau's televised "interview." "Due process of law, preserved for all by our Constitution, commands that no such practice as that disclosed by this record shall send any accused to his death." *Chambers v. Florida,* 309 U.S. 227, 241.
Reversed.

## SAMUEL SHEPPARD'S LONG ORDEAL

In recent years, the *cause celebre* in the lively area of free press and fair trial has been the *Sheppard* case in Ohio. For more than twelve years, this sensational murder case and all the legal byplay that flowed from it was on and off page one of the nation's newspapers. Only the trial of Bruno Richard Hauptmann in the 1930's for kidnapping the Lindbergh baby rivaled it in the extent and excesses of coverage by the press.

Dr. Samuel Sheppard was convicted in 1954 of second-degree murder in the death of his wife. His conviction was upheld by the Ohio courts and his original certiorari appeal to the U.S. Supreme Court was denied in 1956. Ten years later, he again appealed to the Court and this time it ordered a new trial in a decision of prime significance for all those charged with protecting the rights of one accused of a capital crime.

The *Sheppard* case was exceptional—in extent of mass media coverage, in public interest, and in the strong feelings aroused. Yet it is the exceptional case (thousands of criminal cases, especially in the big cities, go unreported in the press) that focuses public attention on the problem and delineates the fundamental issues involved. Justice Clark's decision is an important contribution to the debate over fair trial and free press. While the Court here castigates the excesses of irresponsible news coverage, it would not directly restrict the press. Instead, it places the responsibility for assuring a fair trial squarely in the lap of the trial judge.

SHEPPARD V. MAXWELL, 384 U.S. 333 (1966)

Mr. Justice CLARK delivered the opinion of the Court:

This federal habeas corpus application involves the question whether Sheppard was deprived of a fair trial in his state conviction for the second degree murder of his wife because of the trial judge's failure to protect Sheppard sufficiently from the massive, pervasive and prejudicial publicity that attended his prosecution. The United States District Court held that he was not afforded a fair trial and granted the writ subject to the State's right to put Sheppard to trial again. . . . The Court of Appeals for the Sixth Circuit reversed by a divided vote. . . . We granted certiorari, 382 U.S. 916. . . . We have concluded that Sheppard did not receive a fair trial consistent with the Due Process Clause of the Fourteenth Amendment and, therefore, reverse the judgment.

I

Marilyn Sheppard, petitioner's pregnant wife, was bludgeoned to death in the upstairs bedroom of their lakeshore home in Bay Village, Ohio, a suburb of Cleveland. On the day of the tragedy, July 4, 1954, Sheppard pieced together for several local officials the following story: He and his wife had entertained neighborhood friends, the Aherns, on the previous evening at their home. After dinner they watched television in the living room. Sheppard became drowsy and dozed off to sleep on a couch. Later, Marilyn partially awoke him saying that she was going to bed. The next thing he remembered was hearing his wife cry out in the early morning hours. He hurried upstairs and in the dim light from the hall saw a "form" standing next to his wife's bed. As he struggled with the "form" he was struck on the back of the neck and rendered unconscious. On regaining his senses he found himself on the floor next to his wife's bed. He raised up, looked at her, took her pulse and "felt that she was gone." He then went to his son's room and found him unmolested. Hearing a noise he hurried downstairs. He saw a "form" running out the door and pursued it to the lake shore. He grappled with it on the beach and again lost consciousness. Upon his recovery he was lying face down with the lower portion of his body in the water. He returned to his home, checked the pulse on his wife's neck, and "determined or thought that she was gone." He then went downstairs and called a neighbor, Mayor Houk of Bay Village. The Mayor and his wife came over at once, found Sheppard slumped in an easy chair downstairs and asked, "What happened?" Sheppard replied: "I don't know but somebody ought to try to do something for Marilyn." Mrs. Houk immediately went up to the bedroom. The Mayor told Sheppard, "Get hold of yourself. Can you tell me what happened?" Sheppard then related the above outlined events. After Mrs. Houk discovered the body, the Mayor called the local police, Dr. Richard Sheppard, petitioner's brother, and Aherns. The local police were the first to arrive. They in turn notified the Coroner and Cleveland police. Richard Sheppard then arrived, determined that Marilyn was dead, examined his brother's injuries, and removed him to the nearby clinic operated by the Sheppard family. When the Coroner, the Cleveland police and other officials arrived, the house and surrounding area were thoroughly searched, the rooms of the house were photographed, and many persons, including the Houks and the Aherns, were interrogated. The Sheppard home and premises were taken into "protective custody" and remained so until after the trial.

From the outset officials focused suspicion on Sheppard. After a search of the house and premises on the morning of the tragedy, Dr. Gerber, the Coroner, is reported—and it is undenied—to have told his men, "Well, it is evident the doctor did this, so let's go get the confession out of him." He proceeded to interrogate and examine Sheppard while the latter was under sedation in his hospital room. On the same occasion, the Coroner was given the clothes Sheppard wore at the time of the tragedy together with the personal items in them. Later that afternoon Chief Eaton and two Cleveland police officers interrogated Sheppard at some length, confronting him with evidence and demanding explanations. Asked by Officer Shotke to take a lie detector test, Sheppard said he would if it were reliable. Shotke replied that it was "infallible" and "you might as well tell us all about it now." At the end of the interrogation Shotke told Sheppard: "I think you killed your wife." Still later in the same afternoon a physician sent by the Coroner was permitted to make a detailed examination of Sheppard. Until the Coroner's inquest on July 22, at which time he was subpoenaed, Sheppard made himself available for frequent and extended questioning without the presence of an attorney.

On July 7, the day of Marilyn Sheppard's funeral, a newspaper story appeared in which Assistant County Attorney Mahon— later the chief prosecutor of Sheppard—sharply criticized the refusal of the Sheppard family to permit his immediate questioning. From there on headline stories repeatedly stressed Sheppard's lack of cooperation with the police and other officials. . . . Under the headline "Testify Now In Death, Bay Doctor Is Ordered," one story described a visit by Coroner Gerber and four police officers to the hospital on July 8. When Sheppard insisted that his lawyer be present, the Coroner wrote out a subpoena and served it on him. Sheppard then agreed to submit to questioning without counsel and the subpoena was torn up. The officers questioned him for several hours. On July 8, Sheppard, at the request of the Coroner, re-enacted the tragedy at his home before the Coroner, police officers, and a group of newsmen, who apparently were invited by the Coroner. The home was locked so that Sheppard was obliged to wait outside until the Coroner arrived. Sheppard's performance was reported in detail by the news media along with photographs. The newspapers also played up Sheppard's refusal to take a lie detector test and "the protective ring" thrown up by his family. . . . Front-page newspaper headlines announced on the same day that "Doctor Balks At Lie Test; Retells Story." A column opposite that story contained an "exclusive" interview with Sheppard headlined: " 'Loved My Wife, She Loved Me,' Sheppard Tells News Reporters." The next day, another headline story disclosed that Sheppard had "again late yesterday refused to take a lie detector test" and quoted an Assistant County Attorney as saying that "at the end of a nine-hour questioning of Dr. Sheppard, I felt he was now ruling [a test] out completely." But subsequent newspaper articles reported that the Coroner was still pushing Sheppard for a lie detector test. More stories appeared when Sheppard would not allow authorities to inject him with "truth serum."

On [July] 20th, the "editorial artillery" opened fire with a front-page charge that somebody is "getting away with murder." The editorial attributed the ineptness of the investigation to "friendships, relationships, hired lawyers, a husband who ought to have been subjected instantly to the same third degree to which any person under similar circumstances is subjected. . . ." The following day, July 21, another page-one editorial was headed: "Why No Inquest? Do It Now, Dr. Gerber." The Coroner called an inquest the same day and subpoenaed Sheppard. It was staged the next day in a school gymnasium; the Coroner presided with the County Prosecutor as his advisor and two detectives as bailiffs. In the front of the room was a long table occupied by reporters, television and radio personnel, and broadcasting equipment. The hearing was broadcast with live microphones placed at the Coroner's seat and the witness stand. A swarm of reporters and photographers attended. Sheppard was brought into the room by police who searched him in full view of several hundred spectators. Sheppard's counsel were present during the three-day inquest but were not permitted to participate. When Sheppard's chief counsel attempted to place some documents in the record, he was forcibly ejected from the room by the Coroner, who received cheers, hugs and kisses from ladies in the audience. Sheppard was questioned for five and one-half hours about his actions on the night of the murder, his married life, and love affair with Susan Hayes. At the end of the hearing the Coroner announced that he "could" order Sheppard held for the grand jury, but did not do so.

Throughout this period the newspapers emphasized evidence that tended to incriminate Sheppard and pointed out discrepancies in his statements to authorities. At the same time, Sheppard made many public statements to the press and wrote feature articles asserting his innocence. During the inquest on July 26, a headline in large type stated: "Kerr [Captain of the Cleveland police] Urges Sheppard's Arrest." In the story, Detective McArthur "disclosed that scientific tests at the Sheppard home have definitely established that the killer washed off a trail of blood from the murder bedroom to the downstairs section," a circumstance casting doubt on Sheppard's accounts of the murder. No such evidence was produced at trial. The newspapers also delved into Sheppard's personal life. Articles stressed his extra-marital love affairs as a motive for the crime. The newspapers portrayed Sheppard as a Lothario, fully explored his relationship with Susan Hayes, and named a number of other women who were allegedly involved with him. The testimony at trial never showed that Sheppard had any illicit relationships besides the one with Susan Hayes.

"On July 28, an editorial entitled "Why Don't Police Quiz Top Suspect" demanded that Sheppard be taken to police headquarters. It described him in the following language:

"Now proved under oath to be a liar, still free to go about his business, shielded by his family, protected by a smart lawyer who has made monkeys of the police and authorities, carrying a gun part of the time, left free to do whatever he pleases. . . ."

A front-page editorial on July 30 asked: "Why Isn't Sam Sheppard in Jail?" It was later titled "Quit Stalling—Bring Him In." After calling Sheppard "the most unusual murder suspect ever seen around these parts" the article said that "[e]xcept for some superficial questioning during Coroner Sam Gerber's inquest he has been scot-free of any official grilling. . . ." It asserted that he was "surrounded by an iron curtain of protection [and] concealment."

That night at 10 o'clock Sheppard was arrested at his father's home on a charge of murder. He was taken to the Bay Village City Hall where hundreds of people, newscasters, photographers and reporters were awaiting his arrival. He was immediately arraigned—having been denied a temporary delay to secure the presence of counsel—and bound over to the grand jury.

The publicity then grew in intensity until his indictment on August 17. Typical of the coverage during this period is a front-page interview entitled: "DR. SAM: 'I Wish There Was Something I Could Get Off My Chest—but There Isn't.'" Unfavorable publicity included items such as a cartoon of the body of a sphinx with Sheppard's head and the legend below: "'I Will Do Everything In My Power to Help Solve This Terrible Murder.'—Dr. Sam Sheppard." Headlines announced, *inter alia,* that: "Doctor Evidence Is Ready for Jury," "Corrigan Tactics Stall Quizzing." "Sheppard 'Gay Set' Is Revealed By Houk," "Blood Is Found In Garage," "New Murder Evidence Is Found, Police Claim," "Dr. Sam Faces Quiz At Jail On Marilyn's Fear Of Him." On August 18, an article appeared under the headline "Dr. Sam Writes His Own Story." And reproduced across the entire front page was a portion of the typed statement signed by Sheppard: "I am not guilty of the murder of my wife, Marilyn. How could I, who have been trained to help people and devote my life to saving life, commit such a terrible and revolting crime?" We do not detail the coverage further. There are five volumes filled with similar clippings from each of the three Cleveland newspapers covering the period from the murder until Sheppard's conviction in December 1954. The record includes no excerpts from newscasts on radio and television but since space was reserved in the courtroom for these media we assume that their coverage was equally large.

## II

With this background the case came on for trial two weeks before the November general election at which the chief prosecutor was a candidate for municipal judge and the presiding judge, Judge Blythin, was a candidate to succeed himself. Twenty-five days before the case was set, a list of 75 veniremen were called as prospective jurors. This list, including the addresses of each venireman, was published in all three Cleveland newspapers. As a consequence, anonymous letters and telephone calls, as well as calls from friends, regarding the impending prosecution were received by all of the prospective jurors. The selection of the jury began on October 18, 1954.

The courtroom in which the trial was held measured 26 by 48 feet. A long temporary table was set up inside the bar, in back of the single counsel table. It ran the width of the courtroom, parallel to the bar railing, with one end less than three feet from the jury box. Approximately 20 representatives of newspapers and wire services were assigned seats at this table by the court. Behind the bar railing there were four rows of benches. These seats were likewise assigned by the court for the entire trial. The first row was occupied by representatives of television and radio stations, and the second and third rows by reporters from out of town newspapers and magazines. One side of the last row, which accommodated 14 people, was assigned to Sheppard's family and the other to Marilyn's. The public was permitted to fill vacancies in this row on special passes only. Representatives of the news media also used all the rooms on the courtroom floor, including the room where cases were ordinarily called and assigned for trial. Private telephone lines and telegraphic equipment were installed in these rooms so that reports from the trial could be speeded to the papers. Station WSRS was permitted to set up broadcasting facilities on the third floor of the courthouse next door to the jury room, where the jury rested during recesses in the trial and deliberated. Newscasts were made from this room throughout the trial, and while the jury reached its verdict.

On the sidewalk and steps in front of the courthouse, television and newsreel cameras were occasionally used to take motion pictures of the participants in the trial, including the jury and the judge. Indeed, one television broadcast carried a staged interview of the judge as he entered the courthouse. In the corridors outside the courtroom there was a host of photographers and television personnel with flash cameras, portable lights and motion picture cameras. This group photographed the prospective jurors during selection of the jury. After the trial opened, the witnesses, counsel, and jurors were photographed and televised whenever they entered or left the courtroom. Sheppard was brought to the courtroom about 10 minutes before each session began; he was surrounded by reporters and extensively photographed for the newspapers and television. A rule of court prohibited picture-taking in the courtroom during the actual sessions of the court, but no restraints were put on photographers during recesses, which were taken once each morning and afternoon, with a longer period for lunch.

All of these arrangements with the news media and their massive coverage of the trial continued during the entire nine weeks of the trial. The courtroom remained crowded to capacity with representatives of news media. Their movement in and out of the courtroom often caused so much confusion that, despite the loud speaker system installed in the courtroom, it was difficult for the witnesses and counsel to be heard. Furthermore, the reporters clustered within the bar of the small courtroom made confidential talk among Sheppard and his counsel almost impossible during the proceedings. They frequently had to leave the courtroom to obtain privacy. And many times when counsel wished to raise a point with the judge out of the hearing of the jury it was necessary to move to the judge's chambers. Even then, news media representatives so packed the judge's anteroom that counsel could hardly return from the chambers to the courtroom. The reporters vied with each other to find out what counsel and the judge had discussed, and often these matters later appeared in newspapers accessible to the jury.

The daily record of the proceedings was made available to the newspapers and the testimony of each witness was printed verbatim in the local editions, along with objections of counsel, and rulings by the judge. Pictures of Sheppard, the judge, counsel, pertinent witnesses, and the jury often accompanied the daily newspaper and television accounts. At times the newspapers published photographs of exhibits introduced at the trial, and the rooms of Sheppard's house were featured along with relevant testimony.

The jurors themselves were constantly exposed to the news media. Every juror, except one, testified at *voir dire* to reading about the case in the Cleveland papers or to having heard broadcasts about it. Seven of the 12 jurors who rendered the verdict had one or more Cleveland papers delivered in their home; the remaining jurors were not interrogated on the point. Nor were there questions as to radios or television sets in the talesmen's homes, but we must assume that most of them owned such conveniences. As the selection of the jury progressed, individual pictures of prospective members appeared daily. During the trial, pictures of the jury appeared over 40 times in the Cleveland papers alone. The court permitted photographers to take pictures of the jury in the box, and individual pictures of the members in the jury room. One newspaper ran pictures of the jurors at the Sheppard home when they went there to view the scene of the murder. Another paper featured the home life of an alternate juror. The day before the verdict was rendered—while the jurors were at lunch and sequestered by two bailiffs—the jury was separated into two groups to pose for photographs which appeared in the newspapers.

### III

We now reach the conduct of the trial. While the intense publicity continued unabated, it is sufficient to relate only the more flagrant episodes:

1. October 9, 1954, nine days before the case went to trial, an editorial in one of the newspapers criticized defense counsel's random poll of people on the streets as to their opinion of Sheppard's guilt or innocence in an effort to use the resulting statistics to show the necessity for change of venue. The article said the survey "smacks of mass jury tampering," called on defense counsel to drop it, and stated that the bar association should do something about it. It characterized the poll as "non-judicial, non-legal, and nonsense." The article was called to the attention of the court but no action was taken.

2. On the second day of *voir dire* examination a debate was staged and broadcast live over WHK radio. The participants, newspaper reporters, accused Sheppard's counsel of throwing roadblocks in the way of the prosecution and asserted that Sheppard conceded his guilt by hiring a prominent criminal lawyer. Sheppard's counsel objected to this broadcast and requested a continuance, but the judge denied the motion. When counsel asked the court to give some protection from such events, the judge replied that "WHK doesn't have much coverage," and that "after all, we are not trying this case by radio or in newspapers or any other means. We confine ourselves seriously to it in this courtroom and do the very best we can."

3. While the jury was being selected, a two-inch headline asked: "But Who Will Speak for Marilyn?" The front-page story spoke of the "perfect face" of the accused. "Study that face as long as you want. Never will you get from it a hint of what might be the answer. . . . " The two brothers of the accused were described as [punctuation *sic*] "Prosperous, poised. His two sisters-in-law. Smart, chic, well-groomed. His elderly father. Courtly, reserved. A perfect type for the patriarch of a staunch clan." The author then noted Marilyn Sheppard was "still off stage," and that she was an only child whose mother died when she was very young and whose father had no interest in the case. But the author—through quotes from Detective Chief James McArthur—assured readers that the prosecu-

tion's exhibits would speak for Marilyn. "Her story," McArthur stated, "will come into this courtroom through our witnesses." The article ends:

"Then you realize how what and who is missing from the perfect setting will be supplied.

"How in the Big Case justice will be done.

"Justice to Sam Sheppard.

"And to Marilyn Sheppard."

4. As has been mentioned, the jury viewed the scene of the murder on the first day of the trial. Hundreds of reporters, cameramen and onlookers were there, and one representative of the news media was permitted to accompany the jury while they inspected the Sheppard home. The time of the jury's visit was revealed so far in advance that one of the newspapers was able to rent a helicopter and fly over the house taking pictures of the jurors on their tour.

5. On November 19, a Cleveland police officer gave testimony that tended to contradict details in the written statement Sheppard made to the Cleveland police. Two days later, in a broadcast heard over Station WHK in Cleveland, Robert Considine likened Sheppard to a perjurer and compared the episode to Alger Hiss' confrontation with Whittaker Chambers. Though defense counsel asked the judge to question the jury to ascertain how many heard the broadcast, the court refused to do so. The judge also overruled the motion for continuance based on the same ground, saying:

Well, I don't know, we can't stop people, in any event, listening to it. It is a matter of free speech, and the court can't control everybody. . . . We are not going to harass the jury every morning. . . . It is getting to the point where if we do it every morning, we are suspecting the jury. I have confidence in this jury. . . .

"6. On November 24, a story appeared under an eight-column headline: "Sam Called a 'Jekyll-Hyde' by Marilyn, Cousin To Testify." It related that Marilyn had recently told friends that Sheppard was a "Dr. Jekyll and Mr. Hyde" character. No such testimony was ever produced at the trial. The story went on to announce: "The prosecution has a 'bombshell witness' on tap who will testify to Dr. Sam's display of fiery temper—countering the defense claim that the defendant is a gentle physician with an even disposition." Defense counsel made motions for change of venue, continuance and mistrial, but they were denied. No action was taken by the court.

7. When the trial was in its seventh week, Walter Winchell broadcasted over WXEL television and WJW radio that Carole Beasley, who was under arrest in New York City for robbery, had stated that, as Sheppard's mistress, she had borne him a child. The defense asked that the jury be queried on the broadcast. Two

jurors admitted in open court that they had heard it. The judge asked each: "Would that have any effect upon your judgment?" Both replied, "no." This was accepted by the judge as sufficient; he merely asked the jury to "pay no attention whatever to that type of scavenging. . . . Let's confine ourselves to this courtroom, if you please." In answer to the motion for mistrial, the judge said:

> Well, even so, Mr. Corrigan, how are you ever going to prevent those things, in any event? I don't justify them at all. I think it is outrageous, but in a sense, it is outrageous even if there were no trial here. The trial has nothing to do with it in the Court's mind, as far as its outrage is concerned, but—

> MR. CORRIGAN: I don't know what effect it had on the mind of any of these jurors, and I can't find out unless inquiry is made.

> THE COURT: How would you ever in any jury, avoid that kind of a thing?

8. On December 9, while Sheppard was on the witness stand he testified that he had been mistreated by Cleveland detectives after his arrest. Although he was not at the trial, Captain Kerr of the Homicide Bureau issued a press statement denying Sheppard's allegations which appeared under the headline:
" 'Bare-faced Liar,' Kerr Says of Sam." Captain Kerr never appeared as a witness at the trial.

.  .  .  .  .  .  .  .  .  .  .  .  .  .  .  .  .  .  .

### VI

There can be no question about the nature of the publicity which surrounded Sheppard's trial. We agree, as did the Court of Appeals, with the findings in Judge Bell's opinion for the Ohio Supreme Court:

> Murder and mystery, society, sex and suspense were combined in this case in such a manner as to intrigue and captivate the public fancy to a degree perhaps unparalleled in recent annals. Throughout the preindictment investigation, the subsequent, legal skirmishes and the nine-week trial, circulation-conscious editors catered to the insatiable interest of the American public in the bizarre. . . . In this atmosphere of a "Roman holiday" for the news media, Sam Sheppard stood trial for his life. 165 Ohio St., at 294, 135 N.E.2d, at 342.

Indeed, every court that has considered this case, save the court that tried it, has deplored the manner in which the news media inflamed and prejudiced the public.

Much of the material printed or broadcast during the trial was never heard from the witness stand, such as the charges that Sheppard had purposely impeded the murder investigation and must be guilty since he had hired a prominent criminal lawyer; that Sheppard was a perjurer; that he had sexual relations with numerous women; that his slain wife had characterized him as a "Jekyll-Hyde"; that he was "a bare-faced liar" because of his testimony as to police treatment; and finally, that a woman convict claimed Sheppard to be the father of her illegitimate child. As the trial progressed, the newspapers summarized and interpreted the evidence, devoting particular attention to the material that incriminates Sheppard, and often drew unwarranted inferences from testimony. At one point, a front-page picture of Mrs. Sheppard's blood-stained pillow was published after being "doctored" to show more clearly an alleged imprint of a surgical instrument.

Nor is there doubt that this deluge of publicity reached at least some of the jury. On the only occasion that the jury was queried, two jurors admitted in open court to hearing the highly inflammatory charge that a prison inmate claimed Sheppard as the father of her illegitimate child. Despite the extent and nature of the publicity to which the jury was exposed during trial, the judge refused defense counsel's other requests that the jury be asked whether they had read or heard specific prejudicial comment about the case, including the incidents we have previously summarized. In these circumstances we can assume that some of this material reached members of the jury.

## VII

(6) The court's fundamental error is compounded by the holding that it lacked power to control the publicity about the trial. From the very inception of the proceedings the judge announced that neither he nor anyone else could restrict prejudicial news accounts. And he reiterated this view on numerous occasions. Since he viewed the news media as his target, the judge never considered other means that are often utilized to reduce the appearance of prejudicial material and to protect the jury from outside influence. We conclude that these procedures would have been sufficient to guarantee Sheppard a fair trial and so do not consider what sanctions might be available against a recalcitrant press nor the charges of bias now made against the state trial judge.

(7) The carnival atmosphere at trial could easily have been avoided since the courtroom and courthouse premises are subject to the control of the court. As we stressed in *Estes,* the presence of the press at judicial proceedings must be limited when it is apparent that the accused might otherwise be prejudiced or disadvantaged. Bearing in mind the massive pretrial publicity, the judge should have adopted stricter rules governing the use of the courtroom by newsmen, as Sheppard's counsel requested. The number of reporters in the courtroom itself could have been limited at the first sign that

their presence would disrupt the trial. They certainly should not have been placed inside the bar. Furthermore, the judge should have more closely regulated the conduct of newsmen in the courtroom. For instance, the judge belatedly asked them not to handle and photograph trial exhibits lying on the counsel table during recesses.

Secondly, the court should have insulated the witnesses. All of the newspapers and radio stations apparently interviewed prospective witnesses at will, and in many instances disclosed their testimony. A typical example was the publication of numerous statements by Susan Hayes, before her appearance in court, regarding her love affair with Sheppard. Although the witnesses were barred from the courtroom during the trial the full *verbatim* testimony was available to them in the press. This completely nullified the judge's imposition of the rule. . . .

Thirdly, the court should have made some effort to control the release of leads, information, and gossip to the press by police officers, witnesses, and the counsel for both sides. Much of the information thus disclosed was inaccurate, leading to groundless rumors and confusion. That the judge was aware of his responsibility in this respect may be seen from his warning to Steve Sheppard, the accused's brother, who had apparently made public statements in an attempt to discredit testimony for the prosecution. The judge made this statement in the presence of the jury:

Now, the court wants to say a word. That he was told—he has not read anything about it at all—but he was informed that Dr. Steve Sheppard, who has been granted the privilege of remaining in the courtroom during the trial, has been trying the case in the newspapers and making rather uncomplimentary comments about the testimony of the witnesses for the State.

Let it be now understood that if Dr. Steve Sheppard wishes to use the newspapers to try his case while we are trying it here, he will be barred from remaining in the courtroom during the progress of the trial if he is to be a witness in the case.

The Court appreciates he cannot deny Steve Sheppard the right of free speech, but he can deny him the . . . privilege of being in the courtroom, if he wants to avail himself of that method during the progress of the trial.

Defense counsel immediately brought to the court's attention the tremendous amount of publicity in the Cleveland press that "misrepresented entirely the testimony" in the case. Under such circumstances, the judge should have at least warned the newspapers to check the accuracy of their accounts. And it is obvious that the judge should have further sought to alleviate this problem by imposing control over the statements made to the news media by counsel, witnesses, and especially the Coroner and police officers. The prosecution repeatedly made evidence available to the news media which was never offered in the trial. Much of the "evidence" disseminated in this fashion was clearly inadmissible. The exclusion of such evidence in court is rendered meaningless when a news medium makes it available to the public. For example the publicity about Sheppard's refusal to take a lie detector test came directly from police officers and the Coroner. The story that Sheppard had been called a "Jekyll-Hyde" personality by his wife was attributed to a prosecution witness. No such testimony was given. The further report that there was "a bombshell witness on tap" who would testify as to Sheppard's "fiery temper" could only have emanated from the prosecution. Moreover, the newspapers described in detail clues that had been found by the police, but not put into the record.

The fact that many of the prejudicial news items can be traced to the prosecution, as well as the defense, aggravates the judge's failure to take any action. . . . Effective control of these sources—concededly within the court's power—might well have prevented the divulgence of inaccurate information, rumors, and accusations that made up much of the inflammatory publicity, at least after Sheppard's indictment.

More specifically, the trial court might well have proscribed extra-judicial statements by any lawyer, party, witness, or court official which divulged prejudicial matters, such as the refusal of Sheppard to submit to interrogation or take any lie detector tests; any statement made by Sheppard to officials; the identity of prospective witnesses or their probable testimony; any belief in guilt or innocence; or like statements concerning the merits of the case. See *State v. Van Duyne*, 43 N.J. 369, 389, 204 A.2d 841, 850 (1964), in which the court interpreted Canon 20 of the American Bar Association's *Canons of Professional Ethics* to prohibit such statements. Being advised of the great public interest in the case, the mass coverage of the press, and the potential prejudicial impact of publicity, the court could also have requested the appropriate city and county officials to promulgate a regulation with respect to dissemination of information about the case by their employees. In addition, reporters who wrote or broadcasted prejudicial stories, could have been warned as to the impropriety of publishing material not introduced in the proceedings. The judge was put on notice of such events by defense counsel's complaint about the WHK broadcast on the second day of trial. . . . In this manner, Sheppard's right to a trial free from outside interference would have been given added protection without corresponding curtailment of the news media. Had the judge, the other officers of the court, and the police placed the interest of justice first, the news media would have soon learned to be content with the task of reporting the case as it unfolded in the courtroom—not pieced together from extra-judicial statements.

From the cases coming here we note that unfair and prejudicial news comment on pending trials has become increasingly prevalent. Due process requires that the accused receive a trial by an impartial jury free from outside influences. Given the pervasiveness of modern communications and the difficulty of effacing prejudicial publicity from the minds of the jurors, the trial courts must take strong measures to ensure that the balance is never weighed against the accused. And appellate tribunals have the duty to make an independent evaluation of the circumstances. Of course, there is nothing that proscribes the press from reporting events that transpire in the courtroom. But where there is a reasonable likelihood that prejudicial news prior to trial will prevent a fair trial, the judge should continue the case until the threat abates, or transfer it to another county not so permeated with publicity. In addition, sequestration of the jury was something the judge should have raised *sua sponte* with counsel. If publicity during the proceedings threatens the fairness of the trial, a new trial should be ordered. But we must remember that reversals are but palliatives; the cure lies in those remedial measures that will prevent the prejudice at its inception. The courts must take such steps by rule and regulation that will protect their processes from prejudicial outside interferences. Neither prosecutors, counsel for defense, the accused, witnesses, court staff nor enforcement officers coming under the jurisdiction of the court should be permitted to frustrate its function. Collaboration between counsel and the press as to information affecting the fairness of a criminal trial is not only subject to regulation, but is highly censurable and worthy of disciplinary measures.

Since the state trial judge did not fulfill his duty to protect Sheppard from the inherently prejudicial publicity which saturated the community and to control disruptive influences in the courtroom, we must reverse the denial of the habeas petition. The case is remanded to the District Court with instructions to issue the writ and order that Sheppard be released from custody unless the State puts him to its charges again within a reasonable time.

The state of Ohio tried Sheppard again and this time he was acquitted. On November 16, 1966, Dr. Samuel Sheppard became a free man for the first time in twelve years.

The *Sheppard* decision and others in this chapter and the previous one suggest two generalizations about the relationship between a free press and the administration of justice: first, considerable constitutional freedom exists under the First Amendment to comment upon and even criticize approaching or pending court cases; and second, the Supreme Court in recent years has become increasingly wary of any pre-trial publicity that would deprive a defendant of his constitutional rights to a fair and impartial trial.

Although excessive publicity can interfere with the administration of justice, the Court's limiting of contempt to in-court or "so near thereto" obstructions makes it unlikely that contempt will be applied to the press in such situations. To do so would greatly restrict the press's right to criticize courts and judges.

Yet the *Sheppard* decision makes it clear that judges are very likely going to place increasing restrictions on the amounts and kinds of information released to the press by police, prosecutors, and defense lawyers.

The Freedom of Information Committee of the American Society of Newspaper Editors felt in 1967 that the Supreme Court, whether intentionally or not, had in *Sheppard* "scared a lot of policemen, prosecutors, defense counsel, and especially judges into suppressing legitimate news of the criminal process."[1]

At the same time, the American Bar Association and various state bar organizations recommended stronger controls over pre-trial news. There was evidence too that newspapers were becoming excessively cautious in reporting pre-trial news. Whether or not bar association canons are adopted by trial courts could depend on how well the news media and/or lawyers' groups can carry out self-imposed restraints on prejudicial pre-trial publicity. The rulings of *Sheppard, Irvin,* and *Rideau* are indicative of the modern Supreme Court's deep concern with the rights of individuals caught up in the law enforcement process. A free and responsible press is under increasing obligation to show the same concern.

[1] "Press Freedom Loses Ground, Editors Told," *Wisc. State J.,* April 21, 1967, p. 18.

*Chapter Seven*

FREEDOM TO CRITICIZE PUBLIC OFFICIALS:
LIBEL IMMUNITY

THE RIGHT of the press to criticize government—to serve as a "watchdog" over public officials and their acts—has been a basic tenet of press freedom since the days of Jefferson and Madison. This is, of course, a constitutional right accorded not only to owners of printing presses but to all citizens. In an early debate in the House of Representatives, James Madison said: "If we advert to the nature of republican government, we shall find that the censorial power is in the people over the government, and not in the government over the people." And Justice Hugo Black wrote in *Bridges v. California:* "It is a prized American privilege to speak one's mind, although not always with perfect good taste, on all public institutions." The people, it was reasoned, could not adequately govern themselves unless they had the freedom to scrutinize and to criticize those they had chosen to govern them.

However, it took more than 175 years for the First Amendment's protection to be applied to civil libel cases. This extraordinary time lapse resulted from two circumstances: few legal analysts believed the First Amendment had anything to do with civil libel suits and, further, precedents were lacking; only recently have public officials begun using civil libel suits demanding huge damages to retaliate against press or public criticism. President Theodore Roosevelt was satisfied with a six-cent judgment for libel when he sued a newspaper for saying he cursed and was drunk while campaigning.

129

The civil rights struggles in the South during the 1960's changed this pattern. During April 1963, at least seventeen libel actions were pending in state and federal courts—actions brought by public officials in three southern states against newspapers, magazines, and a television network. Total damages sought exceeded $288,000,000.[1]

Until 1964 and the decision in *New York Times v. Sullivan*, libel suits were a matter for state law, with each state following different rules. Many states, but not all, provided a qualified privilege (limited defense against libel suits) for citizens criticizing their public officials. The *Times* decision placed a uniform national limitation on such libel suits under the First Amendment.

## PUBLIC OFFICIALS LIMITED IN USE OF CIVIL LIBEL SUITS

The *Times* case is an excellent illustration of how the Constitution has been interpreted to accommodate to changing conditions. Until the litigation in Alabama, the Court had not had the opportunity to consider the challenge that excessive libel judgments represent to the press's freedom to criticize public officials. The Court faced the challenge and unanimously expanded the boundaries of press freedom.

As with the Jehovah's Witnesses cases, it was within the context of a social and political struggle—in this case, the Negro's fight for civil rights in the South—from which this new and meaningful delineation of freedom of the press emerged.

### NEW YORK TIMES V. SULLIVAN, 376 U.S. 254 (1964)

*The case arose out of a full-page advertisement published in the New York Times of March 29, 1960. The advertisement, signed by a number of northern supporters of civil rights and (without their knowledge) by four Negro ministers in the South, was critical of the conduct of public officials during racial demonstrations in Montgomery, Alabama. No officials were named, but L. B. Sullivan, police commissioner of Montgomery, brought a libel action against the New York paper and the four Negro ministers. In circuit court of Montgomery, Sullivan won a judgment of $500,000. The property of several of the Negro ministers was seized and sold at sheriff's sale.*

[1] *New York Times*, April 4, 1964, p. 12:3.

*The Alabama Supreme Court upheld the judgment, and the case was carried to the U.S. Supreme Court, where it was reversed unanimously. Justice William J. Brennan, for the Court, announced the constitutional standard that a public official may not recover damages for what he believes to be a libel of his official conduct unless he can prove actual malice —that is, knowledge on the part of the critic that his statement was false, "or showed reckless disregard of whether it was false or not." He carefully traced constitutional history as it related to libel of public officials.*

*Justices Hugo Black, Arthur Goldberg, and William O. Douglas would have liked the Court to uphold a doctrine of unconditional and absolute freedom of the press to criticize official conduct.*

Mr. Justice BRENNAN delivered the opinion of the Court:

We are required for the first time in this case to determine the extent to which the constitutional protections for speech and press limit a state's power to award damages in a libel action brought by a public official against critics of his official conduct.

. . . . . . . . . . . . . . . . . . . .

The second contention is that the constitutional guarantees of freedom of speech and of the press are inapplicable here, at least so far as *The Times* is concerned, because the allegedly libelous statements were published as part of a paid, "commercial" advertisement. The argument relies on *Valentine v. Chrestensen*, 316 U.S. 52, where the Court held that a city ordinance forbidding street distribution of commercial and business advertising matter did not abridge the First Amendment freedoms, even as applied to a handbill having a commercial message on one side but a protest against certain official action on the other. The reliance is wholly misplaced. The Court in *Chrestensen* reaffirmed the constitutional protection for "the freedom of communicating information and disseminating opinion"; its holding was based upon the factual conclusions that the handbill was "purely commercial advertising" and that the protest against official action had been added only to evade the ordinance.

The publication here was not a "commercial" advertisement in the sense in which the word was used in *Chrestensen*. It communicated information, expressed opinion, recited grievances, protested claimed abuses, and sought financial support on behalf of a movement whose existence and objectives are matters of the highest public interest and concern. . . .

That *The Times* was paid for publishing the advertisement is as immaterial in this connection as is the fact that newspapers and books are sold. . . . Any other conclusion would discourage newspapers from carrying "editorial advertisements" of this type, and so might shut off an important outlet for the promulgation of information and ideas by persons who do not themselves have access to publishing facilities—who wish to exercise their freedom of speech even though they are not members of the press. . . . This effect would be to shackle the First Amendment in its attempt to secure "the widest possible dissemination of information from diverse and antagonistic sources." . . . To avoid placing such a handicap upon the freedoms of expression, we hold that if the allegedly libelous statements would otherwise be constitutionally protected from the present judgment, they do not forfeit that protection because they were published in the form of a paid advertisement. . . .

In the only previous case that did present the question of constitutional limitations upon the power to award damages for libel of a public official, the Court was equally divided and the question was not decided. *Schenectady Union Pub. Co. v. Sweeney*, 316 U.S. 642. In deciding the question now we are compelled by neither precedent nor policy to give any more weight to the epithet "libel" than we have to other "mere labels" of state law. . . . Like "insurrection," contempt, advocacy of unlawful act, breach of the peace, obscenity, solicitation of legal business and the various other formulae for the repression of expression that have been challenged in this court, libel can claim no talismanic immunity from constitutional limitations. It must be measured by standards that satisfy the First Amendment.

The general proposition that freedom of expression upon public questions is secured by the First Amendment has long been settled by our decisions. The constitutional safeguard, we have said, "was fashioned to assure the unfettered inter-change of ideas for the bringing about of political and social changes desired by the people." *Roth v. United States*, . . . "The maintenance of the opportunity for free political discussion to the end that government may be responsive to the will of the people and that changes may be obtained by lawful means, an opportunity essential to the security of the Republic, is a fundamental principle of our constitutional system." *Stromberg v. California*, 283 U.S. 359. "It is a prized American privilege to speak one's mind, although not always with perfect good taste, on all public institutions," *Bridges v. California*, . . . and this opportunity is to be afforded for "vigorous advocacy" no less than "abstract discussion." *N.A.A.C.P. v. Button*, 371 U.S. 415.

.  .  .  .  .  .  .  .  .  .  .  .  .  .  .

Thus we consider this case against the background of a profound national commitment to the principle that debate on public issues should be uninhibited, robust, and wide-open, and that it may well include vehement, caustic, and sometimes unpleasantly sharp attacks on government and public officials. . . . The present advertisement, as an expression of grievance and protest on one of the major public issues of our time, would seem clearly to qualify for the constitutional protection. The question is whether it forfeits that protection by the falsity of some of its factual statements and by its alleged defamation of respondent.

Authoritative interpretations of the First Amendment guarantees have consistently refused to recognize an exception for any test of truth, whether administered by judges, juries, or administrative officials—and especially not one that puts the burden of providing truth on the speaker. . . .

The constitutional protection does not turn upon "the truth, popularity, or social utility of the ideas and beliefs which are offered." *N.A.A.C.P. v. Button,* 371 U.S. 415. As Madison said, "Some degree of abuse is inseparable from the proper use of everything; and in no instance is this more true than in that of the press." . . . In *Cantwell v. Connecticut,* 310 U.S. 296, the Court declared:

"In the realm of religious faith, and in that of political belief, sharp differences arise. In both fields the tenets of one man may seem the rankest error to his neighbor. To persuade others to his own point of view, the pleader, as we know, at times resorts to exaggeration, to vilification of men who have been, or are, prominent in church or state, and even to false statement. But the people of this nation have ordained in the light of history, that, in spite of the probability of excesses and abuses, these liberties are, in the long view, essential to enlightened opinion and right conduct on the part of the citizens of a democracy."

That erroneous statement is inevitable in free debate, and that it must be protected if the freedoms of expression are to have the "breathing space" that they "need . . . to survive," *N.A.A.C.P. v. Button,* . . . was also recognized by the Court of Appeals for the District of Columbia Circuit in *Sweeney v. Patterson,* 128 F.2d 457, 458 (1942). Judge Edgerton spoke for a unanimous Court which affirmed the dismissal of a Congressman's libel suit based upon a newspaper article charging him with anti-Semitism in opposing a judicial appointment. He said:

"Cases which impose liability for erroneous reports of the political conduct of officials reflect the obsolete doctrine that the governed must not criticize their governors. . . . The interest of public here outweighs the interest of appellant or any other individual. The protection of the public requires not merely discussion, but information. Political conduct and views which some respectable people approve, and others condemn, are constantly imputed to

Congressmen. Errors of fact, particularly in regard to a man's mental states and processes, are inevitable. . . . Whatever is added to the field of libel is taken from the field of free debate."

. . . . . . . . . . . . . . . . . . .

Criticism of their official conduct does not lose its constitutional protection merely because it is effective criticism and hence diminishes their official reputations.

If neither factual error nor defamatory content suffices to remove the constitutional shield from criticism of official conduct, the combination of the two elements is no less inadequate. This is the lesson to be drawn from the great controversy over the Sedition Act of 1798, . . . which first crystallized a national awareness of the central meaning of the First Amendment. See Levy, *Legacy of Suppression* (1960), at 258 *et seq.,* Smith, *Freedom's Fetters* (1956), at 426, 431, and *passim.* That statute made it a crime punishable by a $5,000 fine and five years in prison, "if any person shall write, print, utter, or publish . . . any false, scandalous and malicious writing or writings against the Government of the United States, or either House of the Congress . . . , or the President, . . . with the intent to defame . . . or to bring them or either of them, into contempt or disrepute; or to excite against them, or either or any of them, the hatred of the good people of the United States."

The act allowed the defendant the defense of truth, and provided that the jury were to be judges both of the law and the facts. Despite these qualifications, the act was vigorously condemned as unconstitutional in an attack joined in by Jefferson and Madison. In the famous Virginia resolutions of 1798, the General Assembly of Virginia resolved that it "doth particularly protest against the palpable and alarming infractions of the Constitution, in the two late cases of the 'Alien and Sedition Acts' passed at the last session of Congress. . . . [the Sedition Act] exercises . . . a power not delegated by the Constitution, but, on the contrary, expressly and positively forbidden by one of the Amendments thereto—a power which more than any other ought to produce universal alarm, because it is leveled against the right of freely examining public characters and measures, and of free communication among the people thereon, which has ever been justly deemed the only effectual guardian of every other right." . . .

Madison prepared the report in support of the protest. His premise was that the Constitution created a form of government under which "the people, not the Government, possess the absolute sovereignty." The structure of the Government dispersed power in reflection of the people's distrust of concentrated power, and of power itself at all levels. This form of government was "altogether different" from the British form, under which the Crown was sovereign and the people were subjects. "Is it not natural and necessary, under such different circumstances," he asked, "that a different degree of freedom in the use of the press should be contemplated?" . . . Earlier, in a debate in the House of Representatives, Madison had said: "If we advert to the nature of republican government, we shall find that the censorial power is in the people over the government, and not in the government over the people." . . . Of the exercise of that power by the press, his report said:

"In every state, probably, in the Union, the press has exerted a freedom of canvassing the merits and measures of public men, of every description, which has not been confined to the strict limits of the common law. On this footing the freedom of the press has stood; on this foundation it yet stands. . . . " . . . The right of free public discussion of the stewardship of public officials was thus, in Madison's view, a fundamental principle of the American form of government.

Although the Sedition Act was never tested in this Court, the attack upon its validity has carried the day in the court of history. Fines levied in its prosecution were repaid by Act of Congress on the ground that it was unconstitutional. . . . Calhoun, reporting to the Senate on Feb. 4, 1836, assumed that its invalidity was a matter "which no one now doubts." . . . Jefferson, as President, pardoned those who had been convicted and sentenced under the act and remitted their fines, stating:

"I discharged every person under punishment or prosecution under the Sedition Law because I considered, and now consider, that law to be a nullity as absolute and palpable as if Congress had ordered us to fall down and worship a golden image." Letter to Mrs. Adams, July 22, 1804. . . . The invalidity of the act has also been assumed by Justices of this Court. Holmes, J., dissenting and joined by Brandeis, J., in *Abrams v. United States,* . . . ; Jackson, J., dissenting in *Beauharnais v. Illinois,* . . . ; Douglas, *The Right of the People* (1958). . . . These views reflect a broad consensus that the act, because of the restraint it imposed upon criticism of government and public officials, was inconsistent with the First Amendment.

. . . . . . . . . . . . . . .

The constitutional guarantees require, we think, a Federal rule that prohibits a public official from recovering damages for a defamatory falsehood relating to his official conduct unless he proves that the statement was made with "actual malice"—that is, with knowledge that it was false or with reckless disregard of whether it was false or not. An oft-cited statement of a like rule, which has been adopted by a number of state courts, is found in the Kansas case of *Coleman v. MacLennan,* 78 Kan. 711, 98 p. 281 (1908). The State Attorney General, a candidate for re-election and a member of the commission charged with the management and control of the state school fund, sued a newspaper publisher for alleged libel in an article purporting to state facts relating to his official conduct in connection with a school-fund transaction. The defendant pleaded privilege and the trial judge, over the plaintiff's objection, instructed the jury that "where an article is published and circulated among voters for the sole purpose of giving what the defendant believes to be truthful information concerning a candidate for public office and for the purpose of enabling such voters to cast their ballot more intelligently, and the whole thing is done in good faith and without malice, the article is privileged, although the principal matters contained in the article may be untrue in fact and derogatory to the character of the plaintiff; and in such a case the burden is on the plaintiff to show actual malice in the publication of the article."

In answer to a special question, the jury found that the plaintiff had not proved actual malice, and a general verdict was returned for the defendant. On appeal the Supreme Court of Kansas, in an opinion by Justice Burch, reasoned as follows:

"It is of the utmost consequence that the people should discuss the character and qualifications of candidates for their suffrages. The importance to the state and to society of such discussions is so vast, and the advantages derived are so great, that they more than counter-balance the inconvenience of private persons whose conduct may be involved, and occasional injury to the reputations of individuals must yield to the public welfare, although at times such injury may be great. The public benefit from publicity is so great, and the chance of injury to private character so small, that such discussion must be privileged."

The Court thus sustained the trial court's instruction as a correct statement of the law, saying:

"In such a case the occasion gives rise to a privilege, qualified to this extent: Anyone claiming to be defamed by the communication must show actual malice or go remediless. This privilege extends to a great variety of subjects, and includes matters of public concern, public men, and candidates for office." 78 Kan., at 723.

Such a privilege for criticism of official conduct is appropriately analogous to the protection accorded a public official when he is sued for libel by a private citizen. In *Barr v. Matteo*, . . . this Court held the utterance of a Federal official to be absolutely privileged if made "within the outer perimeter" of his duties. The states accord the same immunity to statements of their highest officers, although some differentiate their lesser officials and qualify the privilege they enjoy. But all hold that all officials are protected unless actual malice can be proved. The reason for the official privilege is said to be that the threat of damage suits would otherwise "inhibit the fearless, vigorous and effective administration of policies of government" and "dampen the ardor of all but the most resolute, or the most irresponsible, in the unflinching discharge of their duties."

. . . Analogous considerations support the privilege for the citizen-critic of government. It is as much his duty to criticize as it is the official's duty to administer. . . . As Madison said, . . . "The censorial power is in the people over the government, and not in the government over the people." It would give public servants an unjustified preference over the public they serve, if critics of official conduct did not have a fair equivalent of the immunity granted to the officials themselves.

We conclude that such a privilege is required by the First and 14th Amendments.

We hold today that the Constitution delimits a state's power to award damages for libel in actions brought by public officials against critics of their official conduct.

Justice Goldberg would have gone beyond the Court opinion. He urged absolute privilege for comment on official conduct even when malicious. He pointed out that the Constitution, however, did not protect "defamatory statements directed against the private conduct of a public official or private citizens."

Mr. Justice GOLDBERG, with whom Mr. Justice DOUGLAS joined, concurring:

The Court today announces a constitutional standard which prohibits "a public official from recovering damages for a defamatory falsehood relating to his official conduct unless he proves that the statement was made with 'actual malice'—that is with knowledge that it was false or with reckless disregard of whether it was false or not." The Court thus rules that the Constitution gives citizens and newspapers a "conditional privilege" immunizing nonmalicious misstatements of fact regarding the official conduct of a government officer. The impressive array of history and precedent marshaled by the Court, however, confirms my belief that the Constitution affords greater protection than that provided by the Court's standard to citizen and press in exercising the right of public criticism.

In my view, the First and Fourteenth Amendments to the Constitution afford to the citizen and to the press an absolute, unconditional privilege to criticize official conduct despite the harm which may flow from excesses and abuses. The prized American right "to speak one's mind," cf. *Bridges v. California*, 314 U.S. 252, 270, about public officials and affairs needs "breathing space" to survive, *N.A.A.C.P. v. Button*, . . . The right should not depend upon a probing by the jury of the motivation of the citizen or press. The theory of our Constitution is that every citizen may speak his mind and every newspaper express its view on matters of public concern and may not be barred from speaking or publishing because those in control of government think that what is said or written is unwise, unfair, false, or malicious. In a democratic society, one who assumed to act for the citizens in an executive, legislative, or judicial capacity must expect that his official acts will be commented upon and criticized. Such criticism cannot, in my opinion, be muzzled or deterred by the courts at the instance of public officials under the label of libel.

.   .   .   .   .   .   .   .   .   .   .   .   .   .   .   .   .   .   .   .

If individual citizens may be held liable in damages for strong words, which a jury finds false and maliciously motivated, there can be little doubt that public debate and advocacy will be constrained. And if newspapers publishing advertisements dealing with public issues, thereby risk liability, there can also be little doubt that the ability of minority groups to secure publication of their views on public affairs and to seek support for their causes will be greatly diminished. . . . The opinion of the Court conclusively demonstrates the chilling effect of the Alabama libel laws on First Amendment freedoms in the area of race relations. The American Colonists were not willing, nor should we be, to take that risk that "[m]en who injure and oppress the people under their administration [and] provoke them to cry out and complain" will also be empowered to "make that very complaint the foundation for new oppressions and prosecutions." *The Trial of John Peter Zenger,* 17 Howell's St. Tr.

.   .   .   .   .   .   .   .   .   .   .   .   .   .   .   .   .   .   .   .

This is not to say that the Constitution protects defamatory statements directed against the private conduct of a public official or private citizen. Freedom of press and of speech insure that government will respond to the will of the people and that changes may be obtained by peaceful means. Purely private defamation has little to do with the political ends of a self-governing society. The imposition of liability for private defamation does not abridge the freedom of public speech. This, of course, cannot be said "where public officials are concerned or where public matters are involved. . . . [O]ne main function of the First Amendment is to ensure ample opportunity for the people to determine and resolve public issues . . ." Douglas, *The Right of the People* (1958), p. 41.

.   .   .   .   .   .   .   .   .   .   .   .   .   .   .   .   .   .   .   .

If the government official should be immune from libel actions so that his ardor to serve the public will not be dampened and "fearless, vigorous, and effective administration of policies of government" not be inhibited, *Barr v. Matteo* . . . then the citizen and the press should likewise be immune from libel actions for their criticism of official conduct. Their ardor as citizens will thus not be dampened and they will be free "to applaud or to criticize the way public employes do their jobs, from the least to the most important." If liability can attach to political criticism because it damages the reputation of a public official as a public official, then no critical citizen can safely utter anything but faint praise about the government or its officials. The vigorous criticism by press and citizen of the conduct of the government of the day by the officials of the day will soon yield to silence if officials in control of government agencies, instead of answering criticisms, can resort to friendly juries to forestall criticism of their official conduct.

. . . . . . . . . . . . . . . . . .

For these reasons, I strongly believe that the Constitution accords citizens and press an unconditional freedom to criticize official conduct. It necessarily follows that in a case such as this, where all agree that the allegedly defamatory statements related to official conduct, the judgments for libel cannot constitutionally be sustained.

Justice Black had been the first to relate ordinary libel actions to the First Amendment. Several years earlier, he surprised even his friends when he took the position that all libel suits were absolutely forbidden by the First Amendment. In this case, he restated that view.

Mr. Justice BLACK, with whom Mr. Justice DOUGLAS joined, concurring:

I concur in reversing this half-million-dollar judgment against *The New York Times* and the four individual defendants. In reversing the Court holds that "the First and Fourteenth Amendments delimit a state's power to award damages for libel in an action brought by a public official against critics of his official conduct." . . . I base my vote to reverse on the belief that the First and Fourteenth Amendments not merely "delimit" a state's power to award damages to "a public official against critics of his official conduct" but completely prohibit a state from exercising such a power. The Court goes on to hold that a state can subject such critics to damages if "actual malice" can be proved against them. "Malice," even as defined by the Court, is an elusive, abstract concept, hard to prove and hard to disprove. The requirement that malice be proved provides at best an evanescent protection for the right critically to discuss public affairs and certainly does not measure up to the sturdy safeguard embodied in the First Amendment. Unlike the Court, therefore, I vote to reverse exclusively on the ground that *The Times* and the individual defendants had an absolute, unconditional constitutional right to publish in *The Times* advertisement their criticisms of the Montgomery agencies and officials. . . .

The half-million-dollar verdict does give dramatic proof, however, that state libel laws threaten the very existence of an American press virile enough to publish unpopular views on public affairs and bold enough to criticize the conduct of public officials. The factual background of this case emphasizes the imminence and enormity of that threat.

. . . . . . . . . . . . . . . . . . . .

We would, I think, more faithfully interpret the First Amendment by holding that at the very least it leaves the people and the press free to criticize officials and discuss public affairs with impunity. This nation of ours elects many of its important officials; so do the states, the municipalities, the counties, and even many precincts. These officials are responsible to the people for the way they perform their duties. While our Court has held that some kinds of speech and writings, such as "obscenity," *Roth v. United States,* . . . and "fighting words," *Chaplinsky v. New Hampshire,* . . . are not expressions within the protection of the First Amendment, freedom to discuss public affairs and public officials is unquestionably, as the Court today holds, the kind of speech the First Amendment was primarily designed to keep within the area of free discussion. To punish the exercise of this right to discuss public affairs or to penalize it through libel judgments is to abridge or shut off discussion of the very kind most needed. This nation, I suspect, can live in peace without libel suits based on public discussions of public affairs and public officials. But I doubt that a country can live in freedom where its people can be made to suffer physically or financially for criticizing their government, its actions, or its officials. "For a representative democracy ceases to exist the moment that the public functionaries are by any means absolved from their responsibility to their constituents; and this happens whenever the constituent can be restrained in any manner from speaking, writing, or publishing his opinions upon any public measure, or upon the conduct of those who may advise or execute." An unconditional right to say what one pleases about public affairs is what I consider to be the minimum guarantee of the First Amendment.

I regret that the Court has stopped short of this holding indispensable to preserve our free press from destruction.

### *TIMES'* RULE APPLIED TO CRIMINAL LIBEL

*Times v. Sullivan* clearly set the limits of civil libel suits when in conflict with First Amendment interests. Yet there remained the question whether the *New York Times* rule also limited state power to impose criminal sanctions for criticism of the official conduct of public servants. In a later 1964 decision, *Garrison v. Louisiana,* the Supreme Court ruled that it does.

In this important case, both Justices Black and Douglas used the term "seditious libel" for prosecutions brought by public officials against their critics. Historically, seditious libel meant criticism of government, laws, or officials; criminal libel, in early English law, referred to defamation of any individual.

The two concepts tended to merge when there was criticism of a public official. In such a situation, was it an assault on the government or defamation of an individual? *Criminal libel*—less menacing and odious than *seditious* libel—could be the rubric under which the government could punish its critics without fear of the charge of "tyranny." The fight for freedom of the press from the seventeenth to the nineteenth centuries was essentially a struggle to limit the application of the criminal law of seditious libel. One measure of the success of that struggle, in both England and America, is the fact that criminal libel actions, particularly against orthodox news media, have become exceedingly rare.

The American Civil Liberties Union has opposed all criminal prosecutions for libel. In a 1965 statement, the ACLU national board said: "We believe that the award of damages in a civil action provides an adequate remedy for the libelled individual and that the public interest in preventing defamation is not sufficient to justify the effect which criminal libel may have on free expression."

Criminal libel in the form of sedition has disappeared entirely as a Common Law offense and sedition itself is usually legally limited to periods of war or national emergency. However, the state still reserves the right to criminally prosecute those libels considered threats to public peace and welfare. In the vast majority of cases in which private parties seek damages for injury to their reputations, redress is sought through civil action for damages rather than through a criminal complaint filed with the state's attorney. *Garrison v. Louisiana* was an exception and ended with wider application of the *New York Times* rule.

GARRISON V. LOUISIANA, 379 U.S. 64 (1964)

*The Supreme Court held that the Louisiana criminal libel statute incorporated unconstitutional standards in judging criticism of official conduct of public officials. First, the statute directed punishment for true statements made with actual malice. Second, it called for the punishment of false statements made with ill will without considering if they were made with knowledge of their falsity, or in reckless disregard of whether they were true or false, or made in reasonable belief of their truth. Justice Brennan's opinion summarized the facts and stressed the* Times *definition of actual malice.*

Mr. Justice BRENNAN delivered the opinion of the Court:

Appellant is the District Attorney of Orleans Parish, Louisiana. During a dispute with the eight judges of the Criminal District Court of the Parish, he held a press conference at which he issued a statement disparaging their judicial conduct. As a result, he was tried without a jury before a judge from another Parish and convicted of criminal defamation under the Louisiana Criminal Defamation Statute. The principal charges alleged to be defamatory were his attribution of a large backlog of pending criminal cases to the inefficiency, laziness, and excessive vacations of the judges, and his accusation that, by refusing to authorize disbursements to cover the expenses of undercover investigations of vice in New Orleans, the judges had hampered his efforts to enforce the vice laws. In impugning their motives, he said:

"The judges have now made it eloquently clear where their sympathies lie in regard to aggressive vice investigations by refusing to authorize use of the DA's funds to pay for the cost of closing down the Canal Street clip joints. . . . This raises interesting questions about the racketeer influences on our eight vacation-minded judges."

The Supreme Court of Louisiana affirmed the conviction. The trial court and the State Supreme Court both rejected appellant's contention that the statute unconstitutionally abridged his freedom of expression. . . .

We reverse. . . .

At the outset, we must decide whether in view of the differing history and purposes of criminal libel, the *New York Times* rule also limits state power to impose criminal sanctions for criticism of the official conduct of public officials. We hold that it does.

Where criticism of public officials is concerned, we see no merit in the argument that criminal libel statutes serve interests distinct from those secured by civil libel laws, and therefore should not be subject to the same limitations. At common law, truth was no defense to criminal libel. Although the victim of a true but defamatory publication might not have been unjustly damaged in reputation by the libel, the speaker was still punishable since the remedy was designed to avert the possibility that the utterance would provoke an enraged victim to a breach of peace.

. . . . . . . . . . . . . . . . . . .

We next consider whether the historial limitation of the defense of truth in criminal libel to utterances published "with good motives and for justifiable ends" should be incorporated into the *Times* rule as it applies to criminal libel statutes; in particular, we must ask whether this history permits negating the truth defense, as the Louisiana statute does, on a showing of malice in the sense of ill-will. The "good motives" restriction incorporated in many state constitutions and statutes to reflect Alexander Hamilton's unsuccessfully urged formula in *People v. Croswell,* . . . liberalized the common-law rule denying any defense for truth. . . . We need not be concerned whether this limitation serves a legitimate state interest to the extent that it reflects abhorrence that "a man's forgotten misconduct, or the misconduct of a relation, *in which the public had no interest,* should be wantonly raked up, and published to the world, on the ground of its being true." 69 Hansard, *Parl. Hist. Engl.* 1230 (3rd series). In any event, where the criticism is of public officials and their conduct of public business, the interest in private reputation is overborne by the larger public interest, secured by the Constitution, in the dissemination of truth. . . .

Moreover, even where the utterance is false, the great principles of the Constitution which secure freedom of expression in this area preclude attaching adverse consequences to any except the knowing or reckless falsehood. Debate on public issues will not be uninhibited if the speaker must run the risk that it will be proved in court that he spoke out of hatred; even if he did speak out of hatred, utterances honestly believed contribute to the free interchange of ideas and the ascertainment of truth. Under a rule like the Louisiana rule, permitting a finding of malice based on an intent merely to inflict harm through falsehood, "it becomes a hazardous matter to speak out against a popular politician, with the result that the dishonest and incompetent will be shielded." Noel, *Defamation of Public Officers and Candidates,* 49 *Col. L. Rev.* 875, 893 (1949). . . .

We held in *New York Times* that a public official might be allowed the civil remedy only if he establishes that the utterance was false and that it was made with knowledge of its falsity or in reckless disregard of whether it was false or true. The reasons which led us to hold in *New York Times* that the unqualified defense of truth was insufficient apply with no less force merely because the remedy is criminal. The constitutional guarantees of freedom of expression compel application of the same standard to the criminal remedy. Truth may not be the subject of either civil or criminal sanctions where discussion of public affairs is concerned . . . .

The use of calculated falsehood, however, would put a different cast on the constitutional question. Although honest utterance, even if inaccurate, may further the fruitful exercise of the right of free speech, it does not follow that the lie, knowingly and deliberately published about a public official, should enjoy a like immunity. At the time the First Amendment was adopted, as today, there were those unscrupulous enough and skillful enough to use the deliberate or reckless falsehood as an effective political tool to unseat the public servant or even topple an administration. That speech is used as a tool for political ends does not automatically bring it under the protective mantle of the Constitution. For the use of the known lie as a tool is at once at odds with the premises of democratic government and with the orderly manner in which economic, social, or political change is to be effected. Calculated falsehood falls into that class of utterances which "are no essential part of any exposition of ideas, and are of such slight social value as a step to truth that any benefit that may be derived from them is clearly outweighed by the social interest in order and morality. . . ." *Chaplinsky v. New Hampshire*, 315 U.S., 568. Hence the knowingly false statement and the false statement made with reckless disregard of the truth, do not enjoy constitutional protection.

. . . . . . . . . . . . . . . . . . . . . .

Applying the principles of the *New York Times* case, we hold that the Louisiana statute, as authoritatively interpreted by the Supreme Court of Louisiana, incorporates constitutionally invalid standards in the context of criticism of the official conduct of public officials. For, contrary to the *New York Times* rule, which absolutely prohibits punishment of truthful criticism, the statute directs punishment for true statements made with "actual malice." And "actual malice" is defined in the decisions below to mean "hatred, ill will or enmity or a wanton desire to injure. . . ." 244 La. at 851. The statute is also unconstitutional as interpreted to cover false statements against public officials. The *New York Times* standard forbids the punishment of false statements, unless made with knowledge of their falsity or in reckless disregard of whether they are true or false. But the Louisiana statute punishes false statements without regard to that test if made with ill-will; even if ill-will is not established, a false statement concerning public officials can be punished if not made in the reasonable belief of its truth. . . .

Justices Douglas and Black agreed that the prosecution for "seditious libel," as they called it, was unconstitutional. But they were unhappy that "we now hold that proof of actual malice is relevant to seditious libel—that seditious libel will lie for a knowingly false statement or one made with reckless disregard of the truth." Seditious libel, they said, has no standing under our Constitution.

Mr. Justice DOUGLAS, with whom Mr. Justice BLACK joined, concurring:

I am in hearty agreement with the conclusion of the Court that this prosecution for a seditious libel was unconstitutional. Yet I feel that the gloss which the Court has put on "the freedom of speech" in the First Amendment to reach that result (and like results in other cases) makes that basic guarantee almost unrecognizable.

Recently in *New York Times Co. v. Sullivan*, a majority of the Court held that criticism of an official for official conduct was protected from state civil libel laws by the First and Fourteenth Amendments, unless there was proof of actual malice. We now hold that proof of actual malice is relevant to seditious libel—that seditious libel will lie for a knowingly false statement or one made with reckless disregard of the truth.

If malice is all that is needed, inferences from facts as found by the jury will easily oblige. How can we sit in review on a cold record and find no evidence of malice when it is the commonplace of life that heat and passion subtly turn to malice in actual fact? If "reckless disregard of the truth" is the basis of seditious libel, that nebulous standard could be easily met. The presence of "actual malice" is made critical in seditious libel, as well as in civil actions involving charges against public officials, when in truth there is nothing in the Constitution about it, any more than there is about "clear and present danger."

While the First Amendment remains the same, the gloss which the Court has written on it in this field of the discussion of public issues robs it of much vitality.

Why does "the freedom of speech" that the Court is willing to protect turn out to be so pale and tame?

It is because, as my Brother Black has said, the Bill of Rights is constantly watered-down through judicial "balancing" of what the Constitution says and what judges think is needed for a well-ordered society.

As Irving Brant recently said: "The balancing test developed in recent years by our Supreme Court does not *disarm* the Government of power *to trench* upon the field in which the Constitution says "Congress shall make no law." The balancing test does exactly what is done by its spiritual parent, the British "common law of seditious libel," under which (to repeat the words of May), "Every one was a libeler who outraged the sentiments of the dominant party." "Seditious Libel: Myth and Reality." 39 *N.Y.U.L. Rev.* 1, 18–19 (1964).

*Beauharnais v. Illinois,* a case decided by the narrowest of margins, should be overruled as a misfit in our constitutional system and as out of line with the dictates of the First Amendment. I think it is time to face the fact that the only line drawn by the Constitution is between "speech" on the one side and conduct or overt acts on the other. The two often do blend. I have expressed the idea before: "Freedom of expression can be suppressed if, and to the extent that, it is so closely brigaded with illegal action as to be an inseparable part of it." *Roth v. United States.* Unless speech is so brigaded with overt acts of that kind there is nothing that may be punished; and no semblance of such a case is made out here.

I think little need be added to what Mr. Justice Holmes said nearly a half century ago:

"I wholly disagree with the argument of the Government that the First Amendment left the common law as to seditious libel in force. History seems to me against the notion. I have conceived that the United States through many years had shown its repentance for the Sedition Act of 1798 . . . by repaying fines that it imposed." *Abrams v. United States,* 250 U.S. 616, 630 (dissenting opinion).

The philosophy of the Sedition Act of 1798 which punished "false, scandalous and malicious" writings (1 Stat. 596) is today allowed to be applied by the States. Yet Irving Brant has shown that seditious libel was "entirely the creation of the Star Chamber." It is disquieting to know that one of its instruments of destruction is abroad in the land today.

Mr. Justice BLACK, with whom Mr. Justice DOUGLAS joined, concurring:

I concur in reversing the conviction of appellant Garrison, based as it is purely on his public discussion and criticism of public officials. I believe that the First Amendment, made applicable to the States by the Fourteenth, protects every person from having a state or the federal government fine, imprison, or assess damages against him when he has been guilty of no conduct other than expressing an opinion, even though others may believe that his views are unwholesome, unpatriotic, stupid or dangerous. I believe that the Court is mistaken if it thinks that requiring proof that statements were "malicious" or "defamatory" will really create any substantial hurdle to block public officials from punishing those who criticize the way they conduct their office. Indeed, "malicious," "seditious," and other such evil-sounding words often have been invoked to punish people for expressing their views on public affairs. Fining men or sending them to jail for criticizing public officials not only jeopardizes the free, open public discussion which our Constitution guarantees, but can wholly stifle it. I would hold now and not wait to hold later that under our Constitution there is absolutely no place in this country for the old, discredited English Star Chamber law of seditious criminal libel.

The Supreme Court, in the *Garrison* decision, indicated that criminal libel has no social utility at all in prosecutions for criticism of public officials. But both *Garrison* and *New York Times* raised some questions that were not settled until two other well-known libel cases came up to the Supreme Court.

### *TIMES'* RULE EXTENDED TO PUBLIC FIGURES

On June 12, 1967, the Supreme Court handed down a ruling which extended the constitutional protection of freedom of the press to libelous falsehoods about private individuals who willingly take part in public affairs. The Court thus expanded the reach of the 1964 *New York Times v. Sullivan* ruling to embrace public figures as well as public officials.

The two widely publicized libel cases were decided in one opinion. In the case of *Associated Press v. Edwin A. Walker,* the Court overturned by a 9-to-0 vote a $500,000 judgment awarded General Walker by Texas courts. In the case of *Curtis Publishing Co. v. Wallace Butts,* the Court upheld, 5 to 4, a $460,000 award granted to Butts, former athletic director of the University of Georgia.

Chief Justice Earl Warren, who cast the deciding vote in the *Butts* case, explained why the Court felt that public figures who hold no public office should be subject to derogatory criticism, even when based on false statements:

"Our citizenry has a legitimate and substantial interest in the conduct of such persons. . . . Freedom of the press to engage in uninhibited debate over their involvement in public issues and events is as crucial as it is in public officials."

A Texas court had awarded Walker the judgment because of Associated Press reports that he "assumed command" of rioters at the University of Mississippi on September 30, 1962 and that he "led a charge of students against Federal marshals" protesting the admission of James Meredith, a Negro, to the university. The Texas case was one of fifteen suits arising out of the AP dispatch. Walker, who had been active in right wing causes, had asked a total of $33,250,000.

In the *Butts* case, based on an article in the *Saturday Evening Post* charging that the Georgia athletic director had conspired with University of Alabama football Coach Paul Bryant to "fix" a game between the two universities, the Supreme Court sustained the trial court's finding that "what the *Post* did was done with reckless disregard of whether the article was false or not." Justice John Harlan wrote, "the evidence showed that the Butts story was in no sense 'hot news' and the editors of the magazine recognized the need for a thorough investigation of the serious charges. Elementary precautions were, nevertheless, ignored."

Since the *Times v. Sullivan* decision, the lower courts had been trying to determine whether the same immunity from libel damages should extend to statements about prominent persons who, although not holding public office, do participate in discussions about public affairs. The courts have also been trying to define what evidence is necessary to show when libelous remarks stem from outright lies and thus enable plaintiffs to prove malice and collect damages, according to the *Times* rule.

This important 1967 decision clarified to some extent the law on both questions. All nine justices agreed that the constitutional safeguards against libel suits extended beyond public officials to public figures—to those like General Walker, who thrust themselves in public disputes, and those like Butts, who have a status in life that commands wide attention.

From this point, however, the Court divided sharply. In three opinions, five of the Justices—Warren, Brennan, Byron White, Black, and Douglas—held that the same standard as the *Times* case should apply. Hence, the *Times* rule applies to public figures.

But in an opinion written by Justice Harlan and concurred in by Justices Tom Clark, Potter Stewart, and Abe Fortas, a different standard for public figures was proposed. Their opinion would allow damages "on a showing of highly unreasonable conduct constituting an extreme departure from the standards of investigation and reporting ordinarily adhered to by responsible publishers." Such a standard would make it much easier for plaintiffs to collect damages.

CURTIS PUBLISHING CO. V. BUTTS; ASSOCIATED PRESS V. WALKER, 388 U.S. 130 (1967)

Mr. Justice HARLAN announced the judgments of the Court and delivered an opinion in which Mr. Justice CLARK, Mr. Justice STEWART, and Mr. Justice FORTAS joined:

In *New York Times Co. v. Sullivan,* this Court held that "the constitutional guarantees (of freedom of speech and press) require a federal rule that prohibits a public official from recovering damages for a defamatory falsehood relating to his official conduct unless he proves that the statement was made with 'actual malice'— that is, with knowledge that it was false or with reckless disregard of whether it was false or not." We brought these two cases here to consider the impact of that decision on libel actions instituted by persons who are not public officials, but who are "public figures" and involved in issues in which the public has a justified and important interest. . . .

The matter has been passed on by a considerable number of state and lower federal courts and has produced a sharp division of opinion as to whether the *New York Times* rule should apply only in actions brought by public officials or whether it has a longer reach. The resolution of the uncertainty in this area of libel actions requires, at bottom, some further exploration and clarification of the relationship between libel law and the freedom of the press, lest the "New York Times Rule" become a talisman which gives the press constitutionally adequate protection only in a limited field, or, what would be equally unfortunate, one which goes far to immunize the press from having to make just reparation for the infliction of needless injury upon honor and reputation through false publication. These two libel actions, although they rise out of quite different sets of circumstances, provide that opportunity. We think they are best treated together in one opinion.

No. 37, *Curtis Publishing Co. v. Butts,* stems from an article in petitioner's *Saturday Evening Post* which accused respondent of conspiring to "fix" a football game between the University of Georgia and the University of Alabama in 1962. At the time of the article, Butts was athletic director of the University of Georgia and had overall responsibility for the administration of its athletic program. Georgia is a state university, but Butts was employed by the Georgia Athletic Association, a private corporation, rather than by the State itself. Butts had previously served as head football coach of the University and was a well-known and respected figure in coaching ranks. He had maintained an interest in coaching and was negotiating for a position with a professional team at the time of publication.

The article was entitled "The Story of a College Football Fix" and prefaced by a note from the editors stating: "Not since the Chicago White Sox threw the 1919 World Series has there been a sports story as shocking as this. . . . Before the University of Georgia played the University of Alabama . . . Wally Butts . . . gave (to its coach) . . . Georgia's plays, defensive patterns, all the significant secrets Georgia's football team possessed." The text revealed that one George Burnett, an Atlanta insurance salesman, had accidentally overheard, because of electronic error, a telephone conversation between Butts and the head coach of the University of Alabama, Paul Bryant, which took place approximately one week prior to the game. Burnett was said to have listened while "Butts outlined Georgia's offensive plays . . . and told . . . how Georgia planned to defend. . . . Butts mentioned both players and plays by name." The readers were told that Burnett had made notes of the conversation and specific examples of the divulged secrets were set out.

The article went on to discuss the game and players' reaction to the game, concluding that "the Georgia players, their moves analyzed and forecast like those of rats in a maze, took a frightful physical beating," and said that the players, and other sideline observers, were aware that Alabama was privy to Georgia's secrets. It set out the series of events commencing with Burnett's later presentation of his notes to the Georgia head coach, Johnny Griffith, and culminating in Butts' resignation from the University's athletic affairs, for health and business reasons. The article's conclusion made clear its expected impact: "The chances are that Wally Butts will never help any football team again. . . . The investigation by university and Southeastern Conference officials is continuing; motion pictures of other games are being scrutinized; where it will end no one so far can say. But careers will be ruined, that is sure."

Butts brought this diversity libel action in the federal courts in Georgia seeking $5,000,000 compensatory and $5,000,000 punitive damages. . . . The jury returned a verdict for $60,000 in general damages and for $3,000,000 punitive damages. The trial court reduced the total to $460,000 by remittur. . . . For reasons given below, we would affirm.


No. 150, *Associated Press v. Walker,* arose out of the distribution of a news dispatch giving an eyewitness account of events on the campus of the University of Mississippi on the night of September 30, 1962, when a massive riot erupted because of federal efforts to enforce a court decree ordering the enrollment of a Negro, James Meredith, as a student in the University. The dispatch stated that respondent Walker, who was present on the campus, had taken command of the violent crowd and had personally led a charge against federal marshals sent there to effectuate the court's decree and to assist in preserving order. It also described Walker as encouraging rioters to use violence and giving them technical advice on combating the effects of tear gas.

Walker was a private citizen at the time of the riot and publication. He had pursued a long and honorable career in the United States Army before resigning to engage in political activity, and had, in fact, been in command of the federal troops during the school segregation confrontation at Little Rock, Arkansas, in 1957. He was acutely interested in the issue of physical federal intervention, and had made a number of strong statements against such action which received wide publicity. Walker had his own following, the "Friends of Walker," and could be fairly deemed a man of some political prominence.

Walker initiated this libel action in the state courts of Texas, seeking a total of $2,000,000 in compensatory and punitive damages. Associated Press raised both the defense of truth and constitutional defenses. At trial both sides attempted to reconstruct the stormy events on the campus of the University of Mississippi. Walker admitted his presence on the campus and conceded that he had spoken to a group of students. He claimed, however, that he had counseled restraint and peaceful protest, and exercised no control whatever over the crowd which had rejected his pleas. He denied categorically taking part in any charge against the federal marshals.

There was little evidence relating to the preparation of the news dispatch. It was clear, however, that the author of the dispatch, Van Savell, was actually present during the events described and had reported them almost immediately to the Associated Press office in Atlanta. A discrepancy was shown between an oral account given the office and a later written dispatch, but it related solely to whether Walker had spoken to the group before or after approaching the marshals. No other showing of improper preparation was attempted, nor was there any evidence of personal prejudice or incompetency on the part of Savell or the Associated Press. . . . A verdict of $500,000 compensatory damages . . . was returned. . . . For reasons given below, we would reverse.

. . . . . . . . . . . . . . . . . . . . .

The history of libel law leaves little doubt that it originated in soil entirely different from that which nurtured these constitutional values. Early libel was primarily a criminal remedy, the function of which was to make punishable any writing which tended to bring into disrepute the state, established religion, or any individual likely to be provoked to a breach of the peace because of the words. Truth was no defense in such actions and while a proof of truth might prevent recovery in a civil action, this limitation is more readily explained as a manifestation of judicial reluctance to enrich an undeserving plaintiff than by the supposition that the defendant was protected by the truth of the publication. The same truthful statement might be the basis of a criminal libel action.

The law of libel has, of course, changed substantially since the early days of the Republic, and this change is "the direct consequence of the friction between it . . . and the highly cherished right of free speech." The emphasis has shifted from criminal to civil remedies, from the protection of absolute social values to the safeguarding of valid personal interests. Truth has become an absolute defense in almost all cases, and privileges designed to foster free communication are almost universally recognized. But the basic theory of libel has not changed, and words defamatory of another, are still placed "in the same class with the use of explosives or the keeping of dangerous animals." Thus some antithesis between freedom of speech and press and libel actions persists, for libel remains premised on the content of speech and limits the freedom of the publisher to express certain sentiments, at least without guaranteeing legal proof of their substantial accuracy.

. . . . . . . . . . . . . . . . . .

In the cases we decide today none of the particular considerations involved in *New York Times* is present. These actions cannot be analogized to prosecutions for seditious libel. Neither plaintiff has any position in government which would permit a recovery by him to be viewed as a vindication of governmental policy. Neither was entitled to a special privilege protecting his utterances against accountability in libel. We are prompted, therefore, to seek guidance from the rules of liability which prevail in our society with respect to compensation of persons injured by the improper performance of a legitimate activity by another. Under these rules, a departure from the kind of care society may expect from a reasonable man performing such activity leaves the actor open to a judicial shifting of loss. In defining these rules, and especially in formulating the standards for determining the degree of care to be expected in the circumstances, courts have consistently given much attention to the importance of defendants' activities. The courts have also, especially in libel cases, investigated the plaintiff's position to determine whether he has a legitimate call upon the court for protection in light of his prior activities and means of self-defense. We note that the public interest in the circulation of the materials here involved, and the publisher's interest in circulating them, is not less than that involved in *New York Times*. And both Butts and Walker commanded a substantial amount of independent public interest at the time of the publications; both, in our opinion, would have been labeled "public figures" under ordinary tort rules. Butts may have attained that status by position alone and Walker by his purposeful activity amounting to a thrusting of his personality into the "vortex" of an important public controversy, but both commanded sufficient continuing public interest and had sufficient access to the means of counterargument to be able "to expose through discussion the falsehood and fallacies" of the defamatory statements.

These similarities and differences between libel actions involving persons who are public officials and libel actions involving those circumstanced as were Butts and Walker, viewed in light of the principles of liability which are of general applicability in our society, lead us to the conclusion that libel actions of the present kind cannot be left entirely to state libel laws, unlimited by any overriding constitutional safeguard, but that the rigorous federal requirements of *New York Times* are not the only appropriate accommodation of the conflicting interests at stake. We consider and would hold that a "public figure" who is not a public official may also recover damages for a defamatory falsehood whose substance makes substantial danger to reputation apparent, on a showing of highly unreasonable conduct constituting an extreme departure from the standards of investigation and reporting ordinarily adhered to by responsible publishers. Cf. Sulzberger, "Responsibility and Freedom," in Nelson, *Freedom of the Press from Hamilton to the Warren Court,* 409, 412. . . .

Having set forth the standard by which we believe the constitutionality of the damage awards in these cases must be judged, we turn now, as the Court did in *New York Times,* to the question of whether the evidence and findings below meet that standard. We find the standard satisfied in No. 37, *Butts,* and not satisfied by either the evidence or the findings in No. 150, *Walker.*

. . . . . . . . . . . . . . . . . .

The evidence showed that the Butts story was in no sense "hot news" and the editors of the magazine recognized the need for a thorough investigation of the serious charges. Elementary precautions were, nevertheless, ignored. The *Saturday Evening Post* knew that Burnett had been placed on probation in connection with bad check charges, but proceeded to publish the story on the basis of his affidavit without substantial independent support. Burnett's notes were not even viewed by any of the magazine's personnel prior to publication. John Carmichael, who was supposed to have been with Burnett when the phone call was overheard, was not interviewed. No attempt was made to find out whether Alabama had adjusted its plans after the alleged divulgence of information.

The *Post* writer assigned to the story was not a football expert and no attempt was made to check the story with someone knowledgeable in the sport. At trial such experts indicated that the information in the Burnett notes was either such that it would be evident to any opposing coach from game films regularly exchanged or valueless. Those assisting the *Post* writer in his investigation were already deeply involved in another libel action, based on a different article, brought against Curtis Publishing Co. by the Alabama coach and unlikely to be the source of a complete and objective investigation. The *Saturday Evening Post* was anxious to change its image by instituting a policy of "sophisticated muckraking" and the pressure to produce a successful exposé might have induced a stretching of standards. In short, the evidence is ample to support a finding of highly unreasonable conduct constituting an extreme departure from the standards of investigation and reporting ordinarily adhered to by responsible publishers.

The situation in *Walker* is considerably different. There the trial court found the evidence insufficient to support more than a finding of even ordinary negligence and the Court of Civil Appeals supported the trial court's view of the evidence. Ordinarily, we would, under the governing constitutional standard, reverse the decision below on the concurrent findings rule. But, as in *New York Times,* we think it better to face for ourselves the question whether there is sufficient evidence to support the finding we would require.

In contrast to the *Butts* article, the dispatch which concerns us in *Walker* was news which required immediate dissemination. The Associated Press received the information from a correspondent who was present at the scene of the events and gave every indication of being trustworthy and competent. His dispatches in this instance, with one minor exception, were internally consistent and would not have seemed unreasonable to one familiar with General Walker's prior publicized statements on the underlying controversy. Considering the necessity for rapid dissemination, nothing in this series of events gives the slightest hint of a severe departure from accepted publishing standards. We therefore conclude that General Walker should not be entitled to damages from the Associated Press.

The judgment of the Court of Appeals for the Fifth Circuit in No. 37 is affirmed. The judgment of the Texas Court of Civil Appeals in No. 150 is reversed and the case is remanded to that court for further proceedings not inconsistent with the opinions that have been filed herein by The Chief Justice, Mr. Justice Black, and Mr. Justice Brennan. It is so ordered.

Mr. Chief Justice WARREN, concurring in the result:

While I agree with the results announced by Mr. Justice Harlan in both of these cases, I find myself in disagreement with his stated reasons for reaching those results. Our difference stems from his departure from the teaching of *New York Times v. Sullivan* to which we both subscribed only three years ago.

I

In the *New York Times* case, we held that a State cannot, consistently with the First and Fourteenth Amendments, award damages to a "public official" for a defamatory falsehood relating to his official conduct unless the verdict is based on proof of "actual malice"—that is, proof that the defamatory statement was made "with knowledge that it was false or with reckless disregard of whether it was false or not." The present cases involve not "public officials" but "public figures" whose views and actions with respect to public issues and events are often of as much concern to the citizen as the attitudes and behavior of "public officials" with respect to the same issues and events.

All of us agree that the basic considerations underlying the First Amendment require that some limitations be placed on the application of state libel laws to "public figures" as well as "public officials." Similarly, the seven members of the Court who deem it necessary to pass upon the question agree that the respondents in these cases are "public figures" for First Amendment purposes. Having reached this point, Mr. Justice Harlan's opinion departs from the standard of *New York Times* and substitutes in cases involving "public figures" a standard that is based on "highly unreasonable conduct" and is phrased in terms of "extreme departure from the standards of investigation and reporting ordinarily adhered to by responsible publishers." I cannot believe that a standard which is based on such an unusual and uncertain formulation could either guide a jury of laymen or afford the protection for speech and debate that is fundamental to our society and guaranteed by the First Amendment.

To me, differentiation between "public figures" and "public officials" and adoption of separate standards of proof for each has no basis in law, logic, or First Amendment policy. Increasingly in this country, the distinctions between governmental and private sectors are blurred. Since the depression of the 1930's and World War II there has been a rapid fusion of economic and political power, a merging of science, industry, and government, and a high degree of interaction between the intellectual, governmental and business worlds. Depression, war, international tensions, national and international markets and the surging growth of science and technology have precipitated national and international problems that demand national and international solutions. While these trends and events have occasioned a consolidation of governmental power, power has also become much more organized in what we have commonly considered to be the private sector. In many situations, policy determinations which traditionally were channeled through formal political institutions are now originated and implemented through a complex array of boards, committees, commissions, corporations and associations, some only loosely connected with the Government. This blending of positions and power has also occurred in the case of individuals so that many who do not hold public office at the moment are nevertheless intimately involved in the resolution of important public questions or, by reason of their fame, shape events in areas of concern to society at large.

Viewed in this context then, it is plain, that although they are not subject to the restraints of the political process, "public figures," like "public officials," often play an influential role in ordering society. And surely as a class these "public figures" have as ready access as "public officials" to mass media of communication, both to influence policy and to counter criticism of their views and activities. Our citizenry has a legitimate and substantial interest in the conduct of such persons, and freedom of the press to engage in uninhibited debate about their involvement in public issues and events is as crucial as it is in the case of "public officials." The fact that they are not amenable to the restraints of the political process only underscores the legitimate and substantial nature of the interest, since it means that public opinion may be the only instrument by which society can attempt to influence their conduct.

I therefore adhere to the *New York Times* standard in the case of "public figures" as well as "public officials." It is a manageable standard, readily stated and understood, which also balances to a proper degree the legitimate interests traditionally protected by the law of defamation. Its definition of "actual malice" is not so restrictive that recovery is limited to situations where there is "knowing falsehood" on the part of the publisher of false and defamatory matter. "Reckless disregard" for the truth or falsity, measured by the conduct of the publisher, will also expose him to liability for publishing false material which is injurious to reputation. More significantly, however, the *New York Times* standard is an important safeguard for the rights of the press and public to inform and be informed on matters of legitimate interest. Evenly applied to cases involving "public men"—whether they be "public officials" or "public figures"—it will afford the necessary insulation for the fundamental interests which the First Amendment was designed to protect.

Mr. Justice BLACK with whom Mr. Justice DOUGLAS joined, concurring in No. 150 and dissenting in No. 37:

These cases illustrate, I think, the accuracy of my prior predictions that the *New York Times* constitutional rule concerning libel is wholly inadequate to save the press from being destroyed by libel judgments. Here the Court reverses the case of *Associated Press. v. Walker,* but affirms the judgment of *Curtis Publishing Co. v. Butts.* The main reason for this quite contradictory action, so far as I can determine, is that the Court looks at the facts in both cases as though it were a jury and reaches the conclusion that the *Saturday Evening Post,* in writing about Butts, was so abusive that its article is more of a libel at the constitutional level than is the one by the

Associated Press. That seems a strange way to erect a constitutional standard for libel cases. If this precedent is followed, it means that we must in all libel cases hereafter weigh the facts and hold that all papers and magazines guilty of gross writing or reporting are constitutionally liable, while they are not if the quality of the reporting is approved by a majority of us. In the final analysis, what we do in these circumstances is to review the factual questions in cases decided by juries—a review which is a flat violation of the Seventh Amendment.

It strikes me that the Court is getting itself in the same quagmire in the field of libel in which it is now helplessly struggling in the field of obscenity. No one, including this Court, can know what is and what is not constitutionally obscene or libelous under this Court's rulings. Today, the Court will not give the First Amendment its natural and obvious meaning by holding that a law which seriously menaces the very life of press freedom violates the First Amendment. In fact, the Court is suggesting various experimental expedients in libel cases, all of which boil down to a determination of how offensive to this Court a particular libel judgement may be, either because of its immense size or because the Court does not like the way an alleged libelee was treated. . . . I think it is time for this Court to abandon *New York Times v. Sullivan* and adopt the rule to the effect that the first Amendment was intended to leave the press free from the harassment of libel judgements.

The other two Justices, Brennan and White, concurred on overturning the *Walker* award but dissented in the *Butts* case. They felt the *Butts* case should be remanded for a new trial.

By clarifying the "public figure" issue in libel cases, the Court provided answers for some 26 lower court cases in which this was a central question. The combination of opinions—*Times, Garrison,* and *Curtis*—has greatly enlarged the protection the press enjoys when involved in suits for defamation. The press when reporting news of public interest and importance has much less to fear because of the threat of crippling libel judgments. Constitutional law has come much closer to an accommodation of what Justice Harlan called the "antithesis that persists between freedom of speech and press and libel actions."

However, there is one sort of criminal libel which the Supreme Court has upheld—group libel. This earlier decision still stands.

## GROUP LIBEL AS A LIMIT ON FREE EXPRESSION

Group libel laws are aimed at those who engage in false, abusive attacks on racial, religious, or other groups, thereby promoting unreasoning hatred toward such groups. Supporters of group libel laws claim that the ordinary law of libel will not reach defamers of a group except in the unusual case where the group is so small that each member is necessarily libelled by the defamatory statement.

Group libel is distinguished, then, by the special threat to society posed by hate-mongering and the absence of a civil remedy. Opponents of group libel laws, including the American Civil Liberties Union, think that neither of these factors is sufficient to justify group libel legislation. The ACLU national board has declared:

The type of statements sought to be proscribed by group libel laws, like defamatory statements about public officials, require protection because they frequently will pertain to social and political issues of public importance. While the statements involved may well be offensive and hateful, still it is better that they be openly expressed and, therefore, accessible to challenge and debate.

Group libel laws have been enacted in a few states and in recent years federal legislation has been proposed. In 1952, the Supreme Court ruled on a case under the Illinois group libel law and upheld it over vigorous dissent.

BEAUHARNAIS V. ILLINOIS, 343 U.S. 250 (1952)

*Joseph Beauharnais, a professional hate-monger, was found guilty and fined $200 for violating a 1949 Illinois group libel law by distributing anti-Negro leaflets on the streets of Chicago. The law stated:*

It shall be unlawful for any person, firm, or corporation to manufacture, sell, or offer for sale, advertise or publish, present or exhibit in any public place in this state any lithograph, moving picture, play, drama or sketch, which publication or exhibition portrays depravity, criminality, unchastity, or lack of virtue of a class of citizens, of any race, color, creed or religion which said publication or exhibition exposes the citizens of any race, color, creed or religion to contempt, derision, or obloquy or which is productive of breach of the peace or riots.

*Illinois courts upheld the conviction and, by a 5-to-4 decision, so did the Supreme Court. The dissents indicate the dangers that group libel laws present to freedom of the press.*

*In the ruling opinion Justice Felix Frankfurter found ample precedent for group libel laws. The possibility of abuse, he said, is a poor reason for denying Illinois the power—sanctioned by centuries of Anglo-American law—to punish criminal libels.*

Mr. Justice FRANKFURTER delivered the opinion of the Court:

. . . Libel of an individual was a common-law crime, and thus criminal in the colonies. Indeed, at common law, truth or good motives was no defense. In the first decades after the adoption of the Constitution, this was changed by judicial decision, statute or constitution in most States, but nowhere was there any suggestion that the crime of libel be abolished. Today, every American jurisdiction—the forty-eight States, the District of Columbia, Alaska, Hawaii and Puerto Rico—punish libels directed at individuals.

There are certain well-defined and narrowly limited classes of speech, the prevention and punishment of which have never been thought to raise any Constitutional problem. These include the lewd and obscene, the profane, the libelous, and the insulting or "fighting" words—those which by their very utterance inflict injury or tend to incite an immediate breach of the peace. It has been well observed that such utterances are no essential part of any exposition of ideas, and are of such slight social value as a step to truth that any benefit that may be derived from them is clearly outweighed by the social interest of order and morality.

. . . . . . . . . . . . . . . . . . .

Long ago this Court recognized that the economic rights of an individual may depend for the effectiveness of their enforcement on rights in the group, even though not formally corporate, to which he belongs. Such group-protection on behalf of the individual may, for all we know, be a need not confined to the part that a trade union plays in effectuating rights abstractly recognized as belonging to its members. It is not within our competence to confirm or deny claims of social scientists as to the dependence of the individual on the position of his racial or religious group in the community. It would, however, be arrogant dogmatism, quite outside the scope of our authority in passing on the powers of a State, for us to deny that the educational opportunities and the dignity accorded him may depend as much on the reputation of the racial and religious group to which he willy-nilly belongs, as on his own merits. This being so, we are precluded from saying that speech concededly punishable when immediately directed at individuals cannot be outlawed if directed at groups with whose position and esteem in society the affiliated individual may be inextricably involved.

We are warned that the choice open to the Illinois legislature here may be abused, that the law may be discriminatorily enforced; prohibiting libel of a creed or of a racial group, we are told, is but a step from prohibiting libel of a political party. Every power may be abused, but the possibility of abuse is a poor reason for denying Illinois the power to adopt measures against criminal libels sanctioned by centuries of Anglo-American law. "While this Court sits" it retains and exercises authority to nullify action which encroaches on freedom of utterance under the guise of punishing libel. Of course discussion cannot be denied and the right, as well as the duty, of criticism must not be stifled.

Justice Black in dissent rejected Justice Frankfurter's "judicial self restraint" argument. He argued that "no legislature is charged with the duty or vested with the power to decide what public issues Americans can discuss." Group libel laws were, in his view, a constant threat to freedom of speech and press.

Mr. Justice BLACK, with whom Mr. Justice DOUGLAS joined, dissenting:

. . . The Court's holding here and the constitutional doctrine behind it leave the rights of assembly, petition, speech and press almost completely at the mercy of state legislative, executive, and judicial agencies. I say "almost" because state curtailment of these freedoms may still be invalidated if a majority of this Court conclude that a particular infringement is "without reason," or is "a wilful and purposeless restriction unrelated to the peace and well being of the State." But lest this encouragement should give too much hope as to how and when this Court might protect these basic freedoms from state invasion, we are cautioned that state legislatures must be left free to "experiment" and to make "legislative" judgments. We are told that mistakes may be made during the legislative process of curbing public opinion. In such event the Court fortunately does not leave those mistakenly curbed, or any of us for that matter, unadvised. Consolation can be sought and must be found in the philosophical reflection that state legislative error in stifling speech and press "is the price to be paid for the trial-and-error inherent in legislative efforts to deal with obstinate social issues." My own belief is that no legislature is charged with the duty or vested with the power to decide what public issues Americans can discuss. In a free country that is the individual's choice, not the state's. State experimentation in curbing freedom of expression is a startling and frightening doctrine in a country dedicated to self-government by its people. I reject the holding that either state or nation can punish people for having their say in matters of public concern. . . .

This statute imposes state censorship over the theater, moving pictures, radio, television, leaflets, magazines, books and newspapers. No doubt the statute is broad enough to make criminal the "publication, sale, presentation or exhibition" of many of the world's great classics, both secular and religious.

The Court condones this expansive state censorship by painstakingly analogizing it to the law of criminal libel. As a result of this refined analysis, the Illinois statute emerges labeled a "group libel law." This label may make the Court's holding more palatable for those who sustain it, but the sugar-coating does not make the censorship less deadly. However tagged, the Illinois law is not that criminal libel which has been "defined, limited and constitutionally recognized time out of mind." For as "constitutionally recognized" that crime has provided for punishment of false, malicious, scurrilous charges against individuals, not against huge groups. This limited scope of the law of criminal libel is of no small importance. It has confined state punishment of speech and expression to the narrowest of areas involving nothing more than purely private feuds. Every expansion of the law of criminal libel so as to punish discussions of matters of public concern means a corresponding invasion of the area dedicated to free expression by the First Amendment.

. . . . . . . . . . . . . . . . . . . .

Unless I misread history the majority is giving libel a more expansive scope and more respectable status than it was ever accorded even in the Star Chamber. For here it is held to be punishable to give publicity to any picture, moving picture, play, drama, or sketch, or any printed matter which a judge may find unduly offensive to any race, color, creed or religion. In other words, in arguing for or against the enactment of laws that may differently affect huge groups, it is now very dangerous indeed to say something critical of one of the groups. And any "person, firm, or corporation" can be tried for this crime. "Person, firm, or corporation" certainly includes a book publisher, newspaper, radio or television station, or even a preacher.

This act sets up a system of state censorship which is at war with the kind of free government envisioned by those who forced adoption of our Bill of Rights. The motives behind the state law may have been to do good. But the same can be said about most laws making opinions punishable as crimes. History indicates that urges to do good have led to the burning of books and even to the burning of "witches."

No rationalization on a purely legal level can conceal the fact that state laws like this one present a constant overhanging threat to freedom of speech, press and religion. Today Beauharnais is punished for publicly expressing strong views in favor of segregation. Ironically enough, Beauharnais, convicted of crime in Chicago, would probably be given a hero's reception in many other localities, if not in some parts of Chicago itself. Moreover, the same kind of state law that makes Beauharnais a criminal for advocating segregation in Illinois can be utilized to send people to jail in other states for advocating equality and nonsegregation. What Beauharnais said in his leaflet is mild compared with usual arguments on both sides of racial controversies.

We are told that freedom of petition and discussion are in no danger "while this Court sits." This case raises considerable doubt. Since those who peacefully petition for changes in the law are not to be protected "while this Court sits," who is? I do not agree that the Constitution leaves freedom of petition, assembly, speech, press or worship at the mercy of a case-by-case, day-by-day majority of this Court. I had supposed that our people could rely for their freedom on the Constitution's commands, rather than on the grace of this Court on an individual case basis. To say that a legislative body can, with this Court's approval, make it a crime to petition for and publicly discuss proposed legislation seems as farfetched to me at it would be to say that a valid law could be enacted to punish a candidate for President for telling the people his views. I think the First Amendment, with the Fourteenth, "absolutely" forbids such laws without any "ifs" or "buts" or "whereases." Whatever the danger, if any, in such public discussions, it is a danger the Founders deemed outweighed by the danger incident to the stifling of thought and speech. The Court does not act on this view of the Founders. It calculates what it deems to be the danger of public discussion, holds the scales are tipped on the side of state suppression, and upholds state censorship. This method of decision offers little protection to First Amendment liberties "while this Court sits."

If there be minority groups who hail this holding as their victory, they might consider the possible relevancy of this ancient remark:

"Another such victory and I am undone."

Supporting Justice Black, Justice Douglas in his dissenting opinion saw group libel laws as a dangerous erosion of the First Amendment. Free speech and press, he said, are above the police power and not subject to regulation as are factories or the production of oil.

Mr. Justice DOUGLAS dissenting:

. . . My view is that if in any case other public interests are to override the plain command of the First Amendment, the peril of speech must be clear and present, leaving no room for argument, raising no doubts as to the necessity of curbing speech in order to prevent disaster.

The First Amendment is couched in absolute terms—freedom of speech shall not be abridged. Speech has therefore a preferred position as contrasted to some other civil rights. For example, privacy, equally sacred to some, is protected by the Fourth Amendment only against unreasonable searches and seizures. There is room for regulation of the ways and means of invading privacy. No such leeway is granted the invasion of the right of free speech guaranteed by the First Amendment. Until recent years that had been the course and direction of constitutional law. Yet recently the Court in this and in other cases has engrafted the right of regulation onto the First Amendment by placing in the hands of the legislative branch the right to regulate "within reasonable limits" the right of free speech.

This to me is an ominous and alarming trend. The free trade of ideas which the Framers of the Constitution visualized disappears. In its place there is substituted a new orthodoxy—an orthodoxy that changes with the whims of the age or the day, an orthodoxy which the majority by solemn judgment proclaims to be essential to the safety, welfare, security, morality, or health of society. Free speech in the constitutional sense disappears. Limits are drawn—limits dictated by expediency, political opinion, prejudices or some other desideratum of legislative action.

An historic aspect of the issue of judicial supremacy was the extent to which legislative judgment would be supreme in the field of social legislation. The vague contours of the Due Process Clause were used to strike down laws deemed by the Court to be unwise and improvident. That trend has been reversed. In matters relating to business, finance, industrial and labor conditions, health and the public welfare, great leeway is now granted the legislature, for there is no guarantee in the Constitution that the status quo will be preserved against regulation by government. Freedom of speech, however, rests on a different constitutional basis. The First Amendment says that freedom of speech, freedom of the press, and the free exercise of religion shall not be abridged. That is a negation of power on the part of each and every department of government.

Free speech, free press, free exercise of religion are placed separate and apart; they are above and beyond the police power, they are not subject to regulation in the manner of factories, slums, apartment houses, production of oil, and the like.

The Court in this and other cases places speech under an expanding legislative control. Today a white man stands convicted for protesting in unseemly language against our decision invalidating restrictive convenants. Tomorrow a Negro will be haled before a court for denouncing lynch law in heated terms. Farm laborers in the West who compete with field hands drifting up from Mexico; whites who feel the pressure of orientals; a minority which finds employment going to members of the dominant religious group—all these are caught in the mesh of today's decision. Debate and argument even in the courtroom are not always calm and dispassionate. Emotions sway speakers and audiences alike. Intemperate speech is a distinctive characteristic of man. Hotheads blow off and release destructive energy in the process. They shout and rave, exaggerating weaknesses, magnifying error, viewing with alarm. So it has been from the beginning; and so it will be throughout time. The Framers of the Constitution knew human nature as well as we do. They too had lived in dangerous days; they too knew the suffocating influence of orthodoxy and standardized thought. They weighed the compulsions for restrained speech and thought against the abuses of liberty. They chose liberty. That should be our choice today. . . . It is true that this is only one decision which may later be distinguished or confined to narrow limits. But it represents a philosophy at war with the First Amendment—a constitutional interpretation which puts free speech under the legislative thumb. It reflects an influence moving ever deeper into our society. It is notice to the legislatures that they have the power to control unpopular blocs. It is a warning to every minority that when the Constitution guarantees free speech it does not mean what it says.

Justice Robert H. Jackson, who had prosecuted Nazi war criminals, agreed on the dangers of group vilification, but warned of the misuse of group libel legislation.

Mr. Justice JACKSON dissenting:

Group libel statutes represent a commendable desire to reduce sinister abuses of our freedoms of expression—abuses which I have had occasion to learn can tear apart a society, brutalize its dominant elements and persecute, even to extermination, its minorities. While laws or prosecutions might not alleviate racial or sectarian hatreds and may even invest scoundrels with a specious martyrdom, I should be loath to foreclose the States from a considerable latitude of experimentation in this field. Such efforts, if properly applied, do not justify frenetic forebodings of crushed liberty. But these acts present most difficult policy and technical problems, as thoughtful writers who have canvassed the problem more comprehensively than is appropriate in a judicial opinion have well pointed out.

No group interest in any particular prosecution should forget that the shoe may be on the other foot in some prosecution tomorrow. In these, as in other matters, our guiding spirit should be that each freedom is balanced with a responsibility, and every power of the State must be checked with safeguards. Such is the spirit of our American law of criminal libel, which concedes the power to the States, but only as a power restrained by recognition of individual rights. I cannot escape the conclusion that as the Act has been applied in this case it lost sight of the rights.

The prosecutions under group libel laws in recent years have been few and as yet the predictions of Justices Black and Douglas in *Beauharnais* have not come to pass. In fact, when the state of Illinois revised its criminal code in 1961, it deleted from the code the same statute that the Supreme Court upheld in *Beauharnais*. And under the more recent decisions of *Curtis*, *Garrison* and the *New York Times*, the freedom to discuss controversial issues and to criticize official conduct has been greatly enhanced for all.

*Chapter Eight*

✣

# FREEDOM TO REPORT THE NEWS
# VERSUS THE RIGHT OF PRIVACY

✣

PRIVACY, simply stated, is what Judge Thomas Cooley in 1888 called "the right to be let alone." But this simple verbal formula by a noted American jurist does not fit the complexities of life in the latter half of the twentieth century. For a bewildering variety of reasons—including population increases, the activities of the mass media, and the proliferation of electronic gadgets for eavesdropping and spying—it is more and more difficult for Americans to be "let alone." Today, because solitude is often so earnestly sought and so hard to find, privacy is a most timely issue in the law.

## CONFLICTING CLAIMS

Privacy is a personal right which the Supreme Court of the United States has found to have constitutional status. But this personal right poses a tortured dilemma for the American courts and for the communications media: a person's right to be let alone often collides with the constitutionally protected public right, freedom of speech and press. When the courts or legislatures expand the protection given privacy, they may limit the media's freedom to report and the public's right to know.

Privacy, although a precious individual right, is nowhere mentioned in the Constitution itself, and its absence from that

This chapter was prepared by Professor Dwight L. Teeter, University of Wisconsin.

166

document is perhaps understandable. In Revolutionary America, most persons lived on scattered farms. They were often lonely but, nevertheless, secure in their privacy. City dwellers of that time made up little more than 10 per cent of the total population. Philadelphia, then America's largest city, had only 40,000 residents in 1790.

But if privacy was not specifically included in the Constitution, overtones of a "right to be let alone" can nevertheless be found in the Declaration of Independence, which spoke of the right to "life, liberty and the pursuit of happiness." And the Constitution's first ten amendments, including the right to be secure against unreasonable searches and seizures and the principle of due process of law, add up to a moving statement of a right to be let alone.

As Professor James Willard Hurst has noted, American legal history gives ample evidence of a broad *right* to privacy, of which only small pieces are enunciated by the narrower, formalized *law* of privacy which has been set down by judges and legislatures. The broader right was outlined in Justice Louis D. Brandeis' famed dissent in the case of *Olmstead v. United States.* Brandeis attacked a Supreme Court decision which permitted federal agents to tap telephone lines to gather evidence. He wrote that the makers of the Constitution "sought to protect Americans in their belief, their thoughts, their emotions and their sensations. They conferred, as against the Government, the right to be let alone—the most comprehensive of rights and the right most valued by civilized men."[1]

## BACKGROUND OF PRIVACY LAW

The narrower *law* of privacy in America has traditionally been traced to an 1890 *Harvard Law Review* article by two young law partners, Samuel D. Warren and the future Supreme Court Justice Brandeis. Warren was irked by "yellow press" accounts of parties given by him and his wife. This irritation led to the writing of the law journal article titled "The Right to Privacy," which pulled together old decisions taken from established areas of the law such as defamation and trespass to property.

Since 1890, the law of privacy has grown much in acceptance. By 1960, more than 300 privacy cases had been reported.

[1] 277 U.S. 438 (1928).

And by 1967, a Common Law right of privacy had been recognized in the courts of 31 states and in the District of Columbia. Additionally, four states had passed statutes defining a law of privacy.

## GROWTH OF PRIVACY LAW

Privacy law, like its old close cousin, the tort of defamation, is an example of unplanned growth. The tort of invasion of privacy, in its rapid development, covers a wide variety of affronts to the individual. It has been said to have four branches, or, perhaps, to be four separate torts.

1. Intrusion on the plaintiff's physical solitude.
2. Publication of private matters violating the ordinary decencies.
3. Putting plaintiff in a false position in the public eye, as by signing his name to a letter attributing to him views that he does not hold.
4. Appropriation of some element of plaintiff's personality for commercial use.[2]

More than one of these four kinds of invasion of privacy may be found in the same case.

These tort areas have been viewed with concern by the leading authority on privacy, Professor William L. Prosser. He has noted that the law of privacy had thrown aside defenses and limitations which operated in other tort fields to protect freedom of expression. Truth, for example, was *not* a defense to a lawsuit for invasion of privacy except in the third area listed above, "putting plaintiff in a false position in the public eye."[3] Indeed, an invasion of privacy committed by the mass media did not have to be defamatory for a plaintiff to have a successful lawsuit.

For years, the news media's best defense against lawsuits for invasion of privacy has been the concept of "newsworthi-

[2] *Barbieri v. News Journal Co.*, 189 A.2d 773, 774 (1963). The Supreme Court of Delaware here summarized William L. Prosser's analysis of the kinds of actions lumped together by the law of privacy. For fuller treatment, see Prosser's "Privacy," 48 *Calif. Law Rev.* 383 (1960) and his *Handbook of the Law of Torts*, 3rd ed., (St. Paul, Minn.: West Publishing Co., 1964), pp. 829–51.

[3] Prosser, "Privacy," 48 *Calif. Law Rev.*, pp. 407–8. An action for invasion of privacy is much like *"libel per se"*: a plaintiff does not have to plead or prove actual monetary loss in order to have a cause of action and punitive damages may be awarded by a court.

ness." Over the years, American courts have held that the press
has a limited privilege to report about persons or events "in
the public eye." Persons who come to public prominence by
choice (for example, actors or politicians) or by misadventure
(for example, victims of an accident or a crime) have been held
by courts to have lost, in some degree, their right of privacy.
In short, these persons have become news. But news is difficult
to define; one court called news "that indefinable quality of information which arouses public attention." Thus the privilege
of newsworthiness depends to a disquieting extent upon the
courts' ability to define the indefinable, and few newsmen look
with favor toward dependence on courts to define news for
them.

A continuing dilemma in privacy cases involving the news
media has been the "time lapse" problem. Courts have had to
wrestle with such troubled questions as whether a participant
in a notorious criminal trial of yesteryear—now forgotten and
living in obscurity—is still "news." Beyond this, courts have
faced the problem of "fictionalization": how closely must the
media stick to the facts of an actual news event to be able to
plead successfully the newsworthiness of their product? These
were but a few of the problems awaiting the Supreme Court
of the United States when it agreed to hear *Time, Inc. v. Hill*.[4]

TIME, INC. V. HILL, 385 U.S. 374 (1967)

*Early in 1967, the Supreme Court of the United States for
the first time decided a case involving the law of privacy and
the mass media of communications. The case,* Time, Inc. v.
Hill, *dealt with* Life *Magazine's 1955 article about* The Desperate Hours, *a play which was soon to open on Broadway. The
play depicted a family's terror-filled ordeal when held captive
in its home by three escaped convicts. Learning that the White-
marsh, Pennsylvania, house where the James J. Hill family had
faced the convicts was empty, the magazine took pictures of
the play's actors in that house.* Life's *article said that Americans could see the Hill family's story re-enacted in the play.*

*The Hills, however, resented this publicity. Arguing that
the play was not based on their experience—and that* Life knew

[4] Four other decisions excerpted in this book involve other aspects of the
broad right of privacy: *Breard v. Alexandria* in Chapter 10, and the *Gobitis,
Barnette,* and *Public Utilities Commission v. Pollak* cases in Chapter 11. None
of them, however, is directly concerned with conflicts over reporting the news.

*the play was not based on it—the Hills felt that their privacy had been invaded. One point in issue was the article's reference to a son being "roughed up" by one of the convicts, with a picture entitled "brutish convict." Another picture portrayed an actress as the "daughter," biting the hand of a convict to make him drop a gun. This picture was titled "daring daughter." The Hills maintained, however, that the convicts had treated them courteously and had not harmed them or been at all violent.*

*After three trials in New York, that state's highest court affirmed an award of $30,000 damages to the Hills. The Supreme Court of the United States, however, in a 5-to-4 decision, ruled in favor of* Time, Inc.

Mr. Justice William J. BRENNAN delivered the opinion of the Court:

. . . [W]e have had the advantage of an opinion of the Court of Appeals of New York which has materially aided us in our understanding of that court's construction of the [New York privacy] statute. It is the opinion of Judge Keating for the court in *Spahn v. Julian Messner, Inc.,* 18 N.Y. 2d 324, 274 N.Y.S.2d 877, 221 N.E. 2d 543 (1966). The statute was enacted in 1903 following the decision of the Court of Appeals in 1902 in *Roberson v. Rochester Folding Box Co.* . . . *Roberson* was an action against defendants for adorning their flour bags with plaintiff's picture without her consent. It was grounded upon an alleged invasion of a "right of privacy," defined by the Court of Appeals to be 'the claim that a man has the right to pass through this world, if he wills, without having his picture published . . . or his eccentricities commented upon either in handbills, circulars, catalogues, periodicals or newspapers.

. . . [I]t is particularly relevant that the Court of Appeals made crystal clear in the *Spahn* opinion that truth is a complete defense in actions under the statute based upon reports of newsworthy people or events. The opinion states: "The factual reporting of newsworthy persons and events is in the public interest and is protected." Constitutional questions which might arise if truth were not a defense are therefore of no concern.

But although the New York statute affords "little protection" to the "privacy" of a newsworthy person, "whether he be such by choice or involuntarily," the statute gives him a right of action when his name, picture, or portrait is the subject of a "fictitious" report or article. *Spahn* points up the distinction. . . . [T]he well-known professional baseball pitcher, Warren Spahn . . . sought an injunction and damages against the unauthorized publication of what purported to be a biography of his life. The trial judge had found that "[t]he record unequivocally establishes that the book publicizes areas of Warren Spahn's personal and private life, albeit inaccurate and distorted, and consists of a host, a preponderant percentage, of factual errors, disortions and fanciful passages. . . ." The [New York] Court of Appeals sustained the holding.

. . . . . . . . . . . . . . . . . . . . . .

. . . As the instant case [*Time, Inc. v. Hill*] went to the jury, . . . [James Hill] too was regarded to be a newsworthy person "substantially without a right to privacy" insofar as his hostage experience was involved, but to be entitled to his action insofar as that experience was "fictionalized" and "exploited for the defendant's commercial benefit."

. . . The [trial court's] opinion goes on to say that the "establishment of minor errors in an otherwise accurate" report does not prove "fictionalization." Material and substantial falsification is the test. However, it is not clear whether proof of knowledge of the falsity or that the article was prepared with reckless disregard for the truth is also required. In *New York Times Co. v. Sullivan* . . . we held that the Constitution delimits a State's power to award damages for libel in actions brought by public officials against critics of their official conduct. Factual error, content defamatory of official reputation, or both, are insufficient to an award of damages for false statements unless actual malice—knowledge that the statements are false or in reckless disregard of the truth—is alleged and proved.

. . . . . . . . . . . . . . . . . . . . . .

. . . We hold that the constitutional protections for speech and press preclude the application of the New York statute to redress false reports of matters of public interest in the absence of proof that the defendant published the report with knowledge of its falsity or in reckless disregard of truth.

The guarantees for speech and press are not the preserve of political expression or comment upon public affairs, essential as those are to healthy government. One need only pick up any newspaper or magazine to comprehend the vast range of published matter which exposes persons to public view, both private citizens and public officials. Exposure of the self to others in varying degrees is a concomitant of life in a civilized community. The risk of this exposure is an essential incident of life in a society which places a primary value on freedom of speech and press. . . . We have no doubt that the subject of the *Life* article, the opening of a new play linked to an actual incident, is a matter of public interest. "The line between the informing and the entertaining is too elusive for the protection of . . . [freedom of the press]." *Winters v. People of State of New York*, 333 U.S. 507, 510. Erroneous statement is no less inevitable in such case than in the casee of comment upon public affairs, and in both, if innocent or merely negligent, ". . . it must be protected if the freedoms of expression are to have the 'breathing space' that they 'need . . . to survive'. . . . As James Madison said, "Some degree of abuse is inseparable from the proper use of everything and in no instance is this more true than of the press." We create grave risk of serious impairment of the indispensable service of a free press in a free society if we saddle the press with the impossible burden of verifying to a certainty the facts associated in news articles with a person's name, picture or portrait, particularly as related to non-defamatory matter. Even negligence would be a most elusive standard, especially when the content of the speech itself affords no warning of prospective harm to another through falsity. A negligence test would place on the press the intolerable burden of guessing how a jury might assess the reasonableness of steps taken to verify the accuracy of every reference to a name, picture or portrait.

In this context, sanctions against either innocent or negligent misstatement would present a grave hazard of discouraging the press from exercising the constitutional guarantees. Those guarantees are not for the benefit of the press so much as for the benefit of all of us. A broadly defined freedom of the press assures the maintenance of our political system and an open society. Fear of large verdicts in damage suits for innocent or mere negligent misstatement, even fear of the expense involved in their defense, must inevitably cause publishers to "steer far wider of the unlawful zone." *New York Times Co. v. Sullivan*, 376 U.S., at 279. . . .

But the constitutional guarantees can tolerate sanctions against *calculated* falsehood without significant impairment of their essential function. We held in *New York Times* that calculated falsehood enjoyed no immunity in the case of alleged defamation of a public official's conduct. Similarly calculated falsehood should enjoy no immunity in the situation here presented us.

.   .   .   .   .   .   .   .   .   .   .   .   .   .   .   .

We find applicable here the standard of knowing or reckless falsehood not through blind application of *New York Times Co. v. Sullivan,* relating solely to libel actions by public officials, but only upon consideration of the factors which arise in the particular context of the application of the New York statute in cases involving private individuals. This is neither a libel action by a private individual nor a statutory action by a public official. Therefore, although the First Amendment principles pronounced in *New York Times* guide our conclusion, we reach that conclusion only by applying these principles in this discrete context.

.   .   .   .   .   .   .   .   .   .   .   .   .   .   .   .

We do not think . . . that the instructions confined the jury to a verdict of liability based on a finding that the statements in the article were made with knowledge of their falsity or in reckless disregard of the truth.

. . . . . . . . . . . . . . . . . . .

The requirement that the jury also find that the article was published "for trade purposes," as defined in the charge, cannot save the charge from constitutional infirmity. "That books, newspapers, and magazines are published and sold for profit does not prevent them from being a form of expression whose liberty is safeguarded by the First Amendment."

. . . [T]he constitutional command is narrowly limited in this case to the failure of the trial judge to instruct the jury that a verdict of liability could be predicated only on a finding of knowing or reckless falsity in the publication of the *Life* article.

The judgment of the Court of Appeals is set aside and the case is remanded for further proceedings not inconsistent with this opinion.

The concurring opinions of Justices Hugo L. Black and William O. Douglas restated their oft-repeated conviction that the First Amendment is too narrowly interpreted by the majority of the Supreme Court. Although Black and Douglas agreed in the result of *Time, Inc. v. Hill*, these two libertarians were sharply critical of Justice Brennan's use of the "malice test" from *New York Times Co. v. Sullivan*.

Mr. Justice BLACK, with whom Mr. Justice DOUGLAS joined, concurring:

I acquiesce in the application here of the narrower constitutional view of *New York Times* with the belief that this doctrine too is bound to pass away as its application to new cases proves its inadequacy to protect freedom of the press from destruction in libel cases and other cases like this one. The words "malicious" and particularly "reckless disregard of the truth" can never serve as effective substitutes for the First Amendment words: ". . . make no law . . . abridging the freedom of speech, or of the press. . . ." Experience, I think, is bound to prove that First Amendment freedoms can no more be permanently diluted or abridged by this Court's action than could the Sixth Amendment's right to counsel. . . .

I think it not inappropriate to add that it would be difficult, if not impossible, for the Court ever to sustain a judgment against *Time* in this case without using the recently popularized weighing and balancing formula. . . . The prohibitions of the Constitution were written to prohibit certain specific things, and one of the specific things prohibited is a law which abridges freedom of the press. That freedom was written into the Constitution and that Constitution is or should be binding on judges as well as other officers. The "weighing" doctrine plainly encourages and actually invites judges to choose for themselves between conflicting values, even where, as in the First Amendment, the Founders made a choice of values, one of which is a free press. Though the Constitution requires that judges swear to obey and enforce it, it is not altogether strange that all judges are not always dead set against constitutional interpretations that expand their powers, and that when power is once claimed by some, others are loath to give it up.

Finally, if the judicial balancing choice of constitutional changes is to be adopted by this Court, I could wish it had not started on the First Amendment. The freedoms guaranteed by that Amendment are essential freedoms in a government like ours. That Amendment was deliberately written in language designed to put its freedoms beyond the reach of government to change while it remained unrepealed. If judges have, however, by their own fiat today created a right of privacy equal to or superior to the right of a free press that the Constitution created, then tomorrow and the next day and the next, judges can create more rights that balance away other cherished Bill of Rights freedoms. If there is any one thing that could strongly indicate that the Founders were wrong in reposing so much trust in a free press, I would suggest that it would be for the press itself not to wake up to the grave danger to its freedom, inherent and certain in this "weighing process." *Life's* conduct here was at most a mere understandable and incidental error of fact in reporting a newsworthy event. One does not have to be a prophet to foresee that judgments like the one we here reverse can frighten and punish the press so much that publishers will cease trying to report news in a lively and readable fashion as long as there is—and there always will be—doubt as to the complete accuracy of the newsworthy facts. Such a consummation hardly seems consistent with the clearly expressed purpose of the Founders to guarantee the press a favored spot in our free society.

Mr. Justice DOUGLAS, concurring:

. . . It seems to me irrelevant to talk of any right of privacy in this context. Here a private person is catapulted into the news by events over which he had no control. He and his activities are then in the public domain as fully as the matters at issue in *New York Times Co. v. Sullivan.* . . . Such privacy as a person normally has ceases when his life has ceased to be private.

Once we narrow the ambit of the First Amendment, creative writing is imperiled and the "chilling effect" on free expression . . .

is almost sure to take place. That is, I fear, the result once we allow an exception for "knowing or reckless falsity." Such an elusive exception gives the jury, the finder of facts, broad scope and almost unfettered discretion. A trial is a chancy thing, no matter what safeguards are provided. To let a jury on this record return a verdict or not as it chooses is to let First Amendment rights ride on capricious or whimsical circumstances, for emotions and prejudices often do carry the day. The exception for knowing and reckless falsity" is therefore, in my view, an abridgment of speech that is barred by the First and Fourteenth Amendments. But as indicated in my Brother Black's opinion I have joined the Court's opinion in order to make possible an adjudication that controls this litigation. . . .

Justice John Marshall Harlan expressed the fear that the Court was not adequately protecting private citizens from invasions of privacy by the news media.

Mr. Justice HARLAN, concurring in part and dissenting in part:

While I find much with which to agree in the opinion of the Court I am constrained to express my disagreement with its view of the proper standard of liability to be applied on remand. Were the jury on retrial to find negligent rather than, as the Court requires, reckless or knowing "fictionalization," I think that federal constitutional requirements would be met.

. . . . . . . . . . . . . . . . . . .

. . . [W]e have entered an area where the "marketplace of ideas" does not function and where conclusions premised on the existence of that exchange are apt to be suspect. . . . [F]alsehood is more easily tolerated where public attention creates the strong likelihood of a competition among ideas. Here such competition is extremely unlikely. . . . It would be unreasonable to assume that Mr. Hill could find a forum for making a successful refutation of the *Life* material or that the public's interest in it would be sufficient for the truth to win out by comparison as it might in that area of discussion central to a free society. Thus the state interest in encouraging careful checking and preparation of published material is far stronger than in *Times*. The dangers of unchallengeable untruth are far too well documented to be summarily dismissed.

. . . [T]here is a vast difference in the state interest in protecting individuals like Mr. Hill and irresponsibly prepared publicity and the state interest in similar protection for a public official. In *Times* we acknowledged public officials to be a breed from whom hardiness to exposure to charges, innuendoes, and criticisms might

be demanded and who voluntarily assumed the risk of such things by
entry into the public arena. . . . But Mr. Hill came to public attention through an unfortunate circumstance not of his making
rather than his voluntary actions and he can in no sense be considered to have "waived" any protection the State might justifiably
afford him from irresponsible publicity. . . .

[A] state should be free to hold the press to a duty of making a
reasonable investigation of the underlying facts and limiting itself
to "fair comment" on the materials so gathered. Theoretically, of
course, such a rule might slightly limit press discussion of matters
touching individuals like Mr. Hill. But, from a pragmatic standpoint, until now the press, at least in New York, labored under the
more exacting handicap of the existing New York privacy law and
has certainly remained robust. Other professional activity of great
social value is carried on under a duty of reasonable care and there
is no reason to suspect the press would be less hardy than medical
practitioners or attorneys for example. The "freedom of the press"
guaranteed by the First Amendment . . . cannot be thought to
insulate all press conduct from review and responsibility for harm
inflicted. The majority would allow sanctions against such conduct
only when it is morally culpable. I insist that it can also be reached
when it creates a severe risk of irremediable harm to individuals
involuntarily exposed to it and powerless to protect themselves
against it. . . .

Justice Abe Fortas' dissent drew upon other Supreme
Court opinions which have enunciated a right of privacy. He
called privacy a basic right and argued that the guarantees of
freedom of expression do not mean that the press can be beyond punishment if it invades a citizen's privacy.

Mr. Justice FORTAS, with whom THE CHIEF JUSTICE and Mr. Justice Tom
CLARK joined, dissenting:

. . . . . . . . . . . . . . . . .

I fully agree with the views of my Brethren who have stressed
the need for a generous construction of the First Amendment. I,
too, believe that freedom of the press, of speech, assembly, and religion, and the freedom to petition are of the essence of our liberty
and fundamental to our values. . . . But I do not believe that
whatever is in words, however much of an aggression it may be upon
individual rights, is beyond the reach of the law, no matter how
heedless of others' rights—how remote from public purpose, how
reckless, irresponsible, and untrue it may be. I do not believe that
the First Amendment precludes effective protection of the right of
privacy—or, for that matter, an effective law of libel. . . . There

are great and important values in our society, none of which is greater than those reflected in the First Amendment, but which are also fundamental and entitled to this Court's careful respect and protection. Among these is the right to privacy, which has been eloquently extolled by scholars and members of this Court. Judge Cooley long ago referred to this right as "the right to be let alone." In 1890, Warren and Brandeis published their famous article "The Right to Privacy," in which they eloquently argued that the "excesses" of the press in "overstepping in every direction the obvious bounds of propriety and and decency" made it essential that the law recognize a right to privacy, distinct from traditional remedies for defamation, to protect private individuals against the unjustifiable infliction of mental pain and distress. A distinct right of privacy is now recognized, either as a "common-law" right or by statute, in at least 35 States. Its exact scope varies in the respective jurisdictions. It is, simply stated, the right to be let alone; to live one's life as one chooses, free from assault, intrusion or invasion except as they can be justified by the clear needs of community living under a government of law. As Brandeis said in his famous dissent in *Olmstead v. United States,* 277 U.S. 438, 478, (1928), the right of privacy is "the most comprehensive of rights and the right most valued by civilized men."

This Court has repeatedly recognized this principle. As early as 1886, in *Boyd v. United States,* 116 U.S. 616, 630 (1928), this Court held that the doctrines of the Fourth and Fifth Amendments "apply to all invasions on the part of the government and its employes of the sanctity of a man's home and the privacies of life. It is not the breaking of his doors, and the rummaging of his drawers, that constitutes the essence of the offense; but it is the invasion of his indefeasible right of personal security, personal liberty and private property."

. . . . . . . . . . . . . . . . . . . . . .

. . . [I]n the landmark case of *Mapp v. Ohio,* 367 U.S. 643 (1961), this Court referred to "the right to privacy," no less important than any other right carefully and particularly reserved to the people, as "basic to a free society." Mr. Justice Clark, speaking for the Court, referred to "the freedom from unconscionable invasions of privacy" as intimately related to the freedom from convictions based upon coerced confessions. . . .

In *Griswold v. State of Connecticut,* 381 U.S. 479 (1965), the Court held unconstitutional a state law under which petitioners were prosecuted for giving married persons information and medical advice on the use of contraceptives. The holding was squarely based upon the right of privacy which the Court derived by implication from the specific guarantees of the Bill of Rights. . . . As stated in the concurring opinion of Mr. Justice Goldberg . . . :

"the right of privacy is a fundamental personal right, emanating 'from the totality of the constitutional scheme under which we live.'" *Id.*, at 494, 85 S.Ct. at 1637.

Privacy, then, is a basic right. The States may, by appropriate legislation and within proper bounds, enact laws to vindicate that right. . . . Particularly where the right of privacy is invaded by words—by the press or in a book or pamphlet—the most careful and sensitive appraisal of the total impact of the claimed tort upon the congeries of rights is required. I have no hesitancy to say, for example, that where political personalities or issues are involved or where the event as to which the alleged invasion of privacy occurred is in itself a matter of current public interest, First Amendment values are supreme and are entitled at least the types of protection that this Court extended in *New York Times Co. v. Sullivan.* . . . But I certainly concur with the Court that the greatest solicitude for the First Amendment does not compel us to deny to a State the right to provide a remedy for reckless falsity in writing and publishing an article which irresponsibly and injuriously invades the privacy of a quiet family for no purpose except dramatic interest and commercial appeal. My difficulty is that while the Court gives lip-service to this principle, its decision, which it claims to be based on erroneous instructions, discloses hesitancy to go beyond the verbal acknowledgment.

The Court today does not repeat the ringing words of so many of its members on so many occasions in exaltation of the right of privacy. Instead, it reverses a decision under the New York "Right of Privacy" statute because of the "failure of the trial judge to instruct the jury that a verdict of liability could be predicated only on a finding of knowing or reckless falsity in the publication of the *Life* article." In my opinion, the jury instructions, although they were not a text-book model, satisfied this standard.

. . . . . . . . . . . . . . . . . . . . . . .

The courts may not and must not permit either public or private action that censors or inhibits the press. But part of this responsibility is to preserve values and procedures which assure the ordinary citizen that the press is not above the reach of the law— that its special prerogatives, granted because of its special and vital functions, are reasonably equated with its needs in the performance of these functions. For this Court totally to immunize the press— whether forthrightly or by subtle indirection—in areas far beyond the needs of news, comment on public persons and events, discussion of public issues and the like would be no service to freedom of the press, but an invitation to public hostility to that freedom. This Court cannot and should not refuse to permit under state law the private citizen who is aggrieved by the type of assault which we have here and which is not within the specially protected core of the First Amendment to recover compensatory damages for recklessly inflicted invasion of his rights.

Accordingly, I would affirm.

In *Hill*, the Supreme Court stepped gingerly into the no-man's land where the right to privacy and the right to freedom of expression collide. The conflicting claims of privacy and free expression posed here, both based on Bill of Rights provisions, resulted in a cautious decision which carefully adhered to the fact situation before the Court.

The majority opinion turned on the belief that the trial judge had failed to instruct the jury correctly. Instructions to the jury, in Justice Brennan's view, should have included a call for a finding of "knowing or reckless falsehood" to be able to hold the defendant *Life* magazine liable. This standard suggested by Justice Brennan came from the definition of malice in the 1964 libel case of *New York Times v. Sullivan,* discussed in Chapter 7: "knowledge that it was false, or reckless disregard of whether it was false or not." But it should be noted that this case has *not* made truth a trustworthy defense against lawsuits for invasion of privacy. The Court was severely split, and only Justices Potter Stewart and Byron White agreed with Justice Brennan in applying the *"Times* rule," although Justices Black and Douglas concurred in the decision.

As Justice Fortas suggested in his dissent, the majority opinion in *Hill* was perhaps as remarkable for what it did *not* say as for what it did. Ringing affirmations of a constitutionally protected right to privacy were absent, although there were suggestions that, at times, the right to privacy could limit freedom of the press.

Men who wish to see greater freedom for the mass media may continue to fret about the dangers of the law of privacy. Truth is not always a defense to a law suit charging invasion of privacy, and the news media's most useful defense—"newsworthiness"—is so elastic as to be subject to a jury's whims. More definite answers, however, must await further Supreme Court consideration of privacy cases touching the mass media. Unil then, the law of privacy remains a problem area; as Professor Prosser has written, it comes "into head-on collision with the constitutional guaranty of freedom of the press."[5]

[5] *Handbook of the Law of Torts,* 3rd ed., p. 844.

*Chapter Nine*

❧

# PRESS FREEDOM AND THE POST OFFICE

❧

A SPECIAL RELATIONSHIP has always existed between the Post Office and those who exercise their constitutional right to print and distribute publications. Historically, the Post Office has provided the essential service of distributing throughout the nation much of its news and information at low cost. In operating this service, the Post Office, through Congress's powers under Article 1, Section 8 of the Constitution to "establish post offices and post roads" and to make all laws necessary to carry out this function, retains considerable power of potential censorship over printed matter carried in the mails. This power stems from the belief, held by some, that the constitutional grant gives Congress unlimited authority to determine what can be mailed and for what price, and that the use of the mails is not a right but a favor, which can be granted or withheld at the will of those in charge.

So it was for nearly seventy years, from the case of *Ex parte Jackson* in 1877 until *Hannegan v. Esquire* in 1946. The Postmaster General did enjoy great power, mainly through his control of the second-class mailing privilege, which is indispensable to any publication's circulation by mail. If this privilege is denied, a paper or periodical has to pay substantially higher postage rates which places it at a disadvantage with competitors. Before the *Esquire* case, the privilege could be used to impose political, economic, religious, or literary orthodoxy on those using the mails.

In *Esquire* and subsequent decisions, however, the Supreme Court sharply limited the censorship powers of the Postmaster General. In the 1965 case of *Lamont v. Postmaster General* (cited later in the chapter), the Post Office was forbidden to screen political mail from abroad; such screening, the Court decided, was "a limitation on the unfettered exercise of the addressee's First Amendment rights."

## LIBERTY OF CIRCULATION ESSENTIAL TO FREEDOM OF PRESS

Congress does have the power to determine what shall be carried in the mail and at what rates. Yet these determinations, the Supreme Court has ruled, shall not infringe upon the rights of free speech and press. A case involving lotteries started the series of relevant decisions.

### EX PARTE JACKSON, 96 U.S. 727 (1877)

*[A. Orlando] Jackson was tried and found guilty under the penal section of the statute prohibiting the mailing of lottery information. The Supreme Court upheld Jackson's conviction. Justice Stephen Field, in the Court decision, argued that if Congress had the right to decide what was to be carried in the mails, it had the corollary right to decide what to leave out. The Court, however, was aware of the necessity that these powers not conflict with the First Amendment.*

Mr. Justice Stephen FIELD delivered the opinion of the Court:

. . . Nor can any regulation be enforced against the transportation of printed matter in the mail which is open to examination, so as to interfere in any manner with the freedom of the press. Liberty of circulating is as essential to that freedom as liberty of publishing; indeed, without the circulation, the publication would be of little value. If, therefore, printed matter be excluded from the mails, its transportation in any other way cannot be forbidden by Congress.

Another regulation governing the freedom to use the mails, imposed by an act of Congress of August 12, 1912, required disclosure of the ownership of publications enjoying second-class privileges. In *Lewis,* two publishers challenged the constitutionality of the law.

LEWIS PUBLISHING CO. V. MORGAN, 229 U.S. 288 (1913)

*These were two appeals from a U.S. district court to review decrees dismissing suits to enjoin the enforcement of the "newspaper publicity law (the 1912 act)." This law required that every publisher, manager, etc., of every general newspaper, magazine, etc., file twice a year with the Post Office a sworn statement listing the names of the editor, managing editor, publisher, stockholders, etc. All advertising matter had to be plainly marked. Failure to comply could result in a denial of the mails to the publication. The two appellants, both publishers of New York City newspapers, complained that this legislation abridged freedom of the press protected by the First Amendment and constituted a denial of the due process of law guaranteed by the Fifth Amendment. The Supreme Court ruled freedom of the press was not abridged, affirming the lower court judgment. (See Justice Clark's dissent in the 1960 case of* Talley v. California, *p. 200, which seems to run counter to this ruling.)*

Mr. Justice Edward WHITE delivered the opinion of the Court:

We come, then, to determine whether the provision as thus construed is valid. That Congress, in exerting its power concerning the mails, has the comprehensive right to classify which it has exerted from the beginning, and therefore may exercise its discretion for the purpose of furthering the public welfare as it understands it, we think it too clear for anything but statement; the exertion of the power, of course, at all times and under all conditions, being subject to the express or necessarily implied limitations of the Consitution. From this it results that it was and is in the power of Congress, in "the interest of the dissemination of current intelligence," to so legislate as to the mails by classification or otherwise, as to favor the widespread circulation of newspapers, periodicals, etc., even though the legislation on that subject, when considered intrinsically, apparently seriously discriminates against the public and in favor of newspapers, periodicals, etc., and their publishers. Although in the form in which the contentions here made by the publishers which we have at the outset reproduced, as literally stated, seem to challenge this proposition by suggesting that the power of Congress to classify is controlled and limited by conditions intrinsically inhering in the carriage of the mails, we assume that such apparent contention was merely the result of an unguarded form of statement, since we cannot bring our minds to the conclusion that it was intended on behalf of the publishers to generally assail as an infringement of the constitutional prohibition against the invasion of the freedom of the press the legislation which, for a long series of years, has favored the press by discriminating so as to secure to it great pecuniary and other concessions, and a wider circulation and consequently a greater sphere of influence.

If, however, we are mistaken in this view, then, we think, it suffices to say that the contention is obviously without merit. This being true, the attack on the provision in question as a violation of the Constitution because infringing the freedom of the press, and depriving of property without due process of law, rests only upon the illegality of the conditions which the provision exacts in return for the right to enjoy the privileges and advantages of the second-class mail classification. The question, therefore, is only this: are the conditions which were exacted incidental to the power exerted of conferring on the publishers of newspapers, periodicals, etc., the privileges of the second-class classification, or are they so beyond the scope of the exercise of that power as to cause the conditions to be repugnant to the Constitution? We say this is the question, since necessarily if the power exists to legislate by discriminating in favor of publishers, the right to exercise that power carries with it the authority to do those things which are incidental to the power itself, or which are plainly necessary to make effective the principal authority when exerted. In other words, from this point of view, the illuminating rule announced in *McCulloch v. Maryland,* . . . and *Gibbons v. Ogden,* governs here as it does in every other case where an exertion of power under the Constitution comes under consideration.

### POST OFFICE HEARS DISSENTING VOICES

Restrictions in the postal field, as in other areas of civil liberties, reached an apex in the World War I era. In the *Milwaukee Leader* case, Postmaster General A. R. Burleson invoked his classification powers to deny mailing privileges to a paper charged with violating the Espionage Act.

MILWAUKEE SOCIAL DEMOCRATIC PUBLISHING CO. V. BURLESON, 255 U.S. 407 (1921)

*During World War I, the* Milwaukee Leader *published material considered detrimental to the purposes and aims of the United States government in violation of the Espionage Act. Among other things, the paper had charged that the war was unjustifiable and dishonorable and that great numbers of our soldiers were becoming insane. Postmaster General Burleson therefore revoked the paper's second-class mailing privi-*

*lege. The newspaper attempted to obtain a mailing privilege. The attempt failed both in lower courts and in the Supreme Court. However, the dissents of Justices Louis Brandeis and Oliver Wendell Holmes became the basis of the law in the later* Esquire *case.*

Mr. Justice J. H. CLARKE delivered the opinion of the Court:

These publications were not designed to secure amendment or repeal of the laws denounced in them as arbitrary and oppressive, but to create hostility to, and to encourage violation of them. Freedom of the press may protect criticism and agitation for modification or repeal of laws, but it does not extend to protection of him who counsels and encourages the violation of the law as it exists. The Constitution was adopted to preserve our government, not to serve as a protecting screen for those who, while claiming its privileges, seek to destroy it.

The dissent of Justice Brandeis took note of the dangerous censorship potential in the power to deny to one paper a cheaper delivery rate because the Postmaster General felt that past views expressed in the paper were illegal.

Mr. Justice BRANDEIS dissenting:

(a) The power to police the mails is an incident of the postal power. Congress may, of course, exclude from the mails matter which is dangerous or which carries on its face immoral expressions, threats, or libels. It may go further, and through its power of exclusion exercise, within limits, general police power over the material which it carries, even though its regulations are quite unrelated to the business of transporting mails. . . . As stated in *Ex parte Jackson,* 96 U.S. 727, 732:

"The difficulty attending the subject arises, not from the want of power in Congress to prescribe regulations as to what shall constitute mail matter, but from the necessity of enforcing them consistently with rights reserved to the people, of far greater importance than the transportation of the mail."

In other words, the postal power, like all its other powers, is subject to the limitations of the Bill of Rights. . . . Congress may not through its postal police power put limitations upon the freedom of the press which, if directly attempted, would be unconstitutional. This court also stated in *Ex parte Jackson,* that—

"Liberty of circulating is as essential to that freedom as liberty of publishing; indeed, without the circulation, the publication would be of little value."

It is argued that, although a newspaper is barred from the second-class mail, liberty of circulation is not denied, because the first- and third-class mail and also other means of transportation are left open to a publisher. Constitutional rights should not be frittered away by arguments so technical and unsubstantial. "The Constitution deals with substance, not shadows. Its inhibition was leveled at the thing, not the name." . . . The government might, of course, decline altogether to distribute newspapers, or it might decline to carry any at less than the cost of the service, and it would not thereby abridge the freedom of the press, since to all papers other means of transportation would be left open. But to carry newspapers generally at a sixth of the cost of the service, and to deny that service to one paper of the same general character, because to the Postmaster General views therein expressed in the past seem illegal, would prove an effective censorship and abridge seriously freedom of expression.

How dangerous to liberty of the press would be the holding that the second-class mail service is merely a privilege, which Congress may deny to those whose views it deems to be against public policy, is shown by the following contention made in 1912 by the Solicitor General in the *Lewis* Case: . . .

"A possible abuse of power is no argument against its existence, but we may as well observe that a denial of the mails to a paper because of its ownership or the views held by its owners may well be illegal as having no relation to the thing carried in the mails *unless the views are expressed in the paper;* but *if such views are expressed in the paper* Congress can doubtless exclude them, just as Congress could now exclude all papers advocating lotteries, prohibition, anarchy, or a protective tariff if a majority of Congress thought such views against public policy."

Justice Holmes laid the groundwork for the later *Esquire* decision by also seriously questioning the classification rights of the Postmaster General. Here again is an example of how dissenting opinions of one decision become the basis of the ruling opinion of a later one.

Mr. Justice HOLMES dissenting:

. . . To refuse the second-class rate to a newspaper is to make its circulation impossible and has all the effect of the order that I have supposed. I repeat. When I observe that the only powers expressly given to the Postmaster General to prevent the carriage of unlawful matter of the present kind are to stop and to return papers already existing and posted, when I notice that the conditions expressly attached to the second-class rate look only to wholly different matters, and when I consider the ease with which the power claimed by the Postmaster could be used to interfere with very sacred rights, I am of opinion that the refusal to allow the relator the rate to which it was entitled whenever its newspaper was carried, on the ground that the paper ought not to be carried at all, was unjustified by statute and was a serious attack upon liberties that not even the war induced Congress to infringe.

## NO POSTAL POWER TO PRESCRIBE LITERARY STANDARDS

The *Esquire* case is the landmark decision on the postal authority's power to judge the merits of the content when determining a publication's qualification for second-class mailing privileges. Justice William O. Douglas's ruling opinion appealed for diversity and tolerance for "the widest varieties of tastes and ideas."

### HANNEGAN v. ESQUIRE, 327 U.S. 146 (1946)

*The second-class mailing privilege of* Esquire *magazine was revoked under the Classification Act of 1879 which established the requirements for the second-class privilege. Postmaster General Frank C. Walker had originally brought the suit but he was substituted for later by his successor, Robert E. Hannegan.*

Esquire *was charged with failure to meet the act's fourth condition, which read:*

It [the publication] must be originated and published for the dissemination of information of a public character, or devoted to literature, the sciences, arts, or some special industry and having a legitimate list of subscribers. Nothing herein contained shall be so construed as to admit to the second class rate regular publications designed primarily for advertising purposes, or for free circulation, or for circulation at nominal rates.

*The Supreme Court affirmed the lower court ruling that the postal action against* Esquire *should be reversed. The decision has greatly restricted the Postmaster General's powers as a censor.*

Mr. Justice DOUGLAS delivered the opinion of the Court:

. . . An examination of the items makes plain, we think, that the controversy is not whether the magazine publishes "information of a public character" or is devoted to "literature" or to the "arts." It is whether the contents are "good" or "bad." To uphold the order of revocation would, therefore, grant the Postmaster General a power of censorship. Such a power is so abhorrent to our traditions that a purpose to grant it should not be easily inferred.

The second-class privilege is a form of subsidy. From the beginning Congress has allowed special rates to certain classes of publications. The Act of February 20, 1792, . . . granted newspapers a more favorable rate. These were extended to magazines and pamphlets by the Act of May 8, 1794. . . . Prior to the Classification Act of 1879, periodicals were put into the second class, which by the Act of March 3, . . . included "all mailable matter exclusively in print, and regularly issued at stated periods, without addition by writing, mark, or sign." That Act plainly adopted a strictly objective test and left no discretion to the postal authorities to withhold the second-class privilege from a mailable newspaper or periodical because it failed to meet some standard of worth or value or propriety. There is nothing in the language or history of the Classification Act of 1879 which suggests that Congress in that law made any basic change in its treatment of second-class mail, let alone such an abrupt and radical change as would be entailed by the inauguration of even a limited form of censorship.

. . . . . . . . . . . . . . . . . .

We may assume that Congress has a broad power of classification and need not open second-class mail to publications of all types. The categories of publications entitled to that classification had indeed varied through the years. And the Court held in *Ex parte Jackson,* . . . that Congress could constitutionally make it a crime to send fraudulent or obscene material through the mails. But grave constitutional questions are immediately raised once it is said that the use of the mails is a privilege which may be extended or withheld on any grounds whatsoever. See the dissents of Mr. Justice Brandeis and Mr. Justice Holmes in *Milwaukee Publishing Co. v. Burleson.* . . . Under that view the second-class rate could be granted on condition that certain economic or political ideas not be disseminated. The provisions of the Fourth condition would have to be far more explicit for us to assume that Congress made such a radical departure from our traditions and undertook to clothe the Postmaster General with the power to supervise the tastes of the reading public of the country.

It is plain, as we have said, that the favorable second-class rates were granted periodicals meeting the requirements of the Fourth condition, so that the public good might be served through a dissemination of the class of periodicals described. But that is a far cry from assuming that Congress had any idea that each applicant for the second-class rate must convince the Postmaster General that his publication positively contributes to the public good or public welfare. Under our system of government there is an accommodation for the widest varieties of tastes and ideas. What is good literature, what has educational value, what is refined public information, what is good art, varies with individuals as it does from one generation to another. There doubtless would be a contrariety of views concerning Cervantes' *Don Quixote*, Shakespeare's *Venus and Adonis*, or Zola's *Nana*. But a requirement that literature or art conform to some norm prescribed by an official smacks of an ideology foreign to our system. The basic values implicit in the requirements of the Fourth condition can be served only by uncensored distribution of literature. From the multitude of competing offerings the public will pick and choose. What seems to one to be trash may have for others fleeting or even enduring values. But to withdraw the second-class rate from this publication today because its contents seemed to one official not good for the public would sanction withdrawal of the second-class rate tomorrow from another periodical whose social or economic views seemed harmful to another official. The validity of the obscenity laws is recognition that the mails may not be used to satisfy all tastes, no matter how perverted. But Congress has left the Postmaster General with no power to prescribe standards for the literature or the art which a mailable periodical disseminates.

This is not to say that there is nothing left to the Postmaster General under the Fourth condition. It is his duty to "execute all laws relative to the Postal Service." For example, questions may arise whether the publication which seeks the favorable second-class rate is a periodical as defined in the Fourth condition or a book or other type of publication. But the power to determine whether a periodical (which is mailable) contains information of a public character, literature, or art does not include the further power to determine whether the contents meet some standard of the public good or welfare.

## SCREENING OF FOREIGN MAIL IS PROHIBITED

The *Esquire* decision created substantial protection for American newspapers and periodicals but did nothing for periodicals mailed into the United States from overseas. In 1948 the U.S. government began intercepting unsealed Communist propaganda mail from overseas. Unless the addressee made a special request to the Post Office that the mail be delivered, it was destroyed. A holdover of a 1938 law aimed at Nazi literature, the practice was meant to cut the flow of millions of Communist tracts into the United States at cut-rate bulk prices. Many persons felt that the screening interfered with First Amendment rights; most individuals would fear to acknowledge to a disapproving government their interest in the questioned or disapproved reading matter.

On just that ground, President Kennedy abolished mail interception in 1961; however, only a year later it was enacted into law by Congress. Then, in June 1965, for the first time in its 175-year history, the Supreme Court struck down an act of Congress on the explicit ground that it violated the free speech and free press provisions of the First Amendment.

LAMONT V. POSTMASTER GENERAL; FIXA V. HEILBERG, 381 U.S. 301 (1965)

*These were similar actions to enjoin the enforcement of the federal statute relating to Communist political propaganda from foreign countries sent by unsealed mail. The Supreme Court held unconstitutional this law requiring the Post Office to detain and destroy such mail unless the addressee returned a reply card indicating his desire to receive it. The required official act, i.e., return of a card, was deemed a limitation on the "unfettered exercise of the addressee's First Amendment rights."*

Mr. Justice DOUGLAS delivered the opinion of the Court:

. . . We conclude that the Act as construed and applied is unconstitutional because it requires an official act (viz. returning the reply card) as a limitation on the unfettered exercise of the addressee's First Amendment rights. As stated by Mr. Justice Holmes in *United States ex rel. Milwaukee Social Democratic Pub. Co. v. Burleson* . . . : "The United States may give up the post-office when it sees fit, but while it carries it on, the use of the mails is almost as much a part of free speech as the right to use our tongues."

.  .  .  .  .  .  .  .  .  .  .  .  .  .  .  .  .  .  .  .  .

Here the Congress—expressly restrained by the First Amendment from "abridging" freedom of speech and of press—is the actor. The Act sets administrative officials astride the flow of mail to inspect it, appraise it, write the addressee about it, and await a response before dispatching the mail. Just as the licensing or taxing authorities in the *Lovell, Thomas,* and *Murdock* cases sought to control the flow of ideas to the public so here federal agencies regulate the flow of mail. We do not have here, any more than we had in *Hannegan v. Esquire, Inc.,* . . . any question concerning the extent to which Congress may classify the mail and fix the charges for its carriage. Nor do we reach the question whether the standard here applied could pass constitutional muster. Nor do we deal with the right of customs to inspect material from abroad for contraband. We rest on the narrow ground that the addressee in order to receive his mail must request in writing that it be delivered. This amounts in our judgment to an unconstitutional abridgment of the addressee's First Amendment rights. The addressee carries an affirmative obligation which we do not think the Government may impose on him. This requirement is almost certain to have a deterrent effect, especially as respects those who have sensitive positions. Their livelihood may be dependent on a security clearance. Public officials like schoolteachers who have no tenure, might think they would invite disaster if they read what the Federal Government says contains the seeds of treason. Apart from them, any addressee is likely to feel some inhibition in sending for literature which federal officials have condemned as "communist political propaganda." The regime of this Act is at war with the "uninhibited, robust, and wide-open" debate and discussion that are contemplated by the First Amendment.

Justice William J. Brennan argued that the right to receive publications was a fundamental part of the First Amendment.

Mr. Justice BRENNAN, with whom Mr. Justice Arthur GOLDBERG joined, concurring:

It is true that the First Amendment contains no specific guarantee of access to publications. However, the protection of the Bill of Rights goes beyond the specific guarantees to protect from congressional abridgment those equally fundamental personal rights necessary to make the express guarantees fully meaningful. I think the right to receive publications is such a fundamental right. The dissemination of ideas can accomplish nothing if otherwise willing addressees are not free to receive and consider them. It would be a barren marketplace of ideas that had only sellers and no buyers.

. . . . . . . . . . . . . . . . .

The Government asserts that Congress enacted the statute in the awareness that Communist political propaganda mailed to addressees in the United States on behalf of foreign governments was often offensive to the recipients and constituted a subsidy to the very governments which bar the dissemination of publications from the United States. But the sensibilities of the unwilling recipient are fully safeguarded by 39 C.F.R. Sec. 441.1 (a) (Supp. 1965) under which the Post Office will honor his request to stop delivery; the statute under consideration, on the other hand, impedes delivery even to a willing addresse. In the area of First Amendment freedoms, government has the duty to confine itself to the least intrusive regulations which are adequate for the purpose. The argument that the statute is justified by the object of avoiding the subsidization of propaganda of foreign governments which bar American propaganda needs little comment. If the Government wishes to withdraw a subsidy or a privilege, it must do so by means and on terms which do not endanger First Amendment rights. That the governments which originate this propaganda themselves have no equivalent guarantees only highlights the cherished values of our constitutional framework; it can never justify emulating the practice of restrictive regimes in the name of expediency.

Since 1946, the Supreme Court has expanded the freedom of American citizens to use the mails just as it has widened liberties in such areas as contempt or libel suits by public officials. The *Esquire* decision remains a firm protection of a publisher's right to send a wide range of material through the mails. The increasingly libertarian view of the Court toward material once considered obscene means that the Postmaster General no longer has the powers of censorship he once held.

The more recent *Lamont* decision spells out a right of citizens to receive all variety of mail, including Communist propaganda from abroad, without government harassment.

Congress still determines the conditions and rates of mail delivery in a quantitative way, but postal officials may not pass judgment on the worth or value of the mail itself. The use of the mails is now closer to being a basic right belonging to the people rather than a privilege bestowed by government and subject to revocation.

*Chapter Ten*

※

# FREEDOM OF DISTRIBUTION

※

THE RIGHT to freely distribute printed materials without undue government interference is included in the broad concept of freedom of the press. As Justice Stephen Field pointed out in *Ex parte Jackson* in 1877: "Liberty of circulating is as essential to that freedom (of the press) as liberty of publishing; indeed, without the circulation, the publication would be of little value."

Periodicals, handbills, and tracts are often distributed by means other than the mails—by hand, on street corners, in book stores, from door-to-door. Using these methods, distributors occasionally run afoul of local government regulations restricting the place, time, and manner of distribution.

REASONABLE REGULATION IS NOT UNCONSTITUTIONAL

A variety of regulatory problems may be encountered: ordinances against littering, ordinances barring solicitors from going to a residence without prior permission, ordinances for public disclosure of subscription lists, and requirements that handbills carry the names and addresses of those preparing and distributing them. In such situations, legitimate police and health powers have to be reconciled with the right to distribute publications. The following decisions illustrate how the Supreme Court has dealt with these conflicting interests.

MARTIN V. STRUTHERS, 319 U.S. 141 (1943)

*Thelma Martin, a member of Jehovah's Witnesses, was convicted in Mayor's Court in Struthers, Ohio, of violating an* *ordinance which regulated distribution of handbills. She was fined $10. The Supreme Court reversed her conviction, agreeing that the ordinance violated her rights of freedom of press and religion. Justice Hugo Black's decision held that the city of Struthers could not, by ordinance, decide on behalf of all its citizens who may come to their doors. He said the city could not make criminals of those innocently carrying information.*

Mr. Justice BLACK delivered the opinion of the Court:

. . . The right of freedom of speech and press has broad scope. The authors of the First Amendment knew that novel and unconventional ideas might disturb the complacent, but they chose to encourage a freedom which they believed essential if vigorous enlightenment was ever to triumph over slothful ignorance. This freedom embraces the right to distribute literature, and necessarily protects the right to receive it. The privilege may not be withdrawn even if it creates the minor nuisance for a community of clearing litter from its streets. Yet the peace, good order, and comfort of the community may imperatively require regulation of the time, place and manner of distribution. No one supposes, for example, that a city need permit a man with a communicable disease to distribute leaflets on the street or to homes, or that the First Amendment prohibits a state from preventing the distribution of leaflets in a church against the will of the church authorities.

. . . . . . . . . . . . . . . . . . .

While door to door distributors of literature may be either a nuisance or a blind for criminal activities, they may also be useful members of society engaged in the dissemination of ideas in accordance with the best tradition of free discussion. The widespread use of this method of communication by many groups espousing various causes attests its major importance. . . .

Door to door distribution of circulars is essential to the poorly financed causes of little people.

Freedom to distribute information to every citizen whenever he desires to receive it is so clearly vital to the preservation of a free society that putting aside reasonable police and health regulations of time and manner of distribution, it must be fully preserved. The dangers of distribution can so easily be controlled by traditional legal methods, leaving to each householder the full right to decide whether he will receive strangers as visitors, that stringent prohibition can serve no purpose but that forbidden by the Constitution, the naked restriction of the dissemination of ideas.

In dissent, Justice Stanley Reed considered the ordinance

an assurance of privacy that "falls far short of an abridgment of freedom of the press."

Mr. Justice REED, with whom Justices Owen ROBERTS and Robert JACKSON joined, dissenting:

While I appreciate the necessity of watchfulness to avoid abridgments of our freedom of expression, it is impossible for me to discover in this trivial town police regulation a violation of the First Amendment. No ideas are being suppressed. No censorship is involved. The freedom to teach or preach by word or book is unabridged, save only the right to call a householder to the door of his house to receive the summoner's message. I cannot expand this regulation to a violation of the First Amendment.

Freedom to distribute publications is obviously a part of the general freedom guaranteed the expression of ideas by the First Amendment. It is trite to say that this freedom of expression is not unlimited. Obscenity, disloyalty and provocatives do not come within its protection.

. . . . . . . . . . . . . . . . . . . .

The First Amendment does not compel a pedestrian to pause on the street to listen to the argument supporting another's views of religion or politics. Once the door is opened, the visitor may not insert a foot and insist on a hearing. He certainly may not enter the home. A knock or ring, however, comes close to such invasions. To prohibit such a call leaves open distribution of the notice on the street or at the home without signal to announce its deposit. Such assurance of privacy falls far short of an abridgment of the privilege of distributors and the rights of householders.

### MAGAZINE SOLICITATION IS NOT PROTECTED

Another case involving the privacy of the home came several years later and this time Justice Reed wrote the Court opinion. Commercialism is what distinguished *Martin* from *Breard*. The latter case involved the ringing of door bells to solicit subscriptions for national magazines. Municipal ordinances could prohibit door to door solicitation for this commercial purpose, the Court ruled.

BREARD V. ALEXANDRIA, 341 U.S. 622 (1951)

*Jack H. Breard of Keystone Readers Service, Inc. was arrested in Alexandria, Louisiana, soliciting subscriptions door-to-door for nationally circulated magazines. He was charged with violating an ordinance which regulated solicitors and peddlers. This ordinance declared it a nuisance to go to residences without first having been requested to do so. Breard appealed all the way to the Supreme Court, where it was held that the ordinance neither interfered with interstate commerce nor denied freedom of the press. Justice Reed argued for an adjustment of rights so that "we can have both full liberty of expression and an orderly life."*

Mr. Justice REED delivered the opinion of the Court:

First Amendment. —Finally we come to a point not heretofore urged in this Court as a ground for the invalidation of a Green River ordinance. This is that such an ordinance is an abridgment of freedom of speech and the press. Only the press or oral advocates of ideas could urge this point. It was not open to the solicitors for gadgets or brushes. The point is not that the press is free of the ordinary restraints and regulations of the modern state, such as taxation or labor regulation, referred to above at note 24, but, as stated in appellant's brief, "because the ordinance places an arbitrary, unreasonable and undue burden upon a well established and essential method of distribution and circulation of lawful magazines and periodicals and, in effect, is tantamount to a prohibition of the utilization of such method." Regulation necessarily has elements of prohibition. Thus the argument is not that the money-making activities of the solicitor entitle him to go "in or upon private residences" at will, but that the distribution of periodicals through door-to-door canvassing is entitled to First Amendment protection. This kind of distribution is said to be protected because the mere fact that money is made out of the distribution does not bar the publications from First Amendment protection. We agree that the fact that periodicals are sold does not put them beyond the protection of the First Amendment. The selling, however, brings into the transaction a commercial feature.

The First and Fourteenth Amendments have never been treated as absolutes. Freedom of speech or press does not mean that one can talk or distribute where, when and how one chooses. Rights other than those of the advocates are involved. By adjustment of rights, we can have both full liberty of expression and an orderly life.

Justices Black and William Douglas disagreed with the "adjustment of rights" view and regarded the ordinance as a clear violation of the First Amendment.

Mr. Justice BLACK, with whom Mr. Justice DOUGLAS joined, dissenting:

On May 3, 1943, this Court held that cities and states could not enforce laws which impose flat taxes on the privilege of door-to-door sales of religious literature, *Jones v. Opelika,* 319 U.S. 103; *Murdock v. Pennsylvania,* 319 U.S. 105, or which make it unlawful for persons to go from home to home knocking on doors and ringing doorbells to invite occupants to religious, political or other kinds of public meetings. *Martin v. Struthers,* 310 U.S. 141. Over strong dissents, these laws were held to invade liberty of speech, press and religion in violation of the First and Fourteenth Amendments. Today a new majority adopts the position of the former dissenters and sustains a city ordinance forbidding door-to-door solicitation of subscriptions to the *Saturday Evening Post, Newsweek* and other magazines. Since this decision cannot be reconciled with the *Jones, Murdock* and *Martin v. Struthers* cases, it seems to me that good judicial practice calls for their forthright overruling. But whether this is done or not, it should be plain that my disagreement with the majority of the Court as now constituted stems basically from a different concept of the reach of the constitutional liberty of the press rather than from any difference of opinion as to what former cases have held.

Today's decision marks a revitalization of the judicial views which prevailed before this Court embraced the philosophy that the First Amendment gives a preferred status to the liberties it protects. I adhere to that preferred position philosophy. It is my belief that the freedom of the people of this Nation cannot survive even a little governmental hobbling of religious or political ideas, whether they be communicated orally or through the press.

The constitutional sanctuary for the press must necessarily include liberty to publish and circulate. In view of our economic system, it must also include freedom to solicit paying subscribers. Of course, homeowners can if they wish forbid newsboys, reporters or magazine solicitors to ring their doorbells. But when the home-owner himself has not done this, I believe that the First Amendment, interpreted with due regard for the freedoms it guarantees, bars laws like the present ordinance which punish persons who peacefully go from door to door as agents of the press.

## HARASSMENT LIKENED TO CENSORSHIP

The Court has been alert to government activities which apparently involve the government in actions restricting operations of a free press. An official demand for the names of subscribers or persons receiving publications could be an unreasonable restriction on a publisher's right to distribute. One such case involved the Congress of the United States.

UNITED STATES V. RUMELY, 345 U.S. 41 (1953)

*A House of Representatives committee, investigating lobbyists, called Edward A. Rumely, secretary of an organization known as the Committee for Constitutional Government, to testify, and he refused to name those who made bulk purchases of his group's political books for further distribution. Rumely was convicted of contempt of Congress. The Supreme Court set aside the conviction on the technical grounds that the House resolution setting up the committee limited its investigations to lobbying activities only.*

*While agreeing that the conviction should be reversed, Justices Black and Douglas insisted the resolution was intended to vest broad powers but was unconstitutional. Justice Douglas detailed the conflicts that can arise between the investigative powers of Congress and the right of press freedom.*

Mr. Justice DOUGLAS, with whom Mr. Justice BLACK joined, concurring:

. . . Of necessity I come to the constitutional questions. Respondent represents a segment of the American press. Some may like what his group publishes; others may disapprove. These tracts may be the essence of wisdom to some; to others their point of view and philosophy may be anathema. To some ears their words may be harsh and repulsive; to others they may carry the hope of the future. We have here a publisher who through books and pamphlets seeks to reach the minds and hearts of the American people. He is different in some respects from other publishers. But the differences are minor. Like the publishers of newspapers, magazines, or books, this publisher bids for the minds of men in the market place of ideas. The aim of the historic struggle for a free press was "to establish and preserve the right of the English people to full information in respect of the doings or misdoings of their government." *Grosjean v. American Press Co.,* . . . .

If the present inquiry were sanctioned the press would be subjected to harassment that in practical effect might be as serious as censorship. A publisher, compelled to register with the Federal Government, would be subjected to vexatious inquiries. A requirement that a publisher disclose the identity of those who buy his books, pamphlets, or papers is indeed the beginning of surveillance of the press. True, no legal sanction is involved here. Congress has imposed no tax, established no board of censors, instituted no licensing system. But the potential restraint is equally severe. The finger of government leveled against the press is ominous. Once the government can demand of a publisher the names of the purchasers of his publications, the free press as we know it disappears.

Then the spectre of a government agent will look over the shoulder of everyone who reads. The purchase of a book or pamphlet today may result in a subpoena tomorrow. Fear of criticism goes with every person into the bookstall. The subtle, imponderable pressures of the orthodox lay hold. Some will fear to read what is unpopular, what the powers-that-be dislike. When the light of publicity may reach any student, any teacher, inquiry will be discouraged. The books and pamphlets that are critical of the administration, that preach an unpopular policy in domestic or foreign affairs, that are in disrepute in the orthodox school of thought will be suspect and subject to investigation. The press and its readers will pay a heavy price in harassment. But that will be minor in comparison with the menace of the shadow which government will cast over literature that does not follow the dominant party line. If the lady from Toledo can be required to disclose what she read yesterday and what she will read tomorrow, fear will take the place of freedom in the libraries, book stores, and homes of the land. Through harassment of hearings, investigations, reports and subpoenas government will hold a club over speech and over the press.

## THE RIGHT OF ANONYMOUS PUBLICATION

Some have considered a requirement that the publishers be identified to be another type of government harassment. Is there a right of anonymous publication that is an integral part of press freedom? *Talley v. California* indicated that under some circumstances there is.

TALLEY V. CALIFORNIA, 362 U.S. 60 (1960)

*Talley was prosecuted for violating a Los Angeles ordinance absolutely prohibiting the distribution of handbills which did not include the names and addresses of persons who prepared, distributed, or sponsored them. The Supreme Court concluded the Los Angeles ordinance was unconstitutional as an abridgment of free speech and press and reversed the conviction. The dissent, however, pointed out the apparent conflict with another decision upholding identification of publishers. So, apparently, the issue is not completely settled.*

*The Court opinion, through Justice Black, cited the important social and political role that anonymous publications historically have played in the progress of mankind. Persecuted groups have been able to criticize authority either anonymously or not at all. Even the Federalist Papers were published under fictitious names.*

Mr. Justice BLACK delivered the opinion of the Court:

There can be no doubt that such an identification requirement would tend to restrict freedom to distribute information and thereby freedom of expression. "Liberty of circulating is as essential to that freedom as liberty of publishing; indeed, without the circulation, the publication would be of little value." *Lovell v. Griffin*, 303 U.S. at page 452.

Anonymous pamphlets, leaflets, brochures and even books have played an important role in the progress of mankind. Persecuted groups and sects from time to time throughout history have been able to criticize oppressive practices and laws either anonymously or not at all. The obnoxious press licensing law of England, which was also enforced on the Colonies was due in part to the knowledge that exposure of the names of printers, writers and distributors would lessen the circulation of literature critical of the government. The old seditious libel cases in England show the lengths to which government had to go to find out who was responsible for books that were obnoxious to the rulers. John Lilburne was whipped, pilloried and fined for refusing to answer questions designed to get evidence to convict him or someone else for the secret distribution of books in England. Two Puritan ministers, John Penry and John Udall, were sentenced to death on charges that they were responsible for writing, printing or publishing books. Before the Revolutionary War colonial patriots frequently had to conceal their authorship or distribution of literature that easily could have brought down on them prosecutions by English-controlled courts. Along about that time the Letters of Junius were written and the identity of their author is unknown to this day. Even the Federalist Papers, written in favor of the adoption of our Constitution, were published under fictitious names. It is plain that anonymity has sometimes been assumed for the most constructive purposes.

We have recently had occasion to hold in two cases that there are times and circumstances when States may not compel members of groups engaged in the dissemination of ideas to be publicly identified. *Bates v. Little Rock*, 361 U.S. 516; *N.A.A.C.P. v. Alabama*, 357 U.S. 449. The reason for those holdings was that identification and fear of reprisal might deter perfectly peaceful discussions of public matters of importance. This broad Los Angeles ordinance is subject to the same infirmity. We hold that it, like the Griffin, Georgia, ordinance, is void on its face.

In disagreeing with Justice Black, Justice Tom Clark reminded the Court of the earlier *Lewis* case. Then the Court upheld the federal law requiring newspapers using the second-class mailing privilege to publish the names of their executives and stockholders. The question whether the newspaper classi-fication act is still good law in light of the later *Talley* decision has not yet been raised in a case before the Court.

Mr. Justice CLARK, with whom Justices Felix FRANKFURTER and Charles E. WHITTAKER joined, dissenting:

I stand second to none in supporting Talley's right of free speech—but not his freedom of anonymity. The Constitution says nothing about freedom of anonymous speech. In fact, this Court has approved laws requiring no less than Los Angeles's ordinance. I submit that they control this case and require its approval under the attack made here. First, *Lewis Publishing Co. v. Morgan*, 229 U.S. 288, upheld an Act of Congress requiring any newspaper using the second-class mails to publish the names of its editor, publisher, owner, and stockholders. Second, in the Federal Regulation of Lobbying Act, . . . Congress requires those engaged in lobbying to divulge their identities and give a "modicum of information" to Congress. *United States v. Harris*, 1954, 347 U.S. 612, 625. Third, the several States have corrupt practices acts outlawing, inter alia, the distribution of anonymous publications with reference to po-litical candidates. While these statutes are leveled at political campaign and election practices, the underlying ground sustaining their validity applies with equal force here.

No civil right has a greater claim to constitutional protection or calls for more rigorous safeguarding than voting rights. In this area the danger of coercion and reprisals—economic and otherwise—is a matter of common knowledge. Yet these statutes, disallowing anonymity in promoting one's views in election campaigns, have expressed the overwhelming public policy of the Nation. Neverthe-less the Court is silent about this impressive authority relevant to the disposition of this case.

All three of the types of statutes mentioned are designed to prevent the same abuses—libel, slander, false accusations, etc. The fact that some of these statutes are aimed at elections, lobbying, and the mails makes their restraint no more palatable, nor the abuses they prevent less deleterious to the public interest, than the present ordinance.

All that Los Angeles requires is that one who exercises his right of free speech through writing or distributing handbills identify himself just as does one who speaks from the platform. The ordi-nance makes for the responsibility in writing that is present in public utterance. When and if the application of such an ordinance in a given case encroaches on First Amendment freedoms, then will be soon enough to strike that application down. But no such re-straint has been shown here. After all, the public has some rights against which the enforcement of freedom of speech would be "harsh and arbitrary in itself." *Kovacs v. Cooper,* 336 U.S. 77, 88. We have upheld complete proscription of uninvited door-to-door canvassing as an invasion of privacy. *Breard v. Alexandria,* 341 U.S. 622. Is this less restrictive than complete freedom of distribution—regardless of content—of a signed handbill? And commercial handbills may be declared verboten, *Valentine v. Chrestensen,* 316 U.S. 52, regardless of content or identification. Is Talley's anonymous handbill, designed to destroy the business of a commercial establishment, passed out at its very front door, and attacking its then lawful commercial practices, more comportable with First Amendment freedoms? I think not. Before we may expect international responsibility among nations, might not it be well to require individual responsibility at home? Los Angeles' ordinance does not more. . . .

The right of a publisher to distribute his printed materials is recognized as an integral aspect of the broader concept of freedom of the press. Yet the conditions of distribution may be subject to legitimate local regulation in order to avoid such nuisances as littering, invasion of privacy, and intrusive solicitation. As long as local restraints regulate only the conditions of distribution and do not actually block the circulation of information and ideas, then press freedom is protected.

It may be argued that the kind of restrictions upheld against *Breard* represents a substantial diminution of press rights. But the real concern shown for the rights of distributors in *Martin, Rumely, Talley* and in Justice Black's dissent in *Breard,* indicates that the Supreme Court of the United States has consistently supported the individual's right to disseminate printed material.

*Chapter Eleven*

✺

# FREEDOM OF EXPRESSION IN GENERAL

✺

MANY IMPORTANT First Amendment decisions of the Supreme Court are not directly concerned with journalism or mass communications. However, a substantial number involves the broad principles of freedom of expression to a greater or lesser extent. Communication can take many forms. For that reason the views expressed by the Supreme Court in seemingly unrelated cases often have considerable relevance to the mass media.

The decisions in this chapter deal with various facets of human expression. The cases included here are concise and the excerpts emphasize those passages pertinent to press freedom. Those wishing a fuller treatment of each case are urged to consult the collections of reported opinions: *United States Reports, Supreme Court Reporter,* or the excellent casebook, *First Amendment Freedoms.*[1]

When reading this material, it is important to remember that freedom of speech and freedom of the press, as legal concepts, are virtually identical and synonymous.

### PICKETING AS FREE EXPRESSION

The changing conditions of urban industrialized society bring new challenges to the First Amendment. In the context of management/labor disputes, for instance, the Supreme Court has said: "Peaceful picketing is the workingman's means of communication."

[1] Milton R. Konvitz (Ithaca: Cornell University Press, 1963).

202

MILK WAGON DRIVERS UNION V. MEADOWMOOR DAIRIES, 312 U.S. 287 (1941)

*This action by the Meadowmoor Dairies, Inc., against the Milk Wagon Drivers Union of Chicago, Local 753, and others, asked that the union be enjoined from picketing stores where the dairies' products were sold and from doing violence to the stores. The Supreme Court sided with the dairies, and affirmed a permanent injunction against the union.*

Mr. Justice Felix FRANKFURTER delivered the opinion of the Court:

The starting point is *Thornhill's* case. That case invoked the constitutional protection of free speech on behalf of a relatively modern means for "publicizing, without annoyance or threat of any kind, the facts of a labor dispute." *Thornhill v. Alabama,* 310 U.S. 100 (1940). The whole series of cases defining the scope of free speech under the Fourteenth Amendment are facets of the same principle in that they all safeguard modes appropriate for assuring the right to utterance in different situations. Peaceful picketing is the workingman's means of communication.

It must never be forgotten, however, that the Bill of Rights was the child of the Enlightenment. Back of the guarantee of free speech lay faith in the power of an appeal to reason by all the peaceful means for gaining access to the mind. It was in order to avert force and explosions due to restrictions upon rational modes of communication that the guarantee of free speech was given a generous scope. But utterance in a context of violence can lose its significance as an appeal to reason and become part of an instrument of force. Such utterance was not meant to be sheltered by the Constitution.

· · · · · · · · · · · · · · · · · ·

A final word. Freedom of speech and freedom of the press cannot be too often invoked as basic to our scheme of society. But these liberties will not be advanced or even maintained by denying to the states with all their resources, including the instrumentality of their courts, the power to deal with coercion due to extensive violence. If the people of Illinois desire to withdraw the use of the injunction in labor controversies, the democratic process for legislative reform is at their disposal. On the other hand, if they choose to leave their courts with the power which they have historically exercised, within the circumscribed limits which this opinion defines, and we deny them that instrument of government, that power has been taken from them permanently. Just because these industrial conflicts raise anxious difficulties, it is most important for us not to intrude into the realm of policy-making by reading our own notions into the Constitution.

Justice Hugo Black voted with the minority and urged a greater latitude for expression.

Mr. Justice BLACK dissenting:

. . . In determining whether the injunction does deprive petitioners of their constitutional liberties, we cannot and should not lose sight of the nature and importance of the particular liberties that are at stake. And in reaching my conclusion I view the guaranties of the First Amendment as the foundation upon which our governmental structure rests and without which it could not continue to endure as conceived and planned. Freedom to speak and write about public questions is as important to the life of our government as is the heart to the human body. In fact, this privilege is the heart of government. If that heart be weakened, the result is debilitation; if it be stilled, the result is death.

In addition, I deem it essential to our federal system that the states should be left wholly free to govern within the ambit of their powers. Their deliberate governmental actions should not lightly be declared beyond their powers. For us to shear them of power not denied to them by the Federal Constitution would amount to judicial usurpation. But this Court has long since—and I think properly—committed itself to the doctrine that a state cannot, through any agency, either wholly remove, or partially whittle away, the vital individual freedoms guaranteed by the First Amendment. And in solemnly adjudicating the validity of state action touching these cherished privileges we cannot look merely at the surface of things, for were we to do so these constitutional guaranties would become barren and sterile. We must look beneath the surface, and must carefully examine each step in proceedings which lead a court to enjoin peaceful discussion.

.   .   .   .   .   .   .   .   .   .   .   .   .   .   .   .   .   .

But the injunction approved here does not stop at closing the mouths of the members of the petitioning union. It brings within its all-embracing sweep the spoken or written words of any other person "who may . . . now . . . or hereafter . . . agree or arrange with them. . . ." So, if a newspaper should "agree or arrange" with all or some of those here enjoined to publish their side of the controversy, thereby necessarily tending to "discourage" the sale of cut-rate milk, the publishers might likewise be subject to punishment for contempt. Ordinarily the scope of the decree is coextensive with the allegations of the bill, its supporting affidavits or findings of fact. In other words, the acts enjoined are the acts alleged in the bill as the basis for complaint. And the complaint on which the injunction here rests specifically charged that the union had caused "announcement to be made by the public press of the City of Chicago, for the purpose of intimidating the said storekeepers and causing them to cease purchasing the milk sold by said plaintiffs through fear and terror of the renewal of said conspiracy. . . ." Specific reference was made to these newspaper stories as appearing in the *Chicago Tribune* and the *Chicago Evening American*. Proof was made of these publications. And the injunction of the trial judge, set aside by the Supreme Court of Illinois, specifically saved to petitioners—as in effect did Justice Cardozo in the *New York* case—their right to publicize their cause by means of "advertisement or communication." But the injunction sustained here is to be issued as prayed for in the bill of complaint. And since the acts enjoined are the acts alleged in the bill as the basis for complaint, newspaper publications of the type referred to in the complaint are literally enjoined. Since the literal language of the injunction, read in the light of the complaint, the supporting evidence, and the language of the trial judge's saving clause—struck down by action sustained here—thus unconstitutionally abridges the rights of freedom of speech and press, we cannot escape our responsibility by the simple expedient of declaring that those who might be sent to jail for violating the plain language of the injunction might eventually obtain relief by appeal to this Court. To sanction vague and undefined terminologies in dragnet clauses directly and exclusively aimed at restraining freedom of discussion upon the theory that we might later acquit those convicted for violation of such terminology amounts in my judgment to a prior censorship of views. No matter how the decree might eventually be construed, its language, viewed in the light of the whole proceedings, stands like an abstract statute with an overhanging and undefined threat to freedom of speech and the press. All this, of course, is true only as to those who argue on the side of the opponents of cut-rate distribution. No such undefined threat hangs over those who "agree or arrange" with the advocates of the cut-rate system to encourage their method of distribution.

## THE FREEDOM NOT TO SPEAK

If the right of free speech includes the right to express yourself by carrying a picket sign, it also includes the right to keep silent—in this case not to salute the flag—although it took two decisions to establish that freedom.

MINERSVILLE SCHOOL DISTRICT V. GOBITIS, 310 U.S. 586 (1940)

*This was an action by members of Jehovah's Witnesses to stop school officials in Minersville, Pennsylvania, from expelling their children for refusing to salute the American flag. The Circuit Court of Appeals which granted the injunction was reversed by the Supreme Court. It ruled that a Jehovah's Witness could not constitutionally claim exemption on the ground the flag salute would violate religious beliefs and scruples. The lone dissent of Justice Harlan Stone here became the basis of the majority decision in the subsequent Barnette case.*

Mr. Justice STONE dissenting:

The guaranties of civil liberty are but guaranties of freedom of the human mind and spirit and of reasonable freedom and opportunity to express them. They pre-suppose the right of the individual to hold such opinions as he will and to give them reasonably free expression, and his freedom, and that of the state as well, to teach and persuade others by the communication of ideas. The very essence of the liberty which they guarantee is the freedom of the individual from compulsion as to what he shall think and what he shall say, at least where the compulsion is to bear false witness to his religion. If these guaranties are to have any meaning they must, I think, be deemed to withhold from the state any authority to compel belief or the expression of it where that expression violated religious convictions, whatever may be the legislative view of the desirability of such compulsion.

History teaches us that there have been but few infringements of personal liberty by the state which have not been justified, as they are here, in the name of righteousness and the public good, and few which have not been directed, as they are now, at politically helpless minorities. The framers were not unaware that under the system which they created most governmental curtailments of personal liberty would have the support of a legislative judgment that the public interest would be better served by its curtailment than by its constitutional protection. I cannot conceive that in prescribing, as limitations upon the powers of government, the freedom of the mind and spirit secured by the explicit guaranties of freedom of speech and religion, they intended or rightly could have left any latitude for a legislative judgement that the compulsory expression of belief which violates religious convictions would better serve the public interest than their protection. The Constitution may well elicit expressions of loyalty to it and to the government which it created, but it does not command such expressions or otherwise give any indication that compulsory expressions of loyalty play any such part in our scheme of government as to override the constitutional protection of freedom of speech and religion. And while such expressions of loyalty, when voluntarily given, may promote national unity, it is quite another matter to say that their compulsory expression by children in violation of their own and their parents' religious convictions can be regarded as playing so important a part in our national unity as to leave school boards free to exact it despite the constitutional guarantee of freedom of religion. The very terms of the Bill of Rights preclude, it seems to me, any reconciliation of such compulsions with the constitutional guaranties by a legislative declaration that they are more important to the public welfare than the Bill of Rights.

The *Gobitis* decision stood for three years. Then the Court dramatically overruled it.

WEST VIRGINIA STATE BOARD OF EDUCATION V. BARNETTE, 319 U.S. 624 (1943)

*The facts in the* Gobitis *and* Barnette *cases were similar: Jehovah's Witnesses sought to restrain enforcement of a regulation requiring children in public schools to salute the flag. In* Barnette, *the Court declared the compulsory flag salute an invasion of the spirit and intellect which is protected from official control by the First and Fourteenth Amendments.*

Mr. Justice Robert JACKSON delivered the opinion of the Court:

. . . The very purpose of a Bill of Rights was to withdraw certain subjects from the vicissitudes of political controversy, to place them beyond the reach of majorities and officials and to establish them as legal principles to be applied by the courts. One's right to life, liberty, and property, to free speech, a free press, freedom of worship and assembly, and other fundamental rights may not be submitted to vote; they depend on the outcome of no elections.

. . . . . . . . . . . . . . . .

Nor does our duty to apply the Bill of Rights to assertions of official authority depend upon our possession of marked competence in the field where the invasion of rights occurs. True, the task of translating the majestic generalities of the Bill of Rights, conceived as part of the pattern of liberal government in the eighteenth century, into concrete restraints on officials dealing with the problems of the twentieth century, is one to disturb self-confidence. These principles grew in soil which also produced a philosophy that the individual was the center of society, that his liberty was attainable through mere absence of governmental restraints, and that government should be entrusted with few controls and only the mildest supervision over men's affairs. We must transplant these rights to a soil in which the laissez-faire concept or principle of non-interference has withered at least as to economic affairs, and social advancements are increasingly sought through closer integration of society and through expanded and strengthened governmental controls. These changed conditions often deprive precedents of reliability and cast us more than we would choose upon our own judgment. But we act in these matters not by authority of our competence but by force of our commissions. We cannot, because of modest estimates of our competence in such specialties as public education, withhold the judgment that history authenticates as the function of this Court when liberty is infringed.

.  .  .  .  .  .  .  .  .  .  .  .  .  .  .  .  .  .  .

If there is any fixed star in our constitutional constellation it is that no official, high or petty, can prescribe what shall be orthodox in politics, nationalism, religion, or other matters of opinion or force citizens to confess by word or act their faith therein. If there are any circumstances which permit an exception, they do not now occur to us.

## FREEDOM TO SPEAK FOOLISHLY

The right not to speak, then, is part of freedom of speech; so is the right to speak foolishly when one does speak.

BAUMGARTNER V. UNITED STATES, 322 U.S. 665 (1944)

*In a wartime naturalization case involving a former citizen of the German Reich, the Supreme Court upheld the right of a person to express himself foolishly. The view has obvious relevance to some phases of journalism.*

Mr. Justice FRANKFURTER delivered the opinion of the Court:

One of the prerogatives of American citizenship is the right to criticize public men and measures—and that means not only informed and responsible criticism but the freedom to speak foolishly and without moderation. Our trust in the good sense of the people on deliberate reflection goes deep. For such is the contradictoriness of the human mind that the expression of views which may collide with cherished American ideals does not necessarily prove want of devotion to the Nation. It would be foolish to deny that even blatant intolerance toward some of the presuppositions of the democratic faith may not imply rooted disbelief in our system of government.

### FREEDOM TO USE LOUDSPEAKERS

One essential characteristic shared by all media of mass communication is that a mechanical device is involved. Some sort of machine is interposed between the communicator and his audience to reproduce any message a thousandfold—a printing press for print media or broadcasting equipment with radio or television. On this basis, street loudspeakers qualify as mass media and the free speech problems raised by their regulation have proper application to other mass media.

In the *Saia* and *Kovacs* cases, the Supreme Court, within two years, took differing positions on the freedom to use loudspeakers.

SAIA V. NEW YORK, 334 U.S. 558 (1948)

*Samuel Saia was convicted of violating a municipal ordinance governing the use of sound amplification devices. Saia, a minister of Jehovah's Witnesses, lacked the required permission from the Chief of Police to broadcast his lectures. The Supreme Court reversed the lower court conviction and Justice William O. Douglas urged local police not to unduly restrict loudspeakers.*

Mr. Justice DOUGLAS delivered the opinion of the Court:

. . . The right to be heard is placed in the uncontrolled discretion of the Chief of Police. He stands athwart the channels of communication as an obstruction which can be removed only after criminal trial and conviction and lengthy appeal. A more effective previous restraint is difficult to imagine. . . .

Loud-speakers are today indispensable instruments of effective public speech. The sound truck has become an accepted method of political campaigning. It is the way people are reached. Must a candidate for governor or the Congress depend on the whim or caprice of the Chief of Police in order to use his sound truck for campaigning? Must he prove to the satisfaction of that official that his noise will not be annoying to the people?

The present ordinance would be a dangerous weapon if it were allowed to get a hold on our public life. Noise can be regulated by regulating decibels. The hours and place of public discussion can be controlled. But to allow the police to bar the use of loud-speakers because their use can be abused is like barring radio receivers because they too make a noise. The police need not be given the power to deny a man the use of his radio in order to protect a neighbor against sleepless nights. The same is true here.

Any abuses which loud-speakers create can be controlled by narrowly drawn statutes. When a city allows an official to ban them in his uncontrolled discretion, it sanctions a device for suppression of free communication of ideas. In this case a permit is denied because some persons were said to have found the sound annoying. In the next one a permit may be denied because some people find the ideas annoying. Annoyance at ideas can be cloaked in annoyance at sound. The power of censorship interent in this type of ordinance reveals its vice.

Courts must balance the various community interests in passing on the constitutionality of local regulations of the character involved here. But in that process they should be mindful to keep the freedoms of the First Amendment in a preferred position.

Justice Frankfurter, on the other hand, warned of the perils to "cherished privacy" posed by uncontrolled loud-speakers.

Mr. Justice FRANKFURTER, with whom Justices Stanley REED and Harold BURTON joined, dissenting:

The appellant's loud speakers blared forth in a small park in a small city. The park was about 1,600 feet long and from 250 to 400 feet wide. It was used primarily for recreation, containing benches, picnic and athletic facilities, and a children's wading pool and playground. Estimates of the range of the sound equipment varied from about 200 to 600 feet. The attention of a large fraction of the area of the park was thus commanded.

The native power of human speech can interfere little with the self-protection of those who do not wish to listen. They may easily move beyond earshot, just as those who do not choose to read need not have their attention bludgeoned by undesired reading matter. And so utterances by speech or pen can neither be forbidden nor licensed, save in the familiar classes of exceptional situations. . . . But modern devices for amplifying the range and volume of the voice, or its recording, afford easy, too easy, opportunities for aural aggression. If uncontrolled, the result is intrusion into cherished privacy. The refreshment of mere silence, or meditation, or quiet conversation, may be disturbed or precluded by noise beyond one's personal control.

Municipalities have conscientiously sought to deal with the new problems to which sound equipment has given rise and have devised various methods of control to make city life endurable. Surely there is not a constitutional right to force unwilling people to listen. And so I cannot agree that we must deny the right of a State to control these broadcasting devices so as to safeguard the rights of others not to be assailed by intrusive noise but to be free to put their freedom of mind and attention to uses of their own choice.

.  .  .  .  .  .  .  .  .  .  .  .  .  .  .  .  .  .  .  .

The men whose labors brought forth the Constitution of the United States had the street outside Independence Hall covered with earth so that their deliberations might not be disturbed by passing traffic. Our democracy presupposes the deliberative process as a condition of thought and of responsible choice by the electorate. To the Founding Fathers it would hardly seem a proof of progress in the development of our democracy that the blare of sound trucks must be treated as a necessary medium in the deliberative process. In any event, it would startle them to learn that the manner and extent of the control of the blare of the sound trucks by the States of the Union, when such control is not arbitrarily and discriminatorily exercised, must satisfy what this Court thinks is the desirable scope and manner of exercising such control.

We are dealing with new technological devices and with attempts to control them in order to gain their benefits while maintaining the precious freedom of privacy. These attempts, being experimental, are bound to be tentative, and the views I have expressed are directed towards the circumstances of the immediate case. Suffice it to say that the limitations by New York upon the exercise of appellant's rights of utterance did not in my view exceed the accommodation between the conflicting interests which the State was here entitled to make in view of time and place and circumstances. . . .

A year later, the tables were turned and a dissenter in *Saia,* Justice Reed, delivered the Court opinion in a similar case.

KOVACS V. COOPER, 336 U.S. 77 (1949)

*Charles Kovacs was convicted in Trenton, New Jersey, police court for violating a city ordinance prohibiting sound-amplifying devices from making loud and raucous noises on the city streets. In this case the Supreme Court upheld the conviction.*

Mr. Justice REED delivered the opinion of the Court:

City streets are recognized as a normal place for the exchange of ideas by speech or paper. But this does not mean the freedom is beyond all control. We think it is a permissible exercise of legislative discretion to bar sound trucks with broadcasts of public interest, amplified to a loud and raucous volume, from the public ways of municipalities. On the business streets of cities like Trenton, with its more than 125,000 people, such distractions would be dangerous to traffic at all hours useful for the dissemination of information, and in the residential thoroughfares the quiet and tranquility so desirable for city dwellers would likewise be at the mercy of advocates of particular religious, social or political persuasions. We cannot believe that rights of free speech compel a municipality to allow such mechanical voice amplification on any of its streets.

The right of free speech is guaranteed every citizen that he may reach the minds of willing listeners and to do so there must be opportunity to win their attention. This is the phase of freedom of speech that is involved here. We do not think the Trenton ordinance abridges that freedom. It is an extravagant extension of due process to say that because of it a city cannot forbid talking on the streets through a loud speaker in a loud and raucous tone. Surely such an ordinance does not violate our people's "concept of ordered liberty" so as to require federal intervention to protect a citizen from the action of his own local government. Opportunity to gain the public's ears by objectionably amplified sound on the streets is no more assured by the right of free speech than is the unlimited opportunity to address gatherings on the streets. The preferred position of freedom of speech in a society that cherishes liberty for all does not require legislators to be insensible to claims by citizens to comfort and convenience. To enforce freedom of speech in disregard of the rights of others would be harsh and arbitrary in itself. That more people may be more easily and cheaply reached by sound trucks, perhaps borrowed without cost from some zealous supporter, is not enough to call forth constitutional protection for what those charged with public welfare reasonably think is a nuisance when easy means of publicity are open. Section 4 of the ordinance bars sound trucks from broadcasting in a loud and raucous manner on the streets. There is no restriction upon the communication of ideas or discussion of issues by the human voice, by newspapers, by pamphlets, by dodgers. We think that the need for reasonable protection in the homes or business houses from the distracting noises of vehicles equipped with such sound amplifying devices justifies the ordinance.

On this occasion, Justice Frankfurter was somewhat reluctant to accord to the "so-called 'mass communications'" the same protection of the First Amendment that is accorded to the human voice.

Mr. Justice FRANKFURTER concurring:

Some of the arguments made in this case strikingly illustrate how easy it is to fall into the ways of mechanical jurisprudence through the use of oversimplified formulas. It is argued that the Constitution protects freedom of speech: Freedom of speech means the right to communicate, whatever the physical means for so doing; sound trucks are one form of communication; ergo that form is entitled to the same protection as any other means of communication, whether by tongue or pen. Such sterile argumentation treats society as though it consisted of bloodless categories. The various forms of modern so-called "mass communications" raise issues that were not implied in the means of communication known or contemplated by Franklin and Jefferson and Madison. . . . Movies have created problems not presented by the circulation of books, pamphlets, or newspapers, and so the movies have been constitutionally regulated. . . . Broadcasting in turn has produced its brood of complicated problems hardly to be solved by an easy formula about the preferred position of free speech. . . .

Only a disregard of vital differences between natural speech, even of the loudest spellbinders, and the noise of sound trucks would give sound trucks the constitutional rights accorded to the unaided human voice. Nor is it for this Court to devise the terms on which sound trucks should be allowed to operate, if at all. These are matters for the legislative judgment controlled by public opinion. So long as a legislature does not prescribe what ideas may be noisily expressed and what may not be, nor discriminate among those who would make inroads upon the public peace, it is not for us to supervise the limits the legislature may impose in safeguarding the steadily narrowing opportunities for serenity and reflection. Without such opportunities freedom of thought becomes a mocking phrase, and without freedom of thought there can be no free society.

Justices Black, Douglas, and Wiley Rutledge were not willing to let Justice Frankfurter's words pass unchallenged.

Mr. Justice BLACK, with whom Justices DOUGLAS and RUTLEDGE joined, dissenting:

In my view this repudiation of the prior *Saia* opinion makes a dangerous and unjustifiable breach in the constitutional barriers designed to insure freedom of expression. Ideas and beliefs are today chiefly disseminated to the masses of people through the press, radio, moving pictures, and public address systems. To some extent at least there is competition of ideas between and within these groups. The basic premise of the First Amendment is that all present instruments of communication, as well as others that inventive genius may bring into being, shall be free from governmental censorship or prohibition. Laws which hamper the free use of some instruments of communciation thereby favor competing channels. Thus unless constitutionally prohibited, laws like this Trenton ordinance can give an overpowering influence to views of owners of legally favored instruments of communication. This favoritism, it seems to me, is the inevitable result of today's decision. For the result of today's opinion in upholding this statutory prohibition of amplifiers would surely not be reached by this Court if such channels of communication as the press, radio, or moving pictures were similarly attacked.

There are many people who have ideas that they wish to disseminate but who do not have enough money to own or control publishing plants, newspapers, radios, moving picture studios, or chains of show places. Yet everybody knows the vast reaches of these powerful channels of communication which from the very nature of our economic system must be under the control and guidance of comparatively few people. On the other hand, public speaking is done by many men of divergent minds with no centralized control over the ideas they entertain so as to limit the causes they espouse. It is no reflection on the value of preserving freedom for dissemination of the ideas of publishers of newspapers, magazines, and other literature, to believe that transmission of ideas through public speaking is also essential to the sound thinking of a fully informed citizenry.

It is of particular importance in a government where people elect their officials that the fullest opportunity be afforded candidates to express and voters to hear their views. It is of equal importance that criticism of governmental action not be limited to criticisms by press, radio, and moving pictures. In no other way except public speaking can the desirable object of widespread public discussion be assured. For the press, the radio, and the moving picture owners have their favorites, and it assumes the impossible to suppose that these agencies will at all times be equally fair as between the candidates and officials they favor and those whom they vigorously oppose. And it is an obvious fact that public speaking today without sound amplifiers is a wholly inadequate way to reach the people on a large scale. Consequently, to tip the scales against transmission of ideas through public speaking, as the Court does today, is to deprive the people of a large part of the basic advantages of the receipt of ideas that the First Amendment was designed to protect.

There is no more reason that I can see for wholly prohibiting one useful instrument of communication than another. If Trenton can completely bar the streets to the advantageous use of loud-speakers, all cities can do the same. In that event preference in the dissemination of ideas is given those who can obtain the support of newspapers, etc., or those who have money enough to buy advertising from newspapers, radios, or moving pictures. This Court should no more permit this invidious prohibition against the dissemination of ideas by speaking than it would permit a complete blackout of the press, the radio, or moving pictures. It is wise for all who cherish freedom of expression to reflect upon the plain fact that a holding that the audiences of public speakers can be constitutionally prohibited is not unrelated to a like prohibition in other fields. And the right to freedom of expression would be protected from absolute censorship for persons without, as for persons with, wealth and power. At least, such is the theory of our society.

SPEECH THAT CAN CAUSE PUBLIC DISORDER

Loudspeakers can be used by orators both to win approval from a crowd or to antagonize an angry mob and precipitate a riot. The interesting question presented by the *Terminiello* case is whether speech which causes a riot should enjoy the protection of the First Amendment.

TERMINIELLO V. CHICAGO, 337 U.S. 1 (1949)

*Terminiello's conviction for disorderly conduct followed a speech he delivered in a Chicago auditorium. Police outside were unable to prevent a number of disturbances, including rocks being thrown through windows by an angry crowd listening over a loudspeaker. Terminiello had excoriated the crowd outside but the Supreme Court, by a 5-to-4 decision, said Terminiello could not be punished.*

Mr. Justice William O. DOUGLAS delivered the opinion of the Court:

The vitality of civil and political institutions in our society depends on free discussion. Indeed, as Chief Justice Hughes wrote in *DeJonge v. Oregon*, "it is only only through free debate and free exchange of ideas that government remains responsive to the will of the people and peaceful change is effected. The right to speak freely and to promote diversity of ideas and programs is therefore one of the chief distinctions that sets us apart from totalitarian regimes."

Accordingly a function of free speech under our system of government is to invite dispute. It may indeed best serve its high purpose when it induces a condition of unrest, creates dissatisfaction with conditions as they are, or even stirs people to anger. Speech is often provocative and challenging. It may strike at prejudices and and preconceptions and have profound unsettling effects as it presses for acceptance of an idea. That is why freedom of speech, though not absolute, is nevertheless protected against censorship or punishment, unless shown likely to produce a clear and present danger of a serious substantive evil that rises far above public inconvenience, annoyance, or unrest. There is no room under our Constitution for a more restrictive view. For the alternative would lead to standardization of ideas either by legislatures, courts, or dominant political or community groups.

In one of his most famous dissents, Justice Jackson warned against condoning practices that lead to violence.

Mr. Justice JACKSON, with whom Justice BURTON joined, dissenting:

No one will disagree that the fundamental, permanent and overriding policy of police and courts should be to permit and encourage utmost freedom of utterance. It is the legal right of any American citizen to advocate peaceful adoption of fascism or communism, socialism or capitalism. He may go far in expressing sentiments whether pro-semitic or anti-semitic, pro-Negro or anti-Negro, pro-Catholic or anti-Catholic. He is legally free to argue for some anti-American system of government to supersede by constitutional methods the one we have. It is our philosophy that the course of government should be controlled by a consensus of the governed. This process of reaching intelligent popular decisions requires free discussion. Hence we should tolerate no law or custom of censorship or suppression.

But we must bear in mind also that no serious outbreak of mob violence, race rioting, lynching or public disorder is likely to get going without help of some speechmaking to some mass of people. A street may be filled with men and women and the crowd still not be a mob. Unity of purpose, passion and hatred, which merges the many minds of a crowd into the mindlessness of a mob, almost invariably is supplied by speeches. It is naive, or worse, to teach that oratory with this object or effect is a service to liberty. No mob has ever protected any liberty, even its own, but if not put down it always winds up in an orgy of lawlessness which respects no liberties.

Invocation of constitutional liberties as part of the strategy for overthrowing them presents a dilemma to a free people which may not be soluble by constitutional logic alone.

But I would not be understood as suggesting that the United States can or should meet this dilemma by suppression of free, open and public speaking on the part of any group or ideology. Suppression has never been a successful permanent policy; any surface serenity that it creates is a false security, while conspiratorial forces go underground. My confidence in American institutions and in the sound sense of the American people is such that if with a stroke of the pen I could silence every fascist and communist speaker, I would not do it. For I agree with Woodrow Wilson, who said:

"I have always been among those who believed that the greatest freedom of speech was the greatest safety, because if a man is a fool, the best thing to do is to encourage him to advertise the fact by speaking. It cannot be so easily discovered if you allow him to remain silent and look wise, but if you let him speak, the secret is out and the world knows that he is a fool. So it is by the exposure of folly that it is defeated; not by the seclusion of folly, and in this free air of free speech men get into that sort of communication with one another which constitutes the basis of all common achievement." . . .

But if we maintain a general policy of free speaking, we must recognize that its inevitable consequence will be sporadic local outbreaks of violence, for it is the nature of men to be intolerant of attacks upon institutions, personalities and ideas for which they really care. In the long run, maintenance of free speech will be more endangered if the population can have no protection from the abuses which lead to violence. No liberty is made more secure by holding that its abuses are inseparable from its enjoyment. We must not forget that it is the free democratic communities that ask us to trust them to maintain peace with liberty and that the factions engaged in this battle are not interested permanently in either. What would it matter to Terminiello if the police batter up some communists or, on the other hand, if the communists batter up some policemen? Either result makes grist for his mill; either would help promote hysteria and the demand for strong-arm methods in dealing with his adversaries. And what, on the other hand, have the communist agitators to lose from a battle with police?

This Court has gone far toward accepting the doctrine that civil liberty means the removal of all restraints from these crowds and that all local attempts to maintain order are impairments of the liberty of the citizen. The choice is not between order and liberty. It is between liberty with order and anarchy without either. There is danger that, if the Court does not temper its doctrinaire logic with a little practical wisdom, it will convert the constitutional Bill of Rights into a suicide pact.

## THE FREEDOM NOT TO LISTEN

The Court has also ruled that loudspeakers or similar electronic devices can be used even when the audience is "captive" —when it has no alternative but to listen. One such case, which conjured up visions of George Orwell's predictions in 1984, has come before the Supreme Court. Although the unprecedented situation was a fairly innocuous one, it still raised issues that moved Justice Douglas to vigorous dissent.

PUBLIC UTILITIES COMMISSION V. POLLAK, 343 U.S. 451 (1952)

*The Public Utilities Commission of the District of Columbia permitted the Capital Transit Company to broadcast on its street cars and buses radio programs consisting of 90 per cent music and 10 per cent announcements and commercial advertising. Protesting passengers carried the "captive audience" case to the Supreme Court where Justice Harold Burton, for the Court, held that such radio programs did not violate the First and Fifth Amendments. Justice Frankfurter did not participate on the ground that, "as a victim of the practice," his feelings were "so strongly engaged" that he feared his unconscious feelings might "operate in the ultimate judgment" or create the impression that they had.*

Mr. Justice BLACK delivered a separate concurring opinion:

I concur in the Court's holding that this record shows no violation of the Due Process Clause of the Fifth Amendment. I also agree that Capital Transit's musical programs have not violated the First Amendment. I am of the opinion, however, that subjecting Capital Transit's passengers to the broadcasting of news, public speeches, views, or propaganda of any kind and by any means would violate the First Amendment. To the extent, if any, that the Court holds the contrary, I dissent.

Mr. Justice DOUGLAS dissenting:

This is a case of first impression. There are no precedents to construe; no principles previously expounded to apply. We write on a clean slate.

The case comes down to the meaning of "liberty" as used in the Fifth Amendment. Liberty in the constitutional sense must mean more than freedom from unlawful governmental restraint; it must include privacy as well, if it is to be a repository of freedom. The right to be let alone is indeed the beginning of all freedom. Part of our claim to privacy is in the prohibition of the Fourth Amendment against unreasonable searches and seizures. It gives the guarantee that a man's home is his castle beyond invasion either by inquisitive or by officious people. A man loses that privacy, of course, when he goes upon the streets or enters public places. But even in his activities outside the home he has immunities from controls bearing on privacy. He may not be compelled against his will to attend a religious service; he may not be forced to make an affirmation or observe a ritual that violates his scruples; he may not be made to accept one religious, political, or philosophical creed as against another. Freedom of religion and freedom of speech guaranteed by the First Amendment give more than the privilege to worship, to write, to speak as one chooses; they give freedom not to do nor to act as the government chooses. The First Amendment in its respect for the conscience of the individual honors the sanctity of thought and belief. To think as one chooses, to believe what one wishes are important aspects of the constitutional right to be let alone.

If we remembered this lesson taught by the First Amendment, I do not believe we would construe "liberty" within the meaning of the Fifth Amendment as narrowly as the Court does. The present case involves a form of coercion to make people listen. The listeners are of course in a public place; they are on streetcars traveling to and from home. In one sense it can be said that those who ride the streetcars do so voluntarily. Yet in a practical sense they are forced to ride, since this mode of transportation is today essential for many thousands. Compulsion which comes from circumstances can be as real as compulsion which comes from a command.

The streetcar audience is a captive audience. It is there as a matter of necessity, not of choice. One who is in a public vehicle may not of course complain of the noise of the crowd and the babble of tongues. One who enters any public place sacrifices some of his privacy. My protest is against the invasion of his privacy over and beyond the risks of travel.

The government may use the radio (or television) on public vehicles for many purposes. Today it may use it for a cultural end. Tomorrow it may use it for political purposes. So far as the right of privacy is concerned the purpose makes no difference. The music selected by one bureaucrat may be as offensive to some as it is soothing to others. The news commentator chosen to report on the events of the day may give overtones to the news that please the bureau head but which rile the streetcar captive audience. The political philosophy which one radio speaker exudes may be thought by the official who makes up the streetcar programs to be best for the welfare of the people. But the man who listens to it on his way to work in the morning and on his way home at night may think it marks the destruction of the Republic.

One who tunes in on an offensive program at home can turn it off or tune in another station, as he wishes. One who hears disquieting or unpleasant programs in public places, such as restaurants, can get up and leave. But the man on the streetcar has no choice but to sit and listen, or perhaps to sit and to try not to listen.

When we force people to listen to another's ideas, we give the propagandist a powerful weapon. Today it is a business enterprise working out a radio program under the auspices of government. Tomorrow it may be a dominant political or religious group. Today the purpose is benign; there is no invidious cast to the programs. But the vice is inherent in the system. Once privacy is invaded, privacy is gone. Once a man is forced to submit to one type of radio program, he can be forced to submit to another. It may be but a short step from a cultural program to a political program.

If liberty is to flourish, government should never be allowed to force people to listen to any radio program. The right of privacy should include the right to pick and choose from competing entertainments, competing propaganda, competing political philosophies. If people are let alone in those choices, the right of privacy will pay dividends in character and integrity. The strength of our system is in the dignity, the resourcefulness, and the independence of our people. Our confidence is in their ability as individuals to make the wisest choice. That system cannot flourish if regimentation takes hold. The right of privacy, today violated, is a powerful deterrent to any one who would control men's minds.

It is apparent that the Supreme Court faces perplexing problems when it tries to cope with the free speech issues raised by circumstances which, as Justice Frankfurter said, "were not implied in the means of communication known or contemplated by Franklin and Jefferson and Madison."

Organized labor's use of picketing as a form of expression gave a new dimension to free speech. The right to keep silent as upheld in the flag salute cases implies that there is also a right not to publish. And the *Pollak* "captive audience" case suggests that there is a right not to listen. Both are part of the broad concept of the right of privacy.

Street loudspeakers have great potential as nuisances and

privacy invaders in our crowded urban societies, and so are subject to legitimate regulation. But a loudspeaker, just as a radio transmitter or a printing press, may be an essential medium of expression and thus deserving of constitutional protection.

The *Terminiello* case, and the issue it raised of speech that incites violence, was relevant to the often violent controversies of the 1960's, when protests crossed the line from legal expression to illegal obstruction, or when peaceful protesters were themselves confronted by those who would deny their right to speak.

Probably more than any other, this chapter illustrates the complex new situations the Supreme Court has faced in adjudicating claims to free expression. In the adjustments that result, sometimes free expression seems to expand, sometimes it seems to diminish. It usually, however, gets a hearing.

*Chapter Twelve*

✸

# FREEDOM OF MOTION PICTURES

✸

MOTION PICTURES have been a major mass medium in America for the greatest part of this century but only since mid-century have they begun to enjoy the constitutional protection accorded to expression in print. Because of the movies' primary concern with entertainment and their presumed ability to influence the young, efforts to attain full freedom of expression have been thwarted by the exertion of police power of the states and cities under the purpose of protecting the health and morals of their citizens.

The old problem of prior restraint or censorship, apparently settled once and for all for newspapers by the *Near* case has long been an issue with motion pictures. The Supreme Court itself is split over the question of whether the First Amendment permits any prior restraint of motion pictures.

The Court's attitude toward films was for many years determined by the *Mutual Film Corporation* decision of 1915[1] which denied the protection of the First Amendment to a medium it regarded as a "business, pure and simple, originated and conducted for profit." This position prevailed until 1952.

## MOTION PICTURES PROTECTED BY FIRST AMENDMENT

In 1952, the famous *Miracle* case overturned the *Mutual Film Corporation* case, and the Supreme Court ruled for the first time that motion pictures were protected by the First

[1] *Mutual Film Corp. v. Ohio*, 236 U.S. 230 (1915).

Amendment. However, the Court did not outlaw censorship if exercised within narrowly defined boundaries; this matter was left open.

BURSTYN V. WILSON, 343 U.S. 495 (1952)

> *The Italian-made film,* The Miracle, *was denied a license in New York State on the ground that it was "sacrilegious." The Supreme Court held that freedom of speech and press prevented a state censor from banning a film on such a standard. Using a "sacrilegious test," the Court argued, might conflict with the Constitution's guaranty of separation between church and state with freedom of worship for all. Also, as Justice Tom Clark wrote: "It is not the business of government in our nation to suppress real or imagined attacks upon a particular religious doctrine, whether they appear in publications, speeches, or motion pictures."*

Mr. Justice CLARK delivered the opinion of the Court:

As we view the case, we need consider only appellant's contention that the New York statute is an unconstitutional abridgment of free speech and a free press. In *Mutual Film Corp. v. Ohio,* . . . a distributor of motion pictures sought to enjoin the enforcement of an Ohio statute which required the prior approval of a board of censors before any motion picture could be publicly exhibited in the state, and which directed the board to approve only such films as it adjudged to be "of a moral, educational, or amusing and harmless character." The statute was assailed in part as an unconstitutional abridgment of the freedom of the press guaranteed by the First and Fourteenth Amendments. The District Court rejected this contention, stating that the first eight Amendments were not a restriction of state action. . . . On appeal to this Court, plaintiff in its brief abandoned this claim and contended merely that the statute in question violated the freedom of speech and publication guaranteed by the Constitution of Ohio. In affirming the decree of the District Court denying injunctive relief, this Court stated:

"It cannot be put out of view that the exhibition of moving pictures is a business, pure and simple, originated and conducted for profit, like other spectacles, not to be regarded, not intended to be regarded by the Ohio Constitution, we think, as part of the press of the country, or as organs of public opinion."

In a series of decisions beginning with *Gitlow v. New York,* . . . this Court held that the liberty of speech and of the press which the First Amendment guarantees against abridgment by the federal government is within the liberty safeguarded by the Due Process Clause of the Fourteenth Amendment from invasion by state action. That principle has been followed and reaffirmed to the present day. Since this series of decisions came after the *Mutual* decision, the present case is the first to present squarely to us the question whether motion pictures are within the ambit of protection which the First Amendment, through the Fourteenth, secures to any form of "speech" or "the press."

It cannot be doubted that motion pictures are a significant medium for a communication of ideas. They may affect public attitudes and behavior in a variety of ways, ranging from direct espousal of a political or social doctrine to the subtle shaping of thought which characterizes all artistic expression. The importance of motion pictures as an organ of public opinion is not lessened by the fact that they are designed to entertain as well as to inform. As was said in *Winters v. New York*, 1948, 333 U.S. 507:

"The line between the informing and the entertaining is too elusive for the protection of that basic right [a free press]. Everyone is familiar with instances of propaganda through fiction. What is one man's amusement, teaches another's doctrine."

It is urged that motion pictures do not fall within the First Amendment's aegis because their production, distribution, and exhibition is a large-scale business conducted for private profit. We cannot agree. That books, newspapers, and magazines are published and sold for profit does not prevent them from being a form of expression whose liberty is safeguarded by the First Amendment. We fail to see why operation of profit should have any different effect in the case of motion pictures.

It is further urged that motion pictures possess a greater capacity for evil, particularly among the youth of a community, than other modes of expression. Even if one were to accept this hypothesis, it does not follow that motion pictures should be disqualified from First Amendment protection. If there be capacity for evil it may be relevant in determining the permissible scope of community control, but it does not authorize substantially unbridled censorship such as we have here.

For the foregoing reasons, we conclude that expression by means of motion pictures is included within the free speech and free press guaranty of the First and Fourteenth Amendments. To the extent that language in the opinion in *Mutual Film Corp. v. Ohio,* is out of harmony with the views here set forth, we no longer adhere to it.

To hold that liberty of expression by means of motion pictures is guaranteed by the First and Fourteenth Amendments, however, is not the end of our problem. It does not follow that the Constitution requires absolute freedom to exhibit every motion picture of every kind at all times and all places. That much is evident from the series of decisions of this Court with respect to other media of communication of ideas. Nor does it follow that motion pictures are necessarily subject to the precise rules governing any other particular method of expression. Each method tends to present its own peculiar problems. But the basic principles of freedom of speech and the press, like the First Amendment's command, do not vary. Those principles, as they have frequently been enunciated by this Court, make freedom of expression the rule. There is no justification in this case for making an exception to that rule.

The statute involved here does not seek to punish, as a past offense, speech or writing falling within the permissible scope of subsequent punishment. On the contrary, New York requires that permission to communicate ideas be obtained in advance from state officials who judge the content of the words and pictures sought to be communicated. This Court recognized many years ago that such a previous restraint is a form of infringement upon freedom of expression to be especially condemned. *Near v. Minnesota, . . .* The Court there recounted the history which indicates that a major purpose of the First Amendment guaranty of a free press was to prevent prior restraints upon publication, although it was carefully pointed out that the liberty of the press is not limited to that protection. It was further stated that "the protection even as to previous restraint is not absolutely unlimited. But the limitation has been recognized only in exceptional cases." . . .

In seeking to apply the broad and all-inclusive definition of "sacrilegious" given by the New York courts, the censor is set adrift upon a boundless sea amid a myriad of conflicting currents of religious views, with no charts but those provided by the most vocal and powerful orthodoxies. New York cannot vest such unlimited restraining control over motion pictures in a censor. . . . Under such a standard, the most careful and tolerant censor would find it virtually impossible to avoid favoring one religion over another, and he would be subject to an inevitable tendency to ban the expression of unpopular sentiments sacred to a religious minority. Application of the "sacrilegious" test, in these and other respects, might raise substantial questions under the First Amendment's guaranty of separate church and state with freedom of worship for all. However, from the standpoint of freedom of speech and the press, it is enough to point out that the state has no legitimate interest in protecting any or all religions from views distasteful to them which is sufficient to justify prior restraints upon the expression of those views. It is not the business of government in our nation to suppress real or imagined attacks upon a particular religious doctrine, whether they appear in publications, speeches, or motion pictures.

Since the term "sacrilegious" is the sole standard under attack here, it is not necessary for us to decide, for example, whether a state may censor motion pictures under a clearly drawn statute designed and applied to prevent the showing of obscene films. That is a very different question from the one now before us. We hold only that under the First and Fourteenth Amendments a state may not ban a film on the basis of a censor's conclusion that it is "sacrilegious."

## ANY FILM CENSORSHIP IS CALLED UNCONSTITUTIONAL

Other movie censorship cases followed soon after the *Miracle* decision. Two consistent positions in these cases were those of Justices Hugo Black and William O. Douglas, who opposed the censorship of any medium.

### SUPERIOR FILMS V. OHIO, 346 U.S. 587 (1954)

*In this case, an Ohio court banned the American film* M *on the ground it was "tending to promote crime." On appeal from the Ohio Supreme Court, the U.S. Supreme Court in a per curiam decision reversed the Ohio courts, citing the* Miracle *case as precedent.*

*Justices Black and Douglas used a concurring opinion to state their position that any censorship of motion pictures is repugnant to the First Amendment.*

Mr. Justice DOUGLAS, with whom Mr. Justice BLACK agreed, concurring:

The argument of Ohio and New York that the government may establish censorship over moving pictures is one I cannot accept. In 1925 Minnesota passed a law aimed at suppressing before publication any "malicious, scandalous and defamatory newspaper." The Court, speaking through Chief Justice Hughes, struck down that law as violating the Fourteenth Amendment, which had made the First Amendment applicable to the States. *Near v. Minnesota.* . . . The "chief purpose" of the constitutional guaranty of liberty of the press, said the Court, was "to prevent previous restraints upon publication." . . .

The history of censorship is so well known it need not be summarized here. Certainly a system, still in force in some nations, which required a newspaper to submit to a board its news items, editorials, and cartoons before it published them could not be sustained. Nor could book publishers be required to submit their novels, poems, and tracts to censors for clearance before publication. Any such scheme of censorship would be in irreconcilable conflict with the language and purpose of the First Amendment.

Nor is it conceivable to me that producers of plays for the legitimate theatre or for television could be required to submit their manuscripts to censors on pain of penalty for producing them without approval. Certainly the spoken word is as freely protected against prior restraints as that which is written. Such indeed is the force of our decision in *Thomas v. Collins,* 323 U.S. 516. The freedom of the platform which it espouses carries with it freedom of the stage.

The same result in the case of motion pictures necessarily follows as a consequence of our holding in *Joseph Burstyn, Inc. v. Wilson,* . . . that motion pictures are "within the free speech and free press guaranty of the First and Fourteenth Amendments."

Motion pictures are of course a different medium of expression than the public speech, the radio, the stage, the novel, or the magazine. But the First Amendment draws no distinction between the various methods of communicating ideas. On occasion one may be more powerful or effective than another. The movie, like the public speech, radio, or television is transitory—here now and gone in an instant. The novel, the short story, the poem in printed form are permanently at hand to reenact the drama or to retell the story over and again. Which medium will give the most excitement and have the most enduring effect will vary with the theme and the actors. It is not for the censor to determine in any case. The First and the Fourteenth Amendments say that Congress and the States shall make "no law" which abridges freedom of speech or of the press. In order to sanction a system of censorship I would have to say that "no law" does not mean what it says, that "no law" is qualified to mean "some" laws. I cannot take that step.

In this Nation every writer, actor, or producer, no matter what medium of expression he may use, should be free from the censor.

## THE RIGHT TO ADVOCATE UNPOPULAR IDEAS

Many of the persons who have censored motion pictures in America have tended to confuse obscenity with unpopular ideas or with minority viewpoints. Under the First Amendment, obscenity is not protected but unpopular ideas are. In a notable 1959 decision, the Court distinguished between the two.

KINGSLEY INTERNATIONAL PICTURES V. REGENTS OF NEW YORK, 360 U.S. 684 (1959)

*This proceeding contested the New York Regents' refusal of a license to show the film,* Lady Chatterley's Lover. *The*

*New York statute required denial of a license to films which "portray acts of sexual immorality as desirable, acceptable or proper patterns of behavior or which present adultery as being right and desirable for certain people under certain circumstances." These provisions, the U.S. Supreme Court held, violated the distributor's constitutional rights. The lower court decision was reversed. This case illustrated the Supreme Court's close scrutiny of the standards the censor uses to judge films.*

*Discussing what has been called "ideological obscenity," Justice Potter Stewart outlined how such censorship strikes at the heart of the First Amendment which encompasses the right to advocate ideas, however unpopular or even immoral they may be.*

Mr. Justice STEWART delivered the opinion of the Court:

. . . What New York has done, therefore, is to prevent the exhibition of a motion picture because that picture advocates an idea—that adultery under certain circumstances may be proper behavior. Yet the First Amendment's basic guarantee is of freedom to advocate ideas. The State, quite simply, has thus struck at the very heart of constitutionally protected liberty.

It is contended that the State's action was justified because the motion picture attractively portrays a relationship which is contrary to the moral standards, the religious precepts, and the legal code of its citizenry. This argument misconceives what it is that the Constitution protects. Its guarantee is not confined to the expression of ideas that are conventional or shared by a majority. It protects advocacy of the opinion that adultery may sometimes be proper, no less than advocacy of socialism or the single tax. And in the realm of ideas it protects expression which is eloquent no less than that which is unconvincing.

Advocacy of conduct proscribed by law is not, as Mr. Justice Brandeis long ago pointed out, "a justification for denying free speech where the advocacy falls short of incitement and there is nothing to indicate that the advocacy would be immediately acted on." *Whitney v. California,* . . . "Among free men, the deterrents ordinarily to be applied to prevent crime are education and punishment for violations of the law, not abridgment of the rights of free speech. . . ."

The inflexible command which the New York Court of Appeals has attributed to the State Legislature thus cuts so close to the core of constitutional freedom as to make it quite needless in this case to examine the periphery. Specifically, there is no occasion to consider the appellant's contention that the State is entirely without power to require films of any kind to be licensed prior to their exhibition. Nor need we here determine whether, despite problems peculiar to motion pictures, the controls which a State may impose upon this medium of expression are precisely coextensive with those allowable for newspapers, books, or individual speech. It is enough for the present case to reaffirm that motion pictures are within the First and Fourteenth Amendments' basic protection.

Reversed.

Justice Black, condemning any kind of censorship, warned the Court of the problems it would face if it decided to uphold film censorship.

Mr. Justice BLACK concurring:

I concur in the Court's opinion and judgment but add a few words because of concurring opinions by several Justices who rely on their appraisal of the movie *Lady Chatterley's Lover* for holding that New York cannot constitutionally bar it. Unlike them, I have not seen the picture. My view is that stated by Mr. Justice Douglas, that prior censorship of moving pictures like prior censorship of newspapers and books violates the First and Fourteenth Amendments. If despite the Constitution, however, this Nation is to embark on the dangerous road of censorship, my belief is that this Court is about the most inappropriate Supreme Board of Censors that could be found. So far as I know, judges possess no special expertise providing exceptional competency to set standards and to supervise the private morals of the Nation. In addition, the Justices of this Court seem especially unsuited to make the kind of value judgments—as to what movies are good or bad for local communities—which the concurring opinions appear to require. We are told that the only way we can decide whether a State or municipality can constitutionally bar movies is for this Court to view and appraise each movie on a case-by-case basis. Under these circumstances, every member of the Court must exercise his own judgment as to how bad a picture is, a judgment which is ultimately based at least in large part on his own standard of what is immoral. The end result of such decisions seems to me to be a purely personal determination by individual Justices as to whether a particular picture viewed is too bad to allow it to be seen by the public. Such an individualized determination cannot be guided by reasonably fixed and certain standards. Accordingly, neither States nor moving picture makers can possibly know in advance, with any fair degree of certainty, what can or cannot be done in the field of movie making and exhibiting. This uncertainty cannot easily be reconciled with the rule of law which our Constitution envisages.

The different standards which different people may use to decide about the badness of pictures are well illustrated by the contrasting standards mentioned in the opinion of the New York Court of Appeals and the concurring opinion of Mr. Justice Frankfurter here. As I read the New York Court's opinion this movie was held immoral and banned because it makes adultery too alluring. Mr. Justice Frankfurter quotes Mr. Lawrence, author of the book from which the movie was made, as believing censorship should be applied only to publications that make sex look ugly, that is, as I understand it, less alluring.

In my judgment, this Court should not permit itself to get into the very center of such policy controversies, which have so little in common with lawsuits.

But Justice Felix Frankfurter saw a legitimate place for censorship under the Constitution.

Mr. Justice FRANKFURTER concurring:

It is not surprising, therefore, that the pertinacious, eloquent and free-spirited promoters of the liberalizing legislation in Great Britain did not conceive the needs of a civilized society, in assuring the utmost freedom to those who make literature and art possible—authors, artists, publishers, producers, book sellers—easily attainable by sounding abstract and unqualified dogmas about freedom. They had a keen awareness that freedom of expression is no more an absolute than any other freedom, an awareness that is reflected in the opinions of Mr. Justice Holmes and Mr. Justice Brandeis, to whom we predominantly owe the present constitutional safeguards on behalf of freedom of expression. . . .

In short, there is an evil against which a State may constitutionally protect itself, whatever we may think about the questions of policy involved. The real problem is the formulation of constitutionally allowable safeguards which society may take against evil without impinging upon the necessary dependence of a free society upon the fullest scope of free expression. One cannot read the debates in the House of Commons and the House of Lords and not realize the difficulty of reconciling these conflicting interests, in the framing of legislation on the ends of which there was agreement, even for those who most generously espouse that freedom of expression without which all freedom gradually withers.

Justice Douglas, however, said British law had little relevance for our situation.

Mr. Justice DOUGLAS, with whom Mr. Justice BLACK joined, concurring:

While I join in the opinion of the Court, I adhere to the views expressed in *Superior Films Inc. v. Ohio,* . . . that censorship of movies is unconstitutional, since it is a form of "previous restraint" that is as much at war with the First Amendment, made applicable to the States through the Fourteenth, as the censorship struck down in *Near v. Minnesota,* . . . If a particular movie violates a valid law, the exhibitor can be prosecuted in the usual way. I can find in the First Amendment no room for any censor whether he is scanning an editorial, reading a news broadcast, editing a novel or a play, or previewing a movie.

Reference is made to British law and British practice. But they have little relevance to our problem, since we live under a written Constitution. What is entrusted to the keeping of the legislature in England is protected from legislative interference or regulation here. As we stated in *Bridges v. California* . . . , "No purpose in ratifying the Bill of Rights was clearer than that of securing for the people of the United States much greater freedom of religion, expression, assembly, and petition than the people of Great Britain had ever enjoyed." If we had a provision in our Constitution for "reasonable" regulation of the press such as India has included in hers, there would be room for argument that censorship in the interests of morality would be permissible. Judges sometimes try to read the word "reasonable" into the First Amendment or make the rights it grants subject to reasonable regulation . . . . But its language, in terms that are absolute, is utterly at war with censorship. Different questions may arise as to censorship of some news when the Nation is actually at war. But any possible exceptions are extremely limited. That is why the tradition represented by *Near v. Minnesota* . . . , represents our constitutional ideal.

Happily government censorship has put down few roots in this country. The American tradition is represented by *Near v. Minnesota.* . . . We have in the United States no counterpart of the Lord Chamberlain who is censor over England's stage. As late as 1941 only six States had systems of censorship for movies. That number has now been reduced to four—Kansas, Maryland, New York, and Virginia—plus a few cities. Even in these areas, censorship of movies shown on television gives way by reason of the Federal Communications Act. . . . And from what information is available, movie censors do not seem to be very active. Deletion of the residual part of censorship that remains would constitute the elimination of an institution that intrudes on First Amendment rights.

## NO ABSOLUTE FREEDOM TO EXHIBIT MOTION PICTURES

The *Kingsley* decision was one of a series which accorded movies broader freedom of expression. But there was a setback in 1961 in the *Times Film* ruling which was widely criticized by professional and trade organizations in motion pictures, broadcasting, and the press.

TIMES FILM CORP. V. CHICAGO, 365 U.S. 43 (1961)

*This suit was brought by a film distributor to restrain Chicago officials from interfering with the showing of the motion picture* Don Juan. *Times Film Corporation refused to submit the picture for previewing to obtain a license, and was thus prohibited from showing it. The content of the film itself, which was considered innocuous, was never an issue. The district court dismissed the complaint and an appeal was taken. The Court of Appeals affirmed. The U.S. Supreme Court held that there is no complete and absolute freedom to exhibit, even once, any and every kind of motion picture. It held that the Chicago ordinance, requiring submission of films for examination by city officials as a prerequisite to granting a permit for public exhibition, was not a prior restraint in First and Fourteenth Amendment terms. The appeals court action was affirmed by a 5-to-4 decision of the Supreme Court.*

Mr. Justice CLARK delivered the opinion of the Court:

Petitioner's narrow attack upon the ordinance does not require that any consideration be given to the validity of the standards set out therein. They are not challenged and are not before us. Prior motion picture censorship cases which reached this Court involved questions of standards. The films had all been submitted to the authorities and permits for their exhibition were refused because of their content. Obviously, whether a particular statute is "clearly drawn," or "vague," or "indefinite," or whether a clear standard is in fact met by a film are different questions involving other constitutional challenges to be tested by considerations not here involved.

Moreover, there is not a word in the record as to the nature and content of *Don Juan*. We are left entirely in the dark in this regard, as were the city officials and the other reviewing courts. Petitioner claims that the nature of the film is irrelevant, and that even if this film contains the basest type of pornography, or incitement to riot, or forceful overthrow of orderly government, it may nonetheless be shown without prior submission for examination. The challenge here is to the censor's basic authority; it does not go to any statutory standards employed by the censor or procedural requirements as to the submission of the film.

In this perspective we consider the prior decisions of this Court touching on the problem. Beginning over a third of a century ago in *Gitlow v. New York* . . . , they have consistently reserved for future decision possible situations in which the claimed First Amendment privilege might have to give way to the necessities of the public welfare. It has never been held that liberty of speech is absolute. Nor has it been suggested that all previous restraints on speech are invalid. On the contrary, in *Near v. Minnesota* . . . , Chief Justice Hughes, in discussing the classic legal statements concerning the immunity of the press from censorship, observed that the principle forbidding previous restraint "is stated too broadly, if every such restraint is deemed to be prohibited. . . . The protection even as to previous restraint is not absolutely unlimited. But the limitation has been recognized only in exceptional cases." These included, the Chief Justice found, utterances creating "a hinderance" to the Government's war effort, and "actual obstruction to its recruiting service or the publication of the sailing dates of transports or the number and location of troops." In addition, the Court said that "the primary requirements of decency may be enforced against obscene publications" and the "security of the community life may be protected against incitements to acts of violence and the overthrow by force of orderly government." Some years later, a unanimous Court, speaking through Mr. Justice Murphy, in *Chaplinsky v. New Hampshire*, 1942, 315 U.S. 568, held that there were "certain well-defined and narrowly limited classes of speech, the prevention and punishment of which have never been thought to raise any Constitutional problem. These include the lewd and obscene, the profane, the libelous, and the insulting or 'fighting' words—those which by their very utterance inflict injury or tend to incite an immediate breach of the peace." Thereafter, as we have mentioned, in *Joseph Burstyn, Inc., v. Wilson*, we found motion pictures to be within the guarantees of the First and Fourteenth Amendments, but we added that this was "not the end of our problem. It does not follow that the Constitution requires absolute freedom to exhibit every motion picture of every kind at all times and all places." Five years later, in *Roth v. United States*, . . . we held that "in light of . . . history, it is apparent that the unconditional phrasing of the First Amendment was not intended to protect every utterance." Even those in dissent there found that "Freedom of expression can be supressed if, and to the extent that, it is so closely brigaded with illegal action as to be an inseparable part of it." . . . And, during the same Term, in *Kingsley Books, Inc. v. Brown*, after characterizing *Near v. Minnesota* . . . , as "one of the landmark opinions" in its area, we took notice that *Near* "left no doubts that 'liberty of speech, and of the press, is also not an absolute right . . . the protection even as to previous restraint is not absolutely unlimited."

. . . "The judicial angle of vision," we said there, in testing the validity of a statute like (paragraph) 22-a (New York's injunctive remedy against certain forms of obscenity) is "the operation and effect of the statute in substance." And as if to emphasize the point involved here, we added that "The phrase 'prior restraint' is not a self-wielding sword. Nor can it serve as a talismanic test." Even as recently as our last Term we again observed the principle, albeit in an allied area, that the State possesses some measure of power "to prevent the distribution of obscene matter." *Smith v. California.* . . .

The long and brilliant dissent of Chief Justice Earl Warren presented a compelling argument against film censorship. With one more vote, his views would have been accepted as the Court's position. Censorship of movies, he argued, posed a direct threat to all media of communication.

Mr. Justice WARREN, with whom Justices BLACK, DOUGLAS, and William J. BRENNAN joined, dissenting:

I cannot agree either with the conclusion reached by the Court or with the reasons advanced for its support. To me, this case clearly presents the question of our approval of unlimited censorship of motion pictures before exhibition through a system of administrative licensing. Moreover, the decision presents a real danger of eventual censorship for every form of communication, be it newspapers, journals, books, magazines, television, radio or public speeches. The Court purports to leave these questions for another day, but I am aware of no constitutional principle which permits us to hold that the communication of ideas through one medium may be censored while other media are immune. Of course each medium presents its own peculiar problems, but they are not of the kind which would authorize the censorship of one form of communication and not others. I submit that in arriving at its decision the Court has interpreted our cases contrary to the intention at the time of their rendition and, in exalting the censor of motion pictures, has endangered the First and Fourteenth Amendment rights of all others engaged in the dissemination of ideas. . . .

Examination of the background and circumstances leading to the adoption of the First Amendment reveals the basis for the Court's steadfast observance of the proscription of licensing, censorship and previous restraint of speech. Such inquiry often begins with Blackstone's assertion: "The liberty of the press is indeed essential to the nature of a free state; but this consists in laying no previous restraint upon publications, and not in freedom from censure for criminal matter when published." . . . Blackstone probably here referred to the common law's definition of freedom of the press; he probably spoke of the situation existing in England after the disappearance of the licensing systems but during the existence of the law of crown libels. There has been general criticism of the theory that Blackstone's statement was embodied in the First Amendment, the objection being "that the mere exception from previous restraints cannot be all that is secured by the constitutional provisions"; and that "the liberty of the press might be rendered a mockery and a delusion, and the phrase itself a by-word, if, while every man was at liberty to publish what he pleased, the public authorities might nevertheless punish him for harmless publications." . . . The objection has been that Blackstone's definition is too narrow; it had been generally conceded that the protection of the First Amendment extends at least to the interdiction of licensing and censorship and to the previous restraint of free speech. . . .

On June 24, 1957, in *Kingsley Books, Inc. v. Brown* . . . , the Court turned a corner from the landmark opinion in *Near* and from one of the bases of the First Amendment. Today it falls into full retreat.

.   .   .   .   .   .   .   .   .   .   .   .   .   .   .   .   .   .   .   .

A most distinguished antagonist of censorship, in "a plea for unlicensed printing," has said:

"If he [the censor] be of such worth as behoovs him, there cannot be a more tedious and unpleasing Journey-work, a greater loss of time livied upon his head, then to be made the perpetuall reader of unchosen books and pamphlets. . . . we may easily forsee what kind of licensers we are to expect hereafter, either ignorant, imperious, and remisse, or basely pecuniary." *Areopagitica* in the *Complete Poetry and Selected Prose of John Milton.* . . .

There is no sign that Milton's fear of the censor could be dispelled in twentieth century America. The Censor is beholden to those who sponsored the creation of his office, to those who are most radically preoccupied with the suppression of communication. The censor's function is to restrict and to restrain; his decisions are insulated from the pressures that might be brought to bear by public sentiment if the public were given an opportunity to see that which the censor has curbed.

The censor performs free from all the procedural safeguards afforded litigants in a court of law. . . . The likelihood of a fair and impartial trial disappears when the censor is both prosecutor and judge. There is a complete absence of rules of evidence; the fact is that there is usually no evidence at all as the system at bar vividly illustrates. How different from a judicial proceeding where a full case is presented by the litigants. The inexistence of a jury to determine contemporary community standards is a vital flaw. . . .

A revelation of the extent to which censorship has recently been used in this country is indeed astonishing. The Chicago licensors have banned newsreel films of Chicago policemen shooting at labor pickets and have ordered the deletion of a scene depicting the birth of a buffalo in Walt Disney's *Vanishing Prairie*. . . . Before World War II, the Chicago censor denied licenses to a number of films portraying and criticizing life in Nazi Germany including the March of Time's *Inside Nazi Germany*. . . . Recently, Chicago refused to issue a permit for the exhibition of the motion picture *Anatomy of a Murder* based on the best-selling novel of the same title, because it found the use of the words "rape" and "contraceptive" to be objectionable. . . . The Chicago censor bureau excised a scene in *Street With No Name* in which a girl was slapped because this was thought to be a "too violent" episode. . . . *It Happened in Europe* was severely cut by the Ohio censors who deleted scenes of war orphans resorting to violence. The moral theme of the picture was that such children could even then be saved by love, affection and satisfaction of their basic needs for food. . . . The Memphis censors banned *The Southerner* which dealt with poverty among tenant farmers because "it reflects on the south." *Brewster's Millions,* an innocuous comedy of fifty years ago, was recently forbidden in Memphis because the radio and film character Rochester, a Negro, was deemed "too familiar." . . . Maryland censors restricted a Polish documentary film on the basis that it failed to present a true picture of modern Poland. . . . *No Way Out,* the story of a Negro doctor's struggle against race prejudice, was banned by the Chicago censor on the ground that "there's a possibility it could cause trouble." The principal objection to the film was that the conclusion showed no reconciliation between blacks and whites. The ban was lifted after a storm of protest and later deletion of a scene showing Negroes and whites arming for a gang fight. . . . Memphis banned *Curley* because it contained scenes of white and Negro children in school together. . . . Atlanta barred *Lost Boundaries,* the story of a Negro physician and his family who "passed" for white, on the ground that the exhibition of said picture "will adversely affect the peace, morals and good order" in the city. . . .

An early version of *Carmen* was condemned on several different grounds. The Ohio censor objected because cigarette-girls smoked cigarettes in public. The Pennsylvania censor disapproved the duration of a kiss. . . . The New York censors forbade the discussion in films of pregnancy, venereal disease, eugenics, birth control, abortion, illegitimacy, prostitution, miscegenation and divorce. . . . A member of the Chicago censor board explained that she rejected a film because "it was immoral, corrupt, indecent, against my . . . religious principles. . . . A police sergeant attached to the censor board explained, "Coarse language or anything that would be derogatory to the government—propaganda" is ruled out of foreign films. "Nothing pink or red is allowed," he said. . . . The police sergeant in charge of the censor unit has said: "Children should be allowed to see any movie that plays in Chicago. If a picture is objectionable for a child, it is objectionable, period." . . . And this is but a smattering produced from limited research.

.   .   .   .   .   .   .   .   .   .   .   .   .   .   .   .   .   .

Freedom of speech and freedom of the press are further endangered by this "most effective" means for confinement of ideas. It is axiomatic that the stroke of the censor's pen or the cut of his scissors will be a less contemplated decision than will be the prosecutor's determination to prepare a criminal indictment. The standards of proof, the judicial safeguards afforded a criminal defendant and the consequences of bringing such charges will all provoke the mature deliberation of the prosecutor. None of these hinder the quick judgment of the censor, the speedy determination to suppress. Finally, the fear of the censor by the composer of ideas acts as a substantial deterrent to the creation of new thoughts. . . . This is especially true of motion pictures due to the large financial burden that must be assumed by their producers. The censor's sword pierces deeply into the heart of free expression.

It seems to me that the Court's opinion comes perilously close to holding that not only may motion pictures be censored but that a licensing scheme may also be applied to newspapers, books and periodicals, radio, television, public speeches, and every other medium of expression. The Court suggests that its decision today is limited to motion pictures by asserting that they are not "necessarily subject to the precise rules governing any other particular method of expression. Each method . . . tends to present its own peculiar problems. . . ." But, this, I believe, is the invocation of a talismanic phrase. The Court, in no way, explains why moving pictures should be treated differently than any other form of expression, why moving pictures should be denied the protection against censorship—"a form of infringement upon freedom of expression to be especially condemned. . . ." When pressed during oral argument, counsel for the city could make no meaningful distinction between the censorship of newspapers and motion pictures. In fact, the percentage of motion pictures dealing with social and political issues is steadily rising. The Chicago ordinance makes no exception for newsreels, documentaries, instructional and educational films or the like. All must undergo the censor's inquisition. Nor may it be suggested that motion pictures may be treated differently from newspapers because many movies are produced essentially for purposes of entertainment. . . .

"The contention may be advanced that the impact of motion pictures is such that a licensing system of prior censorship is permissible. There are several answers to this, the first of which I think is the Constitution itself. Although it is an open question whether the impact of motion pictures is greater or less than that of other media, there is not much doubt that the exposure of television far exceeds that of the motion picture. . . . But, even if the impact of the motion picture is greater than that of some other media, that fact constitutes no basis for the argument that motion pictures should be subject to greater suppression. This is the traditional argument made in the censor's behalf; this is the argument advanced against newspapers at the time of the invention of the printing press. The argument was ultimately rejected in England, and has consistently been held to be contrary to our Constitution. No compelling reason has been presented for accepting the contention now.

.   .   .   .   .   .   .   .   .   .   .   .   .   .   .   .   .   .

The Court, not the petitioner, makes the "broadside attack." I would reverse the decision below.

Justice Douglas supported this with a historical review of the dangers of censorship.

Mr. Justice DOUGLAS, with whom Justices WARREN and BLACK joined dissenting:

While the problem of movie censorship is relatively new, the censorship device is an ancient one. It was recently stated, "There is a law of action and reaction in the decline and resurgence of censorship and control. Whenever liberty is in the ascendant, a social group will begin to resist it; and when the reverse is true, a similar resistance in favor of liberty will occur." Haney, *Comstockery in America* (1960) pp. 11–12.

Whether or not that statement of history is accurate, censorship has had many champions throughout time.

SOCRATES: "And shall we just carelessly allow children to hear any casual tales which may be devised by casual persons, and to receive into their minds ideas for the most part the very opposite of those which we should wish them to have when they are grown up?"

GLAUCON: "We can not."

SOCRATES: "Then the first thing will be to establish a censorship of the writers of fiction, and let the censors receive any tale of fiction which is good, and reject the bad; and we will desire mothers and nurses to tell their children the authorized ones only. Let them fashion the mind with such tales, even more fondly than they mould the mody with their hands; but most of those which are now in use must be discarded." Plato, *Republic* . . . .

Hobbes was the censor's proponent: ". . . it is annexed to the sovereignty, to be judge of what opinions and doctrines are averse, and what conducing to peace; and consequently, on what occasions, how far, and what men are to be trusted withal, in speaking to multitudes of people; and who shall examine the doctrines of all books before they are published. For the actions of men proceed from their opinions; and in the well-governing of opinions, consisteth the well-governing of men's actions, in order to their peace, and concord." *Leviathan* . . . .

Regimes of censorship are common in the world today. Every dictator has one; every Communist regime finds it indispensable. One shield against world opinion that colonial powers have used was the censor, as dramatized by France in North Africa. Even England has a vestige of censorship in the Lord Chamberlain . . . who presides over the stage—a system that in origin was concerned with the barbs of political satire shifted to a concern with atheism and with sexual morality—the last being the concern evident in Chicago's system now before us.

The problems of the wayward mind concern the clerics, the psychiatrists, and the philosophers. Few groups have hesitated to create the political pressures that translate into secular law their notions of morality. . . . No more powerful weapon for sectarian control can be imagined than governmental censorship. Yet in this country the state is not the secular arm of any religious school of thought, as in some nations; nor is the church an instrument of the state. Whether—as here—city officials or—as in Russia—a political party lays claim to the power of governmental censorship, whether the pressures are for a conformist moral code or for a conformist political ideology, no such regime is permitted by the First Amendment.

The forces that build up demands for censorship are heterogeneous.

"The Comstocks are not merely people with intellectual theories who might be convinced by more persuasive theories; nor are they pragmatists who will be guided by the balance of power among pressure groups. Many of them are so emotionally involved in the condemnation of what they find objectionable that they find rational arguments irrelevant. They must suppress what is offensive in order to stabilize their own tremulous values and consciences. Panic rules them, and they cannot be calmed by discussions of legal rights, literary integrity, or artistic merit." . . .

Yet as long as the First Amendment survives, the censor, no matter how respectable his cause, cannot have the support of government. It is not for government to pick and choose according to the standards of any religious, political, or philosophical group. It is not permissible, as I read the Constitution, for government to release one movie and refuse to release another because of an official's concept of the prevailing need or the public good. The Court in *Near v. Minnesota,* . . . said that the "chief purpose" of the First Amendment's guarantee of freedom of press was "to prevent previous restraints upon publication."

A noted Jesuit has recently stated one reason against government censorship:

"The freedom toward which the American people are fundamentally orientated is a freedom under God, a freedom that knows itself to be bound by the imperatives of the moral law. Antecedently it is presumed that a man will make morally and socially responsible use of his freedom of expression; hence there is to be no prior restraint on it. However, if his use of freedom is irresponsible, he is summoned after the fact to responsibility before the judgment of the law. There are indeed other reasons why prior restraint on communications is outlawed; but none are more fundamental than this." Murray, *We Hold These Truths* (1960), pp. 164–165.

Experience shows other evils of "prior restraint." The regime of the censor is deadening. One who writes cannot afford entanglements with the man whose pencil can keep his production from the market. The result is a pattern of conformity. Milton made the point long ago: "For though a licenser should happen to be judicious more than ordinarily, which will be a great jeopardy of the next succession, yet his very office, and his commission enjoins him to let pass nothing but what is vulgarly received already." *Areopagitica* . . . .

Another evil of censorship is the ease with which the censor can erode liberty of expression. One stroke of the pen is all that is needed. Under a censor's regime the weights are cast against freedom. If, however, government must proceed against an illegal publication in a prosecution, then the advantages are on the other side. All the protections of the Bill of Rights come into play. The presumption of innocence, the right to jury trial, proof of guilt beyond a reasonable doubt—these become barriers in the path of officials who want to impose their standard of morality on the author or producer. The advantage a censor enjoys while working as a supreme bureaucracy disappears. The public trial to which a person is entitled who violated the law gives a hearing on the merits, airs the grievance, and brings the community judgment to bear upon it. If a court sits in review of a censor's ruling, its function is limited. There is leeway left the censor, who like any agency and its expertise, is given a presumption of being correct. That advantage disappears when the government must wait until a publication is made and then prove its case in the accepted manner before a jury in a public trial. All of this is anathema to the censor who prefers to work in secret, perhaps because, as Milton said, he is "either ignorant, imperious, and remisse, or basely pecuniary." *Areopagitica.* . . .

The First Amendment was designed to enlarge, not to limit, freedom in literature and in the arts as well as in politics, economics, law, and other fields. . . . Its aim was to unlock all ideas for argument, debate, and dissemination. No more potent force in defeat of that freedom could be designed than censorship. It is a weapon that no minority or majority group, acting through government, should be allowed to wield over any of us.

By 1964, the composition of the Court had changed; both Justice Frankfurter and Justice Charles E. Whittaker, who voted with the majority in the *Times Film Corporation* case, had left the court. And in that year in another film censorship decision, *Jacobellis v. Ohio,* the Court whittled away still more of the authority of cities and states to censor motion pictures.

## NATIONAL STANDARD MUST BE USED IN OBSCENITY CASES

The *Jacobellis* case involved the French film, *The Lovers,* and the Court upheld the obscenity standard set forth in *Roth* —"whether to the average person, applying contemporary community standards, the dominant theme of the material taken as a whole appeals to prurient interest." Indeed, it went further, saying ". . . the constitutional status of an allegedly obscene work must be determined on the basis of a national standard. It is, after all, a national Constitution we are expounding." This stand weakened the position of local and state censorship groups seeking to ban books, magazines, and motion pictures on the basis of their own local community standards.

JACOBELLIS *v.* OHIO, 378 U.S. 184 (1964)

*Nico Jacobellis, manager of a movie house in Cleveland Heights, Ohio, was convicted in the Court of Common Pleas of Cuyahoga County, Ohio, of possessing and exhibiting an obscene film in violation of the Ohio obscenity law. His conviction was upheld by an intermediate Ohio appellate court and the Supreme Court of Ohio. The U.S. Supreme Court questioned whether the state courts used proper standards to decide that the motion picture* The Lovers *was obscene and therefore not entitled to the free expression guarantees of the First and Fourteenth Amendments. The Court concluded the film was not obscene and reversed the judgment.*

Mr. Justice BRENNAN delivered the opinion of the Court:

Motion pictures are within the ambit of the constitutional guarantees of freedom of speech and of the press. But in *Roth v. United States* and *Alberts v. California,* . . . we held that obscenity is not subject to those guarantees. Application of an obscenity law to suppress a motion picture thus requires ascertainment of the "dim and uncertain line" that often separates obscenity from constitutionally protected expression. It has been suggested that this is a task in which our Court need not involve itself. We are told that the determination whether a particular motion picture, book, or other work of expression is obscene can be treated as a purely factual judgment on which a jury's verdict is all but conclusive, or that in any event the decision can be left essentially to state and lower federal courts, with this Court exercising only a limited review such as that needed to determine whether the ruling below is supported by "sufficient evidence." The suggestion is appealing, since it would lift from our shoulders a difficult, recurring, and unpleasant task. But we cannot accept it. Such an abnegation of judicial supervision in this field would be inconsistent with our duty to uphold the constitutional guarantees. Since it is only "obscenity" that is excluded from the constitutional protection, the question whether a particular work is obscene necessarily implicates an issue of constitutional law. Such an issue, we think, must ultimately be decided by this Court. Our duty admits of no "substitute for facing up to the tough individual problems of constitutional judgment involved in every obscenity case." *Roth v. United States* . . . .

The question of proper standard for making this determination has been the subject of much discussion and controversy since our decision in *Roth-Alberts* seven years ago. Recognizing that the test for obscenity enunciated there—"whether to the average person, applying contemporary community standards, the dominant theme of the material taken as a whole appeals to prurient interest," is not perfect, we think any substitute would raise equally difficult problems, and we therefore adhere to that standard. We would reiterate, however, our recognition in *Roth* that obscenity is excluded from the constitutional protection only because it is "utterly without redeeming social importance," and that "the portrayal of sex, e.g., in art, literature and scientific works, is not itself sufficient reason to deny material the constitutional protection of freedom of speech and press." *Id.,* . . . It follows that material dealing with sex in a manner that advocates ideas, or that has literary or scientific or artistic value or any other form of social importance, may not be branded as obscenity and denied the constitutional protection. Nor may the constitutional status of the material be made to turn on a "weighing" of its social importance against its prurient appeal, for a work cannot be proscribed unless it is "utterly" without social importance. . . .

It has been suggested that the "contemporary community standards" aspect of the *Roth* test implies a determination of the constitutional question of obscenity in each case by the standards of the particular local community from which the case arises. This is an incorrect reading of *Roth*.

.  .  .  .  .  .  .  .  .  .  .  .  .  .  .  .  .  .  .

We do not see how any "local" definition of the "community" could properly be employed in delineating the area of expression that is protected by the Federal Constitution. Mr. Justice Harlan pointed out in *Manual Enterprises, Inc. v. Day*, 370 U.S. at 488, that a standard based on a particular local community would have "the intolerable consequence of denying some sections of the country access to material, there deemed acceptable, which in others might be considered offensive to prevailing community standards of decency." It is true that *Manual Enterprises* dealt with the federal statute banning obscenity from the mails. But the mails are not the only means by which works of expression cross local-community lines in this country. It can hardly be assumed that all the patrons of a particular library, bookstand, or motion picture theater are residents of the smallest local "community" that can be drawn around that establishment. Furthermore, to sustain the suppression of a particular book or film in one locality would deter its dissemination in other localities where it might be held not obscene, since sellers and exhibitors would be reluctant to risk criminal conviction in testing the variation between the two places. It would be a hardy person who would sell a book or exhibit a film anywhere in the land after this Court had sustained the judgment of one "community" holding it to be outside the constitutional protection. The result would thus be "to restrict the public's access to forms of the printed word which the State could not constitutionally suppress directly." *Smith v. California* . . . .

It is true that local communities throughout the land are in fact diverse, and that in cases such as this one the Court is confronted with the task of reconciling the rights of such communities with the rights of individuals. Communities vary, however, in many respects other than their toleration of alleged obscenity, and such variances have never been considered to require or justify a varying standard for application of the Federal Constitution. The Court has regularly been compelled, in reviewing criminal convictions challenged under the Due Process Clause of the Fourteenth Amendment, to reconcile the conflicting rights of the local community which brought the prosecution and of the individual defendant. Such a task is admittedly difficult and delicate, but it is inherent in the Court's duty of determining whether a particular conviction worked a deprivation of rights guaranteed by the Federal Constitution. The Court has not shrunk from discharging that duty in other areas, and we see no reason why it should do so here. The Court has explicitly refused to tolerate a result whereby "the constitutional limits of free expression in the Nation would vary with state lines," *Pennekamp v. Florida*, . . . we see even less justification for allowing such limits to vary with town or county lines. We thus reaffirm the position taken in *Roth* to the effect that the constitutional status of an allegedly obscene work must be determined on the basis of a national standard. It is, after all, a national Constitution we are expounding.

We recognize the legitimate and indeed exigent interest of States and localities throughout the Nation in preventing the dissemination of material deemed harmful to children. But that interest does not justify a total suppression of such material, the effect of which would be to "reduce the adult population . . . to reading only what is fit for children." *Butler v. Michigan*, 352 U.S. 380. State and local authorities might well consider whether their objectives in this area would be better served by laws aimed specifically at preventing distribution of objectionable material to children, rather than at totally prohibiting its dissemination. Since the present conviction is based upon exhibition of the film to the public at large and not upon its exhibition to children, the judgment must be reviewed under the strict standard applicable in determining the scope of the expression that is protected by the Constitution.

We have applied that standard to the motion picture in question. *The Lovers* involves a woman bored with her life and marriage who abandons her husband and family for a young archaeologist with whom she has suddenly fallen in love. There is an explicit love scene in the last reel of the film, and the State's objections are based almost entirely upon that scene. The film was favorably reviewed in a number of national publications, although disparaged in others, and was rated by at least two critics of national stature among the best films of the year in which it was produced. It was shown in approximately 100 of the larger cities in the United States, including Columbus and Toledo, Ohio. We have viewed the film, in the light of the record made in the trial court, and we conclude that it is not obscene within the standards enunciated in *Alberts v. California* and *Roth v. United States,* which we reaffirm here.

Reversed.

Justice Stewart pointed out a marked trend in obscenity decisions.

Mr. Justice STEWART concurring:

It is possible to read the Court's opinion in *Alberts v. California* and *Roth v. United States*, . . . in a variety of ways. In saying this, I imply no criticism of the Court, which in those cases was faced with the task of trying to define what may be indefinable. I have reached the conclusion, which I think is confirmed at least by negative implication in the Court's decisions since *Roth* and *Alberts*, that under the First and Fourteenth Amendments criminal laws in this area are constitutionally limited to hard-core pornography. I shall not today attempt further to define the kinds of material I understand to be embraced within that shorthand description; and perhaps I could never succeed in intelligibly doing so. But I know it when I see it, and the motion picture involved in this case is not that.

### MOVIE CENSORSHIP IS FURTHER RESTRICTED

In a 1965 decision, the Supreme Court made it even more difficult for the official censor to review films before the public has an opportunity to see them. The *Freedman* decision below dealt mainly with legal procedures and not philosophical pronouncements but the effect was to curtail even further the movie censor's authority. In the mid-1960's official prior censorship of motion pictures was fast disappearing. As a friend of the court in *Freedman,* the American Civil Liberties Union pointed out that New York, Virginia, and Kansas were the only states with statutes similar to that of Maryland and also that Chicago, Detroit, Fort Worth, and Providence were the only cities with ordinances similar to that of Maryland. The *Freedman* decision necessarily affected those censorship laws as well as Maryland's.

FREEDMAN V. MARYLAND, 380 U.S. 51 (1965)

*Ronald L. Freedman, a Baltimore theater operator, was convicted in Baltimore Criminal Court of publicly exhibiting a film before submitting it to the board of censors. The Supreme Court held that the procedural aspects of Maryland's movie censorship law didn't contain adequate safeguards against undue restrictions on protected expression. This was because (1) if the censor disapproved a film, it was up to the exhibitor to start judicial proceedings and prove the film was protected expression; (2) once the board had acted against a film, it could not be exhibited until after judicial review, no matter how protracted; and (3) the law contained no assurance of a prompt judicial decision. For these reasons, the conviction was unanimously reversed.*

Mr. Justice BRENNAN delivered the opinion of the Court:

Appellant sought to challenge the constitutionality of the Maryland motion picture censorship statute, and exhibited the film *Revenge at Daybreak* at his Baltimore theatre without first submitting the picture to the State Board of Censors as required by the statute. The State concedes that the picture does not violate the statutory standards and would have received a license if properly submitted, but the appellant was convicted of a violation despite his contention that the statute in its entirety unconstitutionally impaired freedom of expression. The Court of Appeals of Maryland affirmed, and we noted probable jurisdiction. We reverse. . . .

The administration of a censorship system for motion pictures presents peculiar dangers to constitutionally protected speech. Unlike a prosecution for obscenity, a censorship proceeding puts the initial burden on the exhibitor or distributor. Because the censor's business is to censor, there inheres the danger that he may well be less responsible than a court—part of an independent branch of government—to the constitutionally protected interests in free expression. And if it is made unduly onerous, by reason of delay or otherwise, to seek judicial review, the censor's determination may in practice be final.

Applying the settled rule of our cases, we hold that a non-criminal process which requires the prior submission of a film to a censor avoids constitutional infirmity only if it takes place under procedural safeguards designed to obviate the dangers of a censorship system. First, the burden of proving that the film is unprotected expression must rest on the censor. As we said in *Speiser v. Randall*, 357 U.S. 513, "Where the transcendent value of speech is involved due process certainly requires . . . that the State bear the burden of persuasion to show that the appellants engaged in criminal speech." Second, while the State may require advance submission of all films, in order to proceed effectively to bar all showings of unprotected films, the requirement cannot be administered in a manner which would lend an effect of finality to the censor's determination whether a film constitutes protected expression. The teaching of our cases is that, because only a judicial determination in an adversary proceeding ensures the necessary sensitivity to freedom of expression, only a procedure requiring a judicial determination suffices to impose a valid final restraint. To this end, the exhibitor must be assured, by statute or authoritative judicial construction, that the censor will, within a specified brief period, either issue a license or go to court to restrain showing the film. Any restraint imposed in advance of a final judicial determination on the merits must similarly be limited to preservation of the status quo for the shortest fixed period compatible with sound judicial resolution. Moreover, we are well aware that, even after expiration of a temporary restraint, an administrative refusal to license, signifying the censor's view that the film is unprotected, may have a discouraging effect on the exhibitor. Therefore, the procedure must also assure a prompt final judicial decision, to minimize the deterrent effect of an interim and possibly erroneous denial of a license.

Without these safeguards, it may prove too burdensome to seek review of the censor's determination. Particularly in the case of motion pictures, it may take very little to deter exhibition in a given locality. The exhibitor's stake in any one picture may be sufficient to warrant a protracted and onerous course of litigation. The distributor, on the other hand, may be equally unwilling to accept the burdens and delays of litigation in a particular area when, without such difficulties, he can freely exhibit his film in most of the rest of the country; for we are told that only four States and a handful of municipalities have active censorship laws.

It is readily apparent that the Maryland procedural scheme does not satisfy these criteria. First, once the censor disapproves the film, the exhibitor must assume the burden of instituting judicial proceedings and of persuading the courts that the film is protected expression. Second, once the Board has acted against a film, exhibition is prohibited pending judicial review, however protracted. Under the statute, appellant could have been convicted if he had shown the film after unsuccessfully seeking a license, even though no court had ever ruled on the obscenity of the film. Third, it is abundantly clear that the Maryland statute provides no assurance of prompt judicial determination. We hold, therefore, that appellant's conviction must be reversed. The Maryland scheme fails to provide adequate safeguards against undue inhibition of protected expression, and this renders the requirement of prior submission of films to the Board an invalid previous restraint.

How or whether Maryland is to incorporate the required procedural safeguards in the statutory scheme is, of course for the State to decide. But a model is not lacking: In *Kingsley Books, Inc. v. Brown*, 354 U.S. 436, we upheld a New York injunctive procedure designed to prevent the sale of obscene books. That procedure postpones any restraint against sale until a judicial determination of obscenity following notice and an adversary hearing. The statute provides for a hearing one day after joinder of issue; the judge must hand down his decision within two days after termination of the hearing. The New York procedure operates without prior submission to a censor, but the chilling effect of a censorship order, even one which requires judicial action for its enforcement, suggests all the more reason for expeditious determination of the question whether a particular film is constitutionally protected.

The requirement of prior submission to a censor sustained in *Times Film* is consistent with our recognition that films differ from other forms of expression. Similarly, we think that the nature of the motion picture industry may suggest different time limits for a judicial determination. It is common knowledge that films are scheduled well before actual exhibition, and the requirement of advance submission recognizes this. One possible scheme would be to allow the exhibitor or distributor to submit his film early enough to ensure an orderly final disposition of the case before the scheduled exhibition date—far enough in advance so that the exhibitor could safely advertise the opening on a normal basis. Failing such a scheme or sufficiently early submission under such a scheme, the statute would have to require adjudication considerably more prompt than has been the case under the Maryland statute. Otherwise, litigation might be unduly expensive and protracted, or the victorious exhibitor might find the most propitious opportunity for exhibition past. We do not mean to lay down rigid time limits or procedures, but to suggest considerations in drafting legislation to accord with local exhibition practices, and in doing so to avoid the potentially chilling effect of the Maryland statute on protected expression.

Reversed.

Mr. Justice DOUGLAS, with whom Mr. Justice BLACK joined, concurring:

On several occasions I have indicated my views that movies are entitled to the same degree and kind of protection under the First Amendment as other forms of expression. For the reasons there stated, I do not believe any form of censorship—no matter how speedy or prolonged it may be—is permissible. As I see it, a pictorial presentation occupies as preferred a position as any other form of expression. If censors are banned from the publishing business, from the pulpit, from the public platform—as they are—they should be banned from the theatre. I would not admit the censor even for the limited role accorded him in *Kingsley Books, Inc. v. Brown,* 354 U.S. 436. I adhere to my dissent in that case. Any authority to obtain a temporary injunction gives the State "the paralyzing power of a censor." The regime of Kingsley Books "substitutes punishment by contempt for punishment by jury trial." I would put an end to all forms and types of censorship and give full literal meaning to the command of the First Amendment.

The Court has not yet adopted the views of Justices Black and Douglas on censorship, but in *Freedman,* as in *Jacobellis,* it moved much closer to them. In the series of motion picture censorship decisions from the *Miracle* case to *Freedman,* the Supreme Court persistently cut away the props of local and state movie censorship.

One can argue that in a permissive age, the Court was merely responding to social and intellectual pressures by allowing greater freedom (and license) in motion pictures. A more likely explanation, however, is that the Court was following the logic and precedents of its own earlier decisions, and was belatedly moving to give movies the same protection from prior restraint that another medium of expression, the printed word, had long enjoyed.

The Court is still struggling with the problem of establishing a clear and workable definition of obscenity; but aside from obscenity, the day appears to be past when a motion picture can be pre-censored because it propounds a viewpoint that some person or persons consider to be immoral, blasphemous, or against the public interest. We may have arrived at a point where all expression—whether printed, filmed, videotaped, or broadcast—will be judged privileged to enjoy the same freedom and the same constitutional protection.

*Chapter Thirteen*

❖

# FREEDOM OF BROADCASTING

❖

THE BROADCASTING of news and public information on radio and television has become a major means of informing the American people about their government and the world. Television particularly has had a dramatic impact on journalism as well as politics. Unquestionably, more Americans today get more of their news first from television than from any other source. Authorities agree, however, that the broadcasting media really complement rather than displace printed news.

Since a portion of its programming is devoted to news, ideas, and public information, broadcasting is entitled to the protection of the First Amendment. The basic federal law that regulates U.S. broadcasters—the Communications Act of 1934—specifically states in Sec. 326:

> Nothing in this Act shall be understood or construed to give the Federal Communications Commission the power of censorship over the radio communications or signals transmitted by any radio station, and no regulation or condition shall be promulgated or fixed by the Commission which shall interfere with the right of free speech by means of radio communication.

The problem of implementing this protection has concerned the Supreme Court, the Congress, and the Federal Communications Commission (FCC)—the body set up by Congress to regulate broadcasting through the Communications Act.

For a number of technical reasons, broadcasting, of course,

must be regulated by government. But how is the FCC to conduct this necessary regulation without at the same time interfering with program content and thereby violating the admonishment of the First Amendment that "Congress shall make no law . . . abridging freedom of speech or of the press?"

Although the FCC itself decides most of broadcasting's legal questions, the Supreme Court of the United States is the final arbiter on matters involving the FCC's powers over broadcasting. The following cases illustrate how the Court has decided basic constitutional issues arising between broadcasters and the FCC.

## "PUBLIC INTEREST, CONVENIENCE, OR NECESSITY" IS THE STANDARD

In *FCC v. Pottsville,* Justice Felix Frankfurter discussed the intention of Congress in passing the Communications Act of 1934 and in vesting licensing powers in the Federal Communications Commission.

FEDERAL COMMUNICATIONS COMMISSION V. POTTSVILLE BROADCASTING COMPANY, 309 U.S. 134 (1940)

*This was a proceeding by the Pottsville Broadcasting Company against the FCC to obtain a permit to build a radio broadcasting station. An important aspect of this case was the Supreme Court ruling that while the FCC must act according to its standard of "public interest, convenience or necessity," it does not have unlimited power.*

Mr. Justice FRANKFURTER delivered the opinion of the Court:

We are called upon to ascertain and enforce the spheres of authority which Congress has given to the Commission and the courts, respectively, through its scheme for the regulation of radio broadcasting in the Communications Act of 1934. . . .

Adequate appreciation of the facts presently to be summarized requires that they be set in their legislative framework. In its essentials the Communications Act of 1934 derives from the Federal Radio Act of 1927, c. 169, 44 Stat. 1162, as amended, 46 Stat. 844. By this Act Congress, in order to protect the national interest involved in the new and far-reaching science of broadcasting, formulated a unified and comprehensive regulatory system for the industry. The common factors in the administration of the various statutes by which Congress had supervised the different modes of communication led to the creation in the Act of 1934, of the Communications Commission. But the objectives of the legislation have remained substantially unaltered since 1927.

Congress moved under the spur of a wide-spread fear that in the absence of governmental control the public interest might be subordinated to monopolistic domination in the broadcasting field. To avoid this Congress provided for a system of permits and licenses. Licenses were not to be granted for longer than three years. . . . No license was to be "construed to create any right, beyond the terms, conditions, and periods of the license." In granting or withholding permits for the construction of stations, and in granting, denying, modifying or revoking licenses for the operation of stations, "public convenience, interest, or necessity" was the touchstone for the exercise of the Commission's authority. While this criterion is as concrete as the complicated factors for judgment in such a field of delegated authority permit, it serves as a supple instrument for the exercise of discretion by the expert body which Congress has charged to carry out its legislative policy. Necessarily, therefore, the subordinate questions of procedure in ascertaining the public interest, when the Commission's licensing authority is invoked—the scope of the inquiry, whether applications should be heard contemporaneously or successively, whether parties should be allowed to intervene in one another's proceedings, and similar questions—were explicitly and by implication left to the Commission's own devising, so long, of course, as it observes the basic requirements designed for the protection of private as well as public interest. Underyling the whole law is recognition of the rapidly fluctuating factors characteristic of the evolution of broadcasting and of the corresponding requirement that the administrative process possess sufficient flexibility to adjust itself to these factors. Thus, it is highly significant that although investment in broadcasting stations may be large, a license may not be issued for more than three years; and in deciding whether to renew the license, just as in deciding whether to issue it in the first place, the Commission must judge by the standard of "public convenience, interest, or necessity." The Communications Act is not designed primarily as a new code for the adjustment of conflicting private rights through adjudication. Rather it expresses a desire on the part of Congress to maintain, through appropriate administrative control, a grip on the dynamic aspects of radio transmission.

## FCC REGULATION NEED NOT VIOLATE FREE EXPRESSION

The broadcasting industry has sometimes chafed under the regulations imposed by the Federal Communications Commission. The major challenge to the FCC's legal authority came in the early 1940's.

NATIONAL BROADCASTING CO. V. UNITED STATES, 319 U.S. 190 (1943)

*The National Broadcasting Company protested a number of licensing criteria—the Chain Broadcasting Regulations—established by the FCC. For example, Regulation 3.101 dealt with exclusive affiliation of stations. It read:*

No license shall be granted to a standard broadcast station having any contract, arrangement, or understanding, express or implied, with a network organization under which the station is prevented or hindered from or penalized for, broadcasting the programs of any other network organization.

*The Supreme Court found that the establishment of these regulations was a reasonable exercise of authority by the FCC. Expanding on his* Pottsville *decision, Justice Frankfurter explained how freedom of expression is accommodated under the necessary federal regulation of broadcasting.*

*"Freedom of utterance," he admitted, "is abridged to many who wish to use the limited facilities of radio. Unlike other modes of expression, it is subject to governmental regulation. Because it cannot be used by all, some who use it must be denied."*

*But as long as licenses are granted only on the basis of "public interest, convenience, or necessity," which serves the broad interests of free expression, and without consideration of the applicants' political, social, or economic views, denial of a station license is not a denial of free speech. This view has been considered a definitive legal explanation of how the necessary regulation of broadcasting by government can be squared with the requirements of free expression.*

Mr. Justice FRANKFURTER delivered the opinion of the Court:

The Act itself establishes that the Commission's powers are not limited to the engineering and technical aspects of regulation of radio communication. Yet we are asked to regard the Commission as a kind of traffic officer, policing the wave lengths to prevent stations from interfering with each other. But the Act does not restrict the Commission merely to supervision of the traffic. It puts upon the Commission the burden of determining the composition of that traffic. The facilities of radio are not large enough to accommodate all who wish to use them. Methods must be devised for choosing from among the many who apply. And since Congress itself could not do this, it committed the task to the Commission.

The Commission was, however, not left at large in performing this duty. The touchstone provided by Congress was the "public interest, convenience, or necessity," a criterion which "is as concrete as the complicated factors for judgment in such a field of delegated authority permit. . . ." "This criterion is not to be interpreted as setting up a standard so indefinite as to confer an unlimited power. . . . The requirement is to be interpreted by its context, by the nature of radio transmission and reception, by the scope, character, and quality of services. . . ."

The "public interest" to be served under the Communications Act is thus the interest of the listening public in "the larger and more effective use of radio." The facilities of radio are limited and therefore precious; they cannot be left to wasteful use without detriment to the public interest. "An important element of public interest and convenience affecting the issue of a license is the ability of the licensee to render the best practicable service to the community reached by his broadcasts." . . . The Commission's licensing function cannot be discharged, therefore, merely by finding that there are no technological objections to the granting of a license. If the criterion of "public interest" were limited to such matters, how could the Commission choose between two applicants for the same facilities, each of whom is financially and technically qualified to operate a station? Since the very inception of federal regulation by radio, comparative considerations as to the services to be rendered have governed the application of the standard of "public interest, convenience, or necessity." . . .

The avowed aim of the Communications Act of 1934 was to secure the maximum benefits of radio to all the people of the United States. To that end Congress endowed the Communications Commission with comprehensive powers to promote and realize the vast potentialities of radio. Section 303(g) provides that the Commission shall "generally encourage the larger and more effective use of radio in the public interest"; subsection (i) gives the Commission specific "authority to make special regulations applicable to radio stations engaged in chain broadcasting"; and subsection (r) empowers it to adopt "such rules and regulations and prescribe such restrictions and conditions, not inconsistent with law, as may be necessary to carry out the provisions of this Act."

These provisions, individually and in the aggregate, preclude the notion that the Commission is empowered to deal only with technical and engineering impediments to the "larger and more effective use of radio in the public interest." We cannot find in the Act any such restriction of the Commission's authority. Suppose, for example, that a community can, because of physical limitations, be assigned only two stations. That community might be deprived of effective service in any one of several ways. More powerful stations in nearby cities might blanket out the signals of the local stations so that they could not be heard at all. The stations might interfere with each other so that neither could be clearly heard. One station might dominate the other with the power of its signal. . . . But the community could be deprived of good radio service in ways less crude. One man, financially and technically qualified, might apply for and obtain the licenses of both stations and present a single service over the two stations, thus wasting a frequency otherwise available to the area. The language of the Act does not withdraw such a situation from the licensing and regulatory powers of the Commission, and there is no evidence that Congress did not mean its broad language to carry the authority it expresses.

. . . . . . . . . . . . . . . . . . .

Generalities unrelated to the living problems of radio communication of course cannot justify exercises of power by the Commission. Equally so, generalities empty of all concrete considerations of the actual bearing of regulations promulgated by the Commission to the subject-matter entrusted to it, cannot strike down exercises of power by the Commission. While Congress did not give the Commission unfettered discretion to regulate all phases of the radio industry, it did not frustrate the purposes for which the Communications Act of 1934 was brought into being by attempting an itemized catalogue of the specific manifestations of the general problems for the solution of which it was establishing a regulatory agency. That would have stereotyped the powers of the Commission to specific details in regulating a field of enterprise the dominant characteristic of which was the rapid pace of its unfolding. And so Congress did what experience had taught it in similar attempts at regulation, even in fields where the subject-matter of regulation was far less fluid and dynamic than radio. The essence of that experience was to define broad areas for regulation and to establish standards for judgment adequately related in their application to the problems to be solved.

. . . . . . . . . . . . . . . . . . .

"We come, finally, to an appeal to the First Amendment. The regulations, even if valid in all other respects, must fail because they abridge, say the appellants, their right of free speech. If that be so, it would follow that every person whose application for a license to operate a station is denied by the Commission is thereby denied his constitutional right of free speech. Freedom of utterance is abridged to many who wish to use the limited facilities of radio.

Unlike other modes of expression, radio inherently is not available to all. That is its unique characteristic, and that is why, unlike other modes of expression, it is subject to governmental regulation. Because it cannot be used by all, some who wish to use it must be denied. But Congress did not authorize the Commission to choose among applicants upon the basis of their political, economic, or social views, or upon any other capricious basis. If it did, or if the Commission by these Regulations proposed a choice among applicants upon some such basis, the issue before us would be wholly different. The question here is simply whether the Commission, by announcing that it would refuse licenses to persons who engage in specified network practices (a basis for choice which we hold is comprehended within the statutory criterion of "public interest"), is thereby denying such persons the constitutional right of free speech. The right of free speech does not include, however, the right to use the facilities of radio without a license. The licensing system established by Congress in the Communications Act of 1934 was a proper exercise of its power over commerce. The standard it provided for the licensing of stations was the "public interest, convenience, or necessity." Denial of a station license on that ground, if valid under the Act, is not a denial of free speech.

Justice Frank Murphy disagreed with Justice Frankfurter and urged greater restraint in government regulation of this powerful medium which could be used, as it was then in Europe, as an instrument of authority and misrepresentation and even as a means of oppression.

Mr. Justice MURPHY, with whom Justice Owen ROBERTS joined, dissenting:

In the present case we are dealing with a subject of extreme importance in the life of the nation. Although radio broadcasting, like the press, is generally conducted on a commercial basis, it is not an ordinary business activity, like the selling of securities or the marketing of electrical power. In the dissemination of information and opinion, radio has assumed a position of commanding importance, rivalling the press and pulpit. Owing to its physical characteristics radio, unlike the other methods of conveying information, must be regulated and rationed by the government. Otherwise there would be chaos, and radio's usefulness would be largely destroyed. But because of its vast potentialities as a medium of communication, discussion and propaganda, the character and extent of control that should be exercised over it by the government is a matter of deep and vital concern. Events in Europe show that radio may readily be a weapon of authority and misrepresentation, instead of a means of entertainment and enlightenment. It may even be an instrument of oppression. In pointing out these possibilities I do not mean to intimate in the slightest that they are imminent or probable in this country, but they do suggest that the construction of the instant statute should be approached with more than ordinary restraint and caution, to avoid an interpretation that is not clearly justified by the conditions that brought about its enactment, or that would give the Commission greater powers than the Congress intended to confer.

. . . . . . . . . . . . . . . . . . .

If this were a case in which a station license had been withheld from an individual applicant or licensee because of special relations or commitments that would seriously compromise or limit his ability to provide adequate service to the listening public, I should be less inclined to make objection. As an incident of its authority to determine the eligibility of an individual applicant in an isolated case, the Commission has reversed the order of things. Its real objective is to regulate the business practices of the major networks, thus bringing within range of its regulatory power the chain broadcasting industry as a whole. By means of these regulations and the enforcement programs, the Commission would not only extend its authority over business activities which represent interests and investments of a very substantial character, which have not been put under its jurisdiction by the Act, but would greatly enlarge its control over an institution that has now become a rival of the press and pulpit as a purveyor of news and entertainment and a medium of public discussion. To assume a function and responsibility of such wide reach and importance in the life of the nation, as a mere incident of its duty to pass on individual applications for permission to operate a radio station and use a specific wave length, is an assumption of authority to which I am not willing to lend my assent.

## STATIONS CANNOT CENSOR POLITICAL CANDIDATES

In Europe, there are still examples in the 1960's of authoritarian control of broadcasting even in democratic countries. The government-controlled radio and television in France, for instance, have been used to promote the policies and candidacy of President De Gaulle while broadcasting facilities have been almost entirely denied to his political opponents and critics. In America, Congress had provided in the Communications Act that broadcasting facilities should be available equally to all candidates for public office. But this laudable aim, as the next decision indicates, was not without its problems.

FARMERS EDUCATIONAL & COOPERATIVE UNION V. WDAY, INC., 360 U.S.
525 (1959)

*In this libel action, the Supreme Court handled the diffi-
cult question of whether a broadcaster is liable for defamation
broadcast by a candidate for public office. The Court held that
Section 315 of Communications Act of 1934, denying the station power of censorship over material broadcast by a legally
qualified political candidate, barred a broadcasting station
from removing defamatory statements in candidates' speeches
on the air. This granted the station federal immunity from
liability for such libelous statements.*

Mr. Justice Hugo BLACK delivered the opinion of the Court:

. . . More important, it is obvious that permitting a broadcasting station to censor allegedly libelous remarks would undermine
the basic purpose for which (paragraph) 315 was passed—full and unrestricted discussion of political issues by legally qualified candidates. That section dates back to, and was adopted verbatim from,
the Radio Act of 1927. In that Act, Congress provided for the first
time a comprehensive federal plan for regulating the new and expanding art of radio broadcasting. Recognizing radio's potential
importance as a medium of communication of political ideas, Congress sought to foster its broadest possible utilization by encouraging
broadcasting stations to make their facilities available to candidates
for office without discrimination, and by insuring that these candidates when broadcasting were not to be hampered by censorship of
the issues they could discuss. Thus, expressly applying this country's
tradition of free expression to the field of radio broadcasting, Congress has from the first emphatically forbidden the Commission to
exercise any power of censorship over radio communication. It is
in line with this same tradition that the individual licensee has
consistently been denied "power of censorship" in the vital area of
political broadcasts.

The decision a broadcasting station would have to make in
censoring libelous discussion by a candidate is far from easy.
Whether a statement is defamatory is rarely clear. Whether such a
statement is actionably libelous is an even more complex question,
involving as it does, consideration of various legal defenses such as
"truth" and the privilege of fair comment. Such issues have always
troubled courts. Yet, under petitioner's view of the statute, they
would have to be resolved by an individual licensee during the stress
of a political campaign, often, necessarily, without adequate consideration or basis for decision. Quite possibly, if a station were

held responsible for the broadcast of libelous material, all remarks even faintly objectionable would be excluded out of an excess of caution. Moreover, if any censorship were permissible, a station so inclined could intentionally inhibit a candidate's legitimate presentation under the guise of lawful censorship of libelous matter. Because of the time limitation inherent in a political campaign, erroneous decisions by a station could not be corrected by the courts promptly enough to permit the candidate to bring improperly excluded matter before the public. It follows from all this that allowing censorship, even of the attenuated type advocated here, would almost inevitably force a candidate to avoid controversial issues during political debates over radio and television, and hence restrict the coverage of consideration relevant to intelligent political decision. We cannot believe, and we certainly are unwilling to assume, that Congress intended any such result.

## TELEVISING OF "NOTORIOUS" TRIALS IS FORBIDDEN

Broadcasting, particularly television, has had a great impact on American politics, especially the national party conventions and presidential election campaigns. The presence of the television camera at Republican and Democratic national conventions has brought about changes in nomination procedures. Many broadcasters, and others, too, have claimed that the televising of court trials would do much to inform the public on legal processes and help satisfy the Sixth Amendment guarantee that in all criminal prosecutions, "The accused shall enjoy the right to a speedy and public trial." In a far-reaching 1965 decision, the Court issued a ruling which appears likely to prevent televising of most state criminal trials.

ESTES V. TEXAS, 381 U.S. 532 (1965)

*Here, for the first time, the Court considered the effect of courtroom television, radio, and photography upon a defendant's right to a fair trial, an issue which had been debated since the 1937 trial of Bruno Richard Hauptmann for the kidnapping of the Lindbergh baby. (See Chapter 6.)*

*As a result of the free-wheeling sensational press coverage of the Hauptmann trial, all states but Texas and Colorado adopted Canon 35 of the American Bar Association, which holds that broadcasting, or photographing of court proceedings "detract from the essential dignity of court proceedings, distract participants and witnesses in giving testimony and create*

*misconceptions with respect thereto in the mind of the public
and should not be permitted." Press and broadcasting groups
objected to Canon 35 on the ground that the newsman with a
television or still camera is as much a reporter as a newsman
with pencil and paper and has just as much right to be in the
courtroom.*

*In its first ruling on the question, the Supreme Court ex-
ercised the due process clause of the Fourteenth Amendment
in voiding, by a 5-to-4 margin, a Texas district court conviction of Billie Sol Estes, whose trial on a swindling charge had
been televised despite his objections.*

*Chief Justice Earl Warren and Justices William O. Doug-
las, Arthur Goldberg, and Tom Clark declared that "the time-
honored principles of a fair trial" are violated when television
is allowed in any criminal trial. The fifth member of the majority, Justice John Harlan, agreed to overturn the Estes conviction because he felt the case was one of "great notoriety."
However, he said he would reserve judgment on more routine
cases.*

*Dissenting Justices Black, William J. Brennan, Potter
Stewart, and Byron White objected on constitutional grounds
to the blanket ban of television at that stage in the medium's
development. They said there was insufficient proof that
Estes' rights had been violated.*

*The decision is a reminder of the dangers of labeling
members of the Court. In the majority, three reputed libertarians—Chief Justice Warren and Justices Douglas and Goldberg—shared the view of "conservative" Justice Clark. In dissent, "libertarian" Justices Black and Brennan joined "conservative" Justices Stewart and White. Generally speaking,
such apparent shifts in attitude reflect differences in interpretation of the peculiarities of the case before the Court.*

Mr. Justice CLARK delivered the opinion of the Court:

The question presented here is whether the petitioner, who
stands convicted in the District Court for the Seventh Judicial District of Texas at Tyler for swindling, was deprived of his rights
under the Fourteenth Amendment to due process by the televising
and broadcasting of his trial. Both the trial court and the Texas
Court of Criminal Appeals found against the petitioner. We hold
to the contrary and reverse his conviction.

While petitioner recites his claim in the framework of Canon
35 of the Judicial Canons of the American Bar Association, he does

not contend that we should enshrine Canon 35 in the Fourteenth Amendment, but only that the time-honored principles of a fair trial were not followed in this case and that he was thus convicted without due process of law. Canon 35, of course, has of itself no binding effect on the courts but merely expresses the view of the Association in opposition to the broadcasting, televising and photographing of court proceedings. Likewise, Judicial Canon 28 of the Integrated State Bar of Texas which leaves to the trial judge's sound discretion the telecasting and photographing of court proceedings, is of itself not law. In short, the question here is not the validity of either Canon 35 of the American Bar Association or Canon 28 of the State Bar of Texas, but only whether petitioner was tried in a manner which comports with the due process requirement of the Fourteenth Amendment.

Petitioner's case was originally called for trial on September 24, 1962, in Smith County after a change of venue from Reeves County, some 500 miles west. Massive pretrial publicity totaling 11 volumes of press clippings, which are on file with the Clerk, had given it national notoriety. All available seats in the courtroom were taken and some 30 persons stood in the aisles. However, at that time a defense motion to prevent telecasting, broadcasting by radio and news photography and a defense motion for continuance were presented, and after a two-day hearing the former was denied and the latter granted.

These initial hearings were carried live by both radio and television, and news photography was permitted throughout. The videotapes of these hearings clearly illustrate that the picture presented was not one of that judicial serenity and calm to which petitioner was entitled. Indeed, at least 12 cameramen were engaged in the courtroom throughout the hearing taking motion and still pictures and televising the proceedings. Cables and wires were snaked across the courtroom floor, three microphones were on the judge's bench and others were beamed at the jury box and the counsel table. It is conceded that the activities of the television crews and news photographers led to considerable disruption of the hearings. Moreover, a venire of jurymen had been summoned and was present in the courtroom during the entire hearing but was later released after petitioner's motion for continuance had been granted. The court also had the names of the witnesses called, and some answered but the absence of others led to a continuance of the case until October 22, 1962. It is contended that this two-day pretrial hearing cannot be considered in determining the question before us. We cannot agree. Pretrial can create a major problem for the defendant in a criminal case. Indeed, it may be more harmful than publicity during the trial for it may well set the community opinion as to guilt or innocence. Though the September hearings dealt with motions to prohibit television coverage and to postpone the trial, they are unquestionably relevant to the issue before us. All of this two-day affair was highly publicized and could only have impressed those present, and also the community at large, with the notorious character of the petitioner as well as the proceeding. The trial witnesses present at the hearing, as well as the original jury panel, were undoubtedly made aware of the peculiar public importance of the case by the press and television coverage being provided, and by the fact that they themselves were televised live and their pictures rebroadcast on the evening show.

When the case was called for trial on October 22 the scene had been altered. A booth had been constructed at the back of the courtroom which was painted to blend with permanent structure of the room. It had an aperture to allow the lens of the cameras an unrestricted view of the courtroom. All television cameras and newsreel photographers were restricted to the area of the booth when shooting film or telecasting.

Because of continual objection, the rules governing live telecasting, as well as radio and still photos, were changed as the exigencies of the situation seemed to require. As a result, live telecasting was prohibited during a great portion of the actual trial. Only the opening and closing arguments of the State, the return of the jury's verdict and its receipt by the trial judge were carried live with sound. Although the order allowed videotapes of the entire proceeding without sound, the cameras operated only intermittently, recording various portions of the trial for broadcast on regularly scheduled newscasts later in the day and vening. At the request of the petitioner, the trial judge prohibited coverage of any kind, still or television, of the defense counsel during their summations to the jury.

Because of the varying restrictions placed on sound and live telecasting the telecasts of the trial were confined largely to film clips shown on the stations' regularly scheduled news programs. The news commentators would use the film of a particular part of the day's trial activities as a backdrop for their reports. Their commentary included excerpts from testimony and the usual reportorial remarks. On one occasion the videotape of the September hearings were rebroadcast in place of the "late movie."

. . . . . . . . . . . . . . . . . . . . . . . .

We start with the proposition that it is a "public trial" that the Sixth Amendment guarantees to the "accused." The purpose of the requirement of a public trial was to guarantee that the accused would be fairly dealt with and not unjustly condemned. History had proven that secret tribunals were effective instruments of oppression. . . .

It is said, however, that the freedoms granted in the First

Amendment extend a right to news media to televise from the courtroom, and that to refuse to honor this privilege is to discriminate between the newspapers and television. This is a misconception of the rights of the press.

The free press has been a mighty catalyst in awakening public interest in governmental affairs, exposing corruption among public officers and employees and generally informing the citizenry of public events and occurrences, including court proceedings. While maximum freedom must be allowed the press in carrying on this important function in a democratic society, its exercise must necessarily be subject to the maintenance of absolute fairness in the judicial process. . . .

Nor can the courts be said to discriminate where they permit the newspaper reporter access to the courtroom. The television and radio reporter has the same privilege. All are entitled to the same rights as the general public. The news reporter is not permitted to to bring his typewriter or printing press. When the advances in these arts permit reporting by printing press or by television without their present hazards to a fair trial we will have another case.

. . . . . . . . . . . . . . . . . . .

The State contends that the televising of portions of a criminal trial does not constitute a denial of due process. Its position is that because no prejudice has been shown by the petitioner as resulting from the televising, it is permissible; that claims of "distractions" during the trial due to the physical presence of the television are wholly unfounded; and that psychological considerations are for psychologists, not courts, because they are purely hypothetical. It argues further that the public has a right to know what goes on in the courts; that the court has no power to "suppress, edit, or censor events, which transpire in proceedings before it" and that the televising of criminal trials would be enlightening to the public and promote greater respect for the courts.

At the outset the notion should be dispelled that telecasting is dangerous because it is new. It is true that our empirical knowledge of its full effect on the public, the jury or the participants in a trial, including the judge, witnesses and lawyers, is limited. However, the nub of the question is not its newness but, as Mr. Justice Douglas says, "the insidious influences which it puts to work in the administration of justice." . . .

It is true that the public has the right to be informed as to what occurs in the courts, but reporters of all media, including television, are always present if they wish to be and are plainly free to report whatever occurs in open court through their respective media. . . .

The State, however, says that the use of television in the instant case was "without injustice to the person immediately concerned," basing its position on the fact that the petitioner has established no isolatable prejudice and that this must be shown in order to invalidate a conviction in these circumstances. The State paints too broadly in this contention, for this Court itself has found instances in which a showing of actual prejudice is not a prerequisite to reversal. This is such a case.

. . . . . . . . . . . . . . . . . . .

As has been said, the chief function of our judicial machinery is to ascertain the truth. The use of television, however, cannot be said to contribute materially to this objective. Rather its use amounts to the injection of an irrelevant factor into court proceedings. In addition experience teaches that there are numerous situations in which it might cause actual unfairness—some so subtle as to defy detection by the accused or control by the judge. We enumerate some in summary:

1. The potential impact of television on the jurors is perhaps of the greatest significance. They are the nerve center of the fact-finding process. It is true that in States like Texas where they are required to be sequestered in trials of this nature the jurors will probably not see any of the proceedings as televised from the courtroom. But the inquiry cannot end there. From the moment the trial judge announces that a case will be televised it becomes a *cause celebre*. The whole community, including prospective jurors, becomes interested in all the morbid details surrounding it. The approaching trial immediately assumes an important status in the public press and the accused is highly publicized along with the offense with which he is charged. Every juror carries with him into the jury box these solemn facts and thus increases the chance of prejudice that is present in every criminal case. And we must remember that realistically it is only the notorious trial which will be broadcast, because of the necessity for paid sponsorship. The conscious or unconscious effect that this may have on the juror's judgment cannot be evaluated, but experience indicates that it is not only possible but highly probable that it will have a direct bearing on his vote as to guilt or innocence. Where pretrial publicity of all kinds has created intense public feeling which is aggravated by the telecasting or picturing of the trial the televised jurors cannot help but feel the pressures of knowing that friends and neighbors have their eyes upon them. If the community be hostile to an accused, a televised juror, realizing that he must return to neighbors who saw the trial themselves, may well be led "not to hold the balance nice, clear and true between the State and the accused. . . ."

Moreover, while it is practically impossible to assess the effect of television on jury attentiveness, those of us who know juries realize the problem of jury "distraction." The State argues this is *de minimis* since the physical disturbances have been eliminated.

But we know that distractions are not caused solely by the physical presence of the camera and its telltale red lights. It is the awareness of the fact of telecasting that is felt by the juror throughout the trial. We are all self-conscious and uneasy when being televised. Human nature being what it is, not only a juror's eyes but his mind will often be on that fact rather than on the witness stand.

. . . . . . . . . . . . . . . . . .

2. The quality of the testimony in criminal trials will often be impaired. The impact upon a witness of the knowledge that he is being viewed by a vast audience is simply incalculable. Some may be demoralized and frightened, some cocky and given to overstatement; memories may falter, as with anyone speaking publicly, and accuracy of statement may be severely undermined. Embarrassment may impede the search for the truth, as may a natural tendency toward over-dramatization. Furthermore, inquisitive strangers and "cranks" might approach witnesses on the street with jibes, advice or demands for explanation of testimony. There is little wonder that the defendant cannot "prove" the existence of such factors. Yet we all know from experience that they exist.

. . . . . . . . . . . . . . . . . .

While some of the dangers mentioned above are present as well in newspaper coverage of any important trial the circumstances and extraneous influences intruding upon the solemn decorum of court procedure in the televised trial are far more serious than in cases involving only newspaper coverage.

3. A major aspect of the problem is the additional responsibilities the presence of television places on the trial judge. His job is to make certain that the accused receives a fair trial. This most difficult task requires his undivided attention. Still when television comes into the courtroom he must also supervise it. In this trial, for example, the judge on several different occasions—aside from the two days of pretrial—was obliged to have a hearing or enter an order made necessary solely because of the presence of television. Thus where telecasting is restricted as it was here, and as even the States concedes it must be, his task is made much more difficult and exacting. And, as happened here, such rulings may unfortunately militate against the fairness of the trial. In addition, laying physical interruptions aside, there is the ever-present dstraction that the mere awareness of television's presence prompts. Judges are human beings also and are subject to the same psychological reactions as laymen. Telecasting is particularly bad where the judge is elected, as is the case in all save a half dozen of our States. The telecasting of a trial becomes a political weapon, which along with other distractions inherent in broadcasting, diverts his attention from the task at hand—the fair trial of the accused.

. . . . . . . . . . . . . . . . . .

4. Finally, we cannot ignore the impact of courtroom television on the defendant. Its presence is a form of mental—if not physical—harassment, resembling a police line-up or the third degree. The inevitable close-ups of his gestures and expressions during the ordeal of his trial might well transgress his personal sensibilities, his dignity, and his ability to concentrate on the proceedings before him—sometimes the difference between life and death—dispassionately, freely and without the distraction of wide public surveillance. A defendant on trial for a specific crime is entitled to his day in court, not in a stadium, or a city or nation-wide arena. The heightened public clamor resulting from radio and television coverage will inevitably result in prejudice. Trial by television is, therefore, foreign to our system. Furthermore, telecasting may also deprive an accused of effective counsel. The distractions, intrusions into confidential attorney-client relationships and the temptation offered by television to play to the public audience might often have a direct effect not only upon the lawyers, but the judge, the jury, and the witnesses.

The television camera is a powerful weapon. Intentionally or inadvertently it can destroy an accused and his case in the eyes of the public. While our telecasters are honorable men, they too are human. The necessity for sponsorship weighs heavily in favor of the televising of only notorious cases, such as this one, and invariably focuses the beam of the lens upon the unpopular or infamous accused. Such a selection is necessary in order to obtain a sponsor willing to pay a sufficient fee to cover the costs and return a profit. We have already examined the ways in which public sentiment can affect the trial participants. To the extent that television shapes that sentiment, it can strip the accused of a fair trial.

.  .  .  .  .  .  .  .  .  .  .  .  .  .  .  .  .  .  .  .

The facts in this case demonstrate clearly the necessity for the application of the rule announced in Rideau. The sole issue before the court for two days of pretrial hearing was the question now before us. The hearing was televised live and repeated on tape in the same evening, reaching approximately 100,000 viewers. In addition, the courtroom was a mass of wires, television cameras, microphones and photographers. The petitioner, the panel of prospective jurors, who were sworn the second day, the witnesses and the lawyers were all exposed to this untoward situation. The judge decided that the trial proceedings would be telecast. He announced no restrictions at the time. This emphasized the notorious nature of the coming trial, increased the intensity of the publicity on the petitioner and together with the subsequent televising of the trial beginning 30 days later inherently prevented a sober search for the truth. This is underscored by the fact that the selection of the jury took an entire week. As might be expected, a substantial amount of that time was devoted to ascertaining the impact of the pretrial televising on the prospective jurors. As we have noted, four of the jurors selected had seen all or part of those broadcasts. The trial, on the other hand, lasted only three days.

Moreover, the trial judge was himself harassed. After the initial decision to permit telecasting he apparently decided that a booth should be built at the broadcasters' expense to confine its operations; he then decided to limit the parts of the trial that might be televised live; then he decided to film the testimony of the witnesses without sound in an attempt to protect those under the rule; and finally he ordered that defense counsel and their argument not be televised, in the light of their objection. Plagued by his original error—recurring each day of the trial—his day-to-day orders made the trial more confusing to the jury, the participants and to the viewers. Indeed, it resulted in a public presentation of only the State's side of the case.

As Mr. Justice Holmes said: "The theory of our system is that the conclusions to be reached in a case will be induced only by evidence and argument in open court, and not by any outside influence, whether of private talk or public print."

It is said that the ever-advancing techniques of public communication and adjustment of the public to its presence may bring about a change in the effect of telecasting upon the fairness of criminal trials. But we are not dealing here with future developments in the field of electronics. Our judgment cannot be rested on the hypothesis of tomorrow but must take the facts as they are presented today.

In concurring Chief Justice Warren added three more reasons for banning the televising of all criminal trials: it diverts the trial from its proper purposes; it gives the public the wrong impression about the purpose of trials; and it singles out certain defendants and subjects them to trials under prejudicial conditions not experienced by others.

Mr. Chief Justice WARREN, with whom Justices DOUGLAS and GOLDBERG joined, concurring:

While I join the Court's opinion and agree that the televising of criminal trials is inherently a denial of due process, I desire to express additional views on why this is so. In doing this, I wish to emphasize that our condemnation of televised criminal trials is not based on generalities or abstract fears. The record in this case presents a vivid illustration of the inherent prejudice of televised criminal trials and supports our conclusion that this is the appropriate time to make a definitive appraisal of television in the courtroom.

. . . . . . . . . . . . . . . . . . .

I believe that it violates the Sixth Amendment for federal courts and the Fourteenth Amendment for state courts to allow criminal trials to be televised to the public at large. I base this conclusion on three grounds: (1) that the televising of trials diverts the trial from its proper purpose in that it has an inevitable impact on all the trial participants; (2) that it gives the public the wrong impression about the purpose of trials, thereby detracting from the dignity of court proceedings and lessening the reliability of trials; and (3) that it singles out certain defendants and subjects them to trials under prejudicial conditions not experienced by others.

. . . . . . . . . . . . . . . . . . .

I had thought that these days of frontier justice were long behind us, but the courts below would return the theater to the courtroom.

The televising of trials would cause the public to equate the trial process with the forms of entertainment regularly seen on television and with the commercial objectives of the television industry. In the present case, tapes of the September 24 hearing were run in place of the "Tonight Show" by one station and in place of the late night movie by another. Commercials for soft drinks, soups, eye-drops and seatcovers were inserted when there was a pause in the proceedings. In addition, if trials were televised there would be a natural tendency on the part of broadcasters to develop the personalities of the trial participants, so as to give the proceedings more of an element of drama. This tendency was noticeable in the present case.

. . . . . . . . . . . . . . . . . . .

Nor does the exclusion of television cameras from the courtroom in any way impinge upon the freedoms of speech and the press. Court proceedings, as well as other public matters, are proper subjects for press coverage. . . . So long as the television industry, like the other communications media, is free to send representatives to trials and to report on those trials to its viewers, there is no abridgment of the freedom of press. The right of the communications media to comment on court proceedings does not bring with it the right to interject themselves into the fabric of the trial process to alter the purpose of that process.

In summary, television is one of the great inventions of all time and can perform a large and useful role in society. But the television camera, like other technological innovations, is not entitled to pervade the lives of everyone in disregard of constitutionally protected rights. The television industry, like other institutions, has a proper area of activities and limitations beyond which it cannot go with its cameras. That area does not extend into an American courtroom. On entering that hallowed sanctuary, where the lives, liberty and property of people are in jeopardy, television representatives have only the rights of the general public, namely, to be present, to observe the proceedings, and thereafter, if they choose, to report them.

A fifth member of the majority, Justice Harlan, clearly limited his agreement only to "notorious" trials. However, he did not define "notorious." One definition could well be a trial in which there is sufficient public interest to warrant its being televised.

Mr. Justice HARLAN concurring:

I concur in the opinion of the Court, subject, however, to the reservations and only to the extent indicated in this opinion.

The constitutional issue presented by this case is far-reaching in its implications for the administration of justice in this country. The precise question is whether the Fourteenth Amendment prohibits a State, over the objection of a defendant, from employing television in the courtroom to televise contemporaneously, or subsequently by means of videotape, the courtroom proceedings of a criminal trial of widespread public interest. The issue is no narrower than this because petitioner has not asserted any isolatable prejudice resulting from the presence of television apparatus within the courtroom or from the contemporaneous or subsequent broadcasting of the trial proceedings. On the other hand, the issue is no broader, for we are concerned here only with a criminal trial of great notoriety, and not with criminal proceedings of a more or less routine nature.

The question is fraught with unusual difficulties. Permitting television in the courtroom undeniably has mischievous potentialities for intruding upon the detached atmosphere which should always surround the judicial process. Forbidding this innovation, however, would doubtless impinge upon one of the valued attributes of our federalism by preventing the States from pursuing a novel course of procedural experimentation. My conclusion is that there is no constitutional requirement that television be allowed in the courtroom, and at least as to a notorious criminal trial such as this one, the considerations against allowing television in the courtroom so far outweigh the countervailing factors advanced in its support as to require a holding that what was done in this case infringed the fundamental right to a fair trial assured by the Due Process Clause of the Fourteenth Amendment.

.    .    .    .    .    .    .    .    .    .    .    .    .    .    .

The free speech and press guaranties of the First and Fourteenth Amendments are also asserted as embodying a positive right to televise trials, but the argument is greatly overdrawn. Unquestionably, television has become a very effective medium for transmitting news. Many trials are newsworthy, and televising them might well provide the most accurate and comprehensive means of conveying their content to the public. Furthermore, television is capable of performing an educational function by acquainting the public with the judicial process in action. Albeit that these are credible policy arguments in favor of television, they are not arguments of constitutional proportions. The rights to print and speak, over television as elsewhere, do not embody an independent right to bring the mechanical facilities of the broadcasting and printing industries into the courtroom. Once beyond the confines of the courthouse, a news-gathering agency may publicize, within wide limits, what its representatives have heard and seen in the courtroom. But the line is drawn at the courthouse door, and within a reporter's constitutional rights are no greater than those of any other member of the public. Within the courthouse the only relevant constitutional consideration is that the accused be accorded a fair trial. If the presence of television substantially detracts from that goal, due process requires that its use be forbidden.

.    .    .    .    .    .    .    .    .    .    .    .    .    .    .

The probable impact of courtroom television on the fairness of a trial may vary according to the particular kind of case involved. The impact of television on a trial exciting wide popular interest may be one thing; the impact on a run-of-the-mill case may be quite another. Furthermore, the propriety of closed circuit television for the purpose of making a court recording or for limited use in educational institutions obviously presents markedly different considerations. The Estes trial was a heavily publicized and highly sensational affair. I therefore put aside all other types of cases; in so doing, however, I wish to make it perfectly clear that I am by no means prepared to say that the constitutional issue should ultimately turn upon the nature of the particular case involved. When the issue of television in a non-notorious trial is presented it may appear that no workable distinction can be drawn based on the type of case involved, or that the possibilities for prejudice, though less severe, are nonetheless of constitutional proportions. The resolution of those further questions should await an appropriate case; the Court should proceed only step by step in this unplowed field. The opinion of the Court necessarily goes no farther, for only the four members of the majority who unreservedly join the Court's opinion would resolve those questions now.

. . . . . . . . . . . . . . . . . .

Finally, we should not be deterred from making the constitutional judgment which this case demands by the prospect that the day may come when television will have become so commonplace an affair in the daily life of the average person as to dissipate all reasonable likelihood that its use in courtrooms may disparage the judicial process. If and when that day arrives the constitutional judgment called for now would of course be subject to re-examination in accordance with the traditional workings of the Due Process Clause. At the present juncture I can only conclude that televised trials, at least in cases like this one, poses such capabilities for interfering with the even course of the judicial process that they are constitutionally banned. On these premises I concur in the opinion of the Court.

Because of First Amendment considerations, the four dissenters were not willing to go along with a flat ban.

Mr Justice STEWART, with whom Justices BLACK, BRENNAN, and WHITE joined, dissenting:

I cannot agree with the Court's decision that the circumstances of this trial led to a denial of the petitioner's Fourteenth Amendment rights. I think that the introduction of television into a courtroom is, at least in the present state of the art, an extremely unwise policy. It invites many constitutional risks, and it detracts from the inherent dignity of a courtroom. But I am unable to escalate this personal view into a *per se* constitutional rule. And I am unable to find, on the specific record of this case, that the circumstances attending the limited televising of the petitioner's trial resulted in the denial of any right guaranteed to him by the United States Constitution.

. . . . . . . . . . . . . . . . . .

But we do not deal here with mob domination of a courtroom, with a kangaroo trial, with a prejudiced judge or a jury inflamed with bias. Under the limited grant of certiorari in this case, the sole question before us is an entirely different one. It concerns only the regulated presence of television, and still photography at the trial itself, which began on October 22, 1962. Any discussion of pretrial events can do no more than obscure the important question which is actually before us.

It is obvious that the introduction of television and news cameras into a criminal trial invites many serious constitutional hazards. The very presence of photographers and television cameramen plying their trade in a courtroom might be so completely and thoroughly disruptive and distracting as to make a fair trial impossible. Thus, if the scene at the September hearing had been repeated in the courtroom during this jury trial, it is difficult to conceive how a fair trial in the constitutional sense could have been afforded the defendant. And even if, as was true here, the television cameras are so controlled and concealed as to be hardly perceptible in the courtroom itself, there are risks of constitutional dimensions that lurk in the very process of televising court proceedings at all.

. . . . . . . . . . . . . . . . . . . . .

The plain fact of the matter, however, is that none of these things happened or could have happened in this case. The jurors themselves were prevented from seeing any telecasts of the trial, and completely insulated from association with any members of the public who did see such telecasts. . . .

In the courtroom itself, there is nothing to show that the trial proceeded in any way other than it would have proceeded if cameras and television had not been present. In appearance, the courtroom was practically unaltered. There was no obtrusiveness and no distraction, no noise and no special lighting. There is no indication anywhere in the record of any disturbance whatever of the judicial proceedings. There is no claim that the conduct of the judge, or that any deed or word of counsel, or of any witness, or of any juror, were influenced in any way by the presence of photographers or by television.

. . . . . . . . . . . . . . . . . . . .

While no First Amendment claim is made in this case, there are intimations in the opinions filed by my Brethren in the majority which strike me as disturbingly alien to the First and Fourteenth Amendments' guarantees against federal or state interference with the free communication of information and ideas. The suggestion that there are limits upon the public's right to know what goes on in the courts causes me deep concern. The idea of imposing upon any medium of communications the burden of justifying its presence is contrary to where I had always thought the presumption must lie in the area of First Amendment freedoms. And the proposition that nonparticipants in a trial might get the "wrong impression" from unfettered reporting and commentary contains an invitation to censorship which I cannot accept. Where there is no disruption of the "essential requirement of the fair and orderly administration of justice," "freedom of discussion should be given the widest range."

I do not think that the Constitution denies to the State or to individual trial judges all discretion to conduct criminal trials with television cameras present, no matter how unobtrusive the cameras may be. I cannot say at this time that it is impossible to have a constitutional trial whenever any part of the proceedings is televised or recorded on television film. I cannot now hold that the Constitution absolutely bars television cameras from every criminal courtroom, even if they have no impact upon the jury, no effect upon any witness, and no influence upon the conduct of the judge.

For these reasons I would affirm the judgment.

Justice White believed that it is still too early and that too little is known for the Court to take such an unequivocal stand.

Mr. Justice WHITE, with whom Mr. Justice BRENNAN joined, dissenting:

I agree with Mr. Justice Stewart that a finding of constitutional prejudice on this record entails erecting a flat ban on the use of cameras in the courtroom and believe that it is premature to promulgate such a broad constitutional principle at the present time. This is the first case in this Court dealing with the subject of television coverage of criminal trials, our cases dealing with analogous subjects are not really controlling, and there is, on the whole, a very limited amount of experience in this country with television coverage of trials. In my view, the currently available materials assessing the effect of cameras in the courtroom are too sparse and fragmentary to constitute the basis for a constitutional judgment permanently barring any and all forms of television coverage. As was said in another context, "we know too little of the actual impact . . . to reach a conclusion on the bare bones of the evidence before us. . . ."

The opinion of the Court in effect precludes further opportunity for intelligent assessment of the probable hazards imposed by the use of cameras at criminal trials. Serious threats to constitutional rights in some instances justify a prophylactic rule dispensing with the necessity of showing specific prejudice in a particular case. But these are instances in which there has been ample experience on which to base an informed judgment. Here, although our experience is inadequate and our judgment correspondingly infirm, the Court discourages further meaningful study of the use of television at criminal trials. Accordingly, I dissent.

The *Estes* decision doesn't kill television in the courtroom, but it leaves it in a critical condition. In a separate opinion, Justice Brennan pointed out that the decision was "*not* a blanket constitutional prohibition against the televising of state criminal trials." So, though television is only barred from "notorious trials," some observers believe it would be a rare judge who now would take a chance of permitting television in any case tinged, however slightly, with sensationalism. And wouldn't the act of televising a routine case have the effect of turning it into a "notorious" trial?

Although licensing has for centuries been considered anathema to press freedom, decisions in this chapter—*FCC v. Pottsville, NBC v. United States,* and the *WDAY* case—illustrate how the Court has accommodated the First Amendment interests of two media—radio and television—that must of necessity be licensed and regulated by the Federal government.

As the news and public affairs activities of broadcasting increase in scope and importance, so has the First Amendment protection they enjoy. In fact, the FCC has encouraged broadcasters to editorialize on the air, provided they give an opportunity for opposing views to be aired later. For all intents and purposes, the broadcast journalist enjoys the same freedoms as does the pen and pencil journalist. As a result of *Estes,* he may not be able to bring his television camera into the courtroom (and this may be a substantial discrimination against the electronic media), but he has the same right to be there and to report what happens as does any other represnetative of the press.

*Chapter Fourteen*

✿

GOVERNMENT REGULATION
OF BUSINESS ASPECTS OF THE PRESS

✿

DURING the New Deal era the nation's daily newspapers, like other businesses, came under increasing regulation because of the enactment of such laws as the National Industrial Recovery Act (NRA), the National Labor Relations Act (Wagner Act), and the Fair Labor Standards Act (Wage and Hour Act).

To many editors and publishers it seemed that when applied to the press this legislation violated the First Amendment. The pertinent constitutional question was fairly clear: At what point, if any, does government regulation of business actually abridge freedom of the press? Should newspapers be exempt from government restrictions affecting their business activities? These issues have been resolved in several important Supreme Court decisions.

While generous in applying First Amendment protection to the activities of individuals and minority groups, the Court has shown somewhat less latitude in applying that protection to the activities of the corporate complex that the mass media have become. The two major decisions involving the Associated Press illustrate this. It may reflect a feeling of some judges and press critics that the growing tendency towards "bigness, fewness, and likemindedness" in the news media has been itself a deterrent to the free expression of the widest variety of views, ideas, and tastes.

275

## RIGHT TO ORGANIZE IS NOT IN CONFLICT
## WITH PRESS FREEDOM

In the early New Deal period the American Newspaper Guild was established to organize journalists into a labor union. Many newspaper publishers contended that the Guild's activities constituted a threat to freedom of the press. The Court ruled otherwise.

ASSOCIATED PRESS V. NATIONAL LABOR RELATIONS BOARD, 301 U.S. 103 (1937)

*In October, 1935, the Associated Press fired Morris Watson, an employee of its New York office. Subsequently the American Newspaper Guild filed a charge with the National Labor Relations Board claiming his discharge was in violation of Section F of the National Labor Relations Act, which allows employees to organize and to bargain collectively through labor representatives. The NLRB ordered the AP to restore Watson's job. The AP argued that to allow the Guild's position was contrary to the First Amendment as well as a denial of trial by jury in violation of the Seventh Amendment.*

*By a 5–to–4 decision, the Supreme Court upheld the U.S. Circuit Court of Appeals ruling against the AP.*

*The authority for the National Labor Relations Act is based on the powerful commerce clause of the Constitution.[1] The Court held that the Associated Press was indeed in interstate commerce and that its business was not immune from regulation because it was an agency of the press. It further ruled that the action of the NLRB in no way restricted freedom of the press.*

Mr. Justice Owen ROBERTS delivered the opinion of the Court:

The Associated Press is engaged in interstate commerce within the definition of the statute and the meaning of article 1, section 8, of the Constitution. It is an instrumentality set up by constituent members who are engaged in a commercial business for profit, and as such instrumentality acts as an exchange or clearing house of news as between the respective members and as a supplier to members of news gathered through its own domestic and foreign activities. These operations involve the constant use of channels of in-

---

[1] Art. I Sec. 8. "Congress shall have Power . . . to regulate Commerce . . . among the several states."

terstate and foreign communication. They amount to commercial intercourse and such intercourse is commerce within the meaning of the Constitution. Interstate communication of a business nature, whatever the means of such communication, is interstate commerce regulable by Congress under the Constitution. The conclusion is unaffected by the fact that the petitioner does not sell news and does not operate for profit, or that technically the title to the news remains in the petitioner during interstate transmission. Petitioner being so engaged in interstate commerce the Congress may adopt appropriate regulations of its activities for the protection and advancement and for the insurance of the safety of such commerce.

. . . . . . . . . . . . . . . . .

Second. Does the statute, as applied to the petitioner, abridge the freedom of speech or of the press safeguarded by the First Amendment? We hold that it does not. It is insisted that the Associated Press is in substance the press itself, that the membership consists solely of persons who own and operate newspapers, that the news is gathered solely for publication in the newspapers of members. Stress is laid upon the facts that this membership consists of persons of every conceivable political, economic, and religious view, that the one thing upon which the members are united is that the Associated Press shall be wholly free from partisan activity or the expression of opinions, that it shall limit its function to reporting events without bias in order that the citizens of our country, if given the facts, may be able to form their own opinions respecting them. The conclusion which the petitioner draws is that whatever may be the case with respect to employees in its mechanical departments, it must have absolute and unrestricted freedom to employ and to discharge those who, like Watson, edit the news, that there must not be the slightest opportunity for any bias or prejudice personally entertained by an editorial employee to color or to distort what he writes, and that the Associated Press cannot be free to furnish unbiased and impartial news reports unless it is equally free to determine for itself the partiality or bias of editorial employees. So it is said that any regulation protective of union activities, or the right collectively to bargain on the part of such employees, is necessarily an invalid invasion of the freedom of the press.

We think the contention not only has no relevance to the circumstances of the instant case but is an unsound generalization. The ostensible reason for Watson's discharge, as embodied in the records of the petitioner, is "solely on the grounds of his work not being on a basis for which he has shown capability." The petitioner did not assert and does not now claim that he had shown bias in the past. It does not claim that by reason of his connection with the union he will be likely, as the petitioner honestly believes, to show bias in the future. The actual reason for his discharge, as shown by the unattacked finding of the Board, was his Guild activity and his agitation for collective bargaining. The statute does not preclude a discharge on the ostensible grounds for the petitioner's action; it forbids discharge for what has been found to be the real motive of the petitioner. These considerations answer the suggestion that if the petitioner believed its policy of impartiality was likely to be subverted by Watson's continued service, Congress was without power to interdict his discharge. No such question is here for decision. Neither before the Board, nor in the court below nor here has the petitioner professed such belief. It seeks to bar all regulation by contending that regulation in a situation not presented would be invalid. Courts deal with cases upon the basis of the facts disclosed, never with nonexistent and assumed circumstances.

The act does not compel the petitioner to employ any one; it does not require that the petitioner retain in its employ an incompetent editor or one who fails faithfully to edit the news to reflect the facts without bias or prejudice. The act permits a discharge for any reason other than union activity or agitation for collective bargaining with employees. The restoration of Watson to his former position in no sense guarantees his continuance in petitioner's employ. The petitioner is at liberty, whenever occasion may arise, to exercise its undoubted right to sever his relationship for any cause that seems to it proper save only as a punishment for, or discouragement of, such activities as the act declares permissible.

The business of the Associated Press is not immune from regulation because it is an agency of the press. The publisher of a newspaper has no special immunity from the application of general laws. He has no special privilege to invade the rights and liberties of others. He must answer for libel. He may be punished for contempt of court. He is subject to the anti-trust laws. Like others he must pay equable and nondiscriminatory taxes on his business. The regulation here in question has no relation whatever to the impartial distribution of news. The order of the Board in nowise circumscribes the full freedom and liberty of the petitioner to publish the news as it desires it published or to enforce policies of its own choosing with respect to the editing and rewriting of news for publication, and the petitioner is free at any time to discharge Watson or any editorial employee who fails to comply with the policies it may adopt.

Four dissenters regarded the decision as a real threat to freedom of expression. It is worth noting that the strongly "libertarian" views of freedom of the press expressed in Justice Sutherland's dissent spoke for the "conservative" group on the Court which, during this period, blocked much New Deal social legislation.

Mr. Justice George SUTHERLAND, with whom Justices Willis VAN DEVANTER, James C. MC REYNOLDS, and Pierce BUTLER joined, dissenting:

The Associated Press is engaged in collecting, editing, and distributing news to its members, publishers of some 1300 newspapers throughout the United States. These newspapers represent many diverse policies and many differences in point of view. It, obviously, is essential that the news furnished should not only be without suppression, but that it should be, as far as possible, free from color, bias, or distortion. Such is the long-established policy of the Associated Press. If the Congressional act here involved, upon its face or in its present application, abridges the freedom of petitioner to carry its policy into effect, the act to that extent falls under the condemnation of the First Amendment. We shall confine ourselves to that question, the gravity of which is evident; but we do not mean thereby to record our assent to all that has been said with regard to other questions in the case.

The first ten amendments to the Constitution safeguard the fundamental rights therein mentioned from every form of unpermitted federal legislation. The due process clause of the Fifth Amendment protects the person against deprivation of life, liberty, or property except by due process of law. "Liberty" is a word of wide meaning, and, without more, would have included the various liberties guaranteed by the First Amendment. . . .

But the framers of the Bill of Rights, regarding certain liberties as so vital that legislative denial of them should be specifically foreclosed, provided by the First Amendment:

"Congress shall make no law respecting an establishment of religion, or prohibiting the free exercise thereof; or abridging the freedom of speech, or of the press; or the right of the people peaceably to assemble, and to petition the Government for a redress of grievances."

The difference between the two amendments is an emphatic one and readily apparent. Deprivation of a liberty not embraced by the First Amendment, as for example the liberty of contract, is qualified by the phrase "without due process of law"; but those liberties enumerated in the First Amendment are guaranteed without qualification, the object and effect of which is to put them in a category apart and make them incapable of abridgment by any process of law. That this is inflexibly true of the clause in respect of religion and religious liberty cannot be doubted; and it is true of the other clauses save as they may be subject in some degree to rare and extreme exigencies such as, for example, a state of war. Legislation which contravenes the liberties of the First Amendment might not contravene liberties of another kind falling only within the terms of the Fifth Amendment. Thus, we have held that the governmental power of taxation, one of the least limitable of the powers, may not be exerted so as to abridge the freedom of the press . . ., albeit the same tax might be entirely valid if challenged under the "liberty" guaranty of the Fifth Amendment, apart from those liberties embraced by the First. . . .

No one can read the long history which records the stern and often bloody struggles by which these cardinal rights were secured, without realizing how necessary it is to preserve them against any infringement, however slight. For, as Mr. Justice Bradley said in *Boyd v. United States,* 116 U.S. 616, 635, "illegitimate and unconstitutional practices get their first footing in that way, namely, by silent approaches and slight deviations from legal modes of procedure. . . . It is the duty of courts to be watchful for the constitutional rights of the citizen, and against any stealthy encroachments thereon. Their motto should be *obsta principiis.*" "Experience should teach us," it was said in another case, "to be most on our guard to protect liberty when the government's purposes are beneficent. Men born to freedom are naturally alert to repel invasion of their liberty by evil-minded rulers. The greatest dangers to liberty lurk in insidious encroachment by men of zeal, well-meaning but without understanding." *Olmstead v. United States* (dissent), 277 U.S. 471, 479. A little water, trickling here and there through a dam, is a small matter in itself; but it may be a sinister menace to the security of the dam, which those living in the valley below will do well to heed.

The destruction or abridgment of a free press—which constitutes one of the most dependable avenues through which information of public and governmental activities may be transmitted to the people—would be an event so evil in its consequences that the least approach toward that end should be halted at the threshold.

.  .  .  .  .  .  .  .  .  .  .  .  .  .  .  .  .  .  .

Freedom is not a mere intellectual abstraction; and it is not merely a word to adorn an oration upon occasions of patriotic rejoicing. It is an intensely practical reality, capable of concrete enjoyment in a multitude of ways days by day. When applied to the press, the term freedom is not to be narrowly confined; and it obviously means more than publication and circulation. If freedom of the press does not include the right to adopt and pursue a policy without governmental restriction, it is a misnomer to call it freedom. And we may as well deny at once the right of the press freely to adopt a policy and pursue it, as to concede that right and deny the liberty to exercise an uncensored judgment in respect of the employment and discharge of the agents through whom the policy is to be effectuated.

In a matter of such concern, the judgment of Congress—or, still less, the judgment of an administrative censor—cannot, under the Constitution, be substituted for that of the press management in respect of the employment or discharge of employees engaged in editorial work. The good which might come to interstate commerce or the benefit which might result to a special group, however large, must give way to that higher good of all the people so plainly contemplated by the imperative requirement that "Congress shall make no law . . . abridging the freedom . . . of the press." . . .

Do the people of this land—in the providence of God, favored, as they sometimes boast, above all others in the plenitude of their liberties—desire to preserve those so carefully protected by the First Amendment: liberty of religious worship, freedom of speech and of the press, and the right as freemen peaceably to assemble and petition their government for a redress of grievances? If so, let them withstand all beginnings of encroachment. For the saddest epitaph which can be carved in memory of a vanished liberty is that it was lost because its possessors failed to stretch forth a saving hand while yet there was time.

## EVEN SMALL DAILIES ARE IN INTERSTATE COMMERCE

The Associated Press and such giant dailies as the *Chicago Tribune* and *New York Times* are legally—and obviously—in interstate commerce. But what about a small daily or weekly paper serving a limited area? Is it also in interstate commerce and hence subject to federal regulation? The following case provided answers.

MABEE V. WHITE PLAINS PUBLISHING CO., 327 U.S. 178 (1946)

*The circulation of the White Plains Publishing Company's paper in White Plains, New York, during the period involved in this case ranged from 9,000 to 11,000. One half of one per cent of its readers were out-of-state subscribers which the newspaper had made no effort to secure. The petitioners, who were some of the paper's employees, sued to recover overtime pay, liquidated damages, and counsel fees under 16 (6) of the Fair Labor Standards Act of 1938. The Supreme Court found for the employees. Weekly and semi-weekly publications of less than 3,000 circulation (later changed to 4,000 circulation) were exempted from regulation by the Fair Labor Standards Act. One issue was whether this was unfair discrimination against one class of papers.*

Mr. Justice William O. DOUGLAS delivered the opinion of the Court:

Respondent argues that to bring it under the [Fair Labor Standards] Act, Section 13 (a) (8), is to sanction a discrimination against the daily papers in violation of the principles announced in *Grosjean v. American Press Co.*, 297 U.S. 233. Volume of circulation, frequency of issue, and area of distribution are said to be an improper basis of classification. Moreover, it is said that the Act lays a direct burden on the press in violation of the First Amendment. The *Grosjean* case is not in point here. There the press was singled out for special taxation and the tax was graduated in accordance with volume of circulation. No such vice inheres in this legislation. As the press has business aspects it has no special immunity from laws applicable to business in general. And the exemption of small weeklies and semi-weeklies is not a "deliberate and calculated device" to penalize a certain group of newspapers. As we have seen, it was inserted to put those papers more on a parity with other small town enterprises. The Fifth Amendment does not require full and uniform exercise of the commerce power. Congress may weigh relative needs and restrict the application of a legislative policy to less than the entire field.

We hold that respondent is engaged in the production of goods for commerce.

Another decision involving similar issues the same year reinforced the Court's position in the *Mabee* case.

## NEWSPAPERS ARE NOT EXEMPT FROM LABOR LAWS

OKLAHOMA PRESS PUBLISHING CO. V. WALLING, 327 U.S. 186 (1946)

*The Oklahoma Press Company also contested the application of the Fair Labor Standards Act to newspapers—pleading the First, Fourth, and Fifth Amendments as well as the limitation clauses built into the Act itself. The newspaper was overruled by the Supreme Court.*

Mr. Justice Wiley RUTLEDGE delivered the opinion of the Court:

Coloring almost all of petitioners' positions, as we understand them, is a primary misconception that the First Amendment knocks out any possible application of the Fair Labor Standards Act to the business of publishing and distributing newspapers. The argument has two prongs.

The broadside assertion that petitioners "could not be covered by the Act," for the reason that "application of this Act to its newspaper publishing business would violate its rights as guaranteed by the First Amendment," is without merit. If Congress can remove obstructions to commerce by requiring publishers to bargain collectively with employees and refrain from interfering with their rights of self-organization, matters closely related to eliminating low wages and long hours, Congress likewise may strike directly at those evils when they adversely affect commerce. . . . The Amendment does not forbid this or other regulation which ends in no restraint upon expression or in any other evil outlawed by its terms and purposes.

Petitioners' narrower argument, of allegedly invalid classification, arises from the statutory exemptions and may be shortly dismissed. The intimation that the Act falls by reason of the exclusion of seamen, farm workers and others by 13 (a) is hardly more than a suggestion and is dismissed accordingly. . . . The contention drawn from the exemption of employees of small newspapers by 13 (a) (8) deserves only slightly more attention. It seems to be two-fold, that the amendment forbids Congress to "regulate the press by classifying it" at all and in any event that it cannot use volume of circulation or size as a factor in the classification.

Reliance upon *Grosjean v. American Press Co.,* 297 U.S. 233, to support these claims is misplaced. There the state statute singled out newspapers for special taxation and was held in effect to graduate the tax in accordance with volume of circulation. Here there was no singling out of the press for treatment different from that accorded other business in general. Rather the Act's purpose was to place publishers of newspapers upon the same plane with other businesses and the exemption for small newspapers had the same object. . . . Nothing in the *Grosjean* case forbids Congress to exempt some publishers because of size from either a tax or a regulation which would be valid if applied to all.

What has been said also disposes of the contention drawn from the scope of the commerce power and its applicability to the publishing business considered independently of the Amendment's influence.

The newspaper arguments were disallowed in the previous cases because the contested government regulation did not affect the editorial operations or the news itself. But there is a business or property aspect to the "news."

## COPYRIGHT AND PROPERTY IN NEWS

Does news, the report of recent occurrences, have any property value and can it be copyrighted? To what extent does the first reporter of an important news event enjoy a property right to his exclusive story? Copyright is a specialized area of the law rarely involving news gathering, much less freedom of the press. However, the Supreme Court has ruled on the relationship of news to property and copyright, and has identified its constitutional aspects.

INTERNATIONAL NEWS SERVICE V. ASSOCIATED PRESS, 248 U.S. 215 (1918)

*The Associated Press sued the International News Service for copying AP dispatches to redistribute to INS subscribers. The INS procedure, typical of competitive practices of the news services during the era before the anti-trust and fair trade laws, was challenged on the ground of unfair competition. The U.S. district court in southern New York upheld part of AP's complaint. The Supreme Court also held for the Associated Press stating that the law of unfair competition protected non-copyrightable news matter.*

Mr. Justice Mahlon PITNEY delivered the opinion of the Court:

No doubt news articles often possess a literary quality, and are the subject of literary property at the common law; nor do we question that such an article, as a literary production, is the subject of copyright by the terms of the act as it now stands. In an early case at the circuit court Mr. Justice Thompson held in effect that a newspaper was not within the protection of the copyright acts of 1790. . . . But the present act is broader; it provides that the works for which copyright may be secured shall include "all the writings of an author," and specifically mentions "periodicals, including newspapers." . . . Evidently this admits to copyright a contribution to a newspaper, notwithstanding it also may convey news; and such is the practice of the copyright office, as the newspapers of the day bear witness. . . .

But the news element—the information respecting current events contained in the literary production—is not the creation of the writer, but is a report of matters that ordinarily are *publici juris;* it is the "history of the day." It is not to be supposed that the framers of the Constitution, when they empowered Congress "to promote the progress of science and useful arts, by securing for limited times to authors and inventors the exclusive right to their respective writings and discoveries" (Const. Art. 1, sec. 8, par. 8), intended to confer upon one who might happen to be the first to report a historic event the exclusive right for any period to spread the knowledge of it.

. . . . . . . . . . . . . . . . . .

The peculiar value of news is in the spreading of it while it is fresh; and it is evident that a valuable property interest in the news, as news, cannot be maintained by keeping it secret. Besides, except for matters improperly disclosed, or published in breach of trust or confidence, or in violation of law, none of which is involved in this branch of the case, the news of current events may be regarded as common property. What we are concerned with is the business of making it known to the world, in which both parties to the present suit are engaged. That business consists in maintaining a prompt, sure, steady, and reliable service designed to place the daily events of the world at the breakfast table of the millions at a price that, while of trifling moment to each reader, is sufficient in the aggregate to afford compensation for the cost of gathering and distributing it, with the added profit so necessary as an incentive to effective action in the commercial world. The service thus performed for newspaper readers is not only innocent but extremely useful in itself, and indubitably constitutes a legitimate business. The parties are competitors in this field; and, on fundamental principles, applicable here as elsewhere, when the rights or privileges of the one are liable to conflict with those of the other, each party is under a duty so to conduct its own business as not unnecessarily or unfairly to injure that of the other.

In dissenting, Justice Brandeis argued that the general rule of the law is that after words and ideas have been communicated to others, they become the common property of all mankind.

Mr. Justice Louis BRANDEIS dissenting:

News is a report of recent occurrences. The business of the news agency is to gather systematically knowledge of such occurrences of interest and to distribute reports thereof. The Associated Press contended that knowledge so acquired is property, because it costs money and labor to produce and because it has value for which those who have it not are ready to pay; that it remains property and is entitled to protection as long as it has commercial value as news; and that to protect it effectively, the defendant must be enjoined from making, or causing to be made, any gainful use of it while it retains such value. When an essential element of individual property is affected with a public interest, the right of exclusion is qualified. But the fact that a product of the mind has cost its producer money and labor, and has a value for which others are willing to pay, is not sufficient to ensure to it this legal attribute of property. The general rule of law is, that the noblest of human productions— knowledge, truths ascertained, conceptions, and ideas—become, after voluntary communication to others, free as the air to common use. Upon these incorporeal productions the attribute of property is continued after such communication only in certain classes of cases where public policy has seemed to demand it. These exceptions are confined to productions which, in some degree, involve creation, invention, or discovery. But by no means are all such endowed with this attribute of property. The creations which are recognized as property by the common law are literary, dramatic, musical, and other artistic creations; and these have also protection under the copyright statutes. The inventions and discoveries upon which this attribute of property is conferred only by statute are the few comprised within the patent law.

## FIRST AMENDMENT PROTECTION UNAFFECTED BY PROFIT MOTIVE

The first three decisions in this chapter indicate that the business aspects of newspaper operations are not entirely shielded by the First Amendment from laws regulating business. The following *Cammarano* decision provides added perspective—an assurance that those who are out to make money are as much protected by the First Amendment as those "whose advocacy or promotion is not hitched to a profit motive."

CAMMARANO V. UNITED STATES, 358 U.S. 498 (1959)

*This case did not directly involve the press but it provided an opportunity for the Court, through Justice Douglas's concurring opinion, to point out the First Amendment protection given to a protest against a government action that affects a business. William B. Cammarano's action was for refund of federal income taxes. He was a beer wholesaler in the state of Washington. On certiorari to the Supreme Court, Cammarano contested the U.S. Treasury Department regulation that individual or corporate taxpayers could not deduct from gross income any money spent to defeat legislation. The Court upheld the Treasury Department.*

Mr. Justice DOUGLAS concurring:

*Valentine v. Chrestensen,* 316 U.S. 52, 54, held that business advertisements and commercial matters did not enjoy the protection of the First Amendment, made applicable to the States by the Fourteenth. The ruling was casual, almost offhand. And it has not survived reflection. That "freedom of speech or of the press," directly guaranteed against encroachment by the Federal Government and safeguarded against state action by the Due Process Clause of the Fourteenth Amendment, is not in terms or by implication confined to discourse of a particular kind and nature. It has often been stressed as essential to the exposition and exchange of political ideas, to the expression of philosophical attitudes, to the flowering of the letters. Important as the First Amendment is to all those cultural ends, it has not been restricted to them. Individual or group protests against action which results in monetary injuries are certainly not beyond the reach of the First Amendment as *Thornhill v. Alabama*, 310 U.S. 88, which placed picketing within the ambit of the First Amendment, teaches. . . . A protest against government action that affects a business occupies as high a place. The profit motive should make no difference, for that is an element inherent in the very conception of a press under our system of free enterprise. Those who make their living through exercise of First Amendment rights are no less entitled to its protection that those whose advocacy or promotion is not hitched to a profit motive. We held as much in *Follett v. Town of McCormick*, 321 U.S. 573. And I find it difficult to draw a line between that group and those who in other lines of endeavor advertise their wares by different means. Chief Justice Hughes speaking for the Court in *Lovell v. City of Griffin*, . . . defined the First Amendment right with which we now deal in the broadest terms, "The press in its historic connotation comprehends every sort of publication which affords a vehicle of information and opinion."

By the wide range of press activities it has placed under the protection of the First Amendment, the Court during the last quarter century has given real meaning to those words of Chief Justice Charles Evans Hughes. But, as these decisions indicate, legitimate regulation of the business aspects of the press does not conflict with freedom of the press.

Mass communications are in great part involved in interstate commerce and hence subject to such major national legislation (derived from the commerce clause of the Constitution), as the Wagner Act and the Fair Labor Standards Act. When the right of freedom of expression is practiced within the framework of a business activity, that activity is subject to all the general laws that regulate business. As long as those laws

do not interfere with the expression of ideas and information, there is no conflict with the First Amendment.

On the other hand, as the *Cammarano* decision shows,
those who are seeking to make money are as fully protected by
the First Amendment as anyone else. The Court has recognized that a free and vigorous press system essentially must be
one that is privately owned, economically sound, and firmly
anchored in free enterprise.

*Chapter Fifteen*

# THE PRESS AND ANTITRUST LAWS

AS BUSINESS INSTITUTIONS operated for profit, units or combinations of the mass media are subject to the antitrust laws designed to discourage monopolies and conspiracies in restraint of trade.

It can be debated whether the American public really wishes to see the antitrust laws enforced as regards the mass media. In television, viewers enjoy the advantages of standardized network television. There are advantages, too, to readers of the single multipurpose omnibus daily newspaper or newspaper combination so characteristic of American cities today.

However, since antitrust legislation seeks to restore competition, it implies the spirit of diversity or the "market place of ideas" which is so basic to our tradition of freedom of the press. In the 1945 *Associated Press* antitrust case, for example, the Supreme Court applied this principle to answer the AP's claim that the First Amendment is violated by extending the Sherman Act to the press. Here we find government acting in an affirmative way to insure freedom of expression by enlarging the "market place" and to guarantee that the "widest possible diversity of views and ideas" is presented.

In the series of cases excerpted here, the Sherman Anti-Trust Act of 1890 is involved in three strikingly different situations—cooperative news gathering associations, advertising rate practices, and public relations firms.

## POSITIVE GOVERNMENT ACTION TO PROTECT FREEDOM
## FOR ALL

The major antitrust case involving the press was *Associated Press v. United States* in 1945. It affected many units of the newspaper business because the AP is a member-owned cooperative. As with other disputed federal laws, such as the Wagner Act and the Wages and Hours Law, the question here raised was whether the application of the Sherman Act to the press violated the First Amendment.

ASSOCIATED PRESS V. UNITED STATES, 326 U.S. 1 (1945)

*The Associated Press was charged under the Sherman Act with being a combination and conspiracy in restraint of trade and commerce in news among the states, and with attempting to monopolize a part of that trade. The charges cited the AP bylaws allowing members to prohibit the sale of its news to non-AP members and to block the admission of new members. A federal district court in New York ruled that these bylaws unlawfully restricted admission to AP membership and violated the Sherman Act. The Supreme Court agreed by a 5–to–4 margin.*

Mr. Justice Hugo BLACK delivered the opinion of the Court:

In reaching our conclusion on the summary judgment question, we are not unmindful of the argument that newspaper publishers charged with combining cooperatively to violate the Sherman Act are entitled to have a different and more favorable kind of trial procedure than all other persons covered by the Act. No language in the Sherman Act or the summary judgment statute lends support to the suggestion. There is no single element in our traditional insistence upon an equally fair trial for every person from which any such discriminatory trial practice could stem. For equal—not unequal—justice under law is the goal of our society. Our legal system has not established different measures of proof for the trial of cases in which equally intelligent and responsible defendants are charged with violating the same statutes. Member publishers of AP are engaged in business for profit exactly as are other business men who sell food, steel, aluminum, or anything else people need or want. . . . All are alike covered by the Sherman Act. The fact that the publisher handles news while others handle goods does not, as we shall later point out, afford the publisher a peculiar constitutional sanctuary in which he can with impunity violate laws regulating his business practices.

Nor is a publisher who engages in business practices made unlawful by the Sherman Act entitled to a partial immunity by reason of the "clear and present danger" doctrine which courts have used to protect freedom to speak, to print, and to worship. That doctrine, as related to this case, provides protection for utterances themselves so that the printed or spoken word may not be the subject of previous restraint or punishment, unless their expression creates a clear and present danger of bringing about a substantial evil which the government has power to prohibit. . . . Formulated as it was to protect liberty of thought and of expression, it would degrade the clear and present danger doctrine to fashion from it a shield for business publishers who engage in business practices condemned by the Sherman Act. Consequently, we hold that publishers, like all others charged with violating the Sherman Act, are subject to the provisions of the summary judgment statute. And that means that such judgments shall not be rendered against publishers or others where there are genuine disputes of fact on material issues.

. . . . . . . . . . . . . . . . . . .

Inability to buy news from the largest news agency, or any one of its multitude of members, can have most serious effects on the publication of competitive newspapers, both those presently published and those which but for these restrictions, might be published in the future. This is illustrated by the District Court's finding that in 26 cities of the United States, existing newspapers already have contracts for AP news and the same newspapers have contracts with United Press and International News Service under which new newspapers would be required to pay the contract holders large sums to enter the field. The net effect is seriously to limit the opportunity of any new paper to enter these cities. Trade restraints of this character, aimed at the destruction of competition, tend to block the initiative which brings newcomers into a field of business and to frustrate the free enterprise system which it was the purpose of the Sherman Act to protect.

. . . . . . . . . . . . . . . . . . .

Finally, the argument is made that to apply the Sherman Act to this association of publishers constitutes an abridgment of the freedom of the press guaranteed by the First Amendment. . . . It would be strange indeed, however, if the grave concern for freedom of the press which prompted adoption of the First Amendment should be read as a command that the government was without power to protect that freedom. The First Amendment, far from providing an argument against application of the Sherman Act, here provides powerful reasons to the contrary. That Amendment rests on the assumption that the widest possible dissemination of information from diverse and antagonistic sources is essential to the welfare of the public, that a free press is a condition of a free society. Surely a command that the government itself shall not impede the free flow of ideas does not afford non-governmental combinations a refuge if they impose restraints upon that constitutionally guaranteed freedom. Freedom to publish means freedom for all and not for some. Freedom to publish is guaranteed by the Constitution, but freedom to combine to keep others from publishing is not. Freedom of the press from governmental interference under the First Amendment does not sanction repression of that freedom by private interests. The First Amendment affords not the slightest support for the contention that a combination to restrain trade in news and views has any constitutional immunity.

Justice Felix Frankfurter provided several more arguments to justify government intervention in the interests of press diversity.

Mr. Justice FRANKFURTER concurring:

To be sure, the Associated Press is a cooperative organization of members who are "engaged in a commercial business for profit." . . . But in addition to being a commercial enterprise, it has a relation to the public interest unlike that of any other enterprise pursued for profit. A free press is indispensable to the workings of our democratic society. The business of the press, and therefore the business of the Associated Press, is the promotion of truth regarding public matters by furnishing the basis for an understanding of them. Truth and understanding are not wares like peanuts or potatoes. And so, the incidence of restraints upon the promotion of truth through denial of access to the basis for understanding calls into play considerations very different from comparable restraints in a cooperative enterprise having merely a commercial aspect. I find myself entirely in agreement with Judge Learned Hand that "neither exclusively, nor even primarily, are the interests of the newspaper industry conclusive; for that industry serves one of the most vital of all general interests: the dissemination of news from as many different sources, and with as many different facets and colors as is possible. That interest is closely akin to, if indeed it is not the same as, the interest protected by the First Amendment; it presupposes that right conclusions are more likely to be gathered out of a multitude of tongues, than through any kind of authoritative selection. To many this is, and always will be, folly; but we have staked upon it our all." . . .

From this point of view it is wholly irrelevant that the Associated Press itself has rival news agencies. As to ordinary commodities, agreements to curtail the supply and to fix prices are in violation of the area of free enterprise which the Sherman Law was designed to protect. The press in its commercial aspects is also subject to the regulation of the Sherman Law. . . . But the freedom of enterprise protected by the Sherman Law necessarily has different aspects in relation to the press than in the case of ordinary commercial pursuits. The interest of the public is to have the flow of news not trammeled by the combined self-interest of those who enjoy a unique constitutional position precisely because of the public dependence on a free press. A public interest so essential to the vitality of our democratic government may be defeated by private restraints no less than by public censorship.

Equally irrelevant is the objection that it turns the Associated Press into a "public utility" to deny to a combination of newspapers the right to treat access to their pooled resources as though they were regulating membership in a social club. The relation of such restraints upon access to news and the relation of such access to the function of a free press in our democratic society must not be obscured by the specialized notions that have gathered around the legal concept of "public utility."

The short of the matter is that the bylaws which the District Court has struck down clearly restrict the commerce which is conducted by the Associated Press, and the restrictions are unreasonable because they offend the basic functions which a constitutionally guaranteed free press serves in our nation.

But Justice Owen Roberts disagreed arguing that the freedom of the press was not protected when the Court prescribes the conditions under which "news" can be communicated to the public. Justice Roberts' views represent the traditional libertarian view that government should keep its hands off the press.

Mr. Justice ROBERTS dissenting in part:

This case deals with "news." News is information about matters of general interest. The term has been defined as "a report of a recent event." The report may be made to one moved by curiosity or to one who wishes to make some practical use of it. Newspapers obtain such reports and publish them as a part of a business conducted for profit. The proprietor of a newspaper, when he employs a person to inquire and report, engages personal service. I suppose no one would deny that he is entitled to the exclusive use of the report rendered as a result of the service for which he contracts and pays. I suppose that one rendering such service is free to contract with his employer that the product of his inquiries—the news he furnishes his employer—shall be used solely by the employer and not imparted to another.

As I have said, news is the result of effort in the investigation of recent events. Every newspaper is interested in procuring news of happenings in its vicinity, and maintains a staff for that purpose. Such news may have some value to newspapers published in cities outside the locality of the occurrence. I assume that if two publishers agreed that each should supply a transcript of all reports he received to the other, and conditioned their agreement that neither would abuse the privilege accorded by giving away or selling what was furnished under the joint arrangement, there could be no objection under the Sherman Act. I had assumed, although the opinion appears to hold otherwise, that such an arrangement would not be obnoxious to the Sherman Act because many, rather than few, joined in it. I think that the situation would be no different if a machinery were created to facilitate the exchange of the news procured by each of the participants such as a partnership, an incorporated association, or a non-profit corporation.

I assume it cannot be questioned that two or more persons desirous of obtaining news may agree to employ a single reporter, or a staff of reporters, to furnish them news, and agree amongst themselves that, as they share the expense involved, they themselves will use the fruit of the service and will not give it away or sell it. Although the procedure has obvious advantages, and is in itself innocent, I do not know, from the opinion of the court, whether it would be held that the inevitable or necessary operation, or necessary consequence of such an arrangement is to restrain competition in trade or commerce and that it is, consequently, illegal. Many expressions in the opinion seem to recognize that all AP does is to keep for its members that which, at joint expense, its members and employes have produced—its reports of world events. Thus it is said that non-members are denied access to AP news, not, be it observed, to news. Again it is said that the by-laws "block all newspaper non-members from any opportunity to buy news from AP or any of its publisher members"; again that "the erection of obstacles to the acquisition of membership . . . can make it difficult, if not impossible, for non-members to get any of the news furnished by AP. . . ." If these expressions stood alone as the factual basis of decision we should know that the court is condemning a joint enterprise for the production of something—here, news copy—which those who produce it intend to use for their exclusive benefit. But it is impossible to deduce from the opinion that this is the ratio of decision.

The decree may well result not in freer competition but in a monopoly in AP or UP, or in some resulting agency, and thus force full and complete regimentation of all news service to the people of the nation. The decree here approved may well be, and I think threatened to be, but a first step in the shackling of the press, which will subvert the constitutional freedom to print or to withohld, to print as and how one's reason or one's interest dictates. When that time comes, the state will be supreme and freedom of the state will have superseded freedom of the individual to print, being responsible before the law for abuse of the high privilege.

It is not protecting a freedom but confining it to prescribe where and how and under what conditions one must impart the literary product of his thought and research. This is fettering the press, not striking off its chains.

The existing situation with respect to radio points the moral of what I have said. In that field Congress has imposed regulation because, in contrast to the press, the physical channels of communication are limited, and chaos would result from unrestrained and unregulated use of such channels. But in imposing regulation, Congress has refrained from any restraint on ownership of news or information or the right to use it. And any regulation of this major source of information, in the light of the constitutional guarantee of free speech, should be closely and jealously examined by the courts.

Justice Frank Murphy also dissented, showing how one libertarian judge can honestly differ with another—in this case, Justice Black. Justice Murphy hesitated to approve a government action which interfered with the collection and dissemination of news, even though he acknowledged that the press can claim no special immunity from the Sherman Act. He was not quite as willing as Justice Black to regard the publishers' defense as a plea for a "peculiar constitutional sanctuary."

Mr. Justice MURPHY dissenting:

Today is also the first time that the Sherman Act has been used as a vehicle for affirmative intervention by the Government in the realm of dissemination of information. As the Government states, this is an attempt to remove "barriers erected by private combination against access to reports of world news." That newspapers and news agencies are engaged in business for profit is beyond dispute. And it is undeniable that the Associated Press and other press associations can claim no immunity from the application of the general laws or of the Sherman Act in particular. . . . But at the same time it is clear that they are engaged in collecting and distributing news and information rather than in manufacturing automobiles, aluminum or gasoline. We cannot avoid that fact. Nor can we escape the fact that governmental action directly aimed at the methods or conditions of such collection or distribution is an interference with the press, however differing in degree it may be from governmental restraints on written or spoken utterances themselves.

The tragic history of recent years demonstrates far too well how despotic governments may interfere with the press and other means of communication in their efforts to corrupt public opinion and destroy individual freedom. Experience teaches us to hesitate before creating a precedent in which might lurk even the slightest justification for such interference by the Government in these matters. Proof of the justification and need for the use of the Sherman Act to liberate and remove unreasonable impediments from the channels of news distribution should therefore be clear and unmistakable. Only then can the precedent avoid being a dangerous one authorizing the use of the Sherman Act for unjustified governmental interference with the distribution of information.

This does not mean that the Associated Press is entitled to any preferential treatment under the Sherman Act or that the Government must meet any higher degree of proof of a statutory violation when dealing with the press than when dealing with any other field of commercial endeavor. Clear and unmistakable proof of a Sherman Act violation, especially where a summary judgment procedure is followed, is necessary in any case. And failure to insist upon compliance with that standard of proof is unwise under any circumstances. But such a failure has unusually dangerous implications when it appears with reference to an alleged violation of the Act by those who collect and distribute information. We should therefore be particularly vigilant in reviewing a case of this nature, a vigilance that apparently is not shared by the Court today.

## GOVERNMENT ACTION TO END LOCAL MEDIA MONOPOLY

The furor set off in the newspaper business by the Court's decision in the *Associated Press* case soon died down. And the interest of the antitrust division of the Justice Department shifted from news associations to the so-called local newspaper monopoly. Because of economic factors, the number of competing daily newspapers has declined rapidly in urban America since World War I. Many cities, including Minneapolis, Omaha, and Louisville, are served by single newspapers or single ownerships publishing morning and evening newspapers. In some instances, the newspapers also own local radio and television stations.

The *Lorain Journal* and *Times-Picayune* cases were indicative of the Justice Department's concern with business and advertising practices of local combinations of the mass media.

The government won in *Lorain* but lost in *Times-Picayune*. A comparison of the two decisions suggests how the Sherman Act applies to local newspaper advertising practices.

LORAIN JOURNAL V. UNITED STATES, 342 U.S. 143 (1951)

*This was an action by the United States government to enjoin the Lorain Journal Company and others from attempting to monopolize interstate commerce.*

*In 1932, the* Journal *bought out the last competing daily paper in Lorain, Ohio. The* Journal *was reaching 99 per cent of all families in the city in 1948, when new competition appeared in the form of an independent radio station, WEOL, in Elyria, eight miles from Lorain. The* Journal's *competitive practices in dealing with the radio station led to the antitrust charge. A U.S. district court granted an injunction against the* Journal *and the newspaper appealed. In affirming this judgment the U.S. Supreme Court held that the newspaper publisher's attempt to force its advertisers to boycott a competing radio station justified the injunction.*

Mr. Justice Harold BURTON delivered the opinion of the Court:

There can be little doubt today that the immediate dissemination of news gathered from throughout the nation or the world by agencies specially organized for that purpose is a part of interstate commerce. The same is true of national advertising originating throughout the nation and offering products for sale on a national scale. The local dissemination of such news and advertising requires continuous interstate transmission of materials and payments, to say nothing of the interstate commerce involved in the sale and delivery of products sold. The decision in *Blumenstock Bros. v. Curtis Pub. Co.,* 252 U.S. 436, related to the making of contracts for advertising rather than to the preparation and dissemination of advertising. Moreover, the view there stated, that the making of contracts by parties outside of a state for the insertion of advertising material in periodicals of nationwide circulation did not amount to interstate commerce, rested expressly on a line of cases holding "that policies of insurance are not articles of commerce, and that the making of such contracts is a mere incident of commercial intercourse." . . .

The publisher claims a right as a private business concern to select its customers and to refuse to accept advertisements from whomever it pleases. We do not dispute that general right. But the word "right" is one of the most deceptive of pitfalls; it is so easy to slip from a qualified meaning in the premise to an unqualified one in the conclusion. Most rights are qualified. . . . The right claimed by the publisher is neither absolute nor exempt from regulation. Its exercise as a purposeful means of monopolizing interstate commerce is prohibited by the Sherman Act. The operator of the radio station, equally with the publisher of the newspaper, is entitled to the protection of that Act. "*In the absence of any purpose to create or maintain a monopoly, the act does not restrict the long recognized right of trader or manufacturer engaged in an entirely private business, freely to exercise his own independent discretion as to parties with whom he will deal.*" . . .

*The injunction does not violate any guaranteed freedom of the press.* The publisher suggests that the injunction amounts to a prior restraint upon what it may publish. We find in it no restriction upon any guaranteed freedom of the press. The injunction applies to a publisher what the law applies to others. The publisher may not accept or deny advertisements in an "attempt to monopolize . . . any part of the trade or commerce among the several states. . . ." Injunctive relief under paragraph 4 of the Sherman Act is as appropriate a means of enforcing the Act against newspapers as it is against others.

TIMES-PICAYUNE V. UNITED STATES, 345 U.S. 594 (1953)

*In a case similar to* Lorain, *a civil suit brought against the publisher of a morning and evening newspaper combination in New Orleans alleged violation of the Sherman Anti-Trust Act because the publisher required advertisers to buy space in both, not just one, of the newspapers. Such advertising contracts, it was charged, resulted in restraint of trade and were an attempt to monopolize trade. A U.S. district court in Louisiana found violations of the Sherman Act and enjoined the* Times-Picayune *from continuing the practice. The Supreme Court reversed the lower court, holding that the evidence was insufficient to show a violation of the Sherman Act.*

*Justice Tom C. Clark's decision included an excellent description of the recent economic consolidation of the newspaper business and its relation to freedom of expression. The New Orleans papers won because the majority felt there was no unlawful "tying" arrangements whereby an inferior product is forcibly sold with a second desired product. The two papers, under single ownership, were selling indistinguishable prod-*

*ucts: advertising space in the* Times-Picayune *and advertising space in the* States.

Mr. Justice CLARK delivered the opinion of the Court:

At issue is the legality under the Sherman Act of the Times-Picayune Publishing company's contracts for the sale of newspaper classified and general display advertising space. The company in New Orleans owns and publishes the morning *Times-Picayune* and the evening *States*. Buyers of space for general display and classified advertising in its publications may purchase only combined insertions appearing in both the morning and evening paper, and not in either separately. The United States filed a civil suit under the Sherman Act challenging these "unit" or "forced combination" contracts as unreasonable restraints of interstate trade, banned by sec. 1 and as tools in an attempt to monopolize a segment of interstate commerce, in violation of sec. 2.

. . . . . . . . . . . . . . . . .

The daily newspaper, though essential to the effective functioning of our political system, has in recent years suffered drastic economic decline. A vigorous and dauntless press is a chief source feeding the flow of democratic expression and controversy which maintains the institutions of a free society. . . . By interpreting to the citizen the policies of his government and vigilantly scrutinizing the official conduct of those who administer the state, an independent press stimulates free discussion and focuses public opinion on issues and officials as a potent check on arbitrary action or abuse. . . . The press, in fact, serves one of the most vital of all general interests: the dissemination of news from as many different sources, and with as many different facets and colors as is possible. That interest is closely akin to, if indeed it is not the same as, the interest protected by the First Amendment; it presupposes that right conclusions are more likely to be gathered out of a multitude of tongues, than through any kind of authoritative selection. "To many this is, and always will be, folly; but we have staked upon it our all." Yet today, despite the vital task that in our society the press performs, the number of daily newspapers in the United States is at its lowest point since the century's turn: in 1951, 1,773 daily newspapers served 1,443 American cities, compared with 2,600 dailies published in 1,207 cities in the year 1909. Moreover, while 598 new dailies braved the field between 1929 and 1950, 373 of these suspended publication during that period—less than half of the new entrants survived. Concurrently, daily newspaper competition within individual cities has grown nearly extinct: in 1951, 81% of all daily newspaper cities had only one daily paper; 11% more had two or more publications, but a single publisher controlled both or all. In that year, therefore, only 8% of daily newspaper cities enjoyed the clash of opinion which competition among publishers of their daily press could provide.

Advertising is the economic mainstay of the newspaper business. Generally, more than two-thirds of a newspaper's total revenues flow from the sale of advertising space. Local display advertising brings in about 44% of revenues; general—14%; classified—13%; circulation, almost the rest. Obviously, newspapers in 1929 garnered 79% of total national advertising expeditures, by 1951 other mass media had cut newspapers' share down to 34.7%. When the Times-Picayune Publishing Company in 1949 announced its forthcoming institution of unit selling to general advertisers, about 180 other publishers of morning-evening newspapers had previously adopted the unit plan. Of the 598 daily newspapers which broke into publication between 1929 and 1950, 38% still published when that period closed. Forty-six of these entering dailies, however, encountered the competition of established dailies which utilized unit rates; significantly, by 1950, of these 46, 41 had collapsed. Thus a newcomer in the daily newspaper business could calculate his chances of survival as 11% in cities where unit plans had taken hold. Viewed against the background of rapidly declining competition in the daily newspaper business, such a trade practice becomes suspect under the Sherman Act.

.  .  .  .  .  .  .  .  .  .  .  .  .  .  .  .  .  .  .

But every newspaper is a dual trader in separate though interdependent markets; it sells the paper's news and advertising content to its readers. This case concerns solely one of these markets. The Publishing Co. stands not accused of tying sales to its readers but only to buyers of general and classified space in its papers. For this reason, dominance in the advertising market, not in readership, must be decisive in gauging the legality of the Company's unit plan. . . . We do not think that the *Times-Picayune* occupied a "dominant" position in the newspaper advertising market in New Orleans. . . . The common core of the adjudicated unlawful tying arrangements is the forced purchase of a second distinct commodity with the desired purchase of a dominant "tying" product, resulting in economic harm to competition in the "tied" market. Here, however, two newspapers under single ownership at the same place, time, and terms sell indistinguishable products to advertisers; no dominant "tying" product exists (in fact, since space in neither the *Times-Picayune* nor the *States* can be bought alone, one may be viewed as "tying" the other); no leverage in one market excludes sellers in the second, because for present purposes the products are identical and the market the same. . . . In short, neither the rationale nor the doctrines evolved by the "tying" cases can dispose of the Publishing Company's arrangements challenged here.

## PUBLIC RELATIONS PRACTICES PROTECTED BY
## CONSTITUTION

In addition to advertising practices, a related media activity, public relations, has been examined for possible antitrust implications. Public relations, that vigorous and fast-growing offspring of modern mass communications, so far has rarely been involved in Supreme Court decisions. However, a celebrated squabble between the railroads and the truckers in Pennsylvania did bring public relations practitioners to the bar of the high court. In this particular case it was found that their hands were slightly dirty but their practices in Pennsylvania did not violate the Sherman Act and were well within constitutional limits. The decision is of major significance for public relations.

EASTERN RAILROAD PRESIDENTS CONFERENCE V. NOERR MOTOR FREIGHT, 365 U.S. 127 (1961)

*This action was brought by long-distance trucking companies against twenty-four major railroads and the Carl Byoir public relations firm for violation of the Sherman Act. The railroads and Byoir in turn filed a counter claim charging violation of the act by the trucking companies. A lower court found in favor of the trucking companies and their trade association.*

*The Supreme Court, however, held that the publicity campaign of the railroads to obtain governmental action adverse to the trucking interests was not illegal. Even though they may have been trying to gain an unfair competition advantage, and even though they deceived the public and public officials, the railroads' publicity campaign did not, the Court held, violate the Sherman Act. The judgment was reversed. Justice Black's decision placed the public relations activities under the protection of the last clause of the First Amendment—the right to petition government for a redress of grievances.*

Mr. Justice BLACK delivered the opinion of the Court:

We think it equally clear that the Sherman Act does not prohibit two or more persons from associating together in an attempt to persuade the legislature or the executive to take particular action with respect to a law that would produce a restraint or a monopoly. Although such associations could perhaps, through a process of expansive construction, be brought within the general proscription of "combination(s) . . . in restraint of trade," they bear very little if any resemblance to the combinations normally held violative of the Sherman Act, combinations ordinarily characterized by an express or implied agreement or understanding that the participants will jointly give up their trade freedom, or help one another to take away the trade freedom of others through the use of such devices as price-fixing agreements, boycotts, market-division agreements, and other similar arrangements. This essential dissimilarity between an agreement jointly to seek legislation or law enforcement and the agreements traditionally condemned by paragraph 1 of the Act, even if not itself conclusive on the question of the applicability of the Act, does constitute a warning against treating the defendants' conduct as though it amounted to a common-law trade restraint. And we do think that the question is conclusively settled, against the application of the Act, when this factor of essential dissimilarity is considered along with the other difficulties that would be presented by a holding that the Sherman Act forbids associations for the purpose of influencing the passage or enforcement of laws.

In the first place, such a holding would substantially impair the power of government to take actions through its legislature and executive that operate to restrain trade. In a representative democracy such as this, these branches of government act on behalf of the people and, to a very large extent, the whole concept of representation depends upon the ability of the people to make their wishes known to their representatives. To hold that the government retains the power to act in this representative capacity and yet hold, at the same time, that the people cannot freely inform the government of their wishes would impute to the Sherman Act a purpose to regulate, not business activity, but political activity, a purpose which would have no basis whatever in the legislative history of that Act. Secondly, and of at least equal significance, such a construction of the Sherman Act would raise important constitutional questions. The right of petition is one of the freedoms protected by the Bill of Rights, and we cannot, of course, lightly impute to Congress an intent to invade these freedoms. Indeed, such an imputation would be particularly unjustified in this case in view of all the countervailing considerations enumerated above. For these reasons, we think it clear that the Sherman Act does not apply to the activities of the railroads at least insofar as those activities comprised mere solicitation of governmental action with respect to the passage and enforcement of laws. We are thus called upon to consider whether the courts below were correct in holding that, notwithstanding this principle, the Act was violated here because of the presence in the railroads' publicity campaign of additional factors sufficient to take the case out of the area in which the principle is controlling.

The first such factor relied upon was the fact, established by the finding of the District Court, that the railroads' sole purpose in seeking to influence the passage and enforcement of laws was to destroy the truckers as competitors for the long-distance freight business. But we do not see how this fact, even if adequately supported in the record, could transform conduct otherwise lawful into a violation of the Sherman Act. All of the considerations that have led us to the conclusion that the Act does not apply to mere group solicitation of governmental action are equally applicable in spite of the addition of this factor. The right of the people to inform their representatives in government of their desires with respect to the passage or enforcement of laws cannot properly be made to depend upon their intent in doing so. It is neither unusual nor illegal for people to seek action on laws in the hope that they may bring about an advantage to themselves and a disadvantage to their competitors. This Court has expressly recognized this fact in its opinion in *United States v. Rock Royal Co-op.*, where it was said: "If ulterior motives of corporate aggrandizement stimulated their activities, their efforts were not thereby rendered unlawful. If the Act and Order are otherwise valid, the fact that their effect would be to give cooperatives a monopoly of the market would not violate the Sherman Act. . . ." Indeed, it is quite probably people with just such a hope of personal advantage who provide much of the information upon which governments must act. A construction of the Sherman Act that would disqualify people from taking a public position on matters in which they are financially interested would thus deprive the goverment of a valuable source of information and, at the same time, deprive the people of their right to petition in the very instances in which that right may be of the most importance to them. We reject such a construction of the Act and hold that, at least insofar as the railroads' campaign was directed toward obtaining governmental action, its legality was not at all affected by any anti-competitive purpose it may have had.

.  .  .  .  .  .  .  .  .  .  .  .  .  .  .  .  .  .

There may be situations in which a publicity campaign, ostensibly directed toward influencing governmental action, is a mere sham to cover what is actually nothing more than an attempt to interfere directly with the business relationships of a competitor and the application of the Sherman Act would be justified. But this certainly is not the case here. No one denies that the railroads were making a genuine effort to influence legislation and law enforcement practices. Indeed, if the version of the facts set forth in truckers' complaint is fully credited, as it was by the courts below, that effort was not only genuine but also highly successful. Under these circumstances, we conclude that no attempt to interfere with business relationships in a manner proscribed by the Sherman Act is involved in this case.

In rejecting each of the grounds relied upon by the courts below to justify application of the Sherman Act to the campaign of the railroads, we have rejected the very grounds upon which those courts relied to distinguish the campaign conducted by the truckers. In doing so, we have restored what appears to be the true nature of the case—a "no-holds-barred fight" between two industries both of which are seeking control of a profitable source of income. Inherent in such fights, which are commonplace in the halls of legislative bodies, is the possibility, and in many instances even the probability, that one group or the other will get hurt by the arguments that are made. In this particular instance, each group appears to have utilized all the political powers it could muster in an attempt to bring about the passage of laws that would help it or injure the other. But the contest itself appears to have been conducted along lines normally accepted in our political system, except to the extent that each group has deliberately deceived the public and public officials. And that deception, reprehensible as it is, can be of no consequence so far as the Sherman Act is concerned. That Act was not violated by either the railroads or the truckers in their respective campaigns to influence legislation and law enforcement. Since the railroads have acquiesced in the dismissal of their counterclaim by not challenging the Court of Appeals affirmance of that order in their petition for certiorari, we are here concerned only with those parts of the judgments below holding the railroads and Byoir liable for violations of the Sherman Act. And it follows from what we have said that those parts of the judgments below are wrong. They must be and are reversed.

The preceding cases illustrate the kinds of situations which can bring agencies of mass communications into court under the federal antitrust laws.

In the *Times-Picayune* and *Carl Byoir public relations* decisions, the practices in question were held to be within constitutional limits and government intervention was prevented by the Supreme Court.

In the *Associated Press* and *Lorain* decisions, however, the Court acted positively to apply the antitrust laws so that freedom of expression is safeguarded for the many and not just the few. For as Judge Learned Hand wrote in *Associated Press v. U.S.* 52 F. Supp. 362, 372:

> That [newspaper] industry serves one of the most vital of all general interests: the dissemination of news from as many different sources, and with as many different facets and colors as is possible. That interest is closely akin to, if indeed it is not the same as, the interest protected by the First Amendment; it presupposes that right conclusions are more likely to be gathered out of a multitude of tongues, than through any kind of authoritative selection. To many this is, and always will be, folly; but we have staked upon it our all.

More than any others, these words embody the spirit of the First Amendment.

## A CONCLUDING NOTE

THE LEGAL OPINIONS on freedom of the press by the Supreme Court of the United States are marked by both continuity and change. The great principles of free expression enunciated by Justices Oliver Wendell Holmes and Louis Brandeis in the 1920's were restated and reformulated by members of the Warren Court in the 1960's. The consistent concern for the positive values of free expression found eloquent articulation in the views of Justices Charles Evans Hughes, Harlan Stone, Frank Murphy, Felix Frankfurter, Hugo Black, William O. Douglas, Earl Warren, and others quoted in this book. Any new decision on freedom of the press that the Supreme Court hands down today—or tomorrow—must take cognizance of what these modern giants of the law have written. Their words reverberate through the law books.

Yet the decisions included in this book are clearly characterized by change. The direction of that change is unmistakable: at the level of constitutional law, for *all* mass media— newspapers, books, magazines, broadcasting, motion pictures— and for all citizens, there is greater freedom of the press today than at any time in the history of the Republic. The almost seventy decisions included here have given specific legal meaning to the concept of press freedom.

This expanded delineation of freedom of the press is, of course, just one aspect of the modern Supreme Court's concerted efforts in the past thirty years to give legal realization to all the rights named by the first ten amendments to the Constitution.

Committed to making the Bill of Rights meaningful, the

modern Court has produced several important decisions involving great issues of freedom of the press during almost every one of its terms.

The press has re-won battles against its ancient enemies of prior restraint (*Near v. Minnesota* in 1931), discriminatory taxes or "taxes on knowledge" (*Grosjean v. American Press Co.* in 1936), and arbitrary licensing (*Lovell v. Griffin* in 1938).

In *Times v. Sullivan* in 1964, the Court provided powerful new legal support for the right of citizens to criticize their public officials without fear of retaliatory libel actions. In the related case of *Garrison v. Louisiana,* also in 1964, the Court sounded the death knell for criminal, or "seditious," libel trials in state courts.

From the *Miracle* case in 1952 to *Freedman* in 1965, the Court extended First Amendment protection to motion pictures and almost completely whittled away the power of official censors. In the series of decisions from *Roth* in 1957 to *Ginzburg* in 1966, the Court struggled to define obscenity and to separate it from legal expression.

The potential censorship powers of the postal authorities were restrained by *Esquire* in 1946 and other decisions. In 1967, in *Time, Inc. v. Hill,* the Court for the first time extended freedom of the press into the area of suits for invasion of privacy.

A long struggle over the contempt power of judges to punish press critics ended with the *Bridges* decision in 1941, when the Court provided solid protection for the right of the press, and public, to "judge the judges." This immunity of the press from contempt proceedings was not diminished by the Court's later concern for defendants whose rights were jeopardized by pre-trial publicity. *Estes v. Texas* in 1965 barred the televising of "notorious trials." The milestone *Sheppard* case in 1966 placed the responsibility for assuring a fair and impartial trial squarely in the lap of the trial judge.

These last two decisions showed that the Court's consistent support of a free press is sometimes tempered by an implied admonition to the news media: a press that is free must be responsible. Freedom to report news must carry with it a regard and concern for the rights of others whose interests may conflict with those of the press.

Other decisions indicate that the press, as a business entity, is given no special sanctuary by the First Amendment, and is subject to all the general laws regulating business, including the antitrust laws.

But the message is clear: a press that uses its freedom with courage, restraint, and responsibility need not fear curtailment by the Supreme Court of the United States.

Future decisions on freedom of the press will be affected by two factors: the specific legal contests that come before the Court and the composition of the Court itself. Both are exceedingly hazardous if not impossible to predict.

The continuing constitutional difficulties posed by obscenity, defendants' rights and pretrial publicity, status of "public figures" involved in libel and privacy suits, and free speech rights of political dissidents—especially anti-war protestors and Communists—are likely to continue to produce significant litigation.

With five members of the 1967 Court over 67 years of age, several new appointments to the Court are likely to be made in the years just ahead. One change occurred in the summer of 1967, when Justice Tom C. Clark retired. He was replaced by Thurgood Marshall, the first Negro Associate Justice of the Supreme Court. Even if we knew who all the new justices were to be, it would be exceedingly foolhardy to predict their viewpoints. Will some be the intellectual heirs of Hugo L. Black and hold the First Amendment to be a "preferred right" requiring the broadest possible leeway for free expression? Or will the new justices heed Felix Frankfurter's argument for a "balancing of interests" when the First Amendment collided with another right? Only the future will tell.

But regardless of personnel changes on that most remarkable and admirable institution, the Supreme Court of the United States, the tradition of freedom will endure in the great decisions concerning the press that have been quoted in this book.

# SELECTED BIBLIOGRAPHY

BARTH, ALAN. *The Loyalty of Free Men*. New York: The Viking Press, 1951.

BECKER, CARL. *Freedom and Responsibility in the American Way of Life*. New York: Alfred A. Knopf, 1945.

BLACK, HUGO L. "The Bill of Rights." 35 *New York University Law Review* 865 (1960).

BRANT, IRVING. *The Bill of Rights: Its Origin and Meaning*. New York: Bobbs-Merrill, 1965.

CAHN, EDMOND. "Justice Black and First Amendment Absolutes—A Public Interview. 37 *New York University Law Review* 549 (1962).

—— (ed.). *The Great Rights*. New York: Macmillan Co., 1963.

CARR, ROBERT K. *Federal Protection of Civil Rights: Quest for a Sword*. Ithaca: Cornell University Press, 1947.

CAUGHEY, JOHN W. *In Clear and Present Danger*. Chicago: University of Chicago Press, 1958.

CHAFEE, ZECHARIAH, Jr. *The Blessings of Liberty*. New York: Lippincott and Co., 1956.

——. *Free Speech in the United States*. Cambridge: Harvard University Press, 1948.

——. *Government and Mass Communications*. 2 vols. Chicago: University of Chicago Press, 1947.

CHENERY, WILLIAM L. *Freedom of the Press*. New York: Harcourt, Brace and Co., 1955.

COMMISSION ON FREEDOM OF THE PRESS. *A Free and Responsible Press*. Chicago: University of Chicago Press, 1947.

CORWIN, EDWARD S. "Bowing Out 'Clear and Present Danger.' " 27 *Notre Dame Lawyer* 325 (1952).

——. *The Constitution and What It Means Today*. Princeton: Princeton University Press, 1954.

CUSHMAN, ROBERT E. *Civil Liberties in the United States*. Ithaca: Cornell University Press, 1956.

DOUGLAS, WILLIAM O. *The Right of the People*. Garden City, New York: Doubleday and Co., 1958.

309

EMERSON, THOMAS I., and HABER, DAVID. *Political and Civil Rights in The United States.* (2nd ed.) Buffalo: Dennis and Co., 1958.

EMERY, WALTER B. *Broadcasting and Government: Responsibilities and Regulations.* East Lansing: Michigan State University Press, 1961.

ERNST, MORRIS L. *The First Freedom.* New York: Macmillan Co., 1946.

ERNST, MORRIS L., and SCHWARTZ, ALAN U. *Censorship: The Search for the Obscene.* New York: Macmillan Co., 1964.

FELLMAN, DAVID. *The Limits of Freedom.* New Brunswick: Rutgers University Press, 1959.

FRAENKEL, OSMOND K. *The Supreme Court and Civil Liberties.* Dobbs Ferry: Oceana Publications, Inc., 1960.

FREUND, PAUL A. *The Supreme Court of the United States.* New York: Meridian Books, 1961.

GERALD, J. EDWARD. *The Press and the Constitution: 1931–1947.* Minneapolis: University of Minnesota Press, 1948.

GILLMOR, DONALD. *Free Press and Fair Trial.* Washington: Public Affairs Press, 1966.

HAIMAN, FRANKLYN S. *Freedom of Speech: Issues and Cases.* New York: Random House, 1965.

HOCKING, WILLIAM ERNEST. *Freedom of the Press: A Framework of Principle.* Chicago: University of Chicago Press, 1947.

HUDON, EDWARD G. *Freedom of Speech and Press in America.* Washington, D.C.: Public Affairs Press, 1963.

INGLIS, RUTH. *Freedom of the Movies.* Chicago: University of Chicago Press, 1947.

KONVITZ, MILTON R. *First Amendment Freedoms.* Ithaca: Cornell University Press, 1963.

———. *Fundamental Liberties of a Free People: Religion, Speech, Press, Assembly.* Ithaca: Cornell University Press, 1957.

LACY, DAN MABRY. *Freedom and Communications.* Urbana: University of Illinois Press, 1961.

LEVY, LEONARD. *Legacy of Suppression.* Cambridge: Harvard University Press, 1960.

McCLURE, ROBERT C., and LOCKHART, WILLIAM B. "Censorship of Obscenity: The Developing Constitutional Standards." 45 *Minnesota Law Review* 5–121 (1960).

McCORMICK, JOHN, and MacINNES, MAIRI. *Versions of Censorship.* Garden City: Doubleday and Co., 1962.

MAYER, MARTIN (ed.). *The Tradition of Freedom.* Dobbs Ferry: Oceana Publications, 1957.

MEIKLEJOHN, ALEXANDER. *Political Freedom: The Constitutional Power of the People.* New York: Harper and Co., 1960.

MOCK, JAMES R. *Censorship 1917.* Princeton: Princeton University Press, 1941.

NELSON, HAROLD L. *Freedom of the Press from Hamilton to the Warren Court.* New York: Bobbs-Merrill, 1967.

———. *Libel in News of Congressional Investigating Committees.* Minneapolis: University of Minnesota Press, 1961.

PAUL, JAMES C. N. and SCHWARTZ, MURRAY L. *Federal Censorship: Obscenity in the Mail.* New York: Free Press of Glencoe, 1961.

PHELPS, ROBERT H. and HAMILTON, DOUGLAS E. *Libel: Rights, Risks, Responsibilities.* New York: Macmillan Co., 1966.

PROSSER, WILLIAM L. *Handbook of the Law of Torts.* (3rd ed.) St. Paul: West Publishing Co., 1964.

ROCHE, JOHN P. "The Curbing of the Militant Majority," *The Reporter* (July 18, 1963), pp. 35–38.

ROGGE, O. JOHN. *The First and the Fifth.* New York: Thomas Nelson and Sons, 1960.

SIEBERT, FRED. *The Rights and Privileges of the Press.* New York: Appleton Century, 1934.

SIEBERT, FRED; PETERSON, THEODORE; and SCHRAMM, WILBUR. *Four Theories of the Press.* Urbana: University of Illinois Press, 1956.

SMEAD, ELMER S. *Freedom of Speech by Radio and Television.* Washington, D.C.: Public Affairs Press, 1959.

STOUFFER, SAMUEL A. *Communism, Conformity and Civil Liberties.* Garden City: Doubleday and Co., 1955.

SWINDLER, WILLIAM F. *Problems of Law in Journalism.* New York: Macmillan Co., 1955.

THAYER, FRANK. *Legal Control of the Press.* (4th ed.) Brooklyn: The Foundation Press, 1962.

WARREN, SAMUEL D., and BRANDEIS, LOUIS D. "The Right of Privacy." 4 *Harvard Law Review* 193, 1890.

# INDEX

313